P9-DFX-977

GUILTY BY REASON OF INSANITY

DAVID
LIMBAUGH

Guilty by Reason of Insanity

WHY THE DEMOCRATS MUST NOT WIN

REGNERY
PUBLISHING
A Division of Salem Media Group

Cataloging-in-Publication data on file with the Library of Congress

ISBN 978-1-62157-988-5
ebook ISBN 978-1-62157-990-8

Published in the United States by
Regnery Publishing
A Division of Salem Media Group
300 New Jersey Ave NW
Washington, DC 20001
www.Regnery.com

Manufactured in the United States of America

10 9 8 7 6 5 4 3 2 1

Books are available in quantity for promotional or premium use.
For information on discounts and terms, please visit our website:
www.Regnery.com.

To my fellow patriots joined together in our common struggle to save America from the political left's insane and destructive ideas. Only through vigilance, commitment, and faith in God will we succeed in beating back the forces that seek to complete the fundamental—and sinister—transformation of this great nation.

CONTENTS

Introduction

Everything you need to know about America's political division today, and what the two sides really believe in, was evident during President Trump's 2019 State of the Union address.

Originally scheduled for January 29, the speech was postponed by Speaker of the House Nancy Pelosi, who cited security concerns—specifically, that the Secret Service and Department of Homeland Security were lacking funds due to the partial government shutdown then in effect. The shutdown stemmed from congressional Democrats' refusal to grant Trump's request to fund construction of a security wall on the southern border. Many Democrats balked at the wall's $5.7 billion price tag, though within weeks much of the same crowd pledged support for Alexandria Ocasio-Cortez's Green New Deal, whose cost she has projected to be a staggering $10 trillion—which now appears to be a dramatic underestimation.[1]

Homeland Security chief Kirstjen Nielsen quickly debunked Pelosi's reasoning, declaring that both her department and the Secret Service were fully prepared to provide security for the President's speech. That was irrelevant to the left, which cheered Pelosi for ostensibly humiliating Trump. Progressives were less ecstatic a few days later, however, when Trump retaliated by cancelling a weeklong trip Pelosi was scheduled to take overseas. Several Democratic trip participants, including House Intelligence Committee chairman Adam Schiff, Congress's most prominent advocate of the Russia collusion hoax, were filmed exiting a bus that was supposed to take them to an airport but instead merely circled the block several times. At the time Schiff was left speechless by the affair and refused to comment to the press, a rare occurrence for him.[2]

The shutdown was resolved about a week later, and the State of the Union went forward on February 5. The audience featured a large block of Democratic women, including Pelosi, wearing white as an anti-Trump protest. Undaunted, the president delivered a passionate defense of American greatness. He championed border security, deregulation, and lowering prescription drug prices while denouncing radical abortion laws that would allow infanticide. He touted the tremendous economic accomplishments his administration had achieved in just two years, particularly the great strides seen in minority communities.

In pledging common cause with the freedom fighters in Venezuela, Trump roundly denounced the brutality of that nation's regime, tying socialism to totalitarianism and exposing it as a destroyer of prosperity and freedom. He then deftly segued to the alarming calls for socialism in America, noting that America was "founded on liberty and independence—not government coercion, domination, and control." He endorsed America's age-old appeal to liberty, underscoring the incompatibility of freedom and socialism. "We are born free, and we will stay free," proclaimed President Trump. "Tonight, we renew our resolve that America will never be a socialist country."[3]

The speech was a *tour de force* of American exceptionalism and unabashed patriotism. On hearing these remarks, however, Democrats presented themselves in stark relief, with many refusing to stand against socialism. In fact, many Democrats defiantly refused to rise for: American greatness, middle-class prosperity, blue-collar wage increases, low unemployment rates for minorities, the disabled, women, cutting regulations, America's leading the world in oil and natural gas production and becoming a net energy exporter, the USA chant, veterans, the child tax credit, *legal* immigration, an immigrant ICE agent who saved hundreds of women and girls from sex traffickers, ICE itself, angel families, school choice, the reduction of food stamp rolls by five million, the elimination of the Obamacare penalty, the banning of late-term abortion, deescalating tensions with North Korea, and moving the U.S. embassy to Jerusalem.[4] The women in white applauded very little in the speech, but they did give one line an animated reception, replete with hugging and enthusiastic cheering—Trump's lauding of the historic number of women now serving in Congress. In a speech filled with tributes to all sorts of individuals and groups as well as to America itself, they were roused to cheer for themselves.

Trump's optimistic address was filled with calls for unity, promoting American greatness as a benefit to all Americans. For the Democratic response, failed Georgia gubernatorial candidate Stacey Abrams offered an entirely different perspective, one grounded in identity politics—a message that was less optimistic, less hopeful, and decidedly more divisive. Whereas Trump proudly recited America's noble history and emphasized the sacrifices of all Americans, Abrams focused on the shame of the nation's racist history and the continuing prevalence of racism today. She also took a shot at the nation's sexism for good measure. "We fought Jim Crow with the Civil Rights Act and the Voting Rights Act," said Abrams. "Yet we continue to confront racism from our past and in our present.... America achieved a measure of reproductive justice in *Roe v. Wade*, but we must never forget, it is immoral to allow politicians to harm women and families to advance a political agenda."

There could be no sharper contrast between the visions and agendas of the American right and the left today. Conservatives are proud of the amazing economic improvements President Trump has overseen and are delighted that they permeate our whole society, including the poor, minorities, and women. We're pursuing a vision of American greatness in which our government limits its own intrusive powers in order to unleash the awesome power and ingenuity of free American people. We have faith in the inherent goodness, generosity, and kindness of Americans and their dedication to their families, neighbors, and communities. We believe the American nation is exceptional and worth defending, including at the border.

The left, by contrast, is consumed with fury at their own nation. Leftists detest much of the history of our country, which they believe was born in the sins of continental theft, genocide, slavery, white privilege, sexism, and mercenary capitalism. They are on a mission to right all these alleged wrongs and to punish those still benefiting from them. The American people, in their view, are crawling with racists who want to resurrect Jim Crow. Thus, Americans need systematic indoctrination through every conceivable lever—the education system, entertainment, the media, corporate America, and social media, to name a few—to disabuse them of their backward mentality. Every element of American society must be politicized with this goal in mind. Every American must be shamed, publicly and vehemently, for any utterance that strays beyond rigid ideological boundaries. Rejecting the principle of equal opportunity for all, the left pits Americans against one another according to race, class, gender, and other categories in a grim struggle for power and government largess.

The left is emboldened by its cultural dominance and cloistered in its own echo chambers where opposing views are demonized and excluded. Leftists have grown dangerously extreme, dogmatic, and intolerant. Regarding their views as the only acceptable ones, they are increasingly disillusioned with the principle of free speech and seek to suppress ideas they consider offensive—a category in which most conservative expression now belongs.

Crucially, leftists want to punish Americans for the cardinal sin of electing President Trump. They consider anyone who works for Trump, is associated with him, or supports him beyond the pale. In this state of resentful delirium, they have embraced an extremist agenda of socialism, open borders, and legal abortion up to the moment of birth. Contemptuous of constitutional constraints, they propose circumventing measures such as abolishing the Electoral College and packing the Supreme Court to regain and eternalize their political power.

Leftists are stunned and outraged that grassroots Americans are fighting back, through President Trump, to recapture America's freedom tradition and its underlying values. This book chronicles the left's proliferating insanity, born of its extremism and its own frustration with the formidable opposition it is now encountering. It is a wake-up call to anyone who believes the leftists' endgame is anything short of the wholesale conversion of this nation to something only they could love—and something America's founding fathers would abhor.

CHAPTER ONE

The Threat from Within

The world is going crazy and America is rapidly following suit. The left's decades-long assault on our traditional values and constitutional liberties has immeasurably damaged our society and our republic. Up is down. Right is wrong. Good is evil. Words are twisted to represent the opposite of their actual meaning. Intellectual and moral anarchy abound. Radical leftist ideas are hailed as mainstream, while conservative ideas are demonized as extreme.

Every great world power eventually falls, and the process often begins with self-inflicted wounds. There has never been a greater and freer nation than the United States, but it is now tearing itself apart. How long can our nation survive amid the relentless attack on everything that has made it unique?

Well-meaning people say Republicans and Democrats have the same fundamental goals but different ideas and strategies for achieving them. I've always regarded this as wishful thinking, but if it were ever true, it no longer is today. The two parties, as presently constituted, have distinctly different visions for America based on conflicting worldviews. Some will object that all Americans want everyone to be prosperous, safe, free, and to live in harmony, but I'm not sure that's even true anymore, given the left's anti-Americanism, its intolerance and authoritarianism, its romance with socialism, its hysterical environmentalism, its preoccupation with identity politics, its radicalism on race and gender, its attempts to erase our borders, its culture of death, its devaluation of the Constitution, its hostility to Second Amendment rights, and much more.

The Democratic Party is a vehicle of leftist extremism that poses an existential threat to America as founded—because it is at war with our first principles and traditions. It is anti-capitalist and rejects equality of opportunity in favor of a hierarchy of privileges for identity groups ranked according to their levels of alleged historical oppression. It's a brazenly anti-life party that promotes gender anarchy, militant feminism, and hostility toward traditional male roles and masculinity itself. It prosecutes a vicious culture war punctuated by an ongoing assault on Christians' religious liberty.

The left isn't turning to socialism just because its members think it's more equitable than capitalism but also because they seek revenge against America's founding generation and its successor beneficiaries. They want to eradicate the Western tradition that spawned our unique American culture because it allegedly led to continental larceny against Native Americans, is in irredeemable moral debt over slavery, and is forever culpable for oppressing minorities and women through white privilege and the inherent exploitation of capitalism. They are hell-bent on suppressing conservatives and Christians and overturning the entire existing order. Their radicalism is unquenchable. They don't seek solutions but to create permanent turmoil. While holding themselves out as models of tolerance, leftists have become ideological totalitarians, intolerant of dissenting views and contemptuous of those who hold them. It is conservatives who promote a tolerant, optimistic message and still believe in the proverbial melting pot—a truly integrated society. For all the left's talk of tolerance and peace, its power depends on continually pitting Americans against one another.

Progressives have weaponized race to discredit and silence conservatives and to enhance their own power. They are consumed with avenging wrongs allegedly committed by certain groups against other groups. Democrats don't talk about maximizing liberty and prosperity but instead engage in virtue signaling by invoking aggrieved mantras—social justice, income equality, cultural appropriation, intersectionality, white privilege, patriarchy, and toxic masculinity. Having once campaigned for civil rights, they now seek victims to leverage for partisan gain.

It's frightening how rapidly extremists took control of the Democratic Party—and how little resistance they faced. While the party's establishment wing pretends to moderate the radicalism of its newcomers—and there is sometimes spirited infighting between the two groups—the old guard have largely adopted their extremism.[1] Few influential centrists remain. If left unchecked, the Democratic Party would complete—in horrifyingly short order—Obama's twisted vision of fundamentally transforming America. It would drastically redistribute wealth, suppress dissent, dilute and ultimately destroy our national sovereignty, and dismantle our constitutional structure and individual liberties.

AMERICA'S FOUNDING PRINCIPLES

The modern left, then, is in an all-out war against Western civilization and the values and liberties it produced. It is at odds with the Constitution, American sovereignty, and the free market. It does not believe in American exceptionalism. A Gallup poll showed that only 51 percent of Democrats are very proud or extremely proud to be American, compared to 95 percent of Republicans. While a higher percentage of Democrats were proud when Obama was president, Republican pride in the nation remained the same during those years.[2]

"We're not going to make America great again, it was never that great," declared New York governor Andrew Cuomo. "We have not reached greatness, we will reach greatness when every American is fully engaged, we will reach greatness when discrimination and stereotyping against women, 51 percent of our population, is gone."[3] (After taking a deserved rhetorical beating, Cuomo unconvincingly walked back his remarks, claiming he meant America hasn't reached its full potential.)

Cuomo's statement was reminiscent of President Obama's America apology tour, wherein he repeatedly bashed the United States on foreign soil and proclaimed that America is no more exceptional than other nations.[4] This attitude had been telegraphed during the 2008 presidential campaign by Michelle Obama, who exclaimed, "For the first time in my adult lifetime, I'm really proud of my country...not just because Barack has done well, but because I think people are hungry for change."[5] More recently, Democrat Senator Cory Booker expressed similar sentiments. "I'm a big believer that if America, if this country hasn't broken your heart, then you don't love her enough," said Booker. "Because there's things that are savagely wrong in this country. There's a normalcy of injustice that we've accepted."[6] Likewise, former attorney general Eric Holder queried, "When did you think America was great?" This supposedly great American past, said Holder, "never in fact existed."[7]

Congresswoman Alexandria Ocasio-Cortez, the poster girl for America's left and today's Democratic Party, barely conceals her contempt for this nation. She describes America as racist and close to "garbage," insisting that the Reagan presidency was "a perfect example of how special interests and the powerful have pitted white working-class Americans against brown and black working-class Americans in order to just screw over all working-class Americans." She suggests that by promoting an image of black women as "welfare queens," Republicans created a racist caricature of one specific group of people and primed Americans to subconsciously resent them, thus providing a diabolical "logical reason" to "toss out the whole social safety net."[8]

Conservatives aren't angling to eliminate the social safety net; we just want to reasonably limit it because excessive dependency diminishes people's self-worth and productivity. Conservatives deeply value our God-given natural rights and individual liberties guaranteed by the Constitution and sustained by its structure of limited government. The Constitution promotes liberty through the enumerated powers of Congress, the Bill of Rights, the separation of powers among three branches of government, and the federalist system, which divides power between the federal, state, and local governments. Conservatives believe, and history has shown, that the closer people are to the seat of power, the more prudent and responsive the government will be. Accordingly, our freedom, security, and prosperity depend on preserving the Constitution's designed limitations on government, which in turn rely on courts interpreting the Constitution according to its original intent and honoring the rule of law.

The left is far more interested in acquiring power to achieve its political ends than in upholding a system that guarantees personal liberties. Determined to control people's lives and thoughts, leftists push to consolidate power in the federal government—especially when *they* control it. They are untroubled by delegations of power to administrative agencies staffed with career bureaucratic liberals insulated from accountability.

Firmly believing in America's uniqueness, conservatives jealously defend America's sovereignty and its borders and oppose globalism. The overused term "globalism" is often associated with conspiracy theories of one-world governments out of a Robert Ludlum novel. But it's inarguable that leftists often seek to delegate important policy decisions that impact our national sovereignty and personal liberties to like-minded international bodies that hold the United States in contempt.

The disparity in the parties' fidelity to America's freedom tradition partially explains their differing views on illegal immigration. The conservatives' strong opposition to it is not rooted in nativism or racism, as Democrats maliciously allege. Our love for America is based on ideas, not race. We believe America's continued greatness depends on a culture united behind those ideas, which is why we favor the assimilation and integration of legal immigrants.

Squandering the progress memorialized in the 1954 U.S. Supreme Court decision *Brown v. Board of Education of Topeka*,[9] which outlawed racial segregation in our schools, the left incites minorities to obsess on their color and ethnicity. Consequently, in some ways we have come full circle. Universities now foster segregation by making race a criterion for participation in certain student organizations and housing arrangements. Some recommend separate workout rooms for minority students where white students are excluded. Leftists are preoccupied with race, assigning highly paid diversity coordinators to monitor the racial percentages of students, faculty, staff, and contractors. In their racial zealotry they have bastardized the term "diversity," which originally referred to people of different racial and ethnic backgrounds freely interacting and comingling. But heightened race consciousness and the segregation of racial groups on our campuses undermines these goals, fomenting mutual distrust and deterring interracial interaction.[10] This trend is hardly accidental. It's a logical outgrowth of the left's vision for America which, as we've noted, no longer includes people of all races, ethnicities, genders, and religions living together in peace and harmony but sees America as a fractured land of mutually suspicious groups living in uneasy hostility.

Civil rights icon Martin Luther King Jr. not only preached racial harmony but also endorsed America's founding principles—the universal application of the Declaration's guarantees of life, liberty, and the pursuit of happiness. His quarrel was not with the American idea but with its unequal application to African Americans. He envisioned America as a land of equal opportunity for all, not one of government-enforced equal outcomes or perpetual victimhood in which the "aggrieved" continually battle with the "oppressors." "When the architects of our republic wrote the magnificent words of the Constitution and the Declaration of Independence," King proclaimed, "they were signing a promissory note to which every American was to fall heir. This note was a promise that all men—yes, black men as well as white men—would be guaranteed the unalienable rights of life, liberty, and the pursuit of happiness."

ASSAULTING THE CONSTITUTIONAL ORDER

Republicans believe in maximizing our liberties and prosperity through pro-growth policies that expand the economic pie by unshackling people from stifling taxes and regulations and unleashing their entrepreneurial spirit. Democrats see the economic pie as finite and the economy as a zero-sum game where one man's gain is another's loss. They believe enlightened central planners are wiser and more beneficent than the invisible hand of the market, and they support redistributionist schemes to equalize incomes. Just as they exploit racial and gender politics, they employ class warfare to augment their political power. It would be bad enough if they merely sought to pick economic winners and losers, but they also vilify the successful and inspire others to resent them. Some Democrats have conveniently reinterpreted America's founding principles as demands for equal economic outcomes rather than equal opportunity—in other words, as a call for socialism.

The framers warned of another inherent threat to freedom. "Our Constitution," wrote John Adams, "was made only for a moral and religious people. It is wholly inadequate to the government of any other." Constitutions are worth no more than the paper they are written on if the people and their elected representatives don't honor them. The twentieth century is replete with examples of murderous, totalitarian regimes whose organizing documents purported to guarantee liberties to their citizens. While our nation still largely adheres to its constitutional framework, our commitment has measurably softened, as various branches of government have abandoned their fealty to the letter and spirit of the Constitution and usurped other branches' powers or lawlessly delegated their own.

When courts usurp the legislative function and make laws rather than interpret them, when Congress delegates its legislative functions to an unaccountable administrative state, and when presidents issue lawless executive orders, they are abusing their respective constitutional authority. When the other branches fail to rein them in with constitutionally prescribed countermeasures, our government becomes less democratic, responsive, and accountable, and our liberties erode. As America's body politic has grown complacent about the integrity of the Constitution, its prescribed checks and balances, and its federalist system, our freedoms have become imperiled. At the root of this indifference is a festering corruption of our values in which the rule of law is subordinated to the pursuit of raw political power and the political ends of those seeking or wielding that power.

The perpetrators of these assaults on our system maintain that they are honoring the spirit of a "living Constitution" and are interpreting its language progressively to accommodate modernity. They deny distorting its meaning and intent to achieve their policy goals. They rationalize their interpretations in emanations and penumbras that only they can divine, such as their declaration of a constitutional right to privacy as a justification for abortion in the infamous case of *Roe v. Wade*.[11]

An earlier, egregious example of judicial rewriting of the Constitution was the New Deal case of *Wickard v. Filburn*,[12] in which the

Supreme Court sanctioned the federal government's regulation of purely *intrastate* activities under the Interstate Commerce Clause. Having established limits on wheat production to control wheat prices, the federal government imposed a penalty on Ohio farmer Roscoe Filburn for exceeding those limits. Filburn disputed the government's constitutional authority to impose the limitation because he not only didn't engage in interstate commerce, but he didn't engage in commerce at all, since he didn't sell his wheat. Unimpressed, the power-gobbling Court upheld the government's right to regulate Filburn's strictly local farming operations, arguing that even if the activity was local and not commercial, it could have a substantial economic effect on interstate commerce. The Court rationalized that because Filburn's wheat production reduced the amount of wheat he would buy for animal feed on the open market, it was within the federal government's regulatory scope under the Commerce Clause.

The Court knew that the framers never intended such an expansive reading of the clause but justified the federal overreach by presuming that a greater good would come from its decision. The Commerce Clause and *Roe v. Wade* are just a few of the myriad examples of liberal activist jurisprudence inflating the power of government and diminishing our liberties.

A NATION BORN IN HELL?

Conservatives are not indifferent to America's past sins, but we are proud of America's history and its freedom tradition, which has been a remarkable force for good in the world. The left portrays America's history as a morality tale of evil, slavery-loving whites dispossessing Native Americans of the land. In short, America is drenched in evil and born in hell. It must forever atone. We saw this in leftists' reactions to President Trump's Fourth of July "Salute to America." Liberal media networks ABC, CBS, and NBC refused to air the event[13] while progressives roundly denounced the military's participation, revealing their fundamental loathing for traditional patriotic displays. Indeed, the left staged its own counterprogramming: activists burned an American flag in front of the White House, and the *New York Times* produced a video debunking the "myth" that the United States is "the greatest nation on Earth."[14]

The condemnation today of white Europeans for stealing the land from Native Americans is grossly oversimplified—factually and morally. Michael Medved observes that "the 400 year history of American contact with Indians includes many examples of white cruelty and viciousness." But it was a two-way street. "The Native Americans frequently (indeed, regularly) dealt with the European newcomers with monstrous brutality and, indeed, savagery.... But none of the warfare (including an Indian attack in 1675 that succeeded in butchering a full one-fourth of the white population of Connecticut, and claimed additional thousands of casualties throughout New England) on either side amounted to genocide. Colonial and, later, the American government, never endorsed or practiced a policy of Indian extermination; rather, the official leaders of white society tried to restrain some of their settlers and militias and paramilitary groups from unnecessary conflict and brutality."[15]

"One of the things we take for granted today is that it is wrong to take other people's land by force," writes Thomas Sowell. "Neither American Indians nor the European invaders believed that. Both took other people's land by force—as did Asians, Africans and others. The Indians no doubt regretted losing so many battles. But that is wholly different from saying that they thought battles were the wrong way to settle ownership of land."[16] European colonization of the land occurred over four hundred years and was multifaceted. Without question, inexcusable acts of theft and murder occurred, but the typical pattern involved Europeans negotiating with Indian nations for land and the sharing of territory for a period—until war broke out, usually resulting in the Indians losing and being removed. While we mustn't be callous to these hardships, it is unfair to single out Europeans for special opprobrium when what occurred in colonial America was much like what has happened all throughout world history among rival peoples and nations—including among rival nations of Native Americans.[17]

Nor is the issue of slavery in America as simple as the America-hating revisionists would have you believe. Sowell notes that slavery was a worldwide institution for thousands of years. It wasn't a controversial issue, even among intellectuals or political leaders, before the eighteenth century, when it became controversial only in Western civilization. All races of people were both practitioners and victims of slavery.

American history professor Allen Guelzo observes that the Constitution was never pro-slavery. While the Constitution contained concessions to the states on slavery, "nothing in it acknowledged 'men to be property.'" In fact, James Madison said it would be intolerable "to admit to the Constitution the idea that there could be property in men." Thus, writes Guelzo, "the fundamental basis on which the entire notion of slavery rested was barred at the Constitution's door, even while its practical existence slipped through."[18] One member of the Massachusetts Ratifying Convention recognized that the Constitution was written to guarantee that slavery would eventually be abolished even if it was politically impossible to do so then. "It would not do to abolish slavery...in a moment," said Thomas Dawes. But even if "slavery is not smitten with an apoplexy, yet it has received a mortal wound and will die of a consumption."[19]

"To read the Constitution as pro-slavery...requires a suspension of disbelief that only playwrights and morticians could admire," Guelzo concludes. "Yes, the Constitution reduced slaves to the hated three-fifths; but that was to keep slaveholders from claiming them for five-fifths in determining representation, which would have increased the power of slaveholding states. Yes, the Constitution permitted the slave trade to continue; but it also permitted Congress to shut it off, which it did in 1808.... Smearing the Constitution by characterizing it as a contract for the perpetuation of slavery is worse than trying to see as half empty a glass that's half full; it is to see as bone dry a glass that's nearly full, or even to see no glass at all."[20]

Sowell observes that many American leaders, including George Washington, Thomas Jefferson, and Patrick Henry, came to oppose slavery, but maintains that it was much easier to morally oppose slavery in principle than to decide what to do with millions of slaves who were from another continent and had no experience living as free citizens in the United States, where they constituted 20 percent of the population. While the private correspondence of Washington, Jefferson, and many others reveals deep moral misgivings about slavery, Sowell notes that the practical question of what to do about the slavery question had them baffled and would continue to trouble the nation for more than a half a century.[21]

The question, of course, was settled by the American Civil War, in which more than 600,000 men were killed to free almost four million. Sowell cautions against the conceit that there was an easy answer to the problem—"or that those who grappled with the dilemma in the 18th century were some special villains when most leaders around the world saw nothing wrong with slavery."[22] Sowell says it's hypocritical to castigate America as uniquely evil on slavery without so much as mentioning the historical prevalence of slavery worldwide and the millions of people throughout the world still enslaved today—more, in fact, "than were seized from Africa during the four centuries of the trans-Atlantic slave trade."[23]

Despite provisions in the Constitution virtually guaranteeing that the slavery issue would ultimately come to a head and despite the Americans who fought a brutal civil war to end it, the left teaches that America is far from atoning for its original sin. They regard America as an imperialistic and tainted nation dominated by a white patriarchy that enjoys the privileges and benefits of its race while oppressing women, minorities, and homosexuals. They demand that we view everything through the prism of oppressive historical race and gender hierarchies. To them, the idea of the melting pot is passé and even repellent because it distracts our focus from the historical injustices minorities have suffered and the redress to which they are entitled.

IDENTITY POLITICS AS A TICKET TO POWER

Democrats talk a good game of unity and bipartisanship, but their every action aims to divide us into balkanized, competing groups, suspicious and jealous of one another and in constant conflict. They realize their political power depends on convincing identity groups that Republicans are oppressing them and that their only hope is to trust Democrats to protect them. Liberals once abhorred segregation and vigorously advocated integration. Martin Luther King Jr. famously taught that people should be judged not by the color of their skin but the content of their character. Today's left, however, speaks of racial harmony from one side of their mouth, but from the other comes a shrill message of identity politics, which holds that we must fixate on a person's color rather than his character, heart, or personal behavior.

Democrats exploit identity politics not to benefit minorities, women, or the poor, but as a calculated strategy to sustain their power on the currency of minority victimhood. No matter what the issue, they resort to charges of racism, sexism, homophobia, or class warfare when their other arguments fail. They accuse conservatives of supporting border enforcement because they are racists, promoting welfare reform because they despise minorities and the poor, supporting voter ID laws to suppress the minority vote, opposing radical environmental policies to conserve their own wealth, promoting America's national sovereignty and exceptionalism to preserve their "white privilege," defending their Second Amendment rights because they are indifferent to gun deaths, being strict constructionists of the Constitution to preserve our patriarchal system, opposing abortion to undermine women's autonomy and health, opposing state-sanctioned same-sex marriage because they are homophobes, supporting a strong military to impose America's malevolent will on the world, promoting entitlement reform on the backs of seniors and others in need, and opposing the involuntary unionization of workers because they are enemies of the working man. On all these issues there is only one acceptable position and dissenters are aberrant. To enforce these conclusions, the leftist thought police act as cultural hall monitors. Dissent brings consequences, especially for those within the "jurisdiction" of the thought cops, such as university students at the mercy of their professors and public figures and politicians subject to the liberal media's wrath.

Leftist race-baiting works. African Americans overwhelmingly vote Democrat, and their near-unanimous support was critical to electing the last three Democratic presidents—Carter, Clinton, and Obama.[24] A recent study showed that in competitive congressional elections in 2018, 90 percent of black voters supported Democratic House candidates compared to 53 percent of voters overall. It also found that 91 percent of black women and 86 percent of black men believe that President Trump and Republicans are dividing Americans with toxic rhetoric.

How could they not believe that when Democrats and the entire mainstream media hammer this false theme daily with their own toxic rhetoric? They have little else to attract voters.[25]

By contrast, the Republicans' agenda is inherently more unifying because it sees people as individuals, not group members, equal in human dignity as made in God's image and endowed with inalienable rights and equal opportunity under the law. Conservatives believe that these ideas, enshrined in our founding documents, have made America the greatest, freest, and most prosperous nation in history and therefore must be preserved.

THE LEFT'S ACHILLES' HEEL

Progressives project themselves as morally superior guardians of the victim groups conservatives allegedly oppress. This is why they exempt themselves from accountability for their own racist statements, such as former senator Joe Biden's casual description of Barack Obama as "the first mainstream African American who is articulate and bright and clean and a nice-looking guy. I mean that's a storybook, man."[26] Similarly, former senator Harry Reid exclaimed that Obama could win the presidency because he was "light-skinned" and didn't speak with a "negro dialect."[27] According to the left's rule book, one's morality is not determined by his behavior but his political views and group identity. As members of the morally enlightened tribe of progressivism, liberals can be forgiven for an occasional heresy from the established orthodoxy when it's politically expedient to do so.

The left long ago asserted themselves as the sole arbiter of cultural morality, with a monopoly on compassion and "social justice." They adeptly pulled this off in the 1960s, according to author Shelby Steele, when America "finally accepted that slavery and segregation were profound moral failings." This acceptance, Steele argues, "imposed a new moral imperative: America would have to show itself redeemed of these immoralities in order to stand as a legitimate democracy." The left, always quick on the political uptake, seized the moment and anointed themselves the leaders of America's search for redemption—"from shame to decency."[28]

The left parlayed its self-proclaimed moral superiority to institute a staggering panoply of government-funded social programs that would transform America forever. President Johnson assumed office upon President Kennedy's assassination and inaugurated a progressive domestic agenda so ambitious that it shocked and alienated the Kennedy family.[29] If anyone doubts the Democrats' socialist roots, he can go back a few decades earlier and examine FDR's New Deal, not to mention the presidency of Woodrow Wilson, whom some call the "Godfather of Liberalism."[30] Though liberal revisionists maintain that Roosevelt's energetic statism was part of a strategy to save capitalism from the ravages of the Great Depression, his policies exacerbated and prolonged the Depression rather than ameliorating it.[31]

But there is not a hint of ambiguity about the socialistic nature of LBJ's Great Society agenda, even down to its title, which Johnson borrowed from a 1914 socialist screed by British political scientist Graham Wallas.[32] Unlike FDR, Johnson didn't present his grandiose agenda ostensibly to lift America out of a depression but as an unmasked plan of social reengineering. In his first State of the Union address on January 8, 1964, Johnson announced his utopian goal. "This administration today, here and now, declares unconditional war on poverty in America," Johnson pronounced.[33]

Like all socialistic programs, the War on Poverty assumed that Washington elitists have more wisdom and compassion than the people and so could eliminate poverty and racial discrimination, remake cities, and repair our public education system. The sweeping magnitude of LBJ's program was revolutionary, from his education legislation providing aid and benefits for low-income students; to instituting Medicare and Medicaid for the elderly and poor, respectively; to dramatically relaxing immigration laws; to the Voting Rights Act. There were beneficial aspects to some of these laws, undoubtedly, but the Constitution vests state governments with authority over most of them and they were structured to be unsustainable in the long run. As many have argued, this was the defining moment when the Democratic Party permanently established itself as the party of big government and most major institutions in the United States came within the federal government's fiscal and regulatory control.[34] The program also delivered a devastating blow to the constitutional doctrine of federalism, as the federal government swallowed much of the existing power of state and local governments by making them dependent on federal aid and increasingly encumbered by federal regulations.

To capitalize on this moment, Steele observes, the left had to ensure that America's past wrongs were seen as ongoing menaces that threatened the nation's moral legitimacy. Believing their power would increase commensurate with the gravity of the menaces, the left, over time, cleverly developed a list of additional "isms" and "phobias" that had to be defeated, and they positioned themselves to lead the charge against them.

The left also used these bogeymen to legitimize their policy agenda, which they argued, to great success, was directly connected to their moral authority to fight these menaces. As leftists were moral crusaders against America's ills, they deserved to be trusted to remedy them. The left's political agenda thereby acquired greater moral gravity—the policy prescriptions leftists advocated were billed as morally superior to conservatives' proposals, which were deemed to be aligned with the various menaces. So LBJ's Great Society programs were seen as moral necessities, and their supporters—Democrats and the left—were the great saviors. Those opposing them were immoral, uncompassionate, and, of course, racist.

Steele argues that the left's dependence on invoking these menaces became their "Achilles' heel" because the expansion of women's and minorities' rights made these issues less urgent and diminished the left's moral claim to power. As civil rights laws were enacted and enforced and racism gradually subsided, the left, whose *raison d'etre* was crusading against discrimination, faced the crisis of their looming obsolescence, which is the source of their angst and hatefulness. Steele is correct that the left is steeped in hate, which is ironic, considering they always accuse conservatives of spreading hate. It's simple projection.

Unfortunately, negative attitudes are contagious. It is the nature of activists to proselytize. Unlike Christian evangelists who spread the Good News, leftists seek to sow discontent among the groups they depict as aggrieved. This was particularly evident with President Obama.

One would think his election to the presidency would have reassured Americans that racism had greatly diminished in the United States. Instead of treating it in that spirit, though, Obama used his bully pulpit to spread racial division and distrust. He constantly racialized events and fomented ill will among minorities toward cops, from his outburst that the Cambridge police acted stupidly when arresting Harvard professor Henry Gates to his incendiary statements on Trayvon Martin. He demeaned conservatives as bitter clingers who recoil from people who don't look like them.

Taking Obama's cue, the liberal media further fanned the flames of racial disharmony. According to a Rasmussen poll released on July 19, 2016 (around the midpoint of Obama's second term), race relations had reached an all-time low. Sixty percent of the respondents said race relations had deteriorated under Obama and only 9 percent said they had improved.[35] By contrast—and certainly contrary to leftist propaganda—a recent study by Daniel J. Hopkins and Samantha Washington, two University of Pennsylvania sociologists, shows a decrease in racism under President Trump. "Anti-black prejudice . . . declined by a statistically-insignificant degree between 2012 and 2016. . . . But then after 2016 it took a sharp dive that was statistically significant. Moreover, contrary to their expectations, the fall was as evident among Republican voters as it was among Democrats."[36]

DEMOCRAT DENIAL

The left, as noted, developed a comprehensive slate of policies for minorities, the disadvantaged, the poor, women, and children. Their overarching, self-professed righteousness facilitated their gross expansion of government—higher taxes, explosive regulations, income redistribution schemes, exorbitant entitlement programs, government healthcare, and expansive welfare programs—as their policies were assumed to be driven by compassion.

Conservative policies have been far more effective in improving the lives of all people, including disadvantaged groups, than has socialism, which tends to impoverish and enslave the people it ostensibly means to help. Smaller and less intrusive government means more liberty and greater prosperity across the board—a rising tide lifts all boats. The left's domestic policy agenda is fiscally unsustainable and has produced results opposite of those they promised.

After fifty years of experimentation, progressives' domestic policies—welfare, public housing, forced school busing, affirmative action, diversity programs, the Medicare and Medicaid debt bombs, Obamacare, public education, green energy, economic stimulus programs, and environmental boondoggles—have consistently failed. They are angry not only because of their declining relevance on race but also because their policies haven't improved American lives.

But they are in denial about their policy failures. They embrace their ideology with dogmatic fervor, more as a matter of faith than evidence. They reject the inconvenient fact that Jimmy Carter's misery index and pessimistic projections of permanent economic malaise were obliterated by Ronald Reagan's "Morning in America," and that Donald Trump's explosive economy has dwarfed Obama's anemic one, shattering Obama's Carter-like predictions of economic mediocrity. The Democrats' powers of rationalization have grown in proportion to the failure of their policies, so they delude themselves into believing that Trump's robust economy is merely an extension of the Obama "recovery" while ignoring the indisputable fact that Trump's policies have markedly improved the plight of minorities and women. A *Politico* headline summed up the left's self-deception: "Trump Inherits Obama Boom."[37]

This disconnect has frustrated, confused, and outraged leftists—and their outrage is directed not at themselves for clinging to false promises, but at conservatives. They can't accept that people they deem morally inferior have superior solutions for society's problems. Even if conservatives' free-market policies are more effective, why should they get credit when they don't care about people? It would be like praising a robot—except praising conservatives would be worse because human beings, unlike robots, are capable of caring. Besides, if conservative policies work it's only because people are evil. If people weren't so selfish, competitive, and greedy, they'd be content with the government handing them an equal share of society's wealth instead of striving for more. No amount of evidence will disabuse progressives of their sense of moral superiority. It's as if leftists believe in the biblical notion of the Fall, but that it only applies to conservatives.

FEARLESS LIBERALS AND PARANOID CONSERVATIVES

Liberals have bigger hearts, and they've enlisted pop psychology to prove it. Consider, for example, evolutionary psychologist Nigel Barber's "Why Liberal Hearts Bleed and Conservatives Don't." Citing an allegedly scientific study, Barber concludes that "conservatives see the world as a more threatening place because their brains predispose them to being fearful." Conservatives' "brain biology," he argues, inclines them to hate complexity and compromise. "That would help to explain why politics can be so polarized, particularly in a rather conservative era like the present," he wrote in 2012.[38] (I suppose this means, from the leftist perspective, we are born conservative or liberal but not necessarily male or female.)

The biological predisposition to fear "illuminates the conservative take on specific political issues in fairly obvious ways," argues Barber. They are more religious "because religious rituals foster feelings of safety in a dangerous world." Liberals, you see, are less religious because they see the world as less threatening and they rely more on science and education to solve problems. Conservatives "tend to be more hostile to immigrants, foreigners, and racial or ethnic minorities and to view them as more of a threat." Liberals, of course, are more welcoming. "Conservatives are pro-family because being surrounded by close relatives is the best defense against threats that surround them," while "[l]iberals are less interested in family ties as a protective bubble."[39]

Despite liberals' supposedly superior brain power, they do not—if Barber is representative of their thinking—have the faintest clue as to what makes conservatives tick. If conservatives view the world as a more "threatening place," it's because we are more realistic. Is it necessary to have a Judeo-Christian worldview to recognize that we live in a woefully imperfect world? That evil people exist who want to harm us? That the human species, despite our advances in science and technology, is not advancing morally?

Conservatives aren't drawn to Christianity because its rituals are comforting. That theory is frightfully similar to Karl Marx's mantra that religion is the opiate of the masses. Is that a coincidence? People become Christians not to shelter themselves from the world or to inoculate themselves with false feelings of security but because they understand they aren't capable of saving themselves. They understand that man is not the measure of all things, so they trust in Jesus Christ to redeem them from their sins. The feelings of security that flow from their faith are based on the promise of eternal life. But Christianity does not assure the faithful that they'll be spared from earthly problems; in fact, it guarantees them they will not. Happily, however, those struggles often facilitate their spiritual growth.

Nor are conservatives hostile to science, but we oppose its politicization and reject the notion that science can answer all of man's questions or resolve all his problems. We understand that science must be kept within its own sphere and cannot address philosophical or spiritual issues, which are outside its domain.

Conservatives don't view minorities as a threat and are not unwelcoming to immigrants but adamantly oppose illegal immigration. Conservatives don't oppose progressive programs ostensibly aimed at helping the poor and minorities because we are uncompassionate. Rather, we know these programs are harmful to people's welfare and dignity and destructive to society overall. It is more reasonable to conclude that leftists are indifferent to minorities because their programs inevitably harm them. At what point is it fair to judge the left on the results of their policies rather than their professed good intentions?

"BIPARTISAN COMPROMISES LEAD TO EXPANDED GOVERNMENT"

It's time to jettison the myth that liberals are more conciliatory than conservatives. Modern American history shows that political compromise through the decades has invariably advanced leftist ideas, putting America on a steady march toward socialism. But liberals have masterfully sold themselves as being amenable to compromise, while it's the hard-hearted Republicans who supposedly refuse to negotiate. The liberal media have reinforced this canard for years. For example, they have successfully blamed Republicans for all government shutdowns. Some believe this is because the GOP is seen as anti-government and the Democratic Party as pro-government. In reality, the media present Republicans as harsh, extremist, and uncompromising, even though Republicans have not grown more conservative since the Reagan years, while Democrats have moved radically left. Republicans may sometimes appear entrenched, but it's because we have had to ratchet up our resistance in proportion to the left's increasing extremism.

Empirical evidence belies the left's claim that Republicans are less willing to compromise. Michigan State University political scientist Matt Grossmann tested the conventional wisdom that congressional conservatives are the primary culprits in Washington's partisan dysfunction. He examined whether congressional overseers Norman Ornstein and Thomas Mann were correct in 2014 in blaming Republicans for running "the worst Congress ever." After Grossman "combed through hundreds of history books covering American public policy since 1945," he concluded that most policies under debate are liberal, and Republican leaders sacrifice conservative principles when they compromise. "Of the 509 most significant domestic policies passed by Congress," Grossman explained, "only one in five were conservative, in that they contracted the scope of government funding, regulation or responsibility. More than 60 percent were liberal: They clearly expanded government.... The view that normal legislating and bipartisan compromises lead to expanded government is no tea party illusion; it is an accurate reading of the past 70 years."[40]

Grossman found that just 10 percent of the major executive orders and agency rules were conservative.[41] Even if you count those instances of government expansion that advance conservative goals, it makes little difference, says Grossman, because substantial policy changes of this kind rarely occur. When Republicans have succeeded in shrinking a government program it's almost always in exchange for a liberal government expansion elsewhere.

It's natural that conservatives are seen as obstructive because lawmakers derive their worth from taking action, which means more domestic spending, regulation, and increased government control. Not only does the nature of the legislative branch militate toward liberalism, says Grossman, but progressive laws "are self-reinforcing because they create beneficiaries who act as constituencies for their continuation and expansion."[42] Congress creates dependency groups who never ask them to roll back their programs but only to expand them. The legislative process generates its own expansion inertia.

Another force for expanding government is the constant pressure on politicians of both parties to deliver for their respective constituents. They have to be seen as doing something. Macro-level conservative pressure usually favors restricting the size, scope, and role of government—cutting taxes, slashing regulations, and the like. But micro-level pressure, even from red states and communities, is often directed at government expansion, as constituents lobby their congressmen to "bring home the bacon." Conservative congressmen also feel obligated to prove they care about people as much as liberals do by enacting legislation that expands government. Tax cuts are one exceptional example of Republican legislation that reduces the government's scope, but there are far more examples of Republicans expanding government, from wage and price controls under Nixon, to President George W. Bush's "No Child Left Behind" and his Medicare Part D entitlement. Even President Reagan, according to Grossman, signed more government expansion legislation than government contraction legislation. It's the nature of the beast.

Grossman's takeaway is ominous: "The arc of the policy universe is long, but it bends toward liberalism. Conservatives can slow the growth of government but an enduring shift in policy direction would be unprecedented. History shows that a do-nothing Congress is a conservative's best-case scenario."[43] Sadly, a do-nothing Congress doesn't play well with voters.

SUITING UP FOR THE CULTURE WAR

Whether we like it or not, the left is waging a fierce culture war against our traditional values. Its worldview rejects the biblical teaching that man is fallen despite being created in God's image. Most leftists believe that Christianity hindered man's enlightenment for centuries and that the advancement of science and reason alone, particularly in the Enlightenment era, placed man on an inexorable path toward progress and moral perfection. They conveniently ignore the enormous blessings to humanity derived from Christianity as well as the deaths of a hundred million people in the twentieth century alone at the hands of godless Nazi, fascist, and communist regimes. They are trapped in a spiritual void they seek to fill through myriad utopian and idolatrous pursuits, from socialism, to the environment, to social causes. Conservatives oppose the leftists' utopian dreams, which solidifies the left's perception that conservatives are immoral, uncaring, and on the wrong side of history. They view conservatives as heretics who reject the left's secularist worldview and oppose scientific, moral, and quasi-spiritual "progress." Metaphorically, at least, they want to burn us at the stake.

It's true that politics is downstream from culture, but there is also a symbiotic relationship between the two—they influence each other. While the left is diminishing our freedoms through the long arm of government, they are also assaulting them through the culture and obliterating traditional values and institutions. The Democratic Party embraces cultural extremism and institutionally advances it through legislation that codifies new cultural norms. Cultural influences also threaten our liberties beyond the political arena.

Political forces are impotent to stop or even slow most of this cultural corrosion, much less reverse it. Political correctness, even when operating solely within the private sector, is a suffocating suppressor of liberties. Social media giants, from Facebook to Google to Twitter to Instagram, have enormous power, including the unchecked prerogative to regulate speech within their sizable platforms. Leftist vultures hover over every digital acre of America waiting to pounce on conservative commentators and denounce their "hate speech." They lie in wait for any business or industry to support causes they oppose or oppose those they support. They aggressively target Christian businesses that deviate from their secular dogmas, organizing boycotts and judicially harassing those who don't toe the leftist line on same-sex marriage.

Corporate America displays a shocking cowardice in the face of leftist bullying. Just recall Nike's disgraceful cancellation of its plans for patriotic sneakers featuring the Betsy Ross flag due to objections from former NFL quarterback Colin Kaepernick. Nike got cold feet about introducing its Air Max 1 USA shoe after Kaepernick claimed the flag symbolizes slavery.[44] If the left can so easily intimidate our biggest, richest corporations, imagine the pressure it brings to bear when it targets a small Christian bakery[45] or a mom-and-pop convenience store.[46]

The left has waged war on our culture for decades and conservatives have been losing ground, sometimes because they haven't suited up for battle. In recent years, leftists have gained momentum at an alarming rate. The left controls our education system, Hollywood, the mainstream media, social media corporate giants, and the rest of Silicon Valley. Its monolithic voice floods American culture, indoctrinating generations of Americans with progressive propaganda. Conservative counterattacks are disorganized, lack strategic coherence, and are simply overwhelmed by the left's tireless determination to radically alter our culture and impose their values on us. Unless we fight back more effectively on both fronts—political and cultural—we won't be able to save America.

One of the left's many conceits is to anoint as "woke" those who profess to be down with the struggle against alleged racial, gender, and economic discrimination. But being "woke" means being aware, and the left may well be aware of many things that simply aren't true. As Ronald Reagan famously said, "The trouble with our liberal friends is not that they are ignorant, but that they know so much that isn't so."[47] To be "woke" to falsehoods is to be asleep to the truth. But leftists aren't asleep to the reality that the culture war is ongoing and gravely serious. And it's time conservatives "woke" up from their complacency.

GROUNDS FOR OPTIMISM

We deny at our peril the gravity of the threats we face. Will patriots remain mindful of the urgency of these threats? I believe they will—because of their passionate love for this nation and their unwavering dedication to preserving it for their children and their descendants.

Indeed, despite our beleaguered condition, there are reasons for optimism. Trump's election signals that America is finally coming to its senses and patriots want to fight back. Americans didn't elect Trump because he's a celebrity entertainer or because we are bigots, as alleged. Quite the opposite is true. Trump didn't arise in a vacuum. He is not the cause of our nation's division. He didn't start a groundswell movement behind new ideas he was articulating. Rather, he rose to power as a direct result of existing divisions and because establishment Republicans had failed to impede, let alone reverse, the leftist juggernaut.

Under Trump's leadership, conservatives have made great strides toward turning the tide, but progressives are not taking these countermeasures sitting down. They have tenaciously redoubled their resolve to destroy Trump and disable his presidency. Each time they are thwarted, they regroup and re-attack. We must understand that we are locked in a perpetual struggle against relentless opponents and resolve to fight them with equal or greater force.

Our task is enormously difficult. Some conservatives don't want to admit that some of our own fellow Americans, wittingly or unwittingly, are working to change America into something our founding fathers wouldn't recognize. But we mustn't grow numb to what the modern Democratic Party has become.

Some discount the severity of the threat because they believe only part of the party has gone over the starboard side into the deep end. Nancy Pelosi and others from the old guard are battling AOC and her fellow travelers for control of the party, but that fight is more about power than ideology. Some commentators think otherwise—that if the young Turks would just settle down, the old guard would bring the party back to the center. Columnist Niall Ferguson, for example, opined that the Democrats will lose the 2020 presidential election because "they are not one party, but two: a liberal and a socialist. The former can beat Donald Trump—but not if it is associated with the latter."[48]

I believe Trump has a very good chance of being reelected, but not because the Democrats are two parties. Nancy Pelosi and her ilk are certainly more circumspect about their leftist views and would probably take us on a slightly slower path toward socialism if they had their druthers—but they would take us there nevertheless. All twenty-plus Democratic presidential candidates favor socialized medicine, healthcare for illegal immigrants, draconian environmental measures, and the balance of the far-left agenda.[49] Though Pelosi dismisses the party's AOC wing as merely "five people," AOC and her cabal control the narrative, and seventy Democrats have voted with her 95 percent of the time.[50] Not only are they committed believers in socialism, but their hold on power depends on greatly expanding the dependency cycle, including to illegal immigrants. Recall that no less an establishment Democrat than Hillary Clinton based her presidential campaign on a promise to amplify President Obama's decidedly leftist agenda. Ferguson is correct, in my view, that the Democrats will commit political suicide if they embrace AOC's "campus socialism." But regardless of whether they nominate an openly socialist presidential candidate, they've already played their hand, and it's clear they will pursue a radical agenda if they win the presidency or regain full control of the legislative branch.

The 2020 presidential and congressional elections could determine whether this country heads permanently down the dark road of socialism, cultural Marxism, and eventually totalitarianism, or returns to its founding freedom tradition. We must work for the reelection of President Trump and congressional conservatives to reverse this leftist assault on America. To prevail in this war for our nation, which we did not start but have a moral duty to fight, we must present our message more clearly and expose the destructiveness of progressive policies and politics, which requires us to understand the left's thinking and why it is so inimical to the American idea. To that end I have written this book.

CHAPTER TWO

The Victimhood Hierarchy

INTERSECTIONALITY

Progressive activists and their acolytes are bitter and suspicious, always urging people to be wary they're not getting cheated and to ensure they haven't accidentally offended someone and lost their good standing. How can this be healthy? How is it consistent with the American dream? How can it promote prosperity? When you're consumed with paranoia and resentment instead of focusing on bettering yourself, you'll never get past the starting block. It's hard to be constructive when you're always angry. Obsessive victimhood stifles personal growth, and those who foist it on others for political gain or in a personal quest for significance do great harm. Encouraging people to think of themselves solely as members of identity groups instead of unique human beings promotes the soft bigotry of low expectations and perpetuates the very racism and other "isms" that the left purports to condemn.

Today the left exhorts people to dwell on their own race, gender, and sexual orientation along with their group's alleged historical and current oppression. The oppressed are empowered by their identities, and whites, men, and heterosexuals are deemed incapable of understanding their experiences and must be silent and listen.

Historically, most studies of identity groups focused on a single topic, such as race, gender, class, disability, or sexual orientation. But the current trend among leftist scholars is to examine how people are marginalized and endure multiple oppressions based on their multiple identities.[1] This concept of "intersectionality," like many of the left's absurd social theories, began in academia. It establishes hierarchies of victimhood based on combinations of the victims' disadvantages—race, gender, sexual orientation, class, and others. It is a matrix to determine where one fits on the hierarchy of victimhood and privilege. Women, for example, are subject to patriarchal oppression; black women are also subject to racial discrimination, and black lesbian women are victims of heterosexual oppression as well. The more disadvantaged identities you have, the more protection you are afforded. Legal scholar Kimberlé Crenshaw coined the term "intersectionality" in a 1989 paper examining how black women are marginalized by both anti-racist and feminist advocacy because their concerns transcend the individual groups.[2] Intersectionality seeks to form social justice coalitions between different identity groups who can unite to resist discrimination.[3]

As both black men and white women are more privileged than black women, Crenshaw declares, the person who is both female and black has multiple burdens and is marginalized in both feminist theory and anti-racist politics. "Because the intersectional experience is greater than the sum of racism and sexism, any analysis that does not take intersectionality into account cannot sufficiently address the particular manner in which Black women are subordinated," she writes, arrogantly dismissing the relevance of any sort of analysis but her own. Or, as writer Jennifer Kim puts it, "If I'm a black woman, I have some disadvantages because I'm a woman and some disadvantages because I'm black. But I also have some disadvantages specifically because I'm [a] black woman, which neither black men nor white women have to deal with. That's intersectionality; race, gender, and every other way to be disadvantaged interact with each other."[4]

Intersectionality, then, focuses on different types of oppression and how they overlap and are exacerbated if working in combination. Kim says it's important for people to understand this in a time when more companies are paying attention to diversity and inclusion but tend to focus on the specific disadvantages of women or minorities instead of the impact of multiple disadvantages. People are encouraged to advocate for various causes—women's rights, gay rights, racial equity, disability rights, immigration, and more, but they must always do it through the "lens of intersectionality." All oppressed minority factions must see themselves as allies on intersectional issues, which will lead to self-empowerment for all these respective groups.

WOMEN WITHOUT VAGINAS

Crenshaw's concept of intersectionality was embraced on college campuses and weaponized for political effect. In her book *Introducing Intersectionality*, Mary Romero explains that intersectionality is focused on social inequality. It "provides analytical tools for framing social justice issues in such a way as to expose how social exclusion or privilege occurs differently in various social positions, and it does this by focusing on the interaction of multiple systems of oppression."[5] "Class alone does not explain all aspects of poverty or housing segregation," writes Romero. "Gender alone cannot account for wage disparities and occupation segregation. Race by itself does not provide a complete understanding of health disparities or college retention rates. Intersectionality, as an intellectual project, delves deeper into the nuances of social equality by pushing researchers to analyze the various manifestations of inequality." Additional "power systems" and their impact on social identity and economic status must also be examined. These power systems include sexuality, ableism, ethnicity, citizenship, and age.

The study of intersectionality is mainly in the field of sociology. One of its political benefits is that the topic is so broad it can be applied to many different situations. For example, Romero uses intersectionality to examine parenting and childhood, social inequality, life experiences on campus, and other issues.[6]

In practice, intersectionality tends to devolve into a hectoring set of rules that must be strictly followed when applied to political issues or when even talking about them. For example, in another piece by Kim, she identifies mistakes people should avoid while celebrating Women's History Month or when discussing women's issues. The first mistake is knowing just part of the history—it's great to know that women got the right to vote in 1920 with passage of the Nineteenth Amendment, but of course you must recognize that female racial minorities got their voting rights much later. Second, it's unacceptable to discuss women's issues without acknowledging the effect of race, ethnicity, ability/disability, national origin, sexual orientation, religion, class, etc.... And third, you must not exclude transgender women and gender nonconforming people when discussing women's issues. That means you must avoid language that is "cisgendered," which is a term the left manufactured to denote the 99 percent of the population that identifies as the sex they were born. Naturally, instructs Kim, we must retire the "pussy hats" popular at women's marches, which exclude transgender people. After all, not all "women" have vaginas.[7]

A DOWNGRADE FOR FEMINISM

Amusingly, intersectionality has created huge problems for progressives, as aggrieved groups jealously compete for the top rung of the victim hierarchy. This has created particular challenges for feminists. Consider Patricia Arquette, who proclaimed during her acceptance speech for the 2015 Academy Award for Best Supporting Actress, "To every woman who gave birth, to every taxpayer and citizen of this nation, we have fought for everybody else's equal rights. It's our time to have wage equality once and for all and equal rights for women in the United States of America." That may sound like boilerplate feminism, but leftists furiously pounced on Arquette for failing to invoke racial minorities—that is, for callously treating women as one homogenous group without acknowledging the hierarchy of disadvantages.[8]

In a piece titled, "Patricia Arquette's Spectacular Intersectionality Fail," Andrea Grimes denounced Arquette's sins against intersectionality. Grimes says she initially thought Arquette's statement was "a nice thing to say," but something about it "didn't sit right." On further reflection, she concluded that "Arquette thoroughly erases gay women and women of color and all intersecting iterations of those identities by creating these independent identity groups as if they do not overlap—as if, *ahem*, 'all the women are white, all the blacks are men.'"

But that wasn't Arquette's worst sin, says Grimes. She demanded "that 'gay people' and 'people of color' fight for 'us,' a group that Arquette has specifically identified as non-gay and not of color—as very specifically straight and white and 'woman.'"[9] Horrors! Grimes remarks that while white women experience stark wage disparities, the gap between the earnings of white women and white men is smaller than for any other group—except Asian-Americans. "That means white women as a whole do better in terms of wage equality than almost any other group. Got it?"

Grimes ends by admonishing feminists not to protest against intersectionality as being too divisive, which is a favorite ploy of those who pretend that "doors don't close behind straight white women after they've walked through them." In other words, straight white women have made strides in overcoming discrimination, and they must assist other disadvantaged groups in overcoming oppression.

Making people hyperconscious of their various "identities" inevitably stirs resentment among groups and encourages people to keep score along identity lines, rather than to view other people as individuals and unique human beings. Indeed, intersectionality has created a host of troubling contradictions, especially for traditional feminists. In fact, the current leftist notion of gender ideology largely abolishes the entire concept of gender, recognizing only negligible differences between the sexes and insisting that gender is not biologically determined but is a matter of personal identification. If you're a man who really feels you're a woman, then as far as the left is concerned, you *are* a woman, and all of society must recognize that fact. This leaves no basis for women's pride or women's rights, since there is no objective criterion anymore for defining what a woman is. This problem is starkly illustrated in the growing phenomenon of transgender athletes who are biologically male competing in women's sports. When traditional feminists protest the unfairness of biological women having to compete against biological men, they are denounced by the left for disrespecting the transgender experience.

Fortunately conservatives reject intersectionality, so we don't have to exhaust ourselves worrying that our every utterance or action may infuriate the Intersectionality Police. But this is a real problem for traditional feminists. This tension is reflected in a *Washington Post* column by Christine Emba, in which she acknowledges that the feminist movement has delivered gains but questions whether it is for all women or just those in the middle class. She notes that feminism's intersectionality critics use social media hashtags such as #SolidarityIsForWhiteWomen to shame feminists who seek the advancement of only one, relatively privileged group—middle-class white women. Emba cites the Arquette dustup as an example of mainstream feminism's heresy of being insufficiently inclusive.

OUT OF ONE, MANY

Emba observes that despite the rise of intersectionality, some argue that it reinforces identity politics, which she claims the progressive movement was supposed to break down. She also writes that it's leading to infighting within the feminist movement and "encouraging 'privilege-checking' as a form of bullying and silencing." Others contend that intersectionality is spawning academic studies but isn't producing fruit in real life—in law, policy, or day-to-day action.[10]

Whether the progressive movement ever meant to reject identity politics as Emba claims, today identity politics permeates the left's advocacy of almost every policy issue. Race, gender, sexual orientation, and class are the left's driving obsessions. But it's undeniable that intersectionality is causing infighting and "privilege checking." How can constant intramural competition among aggrieved activists not be divisive? Will this friction not impact various causes?

Take slavery reparations. If we're going to make reparation payments to all black Americans, wouldn't it be insensitive not to provide greater compensation for black women, the victims of double oppression? Beyond that, why limit reparations to blacks? Yes, slavery was uniquely horrendous, but intersectionality emphasizes that all women (and men, except for white men, unless they're gay or transgender men) have been oppressed in American society. So why not just cut through all the noise and demand that straight, white men write checks to all non-white groups in varying amounts, as determined by the social justice gods?

Here's another recent example of the absurd contradictions created by intersectionality: the cancellation of the Eureka Women's March in Humboldt County, California, scheduled for January 19, 2019. The organizers released a statement explaining they scrapped the event because "[u]p to this point, the participants have been overwhelmingly white, lacking representation from several perspectives in our community."[11] This would be funny if it weren't so pathetic and destructive. It shows the deep-rooted distrust among these groups—that the fight against oppression and discrimination cannot be advanced by sympathetic surrogates alone. A diversity-identity purity test must be imposed. Unless there is proportional representation among the participants from all identity groups, the cause is compromised. For intersectionality's true believers, it's not just a matter of sufficient diversity among the body of protesters. It's that the causes of oppression of one identity group cannot be properly understood by others, so all must be directly involved or their grievances cannot be adequately presented.

In this sense, intersectionality is self-defeating. It claims to champion inclusiveness but fosters rank exclusiveness by encouraging groups to regard their own experiences as unique and incomprehensible by other groups. It's like saying, "We demand you acknowledge society's sins against us, but don't think you will ever understand what we've been through. We demand your help, but you're incapable of helping us, so just shut up and listen." This impulse is increasingly seen in the ridiculous, growing tendency of leftists to denounce Hollywood actors for playing minority characters if they don't belong to that minority group in real life. Thus, an amputee criticized actor Dwayne Johnson, a.k.a. "The Rock," for portraying an amputee in the movie *Skyscraper* because amputees should be "given the agency to tell our own stories."[12]

How can there ever be closure when true believers are manifestly unforgiving—when they regard historical wrongs as irremediable? How can reconciliation occur when intersectionality encourages various groups to regard one another with suspicion, jealousy, and rivalry? The groveling statement by the organizers of the Eureka Women's March reinforces this mind-set, as they apologize for the event's unforgivable whiteness:

> Our intention with this march is to affect real social change by raising the voices of all women within our community. We recognize the majority of our current leadership team is white, and planning for this event has been centered around our experiences. In recognizing our failure to put enough effort into being more inclusive, we are attempting to make things right by taking this time to create a more balanced leadership team. Our goal moving forward is to ensure the voices of women of color are heard and centered when we come together for the furtherance of the rights and protection of women. Throughout history, women of color have been proven over and over again to be some of the most vulnerable populations. From the suffering of enslaved Black women in early gynecological experiments, to the current epidemic of Missing and Murdered Indigenous Women across the nation and beyond. Having their voices go unheard can be a matter of life and death, and it is imperative that a safe community is created for everyone.[13]

Note that these mostly white organizers sheepishly acknowledge they can't possibly understand the experiences of minority women and can't adequately promote their cause without ample participation by non-whites. Are we expected to believe they truly feel remorse for having organized what they obviously believed was an empowering event? Or are they merely genuflecting to the gods of intersectionality to avoid race-bullying? This is not normal thinking. It's as if they've been reeducated into a real-life *1984*-style groupthink in which dissent is forbidden. Imagine the level of anxiety in that environment—knowing that at any second you might utter the wrong words and be shunned or banished. Thus, another contradiction of this philosophy is exposed—it uses oppression to try to rectify oppression.

This glaring contradiction is also evident in the rabid anti-Semitism of some leaders of the Women's March, a feminist group created to protest the election of President Trump. Intersectionality holds itself out as a champion of all oppressed groups, and who could dispute that Jews have been among the most oppressed people in history? But as they are regarded as members and beneficiaries of the white race, their persecution doesn't count as much as that of other minorities. "On the extreme left, Jews are seen as part of a white-majority establishment that seeks to dominate people of color," writes Emma Green in *The Atlantic*.[14] They are seen as heirs of "white supremacy," which mitigates any suffering they've endured.[15]

This is surely what Women's March co-organizer Tamika Mallory had in mind when she reportedly instructed her Jewish colleague Vanessa Wruble that "Jews needed to confront their own role in racism." Wruble believes she was pushed out of the organization partially because of her Jewish ancestry. Though the Women's March and another co-organizer with a history of anti-Semitic statements, Linda Sarsour, eventually issued separate statements condemning anti-Semitism, their declarations don't square with their association with notorious anti-Semite Louis Farrakhan—Mallory called him the GOAT (greatest of all time) and was notably reluctant to distance herself from him during an appearance on *The View*.[16] Anti-Semitism among Women's March leaders eventually became so acute that Women's March founder Teresa Shook called for four leaders, including Mallory and Sarsour, to leave the organization, while other members launched a petition with a similar goal.[17]

Progressive activism, being rooted in negativity, suspicion, jealousy, and rage, invariably leads advocacy groups to turn on one another. Intersectional ideology demands that everyone constantly keep score and flay himself over past discrimination and its lingering effects on present generations. Assuming nearly every group is being treated unfairly, it engenders perpetual anxiety over who's being treated *more* unfairly, instead of encouraging people to focus on the uplifting aspects of life. Regardless of inequalities among various identity groups, is it healthy for people to endlessly navel gaze, dwelling on their own plight? Will grievance merchants ever be satisfied with progress they've made?

The Civil War, Reconstruction, constitutional amendments, and civil rights legislation were obviously not enough on slavery. But what about the lasting damage caused by salting this wound in perpetuity? Even if you could eradicate all human prejudice and bigotry, what would be next? Would the next generation of malcontent activists demand equal outcomes in every aspect of life to compensate for the different talents and abilities individuals have? If group identity politics could ever reach its logical conclusion, would activists next switch to disparities among individuals?

Progressives essentially reject the notion that every human being is made in God's image and therefore entitled to equal dignity, rights, and protection of the laws. For them, equal opportunity is an unachievable myth, so central planners and social justice warriors must continually interfere in society to "level the playing field."

"WHITE MEN AREN'T PART OF THE PROBLEM; THEY ARE THE PROBLEM"

Leftists believe they serve a higher moral cause and owe no one an explanation. Once they've undertaken a new mission, sundry activists rush to glom on it like flies on dung. In the Star Wars bar scene of the Democratic presidential primary field, former candidate Kirsten Gillibrand showed just how quickly and uncritically Democratic leaders attach themselves to the latest cause to ingratiate themselves to their rabid base. On December 4, 2018, Gillibrand tweeted, "The Future is Female...Intersectional...Powered in our belief in one another...And we're just getting started." Unwittingly, she committed the cardinal sin of championing old-school feminism (the notion of a "female future" was apparently a rallying cry of lesbian separatists in the 1970s) and intersectionality at the same time.[18] She obviously had no clue what intersectionality is but figured she would mouth the popular leftist slogans to boost her campaign. Unsurprisingly, she received a firestorm of criticism in response.

Gillibrand tried to walk it back in an interview with CNN's Van Jones, saying her intended message was, "Please include the ladies in the future, because they're not really included today." Once again, this sentiment, and even her original tweet, may strike conservatives as commonplace left-wing sloganeering. But thanks to intersectionality, yesterday's cliché is today's heresy. In a biting piece denouncing Gillibrand in *The Atlantic*, Caitlin Flanagan proclaimed, "[A]s something that a middle-aged, hyper-successful white woman such as Gillibrand can play around with, [intersectionality is] a hand grenade that's going to explode in her mittens." For example, says Flanagan, when Gillibrand told Jones, "It's worrying that the top three presidential front-runners are white men," she assumed she could leverage just one piece of intersectional theory to wedge her way to the top of the pack. "She's used to feminism being a jet pack that she can fire up any time she needs a boost. Not this time."

Gillibrand clearly didn't understand that white women are a bit of a problem for intersectionalists because they may be oppressed as women, but they're still white, which means they're part oppressor, or at least a partial beneficiary of oppression. Flanagan cites Brittney Cooper, an African American professor and author of *Eloquent Rage*, who argues that intersectionality allows people to confront white women on their notion of feminism if they are using it to have access to the power that white men have. That is not what the fight is about. "White women don't want to change the fundamental paradigm of race and gender in this country," argues Cooper; "they want to exploit it so that they can gain access to the power that white men have." Concerning Gillibrand's worries over white men's dominance in the Democratic Party, Flanagan writes, "If there's anything intersectional feminism has no time for, it's white men—which must have seemed politically useful to her in the moment. According to the intersectional framework, white men aren't part of the problem—they are the problem."

The fanatical intolerance of intersectionality can be seen in the bitterness Flanagan expresses toward Gillibrand—and toward men in general. In her view, Gillibrand can't possibly understand intersectional feminism when she admits to having deferred to her husband and sons as to whether she would ultimately run for president. In the end, Gillibrand's transgression was apparently unforgivable to Flanagan, who suggested she refrain from running altogether and support a "deeply accomplished potential candidate who really would help make the future intersectional: Kamala Harris."[19]

As for white men, they play the role of arch-villain in the intersectionality drama. As Flanagan remarked, they are "the problem." Many leftists will go much further in describing the threat they pose. In an August 2019 CNN appearance, left-wing commentator Angela Rye became offended when Republican strategist Patrick Griffin observed that Reps. Ilhan Omar and Rshida Tlaib were hijacking the Democratic Party from Nancy Pelosi. After berating Griffin for using the word "hijack" in connection with two Muslims, Rye proclaimed, "[T]he greatest terrorist threat in this country is white men, white men who think like you."[20]

"ANOTHER UNPASSABLE PURITY TEST"

Intersectionality, then, requires that only the most identity-disadvantaged can lead the cause. White women, no matter how much they profess their faith in the concept, are disqualified on racial grounds. It is profoundly divisive and alienating to restrict the leadership of a cause to those directly affected by it. Such thinking would have disqualified William Wilberforce and Abraham Lincoln from their abolition advocacy. It violates the biblical principle that we should all serve one another.

Ultimately, this paranoid philosophy might hoist itself on its own petard. CNN's Don Lemon questioned whether Flanagan's favorite presidential candidate, Kamala Harris, is black enough, as Harris descends from an Indian mother and Jamaican father. In an interview with White House correspondent April Ryan, who asked why the "blackness" of mixed-race candidates is relevant, Lemon said it wasn't about being black but whether she was an African-American black—a descendant of slaves. When Ryan noted that some slaves from Africa were taken to the Caribbean, Lemon responded, "Jamaica's not America. Jamaica did not come out of Jim Crow."[21] African-American columnist Renee Graham comments on the absurdity of debating who is black enough. "There is no monolithic way to be black," writes Graham. "Such attacks on Harris are idiotic when there are real and serious policy issues to be discussed.... It's yet another unpassable purity test, not unlike the so-called birthers who sought to undermine Obama's citizenship."[22]

Another columnist, Morgan Jenkins, questions Harris's bona fides from another perspective. Jenkins believes Harris was strong on many issues but had a poor record on criminal justice reform. This causes Jenkins to agonize whether she could possibly be justified in withholding support from a female black candidate. "No candidate is perfect, and the idea that I might not support a black woman who is qualified for the job is excruciating," writes Jenkins. "My life's work is centered on black women and their stories, no matter how complicated those narratives might be. Was my hesitation premature and unfair? But the alternative is almost as painful—giving someone who looks like me a pass on actions that have hurt our communities. I want a black female president. But I want an end to mass incarceration for all black women, for all black families, even more. Who can deliver that? Could it be Harris? Maybe, but I need her to make that case."[23]

Democratic presidential candidate Tulsi Gabbard picked up on this theme, brutally attacking Harris's criminal justice record during one of the presidential debates, prompting columnist Jeff Yang to ask, "Why did a key focal point of a two-hour-long, 10-person debate end up being a confrontation between the only two women of color, despite frontrunner Joe Biden standing at center stage, and a cackling Trump watching the sparks fly from the White House?"[24]

Fundamentally, intersectionality is intellectually dishonest. The ideology purports to be based on one's identity alone—race, gender, class. So shouldn't intersectionality proponents defend Justice Clarence Thomas when he's attacked by white liberal men? Shouldn't everyone be outraged at the abuse heaped on Condoleezza Rice including racist caricatures of her? Shouldn't the opinions of black conservative Thomas Sowell carry more weight than those of white liberal Paul Krugman? Intersectionality peddlers, like other leftists, want it both ways. If they were consistent, they wouldn't treat black conservatives—men and women—white conservative women, and gay Republicans so contemptuously.

Virginia Democrats displayed their hypocrisy as the clashing hierarchies of privilege illustrated that intersectionality is only useful when it serves progressive and Democratic Party causes; otherwise it must yield. In early 2019, wearing blackface became one of the deadly sins. A photo emerged from a yearbook page of Virginia Democratic governor Ralph Northam, depicting someone in blackface standing next to someone in a Ku Klux Klan outfit. Northam offered nonsensical, conflicting explanations, but it was widely understood he was one of the two men. Meanwhile, Virginia attorney general Mark R. Herring admitted to having worn blackface as a young man. Around the same time two black women accused the state's Democratic lieutenant governor, Justin Fairfax, of sexual assault. Most Virginia Democratic leaders and legislators called on Fairfax, an African American, to resign, even though the two white Democrats were resolutely remaining in office. But how could Democrats impeach Fairfax while the white male race-sinners refused to resign?

President Trump succinctly summarized the dilemma. "African Americans are very angry at the double standard on full display in Virginia," he tweeted. The *New York Times* was also exercised over this potential insult to intersectionality. Don't whites have to defer to blacks? Which is worse, sexual assault or racism? Doesn't intersectionality require that female allegations trump male denials? Or must these celebrated causes yield to crass calculations of political power? What should the Democratic Party—the self-proclaimed guardian of all disadvantaged groups—do in the face of these competing interests? How do you mollify the women's movement without alienating blacks, and vice versa? Former DNC chairwoman Donna Brazile expressed the Democrats' quandary well, observing, "There's no playbook for this."[25]

Fairfax defied the new rules of intersectionality, opting instead to fall back on the old norms of race alone. "As a matter of general principle, no one should challenge the fact that African American women have been marginalized regarding sexual assault claims," said Fairfax. "Nor should anyone challenge the fact that African American men have been the targets of false allegations of sexual assault, whoever the accuser. We need a justice system that treats both accusers and the accused fairly and affords both due process."[26] He had a point, though his appeal to fairness, justice, and due process wasn't in line with intersectionality's hierarchical rules. And we certainly didn't hear any Democrats arguing for due process and the presumption of innocence when Judge Brett Kavanaugh was falsely accused of sexual assault.

"YOU DON'T MAKE PROGRESS ON HALF THE RACE"

One convenient aspect of intersectionality is that it can shield victimizers as victims and serve as a perverse type of identity immunity. This is exactly what happened when Representative Ilhan Omar faced allegations of anti-Semitism. As minorities like Omar are among the historically oppressed, they have free rein to dump on historically oppressed whites, to wit: Jews. When Omar was under siege, fellow leftist Linda Sarsour defended her, saying she was "triggered by the constant defensive posture women of color leaders find themselves in.... We are put to higher standards than everyone else." People, said Sarsour, "want to destroy us and liberals always play into it...liberals talk about smashing the patriarchy and standing with people of color and often times are the first people to throw women of color leaders under the bus to show how self-righteous they are and to appease angry white men...this is upholding white supremacy."[27]

If you reject meritocracy, why not reject accountability as well? It's all part of the same logic. Identity trumps behavior. Omar can't be culpable because of her disadvantaged identity. Sarsour's Women's March colleague Tamika Mallory made similar arguments, attempting to turn the tables on Omar's oppressor-accusers. Mallory tweeted that "women of color are held to unreachable standards and scrutinized in a way no one else is." She added that "we are also not given benefit of the doubt. Just based on who we are, people assume ill will. This is NOT okay. There's racism at play."[28] So people are NOT allowed to call out Omar's racist statements lest they be accused of racism themselves.

Similarly, when Representative Rashida Tlaib came under fire for a column she had written in 2006 for Farrakhan's anti-Semitic Nation of Islam, she invoked her identity as a woman of color to portray herself as a victim rather than a victimizer. Tlaib tweeted, "The hardest part of serving in Congress as a WOC [woman of color] & as a 'first' is how people hear you differently. No matter how much we take on the hate & stay true to who we are through our experiences, our voices are shushed and reduced. We aren't perfect, but neither is this institution."[29] Yes, when someone calls you out for your racism, they must be trying to shut you up because of their own racism.

THE SINS OF THE FATHER

The left also uses intersectionality as a lens for examining religious discrimination. Since the American left sees Muslims as non-white and victimized, it overlooks gross violations of civil rights in Muslim countries. Intersectionality is not as forgiving of Christians, who are perceived to represent the top spot on the religious privilege hierarchy. Despite rampant persecution against them, Christians are not seen as victims. Open Doors USA reports that 215 million Christians—about 1 in 12 Christians worldwide—experience high levels of persecution by communist, Islamic, or other nationalist-religious regimes.[30] Yet most of these incidents receive little media attention, much less political condemnation.[31]

Like affirmative action, intersectionality is self-contradictory because it applies racist, sexist, and class solutions to address supposed problems rooted in racism, sexism, and classism. It's one thing to be conscious of wrongs perpetrated against particular groups in history, but it's another to demonize descendants of the identity groups believed responsible for such wrongs based solely on their identities. In effect you are discriminating against people based on their identities, not their behavior, which is as wrong in this case as in any other. Leftists make these classifications based on identity categories and ignore the actions and characters of individuals in the "privileged" groups. Our sense of justice can't help but rebel against condemnation for things we had nothing to do with. Intersectionality encourages us to objectify human beings rather than view them as individuals. It's immoral and destructive to the human spirit to exempt people from personal responsibility for their individual actions because they are a member of a disadvantaged identity group.

Intersectionality's proponents will doubtless claim that they are not demonizing white people or white men in particular but merely seeking redress for the historically disadvantaged. But you can't witness their allegations of privilege and miss the ethos of resentment and blame. This sick thinking dominates the left. For example, the *Library Journal*, founded by Melvil Dewey, who originated the Dewey decimal system, tweeted, "Library collections continue to promote and proliferate whiteness with their very existence and the fact that they are physically taking up space in our libraries."[32] There you go—whiteness is evil. Actress Rosanna Arquette, sister of Patricia Arquette, expressed the same idea when she tweeted, "I'm sorry I was born white and privileged. It disgusts me." In case her feelings weren't clear she added, "And I feel so much shame." Ironically, her self-denunciation provoked criticism from social justice warriors who accused her of taking full advantage of her privilege.[33]

Even pointing out that whites are being categorically maligned can inspire charges of white supremacy. Those who demand an "honest" conversation about race should understand that many people feel they can't speak freely without being wrongly accused of prejudice. As if to prove my point, race-baiting leftists have added another loony term to our dictionaries—"white fragility," defined as "the tendency among members of the dominant white cultural group to have a defensive, wounded, angry, or dismissive response to evidence of racism."[34]

"WHITE WOMEN UPHOLD WHITE SUPREMACY THROUGH THEIR VOTE"

"I don't know if you've heard, but white people are awful," writes *RedState*'s Alex Parker. "They're just the worst. We have a relatively new term for all the people who aren't the worst: people of color. Therefore, there are people who are of color, and there are people who are the worst. Those are the two races in America today." Parker cites an example of how this thinking plays out. Actor Herve Villechaize, a dwarf, played Tattoo in the popular seventies show *Fantasy Island. Game of Thrones* actor Peter Dinklage, also a dwarf, portrayed Villechaize in the HBO movie *My Dinner with Herve.* When social justice warriors heard that Villechaize was a minority and Dinklage was not, they pounced. One person tweeted, "Umm Herve Villechaize is FILIPINO!!!! NOT WHITE!" Another said, "Love Peter Dinklage, but are folks just gonna ignore the fact that Herve Villechaize was Filipino?" He added the hashtag #whitewashedOUT. Yet another went further, tweeting, "No. No. NO. Shame on you, HBO. Herve Villechaize was French-born Filipino and British. Casting Dinklage in a wig and with a fake accent erases his real identity and tragic story and is a crushing blow to APA actors who could've owned this role."[35]

There you have it. One's identity is based on his race, not his common humanity, a buzzword that liberals used to use, ironically, when virtue signaling harmony and solidarity was their thing. But harmony went the way of other liberal pet causes such as global cooling. As it turns out, with regard to Villechaize, the social justice warriors jumped the gun. Villechaize was actually of German, French, and English descent—pretty solidly white, in other words. This entire episode is silly and pathetic. It's wrong for people to obsess over race. It is wretchedly dehumanizing to all concerned, and people who agree should express revulsion toward such thinking rather than standing fearfully silent or pretending to endorse it. It is the height of racism, in the name of purging racism.

Other examples of such divisive nonsense abound. Although Democrats and Never Trumpers hailed the 2018 congressional elections as a repudiation of Trump, some disgruntled leftists were outraged that the white vote trended Republican. Progressive activist Marisa Kabas tweeted, "deleted a couple tweets because I don't think they accurately expressed what I was trying to say. White women uphold white supremacy through their vote. They have no qualms about hurting women of color, and that's an objective truth." If this was her preferred tweet, one wonders what the originals contained. Travon Free tweeted, "Black women voted 95% for [Democrat] Beto [O'Rourke]. White women did what white women do. #ElectionNight." Leftist celebrity Chelsea Handler tweeted, "59% of white women voted for Ted Cruz. I don't know what it is going to take for us to be sisters to other women, but we have to do better than this. We need to vote for the best interests of others, and stop thinking only about ourselves."

Handler was similarly agitated a few weeks before, when she denounced Fox for unveiling its new streaming platform, Fox Nation. She tweeted, "Fox News' new paid streaming service 'Fox Nation' will launch later this year with daily programming from Laura Ingraham and Sean Hannity. It's for when you need a break from watching racists on your TV, so you can watch them on your computer."[36] These tweets illuminate another problem with intersectionality and leftist politics in general. Leftists like Handler get a pass in our culture and from the liberal media for such despicable remarks. They are immune from criticism when falsely alleging that conservatives, by virtue of their conservatism alone, are racist.

On election night, another person tweeted, "Really, truly embarrassed that 76% of white women in Georgia voted for [Republican gubernatorial candidate Brian] Kemp. It's shameful. Humiliating. Thinking about driving my ass down there next election and personally talking to as many of these fools as possible." Another said, "White women: foot soldiers of the patriarchy." There are countless other examples.[37] The message is that white women can't possibly promote their own interests if they vote Republican. Apparently, a robust economy, strong defense, and social conservatism only matter to white male patriarchs.

The election defeats of African-American gubernatorial candidates Stacey Abrams (Georgia) and Andrew Gillum (Florida) triggered socialist icon Bernie Sanders. He told the *Daily Beast* following the election, "I think you know there are a lot of white folks out there who are not necessarily racist who felt uncomfortable for the first time in their lives about whether or not they wanted to vote for an African American. I think next time around, by the way, it will be a lot easier for them to do that." Apparently Bernie was unaware of any whites in either state having voted when Obama was on the ballot. But in the end, Bernie just couldn't resist contradicting himself and blaming racism full-on. "I think [Gillum is] a fantastic politician in the best sense of the word," said Sanders. "He stuck to his guns in terms of a progressive agenda. I think he ran a great campaign. And he had to take on some of the most blatant and ugly racism that we have seen in many, many years. And yet he came within a whisker of winning."[38] It's not about race, but it is.

CHILLING PRIVATE SECTOR SPEECH

Many white progressives revel in attacking conservative whites for their alleged racism and yes, for simply being white. Senator Lindsey Graham became an immediate villain when he staunchly defended Supreme Court Justice nominee Bret Kavanaugh. Protestors accosted Graham when he exited the Senate office building and headed for his car. They called him "despicable" and promised to vote him out of office. They screamed at him, "You old, white, privileged patriarchy!"[39]

Race-shaming is rampant in our culture. Fashion retailer Forever 21 stepped in it when its website showed a white male model wearing a sweater with the words "Wakanda Forever," a reference to the movie *Black Panther.* One critic tweeted, "Hey @Forever21, in what universe did you think it was OK to feature a white model in Wakanda gear? Granted, chances are you knew it wasn't OK, but still. As a Former #21 men brand specialist for the company, I'm highly offended." Being offended is a badge of honor these days, especially if it's for the right reasons and you have the proper pedigree. Another person tweeted, "Wow Forever 21 is tone deaf af. Colonizers aren't praised in Wakanda. Try again." Do you see how deep this goes? The hapless white model with a sweater promoting a black superhero movie is instantly demonized as a colonizer. This is too twisted for words.

Naturally, Forever 21 didn't dare object. The store instantly hit the ground groveling and apologized for offending the left. It deleted a tweet with the photo and deleted pictures of the evil youngster from its website. It tweeted, "Forever 21 takes feedback on our products and marketing extremely seriously. We celebrate all superheroes with many different models of various ethnicities and apologize if the photo in question was offensive in any way."[40]

But in what sane world would the photo be offensive? What is offensive is this entire charade. It's not just the leftist cultural insanity that is so alarming but the widespread capitulation by people who are bullied and intimidated into conforming. Arguably, private sector intimidation is becoming as great a threat to free thought and expression as government encroachments.

Similarly, Columbia University student Julian von Abele ruffled feathers when he filmed a video praising Europeans for building the modern world and expressing his love for white men. The university got wind of the incident and emailed undergraduates, condemning the "racially charged" incident and announcing they had begun an investigation. Von Abele responded on Twitter, denying charges of racism and hatred. "Nobody has explained what I said that was actually negative or racist, or insulting towards anybody else," he said. "I was *theatrically* and *sarcastically* demonstrating that whites are not allowed to embrace their cultural achievements." He added, "As everyone who has known me my whole life knows, I am a kind person and I don't hate anyone, certainly not for their race or ethnicity." The school newspaper, the *Columbia Daily Spectator*, charged von Abele with harassing students of color and "spewing racist, white supremacist rhetoric." Student senate member Alfredo Dominguez attributed the incident to allowing free speech on campus. "You can have arguments all you want about free speech and people being entitled to say what they want," said Dominguez. "But when that bubbles [into] assaulting black or brown people with that and then stalking them . . . you're getting into levels of hate crime and your speech being directly related to violence."

The article reported on a video supposedly showing von Abele berating a group of mainly black underclassmen with racist and white supremacist comments. The Black Student Organization and the Student Organization of Latinxs accused von Abele of physically grabbing another student and asking him if black women like to date white men. The video doesn't corroborate any of these smears, but it does show one student touching von Abele's chest and face.[41] Abele explained that he made the video because he was tired of people using the term "white privilege" and other divisive rhetoric to dismiss others' views. "Every single person should love themselves and their culture, and we should all be allowed to be proud of our heritage," he said. He related that other students told him he had no right to express his views because he was male and white. But he said he was tired of being held personally responsible for others' historical actions and of the divisive rhetoric that blames all society's ills on white men. He added, "At no time did I shove, grab, or physically or verbally assault anyone, nor did I denigrate anyone's race."[42] The alarming attitude of the *Columbia Daily Spectator* vindicates Abele's concerns about his free expression rights. The incident shows that people are frustrated and weary of being blamed for things they had nothing to do with, which violates any reasonable person's innate sense of justice.

Nevertheless, intersectionality has continued to spread from academia to the Democratic Party. Democrat Stacey Abrams, the failed gubernatorial candidate in Georgia, penned an essay in *Foreign Affairs* endorsing intersectionality as a vision for America. She's convinced that white racism is rampant today, mainly among conservatives, and that it must be countered by identity politics, which she laughably denies is divisive. "When the groups most affected by these issues insist on acknowledgment of their intrinsic difference, it should not be viewed as divisive," she wrote. "Embracing the distinct history and identities of groups in a democracy enhances the complexity and capacity of the whole."[43] In her view, all existing inequities are due to bigotry, and identity groups must be empowered to defeat them—which is a formula for a balkanized, bitter, and joyless nation.

"UNEARNED SKIN PRIVILEGE"

The notion of white privilege is fundamental to the ideology of intersectionality. But for allegations of white privilege, intersectionality would have no juice at all. In 1989 sociologist Peggy McIntosh revolutionized the idea in her piece, "White Privilege: Unpacking the Invisible Knapsack."[44] She observed that while men might admit that women are disadvantaged, they won't concede that men are overprivileged. They might be willing to improve women's status but won't agree to lessen their own. She equated men's refusal to reduce their own "privilege" as de facto obstruction of women's progress. In thinking through these issues, she realized there are interlocking hierarchies in our society. White privilege must exist, just as male privilege does, though its existence is denied and protected, as is the existence of male privilege. "As a white person, I realized I had been taught about racism as something which puts others at a disadvantage, but had been taught not to see one of its corollary aspects, white privilege, which puts me at an advantage."[45]

Betraying a conspiracy mind-set, she opines that whites are "carefully taught" not to recognize white privilege, just as males are taught not to recognize male privilege. "I have come to see white privilege as an invisible package of unearned assets which I can count on cashing in each day, but about which I was 'meant' to remain oblivious," she wrote. One wonders who "meant" her—and other whites—to remain oblivious. Adam Smith, perhaps? Ronald Reagan? "White privilege is like an invisible weightless backpack of special provisions, maps, passports, codebooks, visas, clothes, tools and blank checks.... I began to count the ways in which I enjoy unearned skin privilege and have been conditioned into oblivion about its existence."

So she decided to "work on" herself by listing the daily effects of white privilege in her life, which included such items as, "I can if I wish arrange to be in the company of people of my race most of the time.... If I should need to move, I can be pretty sure of renting or purchasing housing in an area which I can afford and in which I would want to live.... I can be pretty sure that my neighbors in such a location will be neutral or pleasant to me. ... I can go shopping alone most of the time, pretty well assured that I will not be followed or harassed.... I can turn on the television or open to the front page of the paper and see people of my race widely represented."[46] This is a small sampling of her "privileges," which she wrote down to force herself to "give up the myth of meritocracy. If these things are true, this is not such a free country; one's life is not what one makes it; many doors open for certain people through no virtues of their own." Here again we see a devaluation of the principles of merit, freedom, and equal opportunity. If leftists succeed in convincing people that a merit-based society is unattainable, they will have destroyed a central pillar of the American idea.

The oppressor–oppressed worldview of white privilege and intersectionality is aligned with neo-Marxism and "privilege theory."[47] It's natural, then, that the neo-Marxist notion of "white privilege" evolved into social doctrine among progressive activists.[48] Karl Marx divided the world into categories of the oppressors and the oppressed with his zero-sum class ideology, which pitted the bourgeoisie against the proletariat and saw capitalism as the systemic oppressor. In modern times, leftists have repackaged Marx's divisive framework and furtively adapted it to forms of oppression beyond the economic class struggle, such as race and gender, pitting identity groups against one another with the ultimate goal of instituting socialism out of the chaos.[49]

Each category has different sets of oppressors and oppressed. With race it's whites versus minorities; with gender it's males versus females and heterosexuals versus gays and transgenders. Philosophy professor Jason Barker, in a *New York Times* op-ed idolatrously titled "Happy Birthday, Karl Marx. You Were Right!," giddily boasts that "racial and sexual oppression have been added to the dynamic of class exploitation. Social justice movements like Black Lives Matter and #MeToo owe something of an unspoken debt to Marx through their unapologetic targeting of the 'eternal truths' of our age. Such movements recognize, as did Marx, that the ideas that rule every society are those of its ruling class and that overturning those ideas is fundamental to true revolutionary progress."[50]

Neo-Marxist philosophy is inherently defeatist and at war with the American idea because it rejects equality of opportunity even as a goal. Because of different privileges enjoyed and disadvantages suffered by various identity groups, meritocracy and opportunity are unattainable. People succeed not because of their efforts or abilities but because of their privilege. The only solution is to replace capitalism with socialism. Only government can remedy the privileges that capitalism confers.

MIDDLE-CLASS FOOT SOLDIERS

Capitalism, according to many neo-Marxists, doesn't just cause class oppression but racial oppression as well. "Capitalism is a system that breeds class oppression and national/racial conquest," writes Edna Bonacich. "The two forms of exploitation operate in tandem. They are part of the same system that creates inequality, impoverishment, and all the other host of social ills that result. I believe you cannot attack capitalism without attacking racism. The two are Siamese twins, joined together from top to bottom."[51] Bonacich regards capitalism as innately flawed and incapable of eliminating poverty—it "depends on exploitation." Private property owners become wealthy on the backs of "propertyless" laborers, who work for them and rent their buildings. But for the have-nots, there could be no "haves." Capitalism can't rid itself of poverty. "It requires poverty. Poverty is the basis of wealth.... To repeat, the wealthy depend on poverty for their riches. They are committed to it, wedded to it. They cannot do without it.... Capital accumulation depends on exploitation, and exploitation both requires and reproduces poverty."[52] Once again, we see the socialist notion of finite wealth, a mind-set that is impervious to the concept of economic growth and wealth creation. With a fixed amount of wealth and no way to expand it, it follows that the social planners must step in and fairly redistribute it. Here we also see the regrettable philosophical basis for the left's contempt for the wealthy.

Bonacich bastardizes the term "racism" to support her theory that capitalism and racism are joined at the hip. For her, "racism is a system of exploitation." It is a mechanism to control and oppress people to extract maximum profits from them. By redefining racism she's able to explain away the rise of the black middle class that was occurring when she wrote her article in 1989. The upward mobility of blacks didn't mitigate racism because the black middle class, "like the white middle class, are part of the structure of oppression of the black poor and working class." She maintains that "the United States continues to be a deeply racist society" in at least two central respects. "First, it consists in the continued exploitation of people of color for profit. Second, it is demonstrated in the demand that people of color must accommodate to the white man's system, rather than vice versa." Capitalism, she insists, "is based on vicious inequality." The ruling class pays lip service to racial equality but openly opposes social equality. It pretends to open the doors of opportunity to blacks, but the system demands that people of color adapt to the white man's culture. "They have to play by the white man's rules."

But what evidence exists that "the system" demands that minorities adapt to "the white man's culture?" If that's the case, why is black culture so popular? Why do politicians like Elizabeth Warren and Beto O'Rourke strain to co-opt minority identities? As Victor Davis Hanson asks, "Why did California congressional candidate Kevin Leon rather abruptly become Kevin de León, emphasizing an ethnic cachet—if 'whiteness' equaled unearned advantage and non-whiteness earned lifelong discrimination?" Other examples include Professor Ward Churchill, who masqueraded as a Native American for career advancement,[53] and Rachel Dolezal, who became Spokane NAACP chapter president while pretending she was black.[54]

Elaborating on her conspiratorial view of capitalism as an innately exploitive system, Bonacich says it's not just the wealthy who exploit the poor but the foot soldiers in the middle class who "are paid out of the profits squeezed from the poor in order to keep the poor under control." The middle class helps to manage the poor. They are the guardians of this pernicious inequality, ensuring that capitalism extends through the generations, and they are paid "handsomely" for their efforts. The education system, whose competitive nature is modeled on capitalism, is a feeder of the middle class and its values. "The schools are a great sorting machine for the unequal hierarchy of wealth and privilege that is American capitalism." The teachers validate this process, and "help to label the poor as incompetents, as failures, as unworthy, and therefore deserving of dispossession."

Bonacich says the great myth of the educational system is that the pursuit of individual achievement will maximize social benefit—that the greatest good comes from selfishness and that the benefits of competition will trickle down to everyone, which she identifies as "the self-delusion of capitalism in general, and imperialism in particular." Once again, she implicates the middle class in this sham. They view their own advancement while others are starving as "a mark of their uprightness," and they claim to be role models to the poor. She also blames capitalism for the ghetto. "It epitomizes the social decay of capitalism. This is what the 'free market' produces."

Bonacich further indicts the black middle class. "They are forced to become police for the white man's system.... They have to participate in supporting capitalist rule. They have to help in the extraction of the surplus from the poor." Like most leftists, Bonacich has a pat answer for everything. The growth of the black middle class, she says, doesn't disprove the reality of America's racial oppression but intensifies it. The existence of a black middle class, you see, impedes the black poor from seeing themselves as victims of racial oppression. Far from showing the decline of racism, it signifies a new chapter in the evolution of American prejudice. Coming close to denouncing the black middle class *en masse* as Uncle Toms, she claims they are putty in the hands of white elites who "are forever devising new strategies to consolidate their rule."

Bonacich sees wealth redistribution and other welfare policies as commendable but inherently limited. As long as our system features private ownership of productive property, which is used to profit the owners, there will always be an impoverished class, likely consisting largely of minorities. "The class relations of capitalism inevitably involve drainage of wealth from the poor to the rich, and no redistributive programs can ever remotely counter the basic direction of this flow." Her solution is not to lobby the government for change but to overthrow it. "Just as the private property in slaves was once confiscated, so the owners of the corporations that rule this nation will one day have to be dispossessed." Bonacich didn't see revolution on the horizon, however, because all the major institutions—schools, media, etc.—were firmly in capitalist hands—which is odd, since the left had long since ensconced itself in the media and schools when she wrote this piece in 1989.

For Bonacich, even large-scale upward mobility among blacks would not improve many black lives. It would just serve to assimilate blacks into the corrupt capitalistic system—"accepting the dominant order and fitting into it.... Jobs in the white man's system is not the answer." Instead, blacks need to build alternative economic systems that they control—not capitalist systems but collective ones. Racism, in her view, is forever intertwined with capitalism. It is "one of the major mechanisms by which private capital retains its rule."[55]

RADICAL IDEAS HAVE BECOME MAINSTREAM

This is a sick, jealous, and loveless ideology whose legitimacy depends on class and race conflict and can permit no meaningful improvement in social mobility or race relations. Socio-economic classes are fixed, and there can be no real assimilation. As such, any objective evidence of improvement is denied or explained away. This us-against-them mind-set is the core of progressive morality. Christian writer Jayme Metzgar articulates it well. "While adherents of progressivism may sincerely believe they're working to end oppression, the fact is that their model of morality *requires oppression in order to exist*," writes Metzgar. "It requires that someone always be cast in the role of oppressor, whether he or she deserves to be or not. Any final end to oppression and evil—any real peace, unity, or brotherhood—is impossible."

This explains why Bonacich felt threatened by successful blacks. "Instead, they needed to rebuild their own communities, with Black, not white, needs and interests, as the central, human concern." In her view, racial harmony and color blindness are not lofty ideals but insidious tricks. Black upward mobility is merely a ruse to entice them to abandon their identity and to be forever relegated to white domination and exploitation.

Some apologists dismiss Bonacich's cohort as radicals who are not representative of leftist or liberal thinking at that time or even now. But if you believe their ideas haven't matriculated into the culture, you haven't been paying attention. This is the stuff of mainstream gender studies and critical race theory classes on nearly every college campus today. Their ideas have now insinuated themselves into mainstream Democratic Party thinking. Democrats are deeply invested in perpetual struggles of race, class, and gender, and are pursuing policies so radical as to annihilate our entire existing economic structure. It is naïve to view these ideas as anything but seminal and today's Democratic initiatives as anything but a logical outworking of this radicalism.

Modern leftism is a secular religion, and there are many denominations that often overlap, from the church of environmentalism to socialism, cultural Marxism, identity politics, and intersectionality. Metzgar notes that many religious traditions seek to answer the question, "What is good, true, and beautiful?" In Christianity, God is the answer to all three. But progressivism, without the benefit of moral absolutes, has settled on a simplistic moral standard that refines sin to the single category of oppression.

Metzgar argues that progressives see history as the moral force that moves toward progress. There is certainly truth in this. Marx clearly subscribed to this general notion, and the progressive worldview rejects the Christian biblical doctrine of man's fall, believing instead that man, through science and reason, marches toward enlightenment. Metzgar contends that the progressive moral framework leads to the inescapable conclusion that victimhood is the highest virtue. "Victims and members of oppressed identity groups are elevated to a kind of sainthood in the progressive religion," writes Metzgar. "Those who are more oppressed have more moral authority and are thus more worthy to speak, set policy, and make demands. This is in fact exactly what intersectionality teaches, complete with a hierarchy of victimhood for comparing everyone's relative righteousness."[56]

Indeed, there is no way to explain their stubborn adherence to an ideology so rife with contradictions other than to understand that it's a matter of faith. This helps to explain why so many Americans are desperately trying to be victims, even to the point of faking their identities or orchestrating hoaxes to validate their victimhood. In the next chapters we'll see how these radical ideas permeate the left's entire political agenda today.

CHAPTER THREE

Turning Color Blindness into a New Heresy

CRITICAL RACE THEORY

While the overwhelming majority of African Americans consistently vote Democrat, this coalition is more fragile than it might appear, as black voters are decidedly more religious and more socially conservative than white liberals.[1] By voting for Democrats they are voting against their own economic interests, as demonstrated by record-low minority unemployment levels and rising wages under President Trump. The left responds by invoking racial politics to distract minorities from bread-and-butter issues—and to ensure they believe the lie that Republicans and conservatives are racist. Black conservative commentator Candace Owens emphasized this in a House hearing on white nationalism and hate crimes, observing that Democrats are using "fear-mongering, power, and control" and terms like "white nationalism" to scare blacks and keep them in the liberal fold.[2]

The left's incessant clamoring for a "national conversation" on race rings hollow because its members don't seek an actual dialogue, just more opportunities to lecture and shame conservatives and score political points. Why would leftists want to converse when they have so much to teach and nothing to learn from us? Based on our political preferences alone, they condemn us as racists. Whether or not leftist leaders actually believe this lie, they convince minorities they believe it, which causes incalculable damage to race relations and the fabric of society. We must pray this begins to change.

Racial politics is a different subject than it was fifty years ago. The left has not only abandoned Martin Luther King Jr.'s vision of a harmonious, color-blind society but now denounces the very concept of color blindness as a right-wing deception. King, as previously noted, wanted African Americans to have full access to the American dream, to enjoy equality of opportunity, and to integrate into society. But seeds were planted in the late 1980s that would steadily undermine this vision.[3]

At that time a concept emerged in legal scholarship known as critical race theory (CRT), which holds that institutional racism is engrained in the fabric and systems of American society and American culture. Our power structures are based on white privilege and white supremacy, which persist despite the rule of law and the constitutional guarantee of equal protection.[4] That is, CRT denies that the law is neutral and colorblind and that minorities who work hard can achieve success. To the contrary, institutional racism ensures systemic, insurmountable inequalities.[5] Egalitarianism and meritocracy are merely parts of a false narrative promoted by people of wealth, power, and privilege. Indeed, critical race theorists maintain that most people only view the more obvious forms of racism as problematic, but there are vast, additional aspects of racism that are concealed beneath an appearance of normality.[6]

According to CRT, racial inequality arises from social, economic, and legal differences that white people create to maintain dominance over minorities, which leads to poverty and criminality among minorities.[7] Consequently, CRT advocates policies and laws designed to benefit minorities and help them overcome the institutional racism they face.[8]

William Voegeli observes that critical race theory is hostile to America's founding ideas. "The left's attitude today toward civil equality, inalienable rights, and government by consent of the governed, ranges from indifference to hostility," writes Voegeli. In their book *Critical Race Theory: An Introduction*, Richard Delgado and Jean Stefancic similarly argue that "critical race theory questions the very foundations of the liberal order, including equality theory, legal reasoning, Enlightenment rationalism and neutral principles of constitutional law."[9]

As we've observed, these theories on race and privilege are no longer the idle musings of academics but have entered the mainstream of progressive thought and now dominate much of the mainstream media. For example, at an August 2019 meeting of the *New York Times* staff, one staffer recommended that racism issues should be much more prominent in every realm of the paper's reporting. "I just feel like racism is in everything," the staffer said. "It should be considered in our science reporting, in our culture reporting, in our national reporting. And so, to me, it's less about the individual instances of racism, and sort of how we're thinking about racism and white supremacy as the foundation of all the systems in the country."[10] Within days of that meeting, with great fanfare the *Times* introduced its 1619 Project. *Times* editorial board member Mara Gay explained the project's concept in simple terms: "In the days and weeks to come, we will publish essays demonstrating that nearly everything that has made America exceptional grew out of slavery."[11]

Critical race theory also prevails in the Democratic Party. Indeed, racial politics are everywhere, as we'll examine in this chapter and the next.

"WHAT INJUSTICE LOOKS LIKE"

New York City's progressives are determined to lower admission standards at New York's top public high schools to promote "diversity," with Mayor Bill de Blasio and Representative Alexandria Ocasio-Cortez leading the way. These super-competitive high schools use just one test score to determine admissions, and activists are concerned that too few black and Hispanic students are admitted because of the privileges of white students. Alexandria Ocasio-Cortez tweeted, "68% of all NYC public school students are Black or Latino. To have only 7 Black students accepted into Stuyvesant (a *public* high school) tells us that this is a system failure. Education inequity is a major factor in the racial wealth gap. This is what injustice looks like."

AOC conveniently omitted that Asian kids, not white kids, are breaking the curve. Seventy-four percent of Stuyvesant students are Asian, although they constitute only 15 percent of all New York students, a statistic that disproves AOC's claim of systemic racial inequity.[12] By gaming the system to achieve a predetermined racial mix, progressives would punish high-achieving Asian students while ignoring the possible reasons that other minorities perform poorly on admissions tests. Engineering the admission of less qualified students could also harm those very students, who will likely struggle with the advanced curriculum. Instead of addressing the root causes, which are probably social and cultural—the Asian community in New York highly values education and has a high rate of two-parent homes—progressives seek to equalize outcomes through state decree, just as they do in our economic system. The left's focus on alleged discrimination and privilege blinds it to other possible causes and any need to address them.

As we've seen, the glorification of the "underprivileged" has created the ridiculous phenomenon of public figures inventing underprivileged backgrounds for themselves. Many well-known people have sought authenticity by separating themselves "from the assumed dominate and victimizing majority of white heterosexual and often Christian males," writes Victor Davis Hanson.[13] They have run from their allegedly privileged positions not to escape the advantages of privilege but to acquire them. Hanson notes that though Puerto Rican American AOC grew up in an upper middle-class family in an affluent suburb in Westchester County, New York, and attended an upscale high school, she passed herself off as a product of the Bronx working class, which is a better fit for Marxist activism.[14]

While some of these charlatans have been publicly ridiculed, they haven't been rejected by the left—because they're still reliable progressives. Yet under the rules of intersectionality, many of them should be disfavored twofold, first for not being an actual member of a disadvantaged group (though AOC, as a Hispanic female, would still rank fairly high in the oppression hierarchy), and secondly for appropriating the disadvantaged identity for themselves. If it is this easy to appropriate an entirely new identity through sleight of hand, shouldn't progressives be less focused on identity in our multiracial culture?

"A SEGREGATION-ERA RACIST"

It should come as little surprise that race-obsessed leftists tend to project their own race fixation on conservative whites. As noted, many Democrats and some Never-Trump Republicans attribute support for border enforcement to racism. The sinister insinuation is that border hawks are white supremacists who want to keep out people "who don't look like them." For them, that was the real message of Trump's pro-American State of the Union address. "The tension between Trump's State of the Union message and his actual record reveals the core of his administration's thinking: Not populism, but ethno-nationalism," writes Zack Beauchamp. "An ideal of a country whose politics center the interests of one ethnic group, the white majority. That is really what the State of the Union was about, and no amount of supposedly race-neutral populism can mask that.... Since people don't want to say they're uncomfortable around minorities, for somewhat obvious reasons, their concerns get articulated through race-neutral language."[15]

Furthermore, Trump offers "white America" the "psychological wage of whiteness," which is a sense of cultural primacy and dominance having nothing to do with wealth. This, argues Beauchamp, is how Trump attracts middle-class workers even though his tax policies radically favor the rich—a favorite canard of the left. So white middle-class people forgo their own upper mobility just to satisfy their racism? When Trump concluded his speech with, "I am asking you to choose greatness," says Beauchamp, we need to ask who the "you" is he was speaking to. "Because as much as Trump might wish us to believe it, he's not speaking to everyone."[16] You have to wonder what inhabits the heart of a person who conjures such deplorable fantasies with zero evidence to support them.

Another despicable example of leftist projection on race and privilege occurred in the confrontation between Covington Catholic High School teenagers in MAGA hats and Native American elder Nathan Phillips. According to initial media reports, Nicholas Sandmann and his classmates attended the 2019 March for Life in Washington, D.C., where they surrounded, ridiculed, and chanted at Phillips. A video of the event, showing Sandmann smiling passively while Phillips banged a drum in front of him, went viral on the internet. The *Washington Post* reported that Phillips felt threatened as the students swarmed around him when he and his group prepared to leave.

The left leapt into outraged action against this bunch of young, white, Christian racists who mocked an elderly Native American, directing particular vituperation against "smirking" Sandmann. Former Democratic presidential candidate Howard Dean tweeted, "#CovingtonCatholic High School seems like a hate factory to me. Why not just close it?"[17] One liberal reporter called Sandmann a "segregation-era racist," and another person tweeted that he was a member of the Ku Klux Klan.[18] NewsBusters reported that CNN and MSNBC spent over fifty-three minutes denouncing the Covington students the weekend following the event.[19] On Sunday's *Kasie DC*, a one-sided panel compared the students to neo-Nazis and segregationists.[20] The *New York Times* castigated the "racist" teens for having "mocked a native American veteran."[21] Commentators on MSNBC equated the students to the KKK, Nazis, and pro-segregationist police officers.[22] HBO's Bill Maher remarked, "I don't blame the kid, the smirking kid. I blame lead poisoning and bad parenting."[23] Rosie O'Donnell posted a photo of Sandmann next to one of Supreme Court Justice Brett Kavanaugh to smear both. Actress Alyssa Milano denounced the students' bigotry, and fellow celebrity Debra Messing tweeted, "Mocking, condescending, disrespecting A**HOLE," with the hashtag #CovingtonShame.[24] CNN contributor Bakari Sellers tweeted about Sandmann, "He is deplorable. Some ppl can also be punched in the face." Though Sellers later deleted the tweet, he neither apologized nor explained the deletion.[25]

Even the kids' school and the Covington diocese joined the parade of condemnation, issuing a joint statement deploring the students' actions, apologizing to Phillips and Native Americans in general, and declaring that the students were under investigation.[26] (Bishop Roger Foys later apologized for the statement, saying the diocese had been bullied into condemning the students.[27])

Amidst this universal damnation of the Covington kids, indications began to spread that the media's account of the confrontation was false and that the viral video omitted crucial context. Sandmann issued a statement explaining that just before the confrontation with Phillips, the students were harassed by demonstrators from a fringe religious-activist group called the Black Hebrew Israelites. These protestors called the students "racists," "bigots," "white crackers," "faggots," and "incest kids," and told one African-American student they would "harvest his organs." One student asked a teacher chaperone for permission to begin school spirit chants to counter the loud, hateful taunts. Sandmann said the chants were positive and that no students chanted "build that wall," as was widely reported, or said anything hateful or racist.

Although the media widely reported that the Covington students accosted Phillips, a fuller video of the incident showed that it was Phillips who waded into the crowd of students, singled out Sandmann, and continually banged a drum in his face while Sandmann did nothing but stand silently and smile. Meanwhile, according to Sandmann, a member of Phillips's group yelled at the students that they "stole our land" and should "go back to Europe."[28] Phillips himself told contradictory versions of the event, including a version to the *Detroit Free Press* in which he admitted having approached the students himself. He also falsely claimed that the students attacked the Black Hebrew Israelites.[29]

The left seized on the false portrayals of the confrontation as proof of America's systemic racism, white privilege, and the vileness of Trump supporters. CNN commentator Keith Boykin tweeted, "The MAGA-hat wearing Covington Catholic High School students mocking Elder Nathan Phillips at the Indigenous Peoples March in Washington are direct descendants of the white privilege that empowered white kids to mock Elizabeth Eckford at Little Rock Central High School in 1957." In another tweet he asked, "When are these people going to learn to stop vilifying the people of color whose suffering and oppression enabled their privilege?" James Fallows of *The Atlantic* compared the students to desegregation protestors. Shaun King said the students' power was centered in their whiteness and that mocking others unlike them made them feel strong. "But it's weak. And despicable." *BuzzFeed's* Anne Helen

Petersen likened one student to the look of white patriarchy. Though some withdrew their derogatory tweets or statements after the full video surfaced, many didn't.

Fallows, for one, simply doubled down. "For a sustained period, a large group of young men, who had chosen by their apparel to identify themselves with a political movement (and a movement whose leader uses 'Pocahontas' as an epithet and recently made a joking reference to a massacre at Wounded Knee), act mockingly to a man their grandfathers' age, who by his apparel and activities represents a racial-minority, indigenous-American group," he declared. "Any such encounter has an implicit edge of menace, intended or not, which everyone understands when younger, bigger, stronger males come close to older, smaller, weaker people." As the *Daily Signal*'s Katrina Trinko observed, "In other words, it is impossible to wear a Make America Great Again hat—a hat that shows solidarity with *the president of the United States*—without coming off as a racist and menacing."[30]

That is exactly the point. Leftists salivated over validating their heinous prejudice against Trump supporters. They so desperately wanted this to be true that they viewed the students' actions through their biased lenses, and some rejected the truth even after the full story emerged. In categorically smearing the students as bigots, they committed the same type of sin they were condemning—judging people on the basis of their identities rather than their individual characters and conduct.

In a bizarre display of projection, *Salon*'s Chauncey DeVega denounced conservatives' outrage at the left's slander of the students and took umbrage at those who defended the students against false charges of racism. In the conservatives' view, said DeVega, "The mere accusation of racism against a white person is worse than the impact of racism on the safety, security, lives and literal existence of nonwhites. White people are the 'real' 'victims' of 'racism' in America. Donald Trump, with the help of Vladimir Putin and Russia, rode this lie to the White House. White people are somehow 'oppressed' by nonwhites, 'political correctness,' and 'civil rights.'"[31]

No one says the accusation of racism against whites is worse than the impact of racism against nonwhites. But why even pose this false choice? Can anyone deny there are few sins more uniformly and severely condemned in the United States today than racism? If so, then why is it so hard to understand how damaging it is to bear false witness against someone as a racist? Does intersectionality deprive white people of due process in the court of public opinion? Does defending innocent whites somehow diminish the legitimacy of racism's impact on nonwhites? This is just one more example of the narrow, zero-sum thinking in which leftists traffic. Reasonable people considering these questions can't avoid concluding that justice and fair play demand that people be judged on their conduct, not on unsupported allegations of bigotry from people with jaundiced predispositions. Individuals have a right to be judged individually and others have a duty to so judge them and to refrain from categorical condemnations.

Hell-bent on villainizing the students, DeVega decries the very thought process he employs, saying, "'Personal responsibility' does not apply to white conservatives." In his twisted perception, the students are being unjustly defended because white conservatives have now made themselves victims. And just a few paragraphs later he proves that he can't stand outside his own biases. "Those who defend and protect the white teens from Covington feel no compassion for the thousands of black migrant and refugee children who have been put in concentration camps by the Trump administration and 'disappeared' into a system that has no intention of reuniting them with their families." Additionally, "A group of white teenage boys donned their MAGA hats—which are overt and intentional symbols of bigotry, racism and ignorance—attended a right-wing Christian rally aimed at denying women their reproductive rights, then happened upon a group of 'Black Israelite' cartoon bigots, and in retaliation decided to harass and insult a Native American by yelling 'war whoops' and making 'tomahawk chop' gestures. They did so because white privilege had trained them from birth that they would likely be able to act in such a way without consequences."[32]

Every one of these pathetically false assertions is born of preconceived and erroneous ideas about groups of people, not individuals. Trump supporters are not bigots, they do not lack compassion for children, and MAGA hats represent to them everything that's positive about America. They are not symbols of bigotry, racism, or ignorance, but those who say they are reveal their own bigotry and ignorance by falsely judging the people who wear them based on false assumptions about them.

Thank God for Christian young men who stand up for the innocent unborn, not to deprive women of rights but to speak up for those who can't speak for themselves. The students were not the wrongdoers in this ordeal and did not yell war whoops. So-called "white privilege" did not train them from birth to be able to misbehave without consequences. Nowhere is personal accountability taught more clearly than in biblical Christianity, and it was in that tradition that the students were raised. In this case, the students behaved in a manner they believed would demonstrate their respect and keep the peace.

In the end, after suffering months of slander in the press and on social media and being ritually flogged nightly throughout cable TV, Sandmann and other Covington students sued a host of celebrities, activists, and media outlets for defamation, including CNN, NBC, the *Washington Post*, Democratic presidential candidate Elizabeth Warren, *New York Times* reporter Maggie Haberman, celebrity Kathy Griffin, and others.[33] Having become unwitting victims of the left's perpetual culture war, and unable to get a modicum of fair coverage from the media, they've turned to the courts for redress. One can only wish them success.

"THE DE FACTO CREED OF THE LEFT"

Columbia University professor Mark Lilla addresses these issues from a different perspective in the *New Statesman*, arguing that the modern left's "addiction to identity politics" fractured it and created the conditions for the rise of Donald Trump. It is a refreshing assessment of the culpability of liberal academics, written by a self-described "centrist liberal." Lilla admits that academia has inadvertently mobilized the right by tolerating limits on speech and debate, stigmatizing and bullying conservatives, and encouraging "a culture of complaint that strikes people outside our privileged circles as comically trivial." He believes his colleagues "have distorted the liberal message to such a degree that it has become unrecognizable."[34]

Lilla maintains that liberals have grown inwardly focused and squandered the opportunity to advance their agenda. Through identity politics, they've alienated Americans from one another and divided them into groups. He contrasts Roosevelt-era liberalism with today's identity liberalism using two images: the former is represented by two hands shaking; the latter by "a prism refracting a single beam of light into its constituent colors, producing a rainbow."[35]

Identity politics, says Lilla, has become the de facto creed of the left, including politicians, professors, teachers, journalists, activists, and the Democratic Party, and has been disastrous for liberalism. He approves of the left's focus on disenfranchised minorities but contends that you don't help them by empty gestures of recognition. You have to win elections by appealing to broad swaths of people and bringing them together, but identity politics does the opposite.

Identity politics initially sought to redress major historical wrongs against large classes of people, argues Lilla, but it devolved into "a pseudo-politics of self-regard and increasingly narrow, exclusionary self-definition that is now cultivated in our colleges and universities." This has turned people inward instead of toward the wider world. They have lost empathy—they don't think about the common good in non-identity terms and how to promote it by convincing others of the merits of their goals. Instead, "every advance of liberal identity consciousness has marked a retreat of effective liberal political consciousness."[36] This is a powerful point. Leftist activism today, from identity politics to abortion, is me-centered. The left's myriad victims are trained to think only of themselves and never about the greater good. It is the politics of graceless, narcissistic self-directedness. For all its boasts about compassion, the left has long since abandoned any pretense of it and replaced it with envy, bitterness, and hate.

This is partly because progressive activists used to come from working-class and farm communities, but now they are mostly academic elitists who are detached socially, culturally, and geographically from the rest of America. Republicans, by contrast, have employed a bottom-up strategy since the Reagan eighties. Lilla sees Republicans as evangelizing their fellow citizens, while liberals strategically spread their message via a top-down strategy in the universities. Lilla believes that liberals forgot their duty to engage with the world outside academia. Their interactions with the world have largely been in their sequestered enclaves—investing "their energies in making their sleepy college towns into socially progressive and environmentally self-sustaining communities." These are nice communities, he says, but their isolated existence doesn't do much to spread the message.[37]

"I AM OFFENDED YOU DISAGREE WITH MY POSITION"

Lilla believes the study of identity politics became an end in itself, which led to an explosion of university studies on the subject and departments, research centers, and professional chairs devoted to it. Though this has been partly positive, it has triggered a single-minded fascination with group differences, which has given students a distorted picture of history and contemporary America. With this shift of focus away from the outer world to the inner self, the purpose of education was transformed as well, from helping students to find themselves by engagement with the wider world to encouraging them to engage with the world (and politics) "for the limited aim of understanding and affirming what one already is."

The more a student becomes ensconced in the identity politics mindset, the less she will be interested in the larger world and uniting people despite their differences. This has caused a distrustful attitude toward certain groups, as professors have convinced students that unifying rhetoric from these groups is a ruse to keep unprivileged groups subordinated. "What matters about these academic trends is that they give an intellectual patina to the narcissism that almost everything else in our society encourages," writes Lilla. "... Intersectionality is too ephemeral to serve as a lasting foundation for solidarity and commitment. The more obsessed with personal identity campus liberals become, the less willing they are to engage in reasoned political debate."[38]

Precisely. Students are taught that their identities exempt them from the responsibility to persuade others of the validity of their positions. Conversations used to begin with a person saying she has a certain opinion and then explaining why. Now they begin with a person saying, "Speaking as an X—a member of a certain identity group—I am offended that you disagree with my position." This leaves no room for discussion. Lilla likens it to religion. Only those with approved identity status are allowed to speak on certain subjects—a development we've noted previously. One's ideas are deemed pure or impure based on the identity connection, not their validity, which no longer has the same significance. By contrast, leftist activists of yesteryear envisioned campuses as being open to robust debates over big ideas, with students having to defend their positions and then go out into the world to change it instead of withdrawing into themselves.

Lilla admits conservatives are correct that colleges are overwhelmingly run by liberals who teach with "a liberal tilt," but disagrees that they are manufacturing leftist radicals to become an effective left-wing political force. This obsession over identity politics, he believes, is a depoliticizing force. It has undermined "the universal democratic 'we' on which solidarity can be built" and is unmaking rather than making citizens. "In the end, this approach just strengthens all the atomizing forces that dominate our age," says Lilla. Regardless of your opinion about the sixties radicals, at least they cared about their fellow citizens and cared when America's democratic principles were violated. Lilla longs for a return to universities that encourage passion, commitment, knowledge, and argument as well as curiosity and concern for other people. You must care for the country and its citizens and seek a better future for all. His lament is not that universities produce liberal students but that they produce self-absorbed, politically impotent ones.

From a different perspective, conservative writer Roger Kimball also grieves the decline of America's universities. "Once upon a time (and it wasn't that long ago), universities were what they claimed to be, institutions dedicated to the preservation and transmission of civilization's highest values," writes Kimball. "Now they are bastions of political correctness, 'intersectionality' and identity politics."[39]

"THE HIRING OF A CDO IS PRIMARILY A VIRTUE-SIGNALING STATEMENT"

Identity politics, sadly, dominates our college campuses and arguably originated there. American universities are bloated with diversity bureaucracies that promote the hiring of minorities and women, initiate campaigns to promote dialogue, and develop strategic plans to increase equity and inclusion on campus. They issue rules on avoiding sexist language, taboo lyrics, politically incorrect party themes, and inappropriate clothing and hairstyles. Many positions come with exorbitant salaries (e.g., the University of Michigan pays its chief diversity officer, or CDO, $385,000), and university spending on these programs has skyrocketed even while state funding for some universities has decreased.[40] Such programs have made diversity complaints a self-fulfilling prophecy, as the media is devoting increasing coverage to claims of mistreatment of minorities and women on campuses and to racial attacks that have a remarkably high tendency to turn out to be hoaxes.

Diversity officials are further required to discourage "microaggressions" and to ensure that campus speech and clothing validates people's identities and cultures. Violators are often sent to diversity training. It's not an infrequent affair; one study of 669 American universities found that almost a third compel faculty to attend diversity training. Bureaucrats outnumber faculty at public universities by a two-to-one margin, and diversity is the primary driver.[41] Ironically, as a result of the diversity racket, many white male professors are limiting campus interaction with minorities and women to avoid violating the rigid guidelines with unintentional perceived slights. Excessive diversity spending can also lead to fewer classes and higher tuition, which harms minorities, a higher percentage of whom are poor.[42]

These expensive programs contribute little, if anything, to fostering interracial interactions and friendships. In fact, they tend to create problems by foisting identity politics on students.[43] Critics argue that the chief diversity officers on campuses are virtually programmed to resist any rational objections to diversity ideology and to perpetuate their empty suppositions by repeating them endlessly.[44] Even with all their monitoring and posturing there is little evidence, according to a study by the National Bureau of Economic Research, that chief diversity officers actually improve faculty and administrator diversity. That's because most deans and provosts have long been responding to pressure to hire applicants who fit diversity categories over those who don't. Furthermore, there are a limited number of minority candidates with the requisite credentials, and no amount of prodding from a diversity official can change that.[45] But George Leef of the James G. Martin Center for Academic Renewal doubts that such findings will lead to reform "because the hiring of a CDO is primarily a virtue-signaling statement—a way for a college's leadership to say, 'Look, our heart is in the right place.'" This is liberalism in a nutshell.

Because progressivism means never being accountable for your failed and costly social engineering experiments, the newly elected Democratic House majority jumped on the diversity and inclusiveness train, prioritizing corporate quotas to increase the number of women and minorities in America's boardrooms. They intend to establish subcommittees on corporate diversity and inclusion and introduce bills to compel public disclosure of the race and gender makeup of corporate boards.[46] But congressional imposition of corporate affirmative action would, like university diversity programs, accomplish few of their stated goals and possibly cause damage. Diversity-based promotions are patronizing, lead to workplace resentment, and undercut morale, including among minorities who advance based on merit.[47]

In reality, diversity officers exist for the sole purpose of advancing identity politics. Just look at the reaction when one diversity officer strayed off the ideological reservation. Denise Young Smith, a former diversity and inclusion officer for Apple, admirably and courageously exclaimed, "I focus on everyone.... Diversity is the human experience. I get a little bit frustrated when diversity or the term 'diversity' is tagged to the people of color, or the women, or the LGBT. There can be 12 white, blue-eyed, blonde men in a room and they're going to be diverse too because they're going to bring a different life experience and life perspective to the conversation." Smith's comments provoked predictable outrage. Some suggested her views were influenced by her Apple paycheck, which is absurd, given Apple's slavish obedience to the diversity gods. If she were mouthing Apple's view, it's doubtful she would have expressed her personal frustration. Other critics were incredulous that a "black woman" could say such a thing. Still others vowed to stop buying Apple products. Leftism permits no dissenting views.[48]

This incident illustrates the fraud of intersectionality and leftist notions of diversity and inclusiveness. The premise is that members of disadvantaged groups must be heard because only they can fully express the experiences of their group. But when a member of such a group deviates from the leftist line, her experience and opinion count for nothing, and she is exposed to the same kind of abuse as members of "privileged" groups and perhaps even more—she must be ostracized and banished, for she has betrayed the cause she was supposed to promote. For all the left's obsession over identity groups, one thing is more important: adhering to the correct ideology. Fail to do this and no minority status will protect you from the ensuing fury.

"A SKIN MELANIN QUOTA SYSTEM"

Identity politics encourages people to be impersonal and robs us of our individuality. At the same time, however, it breeds narcissism, encouraging people to dwell on themselves. It's the worst of both worlds. So as our culture, and especially our universities, pressure young people to view everything through the lens of identity, individuality becomes less important, which diminishes personal accountability. They develop an attitude of entitlement based on a status attributed to them that they've done nothing to earn. This discourages independent thinking and striving for excellence. They will more likely derive their sense of personal morality from their unearned status than from their conduct (apart from their self-glorifying activism) and how they treat others.

This mentality shreds the Golden Rule. The positive side of our moral ledger shouldn't be credited or discredited because of our skin color or gender. It's one thing to have pride in who you are and even your group, but it's another to treat your membership in a group as a license to act irresponsibly, disrespectfully, or unkindly to others. When parents, professors, the media, and others encourage people to think primarily in terms of identities or groups and to contemplate how they are part of those identities and the implications that flow from them, it fosters an unhealthy focus on self. It also tragically pits groups of people against one another purely on the basis of their identities.

Particularly disappointing is the invasion of identity politics, along with other leftist dogmas, into Christian churches. Christian theologian and assistant editor for *Faithfully Magazine* Timothy Isaiah Cho tweeted, "If the references in your pastor's sermons, the books used in small groups, the resources passed between the laity, the music sung in worship, & even the reflection quotes in your worship bulletins are predominantly by White men, your church is promoting a truncated Christianity."[49] Cho argues that these references communicate that "the real gatekeepers of the orthodoxy—and those who are the only ones worth listening to—are White men.... It says that authentic worship—and that which we should rightly emulate—originates from White men. It declares that the church property belongs to, is led by, and influenced by White men. It says that women and people of color are properly always to be listeners, submitters, and passive bystanders in the church who should be grateful for the place they've been allotted by White men. In contrast, Jesus' church is the epicenter of equity and diversity."

Wow. One must pity the person who harbors such bizarre ideas. Imagine a Christian leader focusing on the group identity of a productive church member rather than on the heart of the individual contributor and the blessing of his contribution. Cho substitutes skin color and other identities for Christian love and betrays an unhealthy resentment toward "White men." As writer Peter Heck observes, "Apparently, Cho has determined that his 'gift' is sowing division in the body along the lines of manmade, social constructs like race.... While Christ is instructing His disciples to test all things against the perfect standard of His word alone, social justice theologians like Cho would discard that benchmark in favor of a skin melanin quota system."[50] This message is appallingly divisive for the body of Christ—an evil practice the apostle Paul passionately condemned in his epistles to the churches. It is man-centered, not God-centered, and idolatrously prioritizes superficial and manufactured human concerns above God's will and His Word.

Alveda King, niece of Martin Luther King Jr., discerns the spiritual component in these arguments, and her approach to racial relations is markedly different from the divisive privilege ideology that is prominent today. "What has happened with my uncles' legacy, they forget their spiritual aspect," said King. "... I remember the prayer meetings, how often we came together and prayed. I remember that everything we did was founded on the Bible.... One of his famous quotes [was], 'We must learn to live together as brothers,' and I'll add, as sisters—'or perish together as fools.'" Alveda King said her uncle fully understood Acts 17:26: "Of one blood, God created the human race." "We're not separate races and we're designed to love each other," she said. "... Skin color does not denote or define who we are, and that's the message that's still very relevant today. Treating each other as human beings, having the ability to listen to each other, to communicate with each other, and to resolve our differences nonviolently in a loving, and, for me, a Christ-like manner."[51]

ARTIFICIAL INTELLIGENCE MIMICS HUMAN BIASES

The left's identity mania is frequently asinine. Activists claimed that Amazon's facial recognition software is bigoted because it more accurately recognizes white males than people of other races. Researchers from MIT and the University of Toronto discovered that Amazon's facial-detection technology for law enforcement purposes often misidentifies women and those with darker skin. Privacy and civil rights advocates demanded Amazon desist its marketing of this software because of these concerns about discrimination.

Apparently, the software did have difficulty identifying some groups, such as darker-skinned women, whom it didn't even recognize as women 31 percent of the time. But if you thought that was a simple technological failure, then you're just not woke enough. "Artificial intelligence can mimic the biases of their human creators, as they make their way into everyday life," the study concluded. "If you sell one system that has been shown to have bias on human faces, it is doubtful your other face-based products are also completely bias free," said MIT Media Lab researcher Joy Buolamwini.[52]

No idea is too far-fetched for leftists if it confirms their bias that bigotry is everywhere—except in their own hearts. The automated creations of biased humans must also share those biases. In fact, a study published by New Zealand's University of Canterbury attributed the supposed prevalence of white robots to racism.[53] But don't feel too sorry for the poor robots. In case you missed it, Calvin Klein arranged for supermodel Bella Hadid, a heterosexual, to kiss a female robot in an ad for a T-shirt. Leftists make sure to cover all the bases.[54]

In the next chapter, we'll see more ludicrous examples of the left's destructive preoccupation with race and identity politics.

CHAPTER FOUR

Race Mania: A Compendium of Absurdity

OLE JOE AND CRAZY BERNIE

In September 2018, Democratic presidential candidate Joe Biden, to burnish his identity politics credentials, apologized for his conduct during Clarence Thomas's 1991 Supreme Court confirmation hearings. At the hearings, Anita Hill accused Thomas of having made sexually explicit comments and unwanted advances toward her when she worked under him in the 1980s. Having presided over the hearings as chairman of the Senate Judiciary Committee, Biden has come under fire from the left in recent years for allowing other congressmen to aggressively question Hill and undermine her credibility.

"The woman should be given the benefit of the doubt and not be, you know, abused again, by the system," said Biden. "My biggest regret was I didn't know how I could shut you off if you were a senator and you were attacking Anita Hill's character. Under the Senate rules, I can't gavel you down and say you can't ask that question, although I tried."

Biden groveled further, insisting that Hill, an African American, shouldn't have been forced to face a panel of "a bunch of white guys."[1]

Biden knows that in the #MeToo era he must get in front of any criticisms of his treatment of women, especially since he has a history of awkwardly touching women and sniffing their hair. But he also knows, in reality, he bent over backward to help Hill smear Justice Thomas. If he owes anyone an apology, it's Thomas. Instead, he pretends he's sorry that he couldn't conduct a kangaroo court hearing against Thomas and muzzle Republican senators, insulate Hill from cross-examination, and deny Thomas his right to confront witnesses against him.

The left has done a masterful job of reeducating the old warhorses of the Democratic Party. Biden now understands that he—an old white guy—should have gagged the other white guys. But does he really expect us to swallow that he is sorry he didn't issue a lawless edict to reconstitute the Judiciary Committee on the spot, replacing the old white senators with black ones? This is what passes for seriousness from today's Democratic presidential hopefuls.

Anita Hill wasn't a victim—she was a witness making damning allegations against a Supreme Court nominee. Her race and gender don't entitle her to exemption from rigorous cross-examination. These white male liberals are appallingly patronizing. Anita Hill was an accomplished law professor at the time. Why should Biden have treated her as some vulnerable wallflower? Another contradiction in the women's movement is exposed.

Finding this self-flagellation insufficient, Biden denounced the overall impact of "white man's culture" in America while discussing Anita Hill in March 2019. "We all have an obligation to do nothing less than change the culture in this country," he said. "It's an English jurisprudential culture, a white man's culture. It's got to change."[2] Well, if Democrats have their way, American culture *will* change—identity politics will reign supreme. Biden's capitulation shows that people like him are just puppets of the party's radicals. The old guard isn't reining in AOC; she's shaming them leftward into her cultural Marxist hellhole.

Quintessential socialist Bernie Sanders tried to buck the identity politics trend and stick with pure economic Marxism, but it didn't sit well with leftist thought ministers. When a radio host asked Sanders how he could lead a diverse Democratic Party, he said we shouldn't judge candidates by their skin color, gender, sexual orientation, or age. "I think we have got to try to move us toward a nondiscriminatory society, which looks at people based on their abilities, based on what they stand for."[3] Neera Tanden of the Center for American Progress responded on Twitter, "At a time where folks feel under attack because of who they are, saying race or gender or sexual orientation or identity doesn't matter is not off, it's simply wrong."[4] "This is usually an argument made by people who don't enjoy outsized respect and credibility because of their race, gender, age and sexual orientation," quipped Democratic strategist Jess McIntosh.

Imagine publicly admitting that people should be denied respect and credibility because they don't have a protected identity. And I thought ageism was verboten under intersectionality. But there's the identity politics contradiction rearing its head again. Even if you are a member of a protected group, you forfeit your protection if you challenge leftist orthodoxy. Stephen Colbert revealingly commented about Sanders, "Yes, like Dr. King, I have a dream—a dream where this diverse nation can come together and be led by an old white guy."[5]

CULTURAL APPROPRIATION

Another manifestation of the modern race and privilege ideologies is the concept of "cultural appropriation." The *Oxford English Dictionary* defines cultural appropriation as "the unacknowledged or inappropriate adoption of the customs, practices, ideas, etc. of one people or society by members of another and typically more dominant people or society."[6] It can involve a hairstyle, an item of clothing, a certain way of speaking, or a type of exercise. Sometimes cultural appropriation can clearly be disrespectful. People criticized Gucci, for example, when its models wore white turbans, because many Sikhs objected to their faith symbol being transformed into fashion. Likewise, in 2017 critics denounced Victoria's Secret for placing Native American headdresses on a model.[7]

Predictably, however, the left took this concept to a ridiculous extreme, essentially banning white people from adopting, displaying, or even celebrating any element of a nonwhite culture. For example, two comedy shows banned white comedian Zack Poitras because he wears dreadlocks, a hairstyle associated with black culture. One of the venues, Montreal's Coop les Récoltes, explained on Facebook that its mission is to be "a safe space, free of any link to oppression," and it equated cultural appropriation to violence. "We will not tolerate any discrimination or harassment within our spaces," they wrote.[8] "Privilege" apparently precludes white people from wearing dreadlocks. Though the group admitted Poitras had no racist intent, it insisted his hairstyle "conveys racism." "[C]ultural appropriation is not a debate or an opinion," the group declared, but "a form of passive oppression, a deconstructive privilege and, above all, a manifestation of ordinary racism."[9]

Similarly, Utah teenager Keziah Daum was skewered on Twitter for wearing a Chinese-style dress to her prom. Daum explained she chose the gown because she thought it was "gorgeous" and wanted to show her appreciation for Chinese culture. But this innocent act resulted in a torrent of leftist abuse. "My culture is not your goddamn prom dress," wrote one critic, while another accused Daum of perpetuating "colonial ideology."[10]

Most people would laugh at such bizarre sensitivity unless they were intensely indoctrinated into it, which is why essays on cultural appropriation not only have to explain what the manufactured concept is but why it's wrong. People don't ordinarily think this way. To encourage people to be so easily offended, when no offense or racism is intended, is destructive to society and race relations. It fuels the notion of a never-ending power struggle between alleged oppressors and their victims while doing nothing to ameliorate actual racism.

AN EMBARRASSING SAMPLING

The cultural left is so focused on race that examples of this depressing obsession are too numerous to cover exhaustively. Nevertheless, let me provide a sampling without extended exposition. Race shaming, race-baiting, and utterly spurious accusations of racism are ubiquitous—from professional athletes, to Hollywood, to our Democratic politicians in Washington—and they are taking a toll on our society.

★ Nancy Pelosi alleges President Trump wanted to add a citizenship status question to the census because he wants to "make America white again"[11]—even though some form of citizenship or naturalization question has been included on most censuses since 1820.[12]

★ Lebron James likened the NFL to slavery. "In the NFL, they got a bunch of old white men owning teams, and they got that slave mentality," said James. "And it's like, 'This is my team. You do what the f*** I tell y'all to do or we get rid of y'all.'"[13] Because players are complaining that certain terminology cultivates a "slave-to-master" relationship between the team owners and the players, the NBA is considering replacing the word "owner."[14]

★ In response to a tweet by Senator Marco Rubio, Democratic senator Chris Murphy implied that pushing for a border wall with Mexico and not Canada is driven by racism. "You and Trump are advocating putting up a wall on only one border. No wall for the country filled with mostly white people," Murphy tweeted. Murphy's statement is as specious as it is ugly. Illegal crossings at the southern border dwarf those at the northern border. The Department of Homeland Security reports that more than 500,000 illegal immigrants were apprehended at the southern border in each of the fiscal years 2014, 2016, and 2018. In both fiscal years 2015 and 2017 more than 400,000 were apprehended.[15] By contrast, the number of apprehensions at the northern border in 2017 was around 3,000.[16]

★ Addressing immigration with MSNBC host Chris Hayes, Democratic congresswoman Pramila Jayapal asserted, "This has never been about a wall. [Trump] actually could have gotten funding a couple of years ago, or a year ago, for a wall.... He turned it down because his ultimate goal is, as you said, to make America pure in the sense of not having immigrants, not having folks of color here and shutting down every form of legal immigration, all to throw a bone to those people."[17]

★ Congresswoman Ilhan Omar blamed a migrant caravan's arrival in El Paso at the end of March 2019 on white nationalism. She tweeted, "This is abhorrent and inhumane. It's without a doubt a reflection of what white nationalism is doing to our country. As a country, we have to acknowledge that this is how people are being treated and decide that we are better and we must do better."[18]

★ Freshman Democratic congresswoman Katie Hill admitted that her Democratic colleagues are refusing to fund a new southern border barrier because it would require them to backpedal on their claim that the wall is racist.[19]

★ *The View* cohost Meghan McCain, who supports stronger border security but not a southern border wall, took umbrage at her fellow hosts implying that Republican support for the wall is racist. "When you broad-stroke everyone—all black people think one thing, all Hispanic people think one thing, all Republicans think one thing, that's how we got ourselves into this mess," said McCain. "Please don't paint me, just because I'm for border security, that I'm somehow racist in one way or another, because I don't think that's fair."[20]

★ In decrying alleged racism on the right, MSNBC's Nicole Wallace said, "Part of the problem is we think—this does not have a parallel on the left. There just—it doesn't. There isn't a strain of racism on the left." So, without "anywhere else to go, [white racists].... attach to the Republican Party. The Republican Party doesn't have to let them.... How do Republicans sort of get back to doing something decent?" As *RedState*'s Brandon Morse points out, Democrats can't credibly claim they reject racists considering their embrace of Nation of Islam's Louis Farrakhan, the anti-Semites among the Women's March leadership, and CNN's Don Lemon calling white men the biggest threat in our country.[21]

★ The left, the media, and the Democratic Party uniformly accused Trump of racism when he criticized Democrat

Rep. Elijah Cummings for failing to clean up the "rat and rodent infested mess" in his Baltimore district. Many of Trump's critics, however, had themselves noted the glaring problems facing the city. Bernie Sanders, who denounced Trump as "a racist President who attacks people because they are African Americans," had previously likened a Baltimore neighborhood to a "third world country."[22] The *Baltimore Sun*, which condemned Trump for making "bigoted" arguments and appealing to white supremacists, had published an op-ed bemoaning the city's high crime rate, political scandals, and especially its chronic trash problem—which, the paper noted, "contributes to a rodent problem."[23] And amidst the fulminations against Trump, video emerged of Rep. Cummings himself calling part of his community a "drug-infested area" with people "walking around like zombies."[24] Yet mysteriously, only Trump was accused of racism for pointing out the obvious.

★ White leftists patronizingly dumb down their speech when talking to minorities, according to a study from Cydney Dupree, a Yale assistant professor of organizational behavior.[25] A good example is Hillary Clinton's embarrassing attempt to imitate a black accent at the First Baptist Church of Selma, Alabama, where she exclaimed, "I don't feel no ways tired. I come too far from where I started from…"[26]

★ UCLA professor Corinne Bendersky, a gender bias researcher, argues in the *Harvard Business Review* that there are too many white male firefighters in America. "I find that, when evaluating fit[ness] and competence, firefighters tend to default to a reductive set of traits (physical strength evaluated through strict fitness tests, for example) that serve to maintain white men's dominance in the fire service," writes Bendersky. She argues that because 64 percent of fire department responses are medical emergencies, "stereotypically masculine traits like brawn and courage are simply not enough. Firefighters also need the intellectual, social, and emotional skills required to deliver medical emergency aid, support each other through traumatic experiences, and engage intimately with the communities they serve."[27] She also bizarrely asserts that we must take into account that African Americans are more cheerful than whites: "Joviality—defined as 'markedly good humor' and one that helps process emotional trauma—is a positive trait associated with black Americans somewhat more than with white Americans, so explaining that a jovial culture can increase crew effectiveness may reduce some of the skepticism about and exclusion of black firefighters."[28]

- ★ After a derisive comment by MSNBC leftist Rachel Maddow, Rockefeller University decided to redesign a university wall featuring portraits of Rockefeller scientists who'd won a Nobel Prize or a Lasker Award—because there were too many white men. NPR reports this is part of a trend at universities to redesign such displays or hide them in less conspicuous places.[29]
- ★ Prior to becoming a *New York Times* editorial board member in 2018, Sarah Jeong had posted these tweets:
  - ★ "Dumbass f***ing white people marking up the internet with their opinions like dogs pissing on fire hydrants."
  - ★ It's "kind of sick how much joy I get out of being cruel to old white men."
  - ★ I'm "just imagining being white and waking up every morning with a terrible existential dread about how I have no culture."
  - ★ "Are white people genetically predisposed to burn faster in the sun, thus logically only being fit to live underground like groveling bilious goblins?"
  - ★ "Have you ever tried to figure out all the things that white people are allowed to do that aren't cultural appropriation? There's literally nothing."
  - ★ "The world could get by just fine with zero white people."[30]

Columnist and professor Walter Williams correctly notes that similar statements about black people would provoke outrage, widespread denunciations of Jeong's employer, and demands that she be fired. "Leftists have been taught utter nonsense by their college professors," notes Williams. "The most insidious lesson taught is who can and who cannot be a racist.... According to the thinking of academia's intellectual elite, a minority person cannot be a racist. The reason is that minorities don't have the political, economic and institutional power to adversely affect the lives of whites."[31] Williams thus captures the essence of intersectionality thinking.

★ Some leftists are offended that Democratic presidential candidates include old white men. When Ohio senator Sherrod Brown was considering running, CNN contributor Harry Enten remarked, "This is an interesting guy for Democrats. Another white male, I am very suspect of that going into a Democratic primary with women doing well, I am not sure it's the time to nominate a white man."[32]

★ A nine-year-old black girl in Linden, Alabama, committed suicide, allegedly because classmates had persistently bullied her for being friends with a white boy.[33]

★ Seventy-nine teaching assistants and instructors at the University of North Carolina at Chapel Hill threatened to withhold more than two thousand students' final grades unless the university agreed not to house Silent Sam, a statue of a Confederate soldier that activists pulled down a few months before, in its history center. The group demanded that the university keep the statue off campus and that the university's board of governors hold "listening sessions in good faith with the campus community."[34]

★ University of Oregon students and faculty demanded removal of an American pioneer statue on its one-hundred-year anniversary because many "students feel oppressed" by it. "I know when I walk under it I feel very inferior," said Bret Gilbert, co-leader of the University's

Native American Student Union. "I don't feel that way when I'm at other places on campus. I don't think that's what the university community wants us to feel like when we're here."[35]

- The University of Texas at San Antonio removed white biology instructor Anita Moss from class for a semester for warning her students to "be respectful in class" by keeping their feet off chairs, putting away their phones, and not talking, and for having one student, who was black, removed from class for putting her feet up. Though two university investigations revealed that Moss was not motivated by racial bias, the university president issued a statement, according to the *College Fix*, "drawing explicit racial connections to the incident."[36] President Eighmy pronounced, "The reactions expressed through social media, emails, phone calls and group meetings I've attended confirm that feelings of marginalization on the part of some students—especially our African American students—are real and profound. The bottom line: regardless of the final outcomes regarding yesterday's incident, we have an obligation as an institution to take a hard look at our campus climate—especially for students of color—and enact a system change to make UTSA a more inclusive campus."[37] Why do they have to reform the system when the investigations revealed no racial bias? Conceding unsubstantiated claims of racism does more to perpetuate racial issues than alleviate them. Such race pandering trivializes actual racism.
- A Dartmouth student complained in the university newspaper, *The Dartmouth*, that students of color are victimized by the system of student–faculty office hours, partly because upperclassmen urge freshmen to attend without telling them how to go about it. Because of their backgrounds some students lack confidence to raise questions and exchange ideas with professors. "Minoritarian subjects may feel undeserving of space because of an inherent

lack of self-confidence, victim complex or innate helplessness," writes Clara Chin. "It is because institutions, such as academia, can send an implicit message that ideas out of the white, normative mainstream are unimportant by erasing these other narratives. One form of this is the lack of faculty of color at elite institutions like Dartmouth."[38]

★ ESPN host Molly Qerim was concerned that President Trump evinced racism by serving burgers and pizza to Clemson's national-championship-winning football team. "When I saw him giving the football players—it's a predominantly black sport—fast food my thought went a very different place. I mean, come on." Clay Travis of Outkick the Coverage tweeted, "ESPN host argues Donald Trump giving fast food to Clemson players was racist because the team is majority black. Really. Fast food is racist, y'all."[39] Does it ever occur to these race cops that their characterization of fast food as particularly associated with blacks might itself be racist?

★ We reap what we sow. A group of more than a dozen Asian Americans sued Harvard for unconstitutionally discriminating against them by penalizing their high achievement as a group while giving preferences to other racial and ethnic minorities. They claim Harvard's admission process is an illegal quota system. In 2016 the Supreme Court held that a university may constitutionally use race as one of many factors in admission decisions, though that case involved a white applicant suing the University of Texas at Austin.[40]

★ On David Webb's SiriusXM radio show, CNN legal analyst Areva Martin, an African American, lectured Webb on his white privilege. "Well, David, that's a whole 'nother long conversation about white privilege, the things that you have the privilege of doing that people of color don't have the privilege of," said Martin. An incredulous Webb asked her exactly how he benefits, and Martin responded, "by virtue of being a white male." Webb responded,

"Areva, I hate to break it to you, but you should've been better prepped. I'm black."[41] Ouch!

★ The left's habitual demonization of whites for their alleged "privilege" gives license to subject whites to racist ridicule with impunity. In *BuzzFeed*, multicultural beauty writer Patrice Peck identified "37 Things White People Need to Stop Ruining In 2018." Included in the list were the United States of America, the National Anthem, the Oscars, and the Grammy Awards. Peck mocked the "plague" of "white people" populating the planet. One reader commented, "Another racist article. Live, let live, stop blaming everyone else for your issues, and shut the hell up. In a nation where people of color have sat in the highest office on the planet, are some of the biggest names in entertainment, are world-renowned neurosurgeons, business owners, highest paid athletes, etc., the only thing keeping you from success is your own racist and 'woe-is-me' attitudes."[42] Consider the ensuing scandal if a white person had penned this article about a minority group.

★ Ravelry, one of the world's biggest knitting websites with some eight million members, banned its users from expressing support for President Trump, likening it to "white supremacy." "We cannot provide a space that is inclusive of all and also allow support for open white supremacy. Support of the Trump administration is undeniably support for white supremacy," the company's administrators said in a post. Setting aside their hysterically absurd claim that supporting Trump constitutes white supremacy, consider the logic in their position: "We must be exclusive to prove we are inclusive."

★ In an op-ed in the *New York Times*, Ekow N. Yankah questioned whether her children could even be friends with white people in light of the election of Donald Trump. "For people of color, the stakes are different. Imagining we can now be friends across this political line is asking us to ignore our safety and that of our children, to abandon personal regard and self-worth.... [Trump's] election and the year that has followed have fixed the awful thought in my mind too familiar to black Americans: 'You can't trust these people.'" It is not Trump who has done this, said Yankah, but "the ranks of Mr. Trump's many allies and apologists" who "are practiced at purposeful blindness. . . . I do not write this with liberal condescension or glee. My heart is unbearably heavy when I assure you we cannot be friends. . . . Don't misunderstand: White Trump supporters and people of color can like one another. But real friendship?... For African-Americans, race has become a proxy not just for politics but also for decency. White faces are swept together, ominous anxiety behind every chance encounter at the airport or smiling white cashier. If they are not clearly allies, they will seem unsafe to me.... We can still all pretend we are friends. If meaningful civic friendship is impossible, we can make do with mere civility—sharing drinks and watching the game.... In coming years, when my boys ask again their questions about who can be their best friend, I pray for a more hopeful answer."[43]

★ Considering their divisive racial politics, it's remarkable that Democratic politicians believe they have standing to complain about President Trump's alleged racism and divisiveness. Presidential candidate Bernie Sanders, having taken some heat for not infusing his socialist rhetoric with privilege ideology, sought to make amends with his base. "Today we say to Donald Trump—We are not going back to more bigotry, discrimination and division," Sanders told an audience in South Carolina. "Instead of bringing us together as Americans, he has purposely and aggressively attempted to divide us up by the color of our skin, by our gender, by our nationality, by our religion and by our sexual orientation."[44] The irony of Sanders creating the very divisiveness he decries is completely lost on him.

★ Sanders is just one of many Democrat leaders pretending to fight divisiveness with their own despicable divisiveness.

"We have a hater in the White House," said Rep. Hakeem Jeffries. "The birther in chief. The grand wizard of 1600 Pennsylvania Avenue.... While Jim Crow may be dead, he's still got some nieces and nephews that are alive and well." "Our government is shut down for one reason," declared Senator Elizabeth Warren. "So the president of the United States can fund a monument to hate and division along our southern border." Senator Kirsten Gillibrand said that President Trump has "inspired a hate and a darkness in this country that I have never experienced myself."[45]

★ In a CNN op-ed about the incident between the Covington kids and Nathan Phillips, Issac Bailey announced he wasn't interested in who started the confrontation or who the real victims were. For Bailey, the central issue was not that Black Hebrew Israelite demonstrators harassed the Covington students, or that Phillips accosted them and lied about it, or that the kids were subject to endless vituperation based on false media reports. No, for him, the real wrongdoing was that the teenagers wore MAGA hats, thus endorsing Trump's alleged racism. Wearing those hats sends a signal, you see, that they want to return to the days of American greatness when "it was worse for people of color," whether during slavery, the days of Jim Crow, the height of lynching, or others.[46] To the contrary, Trump supporters flatly reject that Trump is a racist and understand he is trying—successfully—to improve conditions in America for everyone regardless of race, creed, color, or gender. "Wearing MAGA hats, of course, does not automatically make someone evil, yet almost half of the country's population...are considered such," writes Sumantra Maitra. "[The hat] is simply a choice of apparel that denotes someone's political preference, and he or she should be allowed to, because that is the sign of a healthy democracy."[47]

★ Adam Serwer, in *The Atlantic*, critiqued the *Rocky* movie series in light of the latest installment, *Creed II*, which he argued redeems the series from its racist themes. Prior to the two *Creed* movies, the *Rocky* series "sees a black boxer humbled by a white challenger in every single movie." They gave "a resentful white audience the catharsis of seeing a white boxer humble [Muhammad] Ali.... The *Rocky* films are a product of a sense of white pride and humiliation, and the desire to overcome it by restoring the proper order of things."[48] Serwer grudgingly gives Sylvester Stallone credit for *Creed II* because he allowed "his career-defining character, an avatar of white masculinity, to be transformed into a vehicle of redemption for *Creed*'s black protagonist—a role traditionally played by black actors.... Stallone's decision to accede to fundamentally altering the most important fictional creation of his career, to elevate Apollo above Rocky as a fighter, and to make his journey subordinate to that of the young black man on the screen, is worthy of recognition."

I've watched every *Rocky* movie, and race never entered my mind. Like most people, I rooted for Rocky because he was an underdog, not because of some racist antipathy for Muhammad Ali. In fact, like many whites, I was a fan of Muhammad Ali and rooted for him in every fight regardless of his opponent's race. I doubt, too, that Sylvester Stallone, in the original *Rocky* series, had the motive Serwer imputes to him.

★ In anticipation of Republican senator Cindy Hyde-Smith winning the Mississippi runoff election, there was discussion about Democratic senator Kamala Harris being removed from the Senate Judiciary Committee because Republicans would be entitled to another committee seat. Although this would have been purely a matter of seniority and in accordance with past practice, Democrats turned it into a race issue. "Not only would it be unconscionable to remove the only African American woman from the committee, but Senator Harris also is the most skilled questioner on the entire panel," said Brian Fallon, former press secretary for Hillary Clinton's 2016 presidential campaign.[49] Reportedly, Minority Leader Chuck Schumer later negotiated a deal to give Republicans an extra seat on the committee in exchange for not kicking off any Democrats.[50]

- ★ In Dickinson College's student newspaper *The Dickinsonian*, a black female student wrote that American society tells men, especially white men, that their opinions have merit and their voice is valuable, "but after four years of listening to white boys in college, I am not so convinced.... The list of what white boys think they are qualified to talk about is endless.... I am so g****mned tired of listening to white boys. I cannot describe to you how frustrating it is to be forced to listen to a white boy explain his take on the Black experience in the Obama-era. Hey Brian.... [y]ou do not speak alone, you speak with the weight of every other white man who has ever spoken over a woman, erased the contributions of queer people from history, or denigrated 'broken English' as unintelligent.... So, should white boys still be allowed to share their 'opinions'? Should we be forced to listen? In honor of Black History Month, I'm gonna go with a hell no. Go find someone whose perspective has been buried or ignored and listen to them, raise up their voice."[51] It seems that some leftists will not be satisfied until, as the writer suggested here, white men are censored and silenced.
- ★ Wake Forest University hosted a series of "listening sessions" for minority faculty and staff to promote campus inclusiveness. The *College Fix* notes the irony in "no-whites-allowed" faculty and listening sessions—to promote inclusivity.[52]
- ★ Jennifer Lopez was savaged on social media for performing a tribute to Motown at the Grammy Awards because she is Puerto Rican, not black. Critics said any number of black performers could have done the tribute and "[n]o doubt Latinos would be upset if they had a black soul singer doing a tribute to Latin music." Lopez responded

without apology, and her answer could serve as a template response to criticisms of so-called cultural appropriation. "Any type of music can inspire any type of artist," she said. "You can't tell people what to love. You can't tell people what they can and can't do—what they should sing or not sing." What kind of joyless ideology renders that a controversial statement? Motown legend Smokey Robinson defended Lopez. "I don't think anyone who is intelligent is upset," said Robinson. "I think anyone who is upset is stupid. Motown was music for everybody. Everybody. Who's stupid enough to protest Jennifer Lopez for doing anything for Motown?"[53] What a refreshingly defiant rejoinder to race-obsessed virtue signalers.

★ In an op-ed in the *Yale Daily News*, a female student, apparently upset by Judge Brett Kavanaugh's confirmation to the Supreme Court, implied that students should start collecting opposition research on future Kavanaugh types. Calling out classmates is not enough because it wasn't enough to stop Kavanaugh's confirmation. "But I can't do that anymore—I can't let things slip by," the student wrote. "I'm watching you, white boy. And this time, I'm taking the screenshot."[54]

★ CNN's Don Lemon, one of the most racially obsessed media figures, is quite open about his rejection of color blindness. Lemon was appalled by Howard Schultz's comment at a CNN-hosted town hall that "I didn't see color as a young boy, and I honestly don't see color now." "Is Howard Schultz completely out of touch," asked Lemon in teasing the segment. "What is this so-called color-blind ideology? What does it tell us about Howard Schultz and his views on race?" Lemon said that it is not okay to say "I don't see color" in 2019, and that a better answer would have been, "Color has never been a defining characteristic for me, either qualifying or non-qualifying in this culture or in society." CNN's Bakari Sellers, who is black, complained that not seeing his color erases his blackness. It's ignorant not to see black people's color, he said, because you must see "the benefit of the diversity we bring to the table."[55]

- University of Washington "white studies" professor Robin DiAngelo said that a white American who sees people as individuals rather than defining them by skin color is a "dangerous white person."[56]
- Democratic presidential candidates Senators Kamala Harris and Elizabeth Warren both publicly support paying reparations for blacks, a proposal that until recently was found almost exclusively among obscure, radical academics. Previous Democratic presidential candidates have never taken that position, according to the *New York Times*—which shows how far left the party has moved and how immersed it is in racial politics. In light of her fraudulent claim of American Indian ancestry, some wondered whether Warren would support a similar measure for Native Americans.[57]
- Kamala Harris insists that America hasn't yet had an honest conversation about race. *National Review*'s Jim Geraghty soundly refuted Harris in a post chronicling the "perpetual and ubiquitous" conversations we've had, including after Charlottesville, Ferguson, Baltimore's riots, Ralph Northam, Jussie Smollett, Roseanne Barr, Kanye West's rants, and a dozen others. Moreover, we never stopped talking about race during the entire Obama presidency.[58] The problem isn't that we haven't had honest discussions about race but that the left isn't satisfied unless everyone agrees with its analysis and proposed solutions. Until the entire nation embraces the leftists' worldview on race they will always warn of a crisis-level race problem in America. For them, there is only one legitimate opinion. All others are not just wrong but immoral.

One discouraging aspect of identity politics is that the left shows they don't really want these problems solved. They will never acknowledge progress in civil rights, women's rights, or overall interracial tolerance. It is not in their political interests to do so because their political power, which they crave above all else, depends on the existence of perpetual classes of victims. Their lust for social justice (read: revenge) is insatiable.

In sharp contrast to the left's racial McCarthyism, John McWhorter, an African-American linguistics professor at Columbia University, sees substantial progress in our culture on race. He discusses the case of Jussie Smollett, the African-American gay male initially charged with fabricating a story about being attacked by MAGA–hat wearing homophobes. McWhorter doesn't deny that racism exists but notes that "one might argue ... that there is a degree of exaggeration in how Americans today discuss and process race." Victimhood chic, says McWhorter, has taken hold so deeply that Smollett might have assumed he didn't have to be that careful in choreographing his scam. McWhorter was particularly incredulous that Smollett didn't remove the rope from around his neck by the time the police arrived. He notes that if Smollett was playacting, it might be that for him, "being a successful actor and singer" wasn't "quite as exciting as being a poster child for racist abuse in Trump's America."

Smollett, McWhorter continues, would have realized that "very important people would find him more interesting for having been hurt on the basis of his identity than for his fine performance on an interesting hit television show. He would have known this so well that it didn't even occur to him that his story would have to be more credible than the dopey one he threw together about being jumped in near-Arctic temperatures by the only two white bullies in America with a mysterious fondness for a black soap hip-hopera." McWhorter argues that this incident demonstrates that in America, "matters of race are not as utterly irredeemable as we are often" led to believe. "That anyone could feel this way and act on it in the public sphere is, in a twisted way, a kind of privilege, and a sign that we have come further on race than we are often comfortable admitting."[59]

We must pray that Professor McWhorter's optimism is warranted. But it's sobering to recognize that race is far from the only sensitive issue the left exploits in their divide-and-rule strategy of pitting Americans against one another. In the next two chapters we'll examine the left's destructive ideas and initiatives on gender.

CHAPTER FIVE

Gender Madness

In the past several decades we have witnessed a sexual revolution. Whereas the sexual revolt of the sixties was characterized by sexual liberation and licentiousness, this new revolution attacks the idea that there are two distinct sexes. The assault has come in distinct but overlapping stages: the feminist movement, the homosexual movement, and the transgender movement. "The third wave of this assault on the sexes [the transgender movement] has been an attack on a basic reality—that all people have a biological sex, identifiable at birth and immutable through life, which makes them either male or female," write Dale O'Leary and Peter Sprigg.[1]

Conceding that a tiny percentage of people suffer from sexual development disorders, referred to as an intersex condition or hermaphroditism, O'Leary and Sprigg argue that the vast majority of transgender people are not "intersexed." Regardless of all the methods, devices, and surgical procedures people use today, "no one can change his or her sex," they write. "The DNA in every cell in the body is marked clearly male or female. Hormones circulating in an unborn child's brain and body shape his or her development. Psychiatrists and surgeons who have served transsexual clients know surgery does not change sex. Georges Burou, a Moroccan physician, admitted: 'I don't change men into women. I transform male genitals into genitals that have a female aspect. All the rest is in the patient's mind.'"[2] "A person's sex (male or female) is an immutable biological reality," say O'Leary and Sprigg. "It is unambiguously identifiable at birth. There is no compassionate reason to affirm a distorted psychological self-concept that one's 'gender identity' is different from one's biological sex."[3]

In this chapter and the next we'll trace this assault on the sexes and the various manifestations and consequences of the modern left's militant gender activism.

INVADING WOMEN'S SPACES

Not long ago, feminism was center stage, characterized by the slogan, "I am woman. Hear me roar!" Feminists sought equal rights—equal job opportunity, equal pay for equal work, and redress for sexual harassment. In some ways feminism pitted women against men, fostering suspicion, distrust, and competition. But at least the movement acknowledged differences between the sexes. Today, gender politics has descended into intellectual and moral anarchy. Though they claim to champion science, leftists are science deniers when it comes to gender. They promote "gender ideology"—the notion that gender is a social construct and that one's biological sex is independent from one's gender identification. Gender ideology advocates maintain that gender is more a matter of choice than biology. Gender is not biologically determined at birth but merely "assigned," remaining fluid until a person identifies as male, female, or something else.

The left has strived to normalize these ideas in our culture: men and women are not different; a man can be trapped in a woman's body; a person can be both male and female; some people are neither male nor female; there are numerous genders; one may have an infinite number of genders inside oneself; and people may choose their own genders.[4] It's one thing to say there is genuine gender confusion in the world; it's another to accept the foregoing assertions as undeniable truths. But in today's society you challenge them at your own risk.

The advent of gender ideology and intersectionality has in some ways left the gay lobby in the lurch. The idea that one can freely swap genders is troubling to gay activists, who have long maintained that some people are born homosexual. "The LGBT lobby is dead set against anything that smacks of conversion therapy—the idea that you could convert someone who has a primarily homosexual identity to someone who has a primarily heterosexual [identity]," notes psychologist and author Jordan Peterson of the University of Toronto. "But if there's complete independence between the biology, the identity, the expression and the sexual preference, then there's no reason to assume that it can't be changed." Peterson likens modern laws recognizing gender as a matter of subjective choice, independent of biological realities, to destructive laws in the Soviet Union based on utopian fantasies.[5]

Before further examining gender ideology, let's look at the left's ideas on feminism, patriarchy, and toxic masculinity. Feminism too is taking a hit from gender ideology and intersectionality. Until recently feminists could "roar" about the glories of women, the horrors of discrimination against them, and their campaign to rectify these historical injustices. But as we've seen, today they might run into the buzz saw of militant transgenders or the intersectionality police if they focus on injustices specifically against women, if they rally only women to their cause, or if white women don't acknowledge their racial privilege.

Furthermore, transgender men are now entering women's spaces, including their locker rooms, bathrooms, prisons, beauty pageants, and sporting events. Some feminists, like tennis star Martina Navratilova, have been denounced for objecting to these encroachments by biological males. Freelance writer Selwyn Duke notes the irony in feminists having laid the groundwork for ideas that are now backfiring on them. Feminists essentially argued that aside from certain superficial physical differences, men and women are the same. Transgender activists then came along, claiming that if you change these superficial physical differences (and in some cases, even if you don't), you can transform into the opposite sex.

The transgenders' assertion, argues Duke, logically follows from the feminists' viewpoint. For example, feminists traditionally argued that they were fully capable of competing with men in sports, and now transgenders are increasingly making them do so. Feminists for years elbowed their way into exclusively male spaces—from locker rooms to men's clubs—and even into the Virginia Military Institute and the Citadel. But now, biological men identifying as women are forcing their way into women's spaces. Many feminists have been bullied into submission and don't dare object. Others complain that transgenderism is really a "men's rights movement." What they miss is that these are all leftist developments—the intellectual, moral, and cultural chaos naturally flowing from their abnormal ideas. "It apparently eludes them," notes Duke, "that women currently have greater complicity in advancing transgenderism because they tend to support the leftists pushing it."[6]

"THE WILLFUL OPPRESSION OF WOMEN"

Feminism is not only facing assaults from outside forces but is struggling internally as well. It seems to be unsure even how to define itself anymore. In *A Guide to Gender: The Social Justice Advocate's Handbook*, Sam Killermann acknowledges that feminism has many different meanings, but "what matters is that feminism, distilled down to its absolute core, is about gender equity. The goal of feminism is to create a society in which individuals' genders don't restrict them from an equitable shot at success and happiness."[7] Actor Emma Watson expressed these sentiments amid criticism for doing a topless photo shoot in *Vanity Fair*. Defending her decision to display her feminine biology, Watson declared, "Feminism is about giving women choice. It's about freedom. It's about liberation. It's about equality."[8]

But this is simply no longer true among many leftists. In their mind, that view upholds the patriarchy. Thus a writer identifying as "RadFemFatale" instructed Watson, "When feminism is defined as becoming equal to men, it is a clear admission that men are the default by which we ought to measure ourselves, and therefore, no longer feminism at all."[9]

RadFemFatale rejects so-called "neoliberal feminism," which focuses on the sexist behavior of individuals rather than on the systemic effects of sexism. Just as a person, by virtue of his race alone, can be considered racist without having a racist bone in his body, someone can also, by virtue of his gender, be considered sexist. The leftist march toward dehumanization transcends the multiple categories of victimhood.

RadFemFatale contends that we live in a patriarchal system in which "the mistreatment of women and girls is intended to keep us in a subordinate position to men.... Any definition of feminism that removes 'women' or 'patriarchy' is inaccurate and is pandering to the idea that male rule doesn't exist; such definitions erase the willful oppression of women by men."[10] The writer continues, "In every aspect of our lives we are policed: existing in public is enough to invite harassment; female sexuality is robbed and used to sell products for which men largely see the gains; we are treated as reproductive chattel; when we are raped, it's the perceived sexuality of females that is blamed, rather than male entitlement to our bodies." RadFemFatale's unfavorable opinion of men, male rule, and the "patriarchy" aside, ironically, she does emphasize the differences between men and women, an idea that modern gender ideology rejects. "We do not need to be seen as equal to men: we need to be seen as worthy and valid not in spite of, but because of our differences," she writes.

RadFemFatale exhibits some of the bitterness that characterized traditional feminists, who claimed to advocate equal rights but often seemed to be primarily motivated by animus against men. We still see that hostility today, especially in the pro-abortion movement and at women's marches, replete with angry women wearing vagina hats while strenuously decrying the patriarchy. Perpetually furious at men, they constantly invent new transgressions to denounce such as "mansplaining," which is when a man explains something to a woman. Yes, they claim the term refers to explanations offered in a condescending or patronizing way, but even the most innocuous remarks are now condemned as mansplaining since, of course, patriarchs will be patronizing. Sorry, feminists, but men explain things to other men all the time, and in fact women do as well.

Feminists seem determined to suck the joy out of every occasion, turning the most trivial interaction into a grim hunt for subtle oppression. *New York Times* columnist Jennifer Weiner, for example, is not a big fan of Christmas parties because of—you guessed it—men. "It's the least wonderful time of the year," she whines, begrudging all the agonizing clothing choices that confront women while men can get ready in five minutes. "Whatever the reason, you have to navigate the journey from professional to party, choosing clothes that signal that you are polished without being boring, attractive without being provocative, and that you're looking to be promoted, not propositioned. For women, it's never easy."[11]

"A REPREHENSIBLE IDEOLOGICAL REWRITE OF HISTORY"

Let's consider the feminist concept of villainous patriarchy. In *Key Concepts in Gender Studies*, Jane Pilcher and Imelda Whelehan define "patriarchy" as "rule by a male head of a social unit...over other...men, all women, and children." They explain that since the early twentieth century, feminists have used the term to describe the social system of men's domination over women. Radical feminists regard patriarchy as the fundamental social division in society. Men achieve domination through the family unit and their control of women's bodies. Some, called Marxist feminists, argue that patriarchy is an outgrowth of capitalism, which relies on women's unpaid labor in the home.[12]

Charlotte Higgins, the *Guardian's* chief culture writer, maintains that the patriarchy oppresses women on multiple layers, including inequalities in the law, the home, and the workplace. It is upheld and reinforced by cultural norms, tradition, education, and religion. Some argue that it is so pervasive that it seems natural and inevitable, to the extent that even if women were to gain equal rights in society, patriarchy would persist "because institutions—political, legal, educational, cultural—are themselves, in their bones, patriarchal structures."[13] Higgins claims the idea of patriarchy has ebbed and flowed over time but is resilient, having "survived its biggest theoretical challenge—that of intersectionality, which argues that 'patriarchy' universalizes and oversimplifies the realities of oppression."

Once again, we see how leftist cliques turn on each other, with the politics of transgenderism and race stealing the oxygen of feminism. Intersectionality, as we've seen, requires feminism and patriarchy to be folded into the larger hierarchy of oppression. Additionally, the feminist worldview must expand to recognize the gender identity confusion now in vogue. Nevertheless, Higgins maintains that despite the advent of intersectionality, the ideas of feminism and patriarchy have survived and are thriving, aided to some degree by online global campaigning. These causes also are fueled by the presidency of Donald Trump, the quintessential symbol of the evils of patriarchy. Higgins acknowledges that "the eradication of patriarchy looks like a task of enormous complexity; when it is smashed it will take a lot down with it. And so the patriarchs—from the bully in the White House to the bully in your workplace—are still in charge. For now."[14]

Jordan Peterson challenges the concept of patriarchy as well. The notion of patriarchy, he argues, "is part of an ideological worldview that sees the entire history of mankind as the oppression of women by men, which is a dreadful way of looking at the world, a very pathological way of looking at the world." Human history, he says, has been a cooperative endeavor between men and women, and to portray it simply as centuries of oppression is "an absolutely reprehensible ideological rewrite of history. And it's what's taught in the humanities at universities and increasingly in the public education system. It's taken as an unassailable fact."[15] Peterson has stern advice for parents whose children are being taught white privilege, equity, diversity, inclusivity, and systemic racism: take them out of the class because they are not being educated but indoctrinated.[16]

Peterson argues that lessons on patriarchy tend to demonize boys, suppressing their natural competitive drive. "Our culture confuses men's desire for achievement and competence with the patriarchal desire for tyrannical power, and that's a big mistake," he says. When an interviewer asserts that men own the vast majority of wealth and that women do more unpaid labor, Peterson responds that it is a tiny proportion of men. "A huge proportion of people who are seriously disaffected are men; most people in prison are men; most people who are on the street are men; most victims of violent crime are men; most people who commit suicide are men; most people who die in wars are men; people who do worse in school are men. Where's the dominance here, precisely? What you are doing is taking a tiny substratum of hyper-successful men and using that to represent the entire structure of Western society. There's nothing about that that's vaguely appropriate."[17] Peterson says the feminists' labeling of the entirety of Western civilization as a patriarchy just because it contains some corruptions and imperfections that might be called "patriarchal" is irrational and unjust.[18]

TURNING OUR CHILDREN'S EDUCATION OVER TO IDIOT IDEOLOGUES

Another concept polluting the national dialogue is "toxic masculinity." Formerly a subject mostly for women's studies classes, it has been mainstreamed today, along with so many absurd leftist ideas. Experts describe toxic masculinity as a set of behaviors and beliefs that includes suppressing emotions or concealing distress, maintaining an appearance of hardness, and equating violence with power. "In other words," writes *New York Times* columnist Maya Salam, "toxic masculinity is what can come of teaching boys that they can't express emotion openly; that they have to be 'tough all the time'; that anything other than that makes them 'feminine' or weak. (No, it doesn't mean that all men are inherently toxic.)"[19] The idea is that our culture grooms men to be more aggressive and violent, which puts them at higher risk for school disciplinary issues, academic challenges, and health disparities such as cardiovascular disease and substance abuse.[20]

Psychologists and psychotherapists suggest that men are under cultural pressure to live up to these masculine stereotypes—that men should be strong and stoic, emotionally and physically.[21] In addition to the problems of academic discipline and achievement, violence, and health issues, societal pressure on men can keep them from seeking help because that signals weakness. Some experts insist that in calling attention to "toxic masculinity" they aren't demonizing men or all aspects of masculinity. Leftists must have missed the memo, because they have exploited the idea for that very purpose. It's just one more hook they use to solidify man's top rung on the infamous hierarchy of privilege.

Leftists are clearly demonizing most of the qualities that make men different from women. Some argue that men aren't inherently evil but masculinity itself is, and because of these acquired traits a high percentage of men become evil and violent. If they can be reprogrammed at a young age to shed their machismo and tap into their inner woman, they will be better people. Consider, for example, the title of a prominent book on the subject: *The Mask of Masculinity: How Men Can Embrace Vulnerability, Create Strong Relationships, and Live Their Fullest Lives.*[22] Leftists cleverly have it both ways with this line of reasoning: men and women aren't that different biologically, but men are evil anyway.

"After decades of study, I deeply believe that men are not naturally violent," writes Colleen Clemens, a director of women's and gender studies at Kutztown University in Pennsylvania. "But in a culture that equates masculinity with physical power, some men and boys will invariably feel like they are failing at 'being a man.' For these particular men and boys, toxic masculinity has created a vacuum in their lives that can be filled through violence: through the abuse of women and of children in their care, through affiliation with the so-called 'alt-right' or ISIS, through gun violence or any other promise of restored agency that those parties wrongly equate with manhood."[23] Here we see how leftists have weaponized toxic masculinity to villainize men and then link the concept to right-wing politics.

In an interview with Fox News's Tucker Carlson, Jordan Peterson also challenges the leftist notion of toxic masculinity and questions why we are even talking about it, considering that the crime rates in the United States and all of North America have fallen by 50 percent in the last twenty-five years, including every category of violent crime. "So, where's the crisis, and why in the world would we turn our children's education over to idiot ideologues? Even the academics are waking up to this. There was an article in the *Chronicle of Higher Education* just two weeks ago excoriating the faculties of education for their appalling standards and their absolute ideological obssession. And this idea that we should address toxic masculinity from K to 12 is just an extension of that."[24]

"The term [toxic masculinity] itself is terribly defined," observes Peterson. "I think it's appalling that faculties of education are pushing this sort of nonsense and I think that if your kids are exposed to that type of idiot social justice, pseudo education, you should pull them out of the schools. Everything about the idea is ridiculous.... They are not being educated; they are being propagandized. There's also no evidence that we construct our identities as masculine and feminine by being expressly taught them by teachers. Almost all that is learned by example, to the degree that it's learned, and a tremendous amount of it is a consequence of biological inclination."[25] Peterson's assertion on biological inclination, of course, radically differs from the leftist notion that men and women are not that different biologically.

"MEN WHO DO EVIL THINGS AREN'T POISONED BY TESTOSTERONE, BUT CORRUPTED BY SIN"

Toxic masculinity got a professional credibility boost when the American Psychological Association issued its first-ever guidelines to help psychologists work with men and boys. The APA purportedly relied on forty years of research showing that traditional masculinity is psychologically harmful. Men are conditioned to suppress their emotions, so when a boy or man observes other men, he mistakenly thinks they are free of conflict and then assumes his own conflicts are abnormal. Unaware that other males experience the same doubts, he begins to feel weak and isolated.[26]

All this psychobabble is tantamount to declaring manhood a mental disorder, notes writer Rod Dreher.[27] Writer David French argues it is harmful to teach boys to avoid their masculine impulses. "We do our sons no favors when we tell them that they don't have to answer that voice inside them that tells them to be strong, to be brave, and to lead," says French. "We do them no favors when we let them abandon the quest to become a grown man when that quest gets hard.... When it comes to the crisis besetting our young men, traditional masculinity isn't the problem; it can be part of the cure."[28]

Not all psychologists are buying what the APA is selling. Mental health counselor Michael Gurian argues its guidelines fall into an "ideological swamp," lacking hard science and ignoring male nature, the male brain, and "the need to contextualize boyhood into an important masculine journey to manhood." The APA blames "too much masculinity" for most problems males experience, from suicide to early death to depression and substance abuse. While these experts contend that masculinity destroys male development, they don't consult the hundreds of scientists worldwide who use brain scan technology to discern the differences between the male and female brain. The guidelines include no contributions from such experts or other practitioners "who have conducted multiple studies in science-based practical application of neuroscience to male nurturance in schools, homes, and communities."[29]

Gurian notes we can't improve society by condemning the very male characteristics that enable them to succeed, heal, and grow. Similarly to Peterson, Gurian maintains that masculinity is more than culture. It "is an amalgam of nature, nurture, and culture." It is about "developing and exercising strength, perseverance, hard work, love, compassion, responsibility for others, service to the disadvantaged, and self-sacrifice.... What professional in the psychological field would not want to embolden these characteristics?... Not the erasure of masculinity but the accomplishment of it is required." Only by embracing masculinity will we be able to save our sons from the crises that the APA guidelines detail. Gurian highlights the danger in teaching mental health professionals that masculinity is the problem, that males do not need nurturing in male-specific ways, and that manhood is not a healthy way of being but a form of oppression.[30]

"Men don't do evil things with their masculinity because they're poisoned by testosterone, but because they're corrupted by sin," states Hans Fiene, a Lutheran pastor and writer. "So, when you grow up and encounter such men, don't disavow your manliness. Embrace it and use it to defeat them as you pray for their conversion. Bad men will always be out there.... Big, strong, evil men need to know that if they use their size and strength to do something evil, big, strong, righteous men will make them regret it."[31] Pastor Fiene's point is that we shouldn't try to emasculate young men but teach them to develop their strength and their righteousness and use them for good.

Similarly, D. C. McAllister argues that masculinity is good, or at worst, morally neutral. Masculine characteristics can be used for good or evil. Leftists who buy into feminist ideology misperceive masculinity, associating bad behavior by men with masculinity itself. That's why they are trying to reeducate boys and men into rejecting their maleness in favor of something more feminine, which they deceptively call a new kind of masculinity. Their effort to destroy masculinity is dangerous and disruptive to our social cohesiveness and to relationships that flourish because of the complementary nature of masculinity and femininity. Like Dr. Peterson, McAllister notes that if masculinity really is toxic, we wouldn't see a sharp decline in individual violence when it is fostered and held in high esteem.[32]

Discussing the dangers inherent in this misguided, ideological approach to raising boys, Melissa Langsam Braunstein, a mother of three daughters and one son, asks, "How do you parent a boy when political grenades are constantly being lobbed at their entire sex, due to no fault of their own?" Describing the new APA guidelines as "hair-raising," she strongly objects to the APA telling boys they are inherently damaged and that they should shoulder blame for centuries of perceived wrongs by the so-called patriarchy. "I certainly don't want them being asked to leave a public playground," she says, "because another mother wants to host a girls-only playtime to compensate for decades- or centuries-old injustices."[33] She wonders why people can't support girls and women without shaming boys and men. Not everything has to be a zero-sum game.

Gillette's notorious online ad sparked much debate on toxic masculinity. The ad shows a series of badly behaving males—bullies chasing a scared classmate, text-message bullying, young men acting violently, rude chauvinistic guys, and arrogant men in a corporate environment. All this is followed by various men callously mouthing, "Boys will be boys." In the end, more well-behaved men come to the rescue, police the bad guys, and restore order and civility. In different times one might conclude that Gillette was endorsing the Christian belief that good men should use their strength to corral the bad ones. But the message isn't to inspire men to be good but to shame them for allowing the unbridled mushrooming of toxic masculinity. If they were less like men, you see, we wouldn't have these problems. This is hardly a Christian message.

Consider the audacity of a company lecturing its own customers about their moral behavior as if the company is their conscience. "The unblinking temerity of a brand believing it's somehow its duty not merely to make an appeal for commercial inclusion, but rather to instruct millions of people on how to lead their lives," writes Damian Reilly. "If the ideological vacuum left by the decline of Christianity in the West really is being filled with a rush of competing forces, then surely we can view Gillette's ad as consumerism's most blatant effort from the pulpit of modernity to claim the hearts and minds (and souls) of the lumpen masses."[34]

One by one our major corporations and cultural institutions are groveling to the madness of political correctness, the redefinition of words, the inversion of truth, and the restructuring of society—even the unraveling of the biblical and scientific distinction between man and woman. "Where will it stop, this handling of the great levers of our culture to people defined and motivated by nothing so much as their disdain for unarguable truths of mankind?" asks Reilly. "Gillette isn't the first outwardly credible institution to bend the knee to this typically man-hating craziness—increasingly it's happening everywhere, from business to academia—but it's shameful nonetheless.... Is this ad the best a brand can get? No chance. Masculinity isn't toxic. Woke advertising is. Go away, Gillette, and try again."[35] In case anyone was wondering whether Gillette's message may have somehow been misinterpreted, David Taylor, the CEO of its parent company, Proctor & Gamble, clarified the point. Referring to the ad, he said, "It started a conversation.... There is an issue with toxic masculinity."[36]

"GENDER IDENTITY"

Dr. John Money coined the term "gender identity" in the 1950s to distinguish between biological sex and gender—describing it as a psychological or spiritual condition that includes a person's thoughts, beliefs, and feelings about being male or female. Money taught that children are blank slates when it comes to gender, and gender is socially determined and learned irrespective of biological sex. The term "gender" evolved to also describe the ways people express their genders through language, dress, and behavior.[37] Money not only pioneered the thinking that gender and identity are separate but also that six or more variables define one's gender, including chromosomes, internal reproductive organs, and a person's "assigned" sex.

Jeff Johnston of *Focus on the Family* argues that in separating biological reality (male or female) from a person's thoughts, decisions, feelings, and beliefs (roughly, the Christian concept of the human soul), Money indulged a form of an ancient Gnostic heresy that taught that the human soul is good and the body is evil.[38] Indeed, the Gnostics believed they had a special knowledge of the truth and that man's main spiritual problem is not sin but ignorance. Gnostics believed the entire material world is evil and that Christ was not human, so His crucifixion was illusory.[39] Johnston correctly notes that this contradicts Christian teachings that our body, soul, and spirit are connected and that Christ's incarnation affirms the value of our bodies. "Or do you not know that your body is a temple of the Holy Spirit within you, whom you have from God?" writes the apostle Paul. "You are not your own, for you were bought with a price. So glorify God in your body."[40]

Money's trendy idea collapsed back on itself when he imposed his theory on a real-life human subject, David Reimer, a twin boy whose penis was badly damaged during circumcision. Reimer's parents sought Money's advice, and he recommended raising David as a girl. So the Reimers, under Money's guidance, made extensive socialization efforts to "nurture" David into a girl, giving him girl toys and pushing him toward feminine interests such as baking cookies and putting on makeup, though he eventually wanted to play with his brother's toys. In his treatment, Money interviewed the twins about their sexuality and feelings about life and gave them physicals including genital inspections. He performed experiments on them, including their performing sexual acts upon one another. If they refused, he pressured them into it. Money did this for years, believing such "sexual rehearsals" would lead to a healthy adult life for the boys.[41]

David struggled and ultimately reverted to his maleness.[42] He realized he wasn't a girl by age ten, and as teenagers both twins experienced depression and eventually committed suicide.[43] Many scholars concluded that the brothers took their own lives due to Money's abusive practices—and yet his research had a huge impact on the study of sex and gender.[44] With leftism, no bad deed goes unrewarded.

Such denial of biological reality is alarming but no more so than societal elites' unquestioning acceptance of it. One writer notes the disturbing scene in Orwell's novel *1984* in which Big Brother tortures the hero into conceding that the four fingers he sees being held up are actually five. But what is happening today is worse because the distortions of reality are occurring without torture. "Every moronic and anti-reality bit of nonsense the militants throw our way," writes Bill Muehlenberg, "the authorities and politicians cheerily acquiesce to."[45] The American-born Muehlenberg lives in Australia and cites examples of incidents that occurred in Queensland. In one case transport authorities eliminated gender on all Queensland licenses following complaints by the LGBTQI (the "I" stands for "intersex") community.[46]

Rather than using torture, leftists are employing indoctrination and intimidation to alter reality right before our eyes. They are consciously chipping away at our biological identities and the biblical teaching that God created mankind in His own image, as man and woman (Gen. 1:27). This is part of a concerted attack by the left on the nuclear family. Leftists don't merely seek to make gender nonconforming people feel more at ease; they also want to force everyone else to adopt their views. If this weren't the case, why would they try to suppress dissent?

YOU CAN'T MAKE THIS UP

Gender ideology preposterously recognizes some seventy genders—and counting. In 2016, the New York City Commission on Human Rights identified at least thirty-one genders that must be recognized in the workplace, including bi-gendered, cross-dresser, drag queen, femme queen, female-to-male, FTM, gender bender, genderqueer, male-to-female, MTF, non-op, HIJRA, pangender, transexual/transsexual, trans person experience, woman, man, butch, two-spirit, trans, agender, third sex, gender fluid, non-binary transgender, androgyne, gender gifted, gender blender, femme, androgynous, and person of transgender experience. The commission declared, "In New York City, it's illegal to discriminate on the basis of gender identity and gender expression in the workplace, in public spaces, and in housing. The NYC Commission on Human Rights is committed to ensuring that transgender and gender nonconforming New Yorkers are treated with dignity and respect and without threat of discrimination."[47] Reaction against the law was swift and critical, as many outlets reported that accidental misidentification of someone's gender (called "misgendering") could result in a fine of up to $250,000. Commissioner Carmelyn P. Malalis was forced to clarify that accidental misuse of pronouns is not illegal.[48]

What are the free-speech implications for such edicts? What if a person feels uncomfortable referring to another person with a plural pronoun, such as "they"? In the Gresham-Barlow School District in Oregon a female teacher decided she was genderqueer, or transmasculine, so she changed her name to Leo and insisted her colleagues refer to her as "they." When some didn't comply, "they" filed a gender harassment complaint with the school district, which was eventually settled with the district paying "them" $60,000 for emotional distress and agreeing to provide "them" with gender-neutral restrooms. Henceforth "their" colleagues must use the proper pronouns with "them" or face discipline or dismissal.[49]

Similarly, a Virginia high school teacher paid an enormous price for refusing to use the preferred pronoun of a female student identifying as male. All five members of the West Point School Board agreed to fire West Point High School French teacher Peter Vlaming following a four-hour hearing. Vlaming did address the person by her chosen name but wouldn't use her new pronoun because he believed it conflicted with his Christian faith. Illustrating the absurdity of this inquisition, the school principal, Jonathan Hochman, referred to the student as female during the hearing. Hochman testified that he told Vlaming, "You need to say sorry for that. And refer to her by the male pronoun."[50] You can't make this up.

"CHALLENGING THE GENDER BINARY"

For many years Facebook was just as gender insensitive as the rest of us, offering its users only two options for declaring their gender—plain vanilla male and female. In early 2014, it expanded its options to fifty-eight. It offers three pronoun options: "her," "him," or "them." "There's going to be a lot of people for whom this is going to mean nothing, but for the few it does impact, it means the world," says Facebook software engineer Brielle Harrison, who personally transformed her gender from male to female and changed her Facebook identity from Female to TransWoman. "All too often transgender people like myself and other gender nonconforming people are given this binary option, do you want to be male or female?" says Harrison. "What is your gender?

And it's kind of disheartening because none of those let us tell others who we really are. This really changes that, and for the first time I get to go to the site and specify to all the people I know what my gender is."[51] That she has to identify her gender to her friends, who apparently otherwise may not know, is instructive.

Facebook UK upped the ante and offered its users seventy-one gender options and the pronoun choices "he/his," "she/her," and "they/their." "Gender identities are complex and for many people, describing themselves as just a man or just a woman has always been inadequate," explained Professor Stephen Whittle. "By challenging the gender binary, Facebook will finally allow thousands of people to describe themselves as they are now and it will allow future generations of kids to become truly comfortable in their own skins."[52] In light of the rapid proliferation of genders, it seems Joe Biden has some serious ground to cover, since at the moment he only recognizes "at least three."[53] While an increasing number of gender identities may sound liberating and innocuous, social psychologist Barry Schwartz notes that telling people who are struggling with their gender identity that they have complete autonomy to define themselves may increase their confusion and suffering.[54]

"A CRIME AGAINST HUMANITY"

Walt Heyer, a former transgender person, is concerned that activists are changing gender vocabulary.[55] Public and private universities are teaching these concepts in their human sexuality and public health courses. Professors are teaching that gender is more than male and female, which have become passé terms. As noted, activists are so determined to make the unorthodox normal and vice versa that they manufactured a new term, "cisgender," for a person without gender hang-ups—that is, for a person "whose gender identity corresponds with the sex the person had or was identified as having at birth."[56] One of Webster's usage examples shows how leftists are proactively trying to de-normalize heterosexual reality. Webster's quotes Hugh Ryan, who says, "In a very real and measurable way, cisgender identity is no longer unmarked, universal, or assumed. It is denoted, limited, and in conversation with trans identities—or at least we're moving in that direction." In other words, they don't want normal to be considered normal because that will make any other identity seem abnormal.

Heyer observes that while people who suffer from gender confusion were formerly considered to have a mental disorder, the American Psychiatric Association's *Diagnostic and Statistical Manual of Mental Disorders* has been politicized to treat it as "dysphoria" rather than a disorder. Dysphoria is a state of unease or dissatisfaction with life—the opposite of euphoria[57]—and, as such, is not viewed as something to overcome. Heyer contends that gender "confusion" is not biological but psychological. He disputes the claim that "transgenders are born that way," saying that "not a smidgeon of abnormality can be found in the genetic makeup of transgenders, so, no, transgenders are not born that way. They are normal males and females."

"What researchers *have* found," however, "is that transgenders attempt suicide at an alarming rate" and that a majority of them have at least one psychiatric co-existing (co-morbid) disorder, the most common of which are major depressive disorder, specific phobia, and adjustment disorder. Researchers, Heyer says, have found that 30 percent of gender dysphoria patients have a lifetime diagnosis of dissociative disorder, which used to be known as multiple personality disorder. Heyer says he was diagnosed with gender dysphoria by the most highly regarded gender specialist in America, who recommended surgery to transition from male to female. The doctor said "all my discomfort would go away after surgery.... He was wrong."[58] Heyer says he lived eight years successfully as a transgender female, but after the euphoria wore off he was confused and even more depressed. Later, when he received the proper diagnosis and treatment of his dissociative disorder, he no longer needed to play the role of a woman and felt betrayed by "the redefinition madness.... The surgery can't define who I am," he said. "The idea of 56 different genders is repugnant to this former transgender. I am a man, not some nonsense name contrived by the LGBT."[59]

"People who pursue a cross-sex identity aren't born that way, and children should not be encouraged to 'transition' to the opposite sex, according to a reference work endorsed by the American Psychological Association," says Heyer. Many parents tell him their children's therapist recommends the child change his or her name or personal pronouns, live as the opposite sex, and begin "irreversible medical interventions"—after only a few appointments.[60]

Based on studies of transgender children, the *APA Handbook of Sexuality and Psychology* finds that gender dysphoria persists to adulthood in no more than 25 percent of children; most of the boys and about half of the girls later identify as gay, not transgender. Early social transition (change of gender role) should be approached with caution, as the stress involved with a later reversal is substantial. Heyer says that despite these findings, sex-change advocates claim the opposite—that the science is settled that those who identify as the opposite sex will never change their minds—and so they are adamant that the transition must be made as early as possible.[61] This is further proof that the tendency to declare something as settled science is a recurring practice for leftists.

Heyer had a "sex change" in 1983, unaware that evidence was surfacing against the notion that people are "born that way." In 1979 Dr. Charles L. Ihlenfeld, an endocrinologist, warned against using hormones and surgery on the transgender population, based on his own experimentation. Ihlenfeld flatly said that 80 percent of the people who want to change their sex shouldn't do it—that this strong desire most likely arises from powerful psychological factors they experienced in the first eighteen months of their lives. Heyer says Ihlenfeld's conclusions foreshadowed the findings of the APA handbook, including that identifying as the opposite sex is "most likely the result of a complex interaction between biological and environmental factors."

Heyer says the evidence does not demonstrate the effectiveness of using cross-sex hormones and sex-change surgery to treat gender dysphoria. He is troubled that the medical and psychological communities ignore their own research and continue to experiment with real lives, including the lives of children. He strongly rejects the battle cry of the "sex-change cheerleaders" who "falsely claim, 'Affirmation is the only solution.'... We must wake up and use the evidence provided in the APA handbook to counter those who say transgender people are born that way."[62]

Feminist author and professor Camille Paglia maintains that "the transgender propagandists make wildly inflated claims about the multiplicity of gender." Regardless of how you define your gender or even if you have sex reassignment surgery, says Paglia, "ultimately, the DNA in that cell, remains coded for your biological birth. So there are a lot of lies being propagated...which...is not in anyone's best interest.... Parents are now encouraged to subject the child to procedures that I think are a form of child abuse.... People should not be doing this to their children, and I think that even in the teenage years is too soon to be making this leap. People change, people grow, and people adapt."[63] Paglia describes assisting children to undergo sex reassignment surgery as a "crime against humanity."[64]

A 2016 study by Johns Hopkins University scientists Dr. Lawrence S. Mayer and Dr. Paul R. McHugh corroborates Heyer's and Paglia's claims. Its findings include: scientific evidence does not support the claim that sexual orientation is an innate, biologically fixed property (that people are "born that way"); some 80 percent of male adolescents who report same-sex attractions do not do so as adults; non-heterosexuals are two to three times more likely to have been sexually abused in childhood; gay people have an increased risk of adverse health and mental health outcomes; gay-identified people have a nearly two-and-a-half times greater risk of suicide; the notion that gender identity is fixed (that a man might be trapped in a woman's body or a woman in a man's body) is unsupported by scientific evidence; studies of brain structures show no evidence for a neurological basis for cross-gender identification; sex-reassigned people are five times more likely to attempt suicide and nineteen times more likely to die by suicide; the rate of lifetime suicide attempts by transgenders is 41 percent compared to 5 percent among the entire U.S. population; and only a minority of children who experience cross-gender identification continue to do so into adolescence or adulthood.[65]

THE SUDDEN BLOOMING OF TRANSGENDER CLINICS

But Heyer's and Paglia's view is not prevailing. In April 2017 the *New York Times* featured an op-ed by Yale School of Medicine research fellow Jack Turban, who lectures on the treatment of transgender and gender-nonconforming youth. Turban criticized President Trump for eliminating supportive policies for transgender students at public schools and opposing laws allowing transgenders to use bathrooms not corresponding with their birth genders. "Politicians could learn something from the doctors who treat these patients," says Turban. "If we support these children in their transgender identities instead of trying to change them, they thrive instead of struggling with anxiety and depression." It's noteworthy that Turban views treating a person as a member of his biological gender as trying to change him, leading to anxiety and depression. Turban describes Hannah, a fourteen-year old girl who was born a boy.[66] He says that Hannah is using a puberty-blocking implant as she prepares to develop a female body by starting estrogen hormone therapy. "Ten years ago most doctors would have called this malpractice," he writes. "New data has now made it the protocol for thousands of American children."

Turban argues that transforming kids' bodies at a younger age would prevent societal stigma, which leads to higher rates of suicide and depression now associated with gender dysphoria. "But there's no hard data to support that notion," writes columnist Ben Shapiro. "A study from professors at the American Foundation for Suicide Prevention and the Williams Institute at the UCLA School of Law, for example, found that 46 percent of transgender men and 42 percent of transgender women had attempted suicide.... Surgery doesn't militate against suicide either."[67] Shapiro notes that this is "science with an agenda." It's one thing for adults to make decisions about their sexualities and their bodies, but these decisions should not be imposed on children, especially since 80 percent of children with gender confusion outgrow it.[68]

Social conservatives warned that the left would not be satisfied with "equal rights" for homosexuals or even with the legalization of same-sex marriage. Just a few years ago, activists were focused on "gay rights." But once they triumphed, they moved on to their new obsession, "transgender rights." There has been a concerted effort to increase the previously minuscule population of people with "gender dysphoria" and prioritize their demands above all others. There is an all-out push for dysphoric children to be given medical treatment to enable their bodies to simulate those of the opposite sex, often with the use of puberty blockers that disrupt the body's natural maturation processes. Other treatments include cross-sex hormones—flooding the body with hormones of the opposite sex—and invasive surgery to remove healthy reproductive organs and sometimes implant fake organs of the opposite sex. Even some homosexuals are troubled by research showing that the large majority of children with this dysphoria will outgrow it without potentially dangerous and irreversible treatments.

Sadly, many physicians succumb to the PC pressure and support "gender-affirming treatment" or cower in silence before the thought police. As early as 2008, the American Medical Association officially supported increased access to hormonal and surgical treatment for patients with gender identity disorder, which the condition used to be called until 2013, when the American Psychiatric Association changed it to gender dysphoria, as noted. In *The Federalist*, Jane Robbins observes that these attitudinal changes in the medical community "fertilized the soil for the sudden blooming of 'transgender clinics'" to help the mushrooming number of gender dysphoric patients get medical alterations—and "by happy coincidence, create a lucrative new specialty for physicians willing to push the Hippocratic envelope."

Robbins argues that the Endocrine Society has yielded to political ideology in lieu of sound medical practice and encourages its members to "ride the gender dysphoria wave regardless of concerns about safety and ethics." Some brave endocrinologists are standing up to the gender bullies and the Endocrine Society by opposing "gender affirmation treatment (GAT)." They claim the risks in the treatment make truly informed consent for children, adolescents, and parents unlikely. In their letter to the *Journal of Clinical Endocrinology and Metabolism*, these dissenting physicians state, "Physicians need to start examining GAT through the objective eye of the scientist-clinician rather than the ideological lens of the social activist. Far more children with gender dysphoria will ultimately be helped by this approach."[69]

"GENDER BINARISM VIOLATES MY VALUES"

The insanity marches on as the left aggressively pushes the transgender lifestyle. In the summer of 2018, the Boston Public Library allowed the "Sisters of Perpetual Indulgence," who are drag queens dressed as

Catholic nuns, to read stories to kids. Is nothing sacred anymore? Princeton professor Robert P. George argues that it's dangerous for the state to promote ideas that defy normal notions about gender. "It's a message about power," says George. "The group in question ... is sending a message that they have the power to enter into the public domain, a publicly funded institution ... and to essentially hold a catechism class for this new religion that they've created—a religion of hedonism, of self-indulgence, Sisters of Perpetual Indulgence, say a religion of licentiousness."[70] In another case, the Houston Public Library allowed a man to entertain children during "drag queen story time" without conducting a background check on him. It turns out he was a registered sex offender who was convicted of assaulting an eight-year-old child in 2009, and the library issued an apology.[71]

At a separate reading event, a man dressed in drag encouraged a young child to become a drag queen. A video shows a little girl saying, "I want to be a superhero," and the drag queen responds, "You can be a drag queen superhero."[72] Surely we can acknowledge this isn't merely a live-and-let-live attitude but one of proselytizing and recruitment.

There are now parent-and-children teams transitioning to the opposite sex in tandem, as if it's some hot new trend. In one case, a Detroit mother and her son transitioned to father and daughter. One writer glowed, "The family that transgenders together stays together."[73] In another reported case, a mother and daughter became father and son.[74]

Today, many parents have "gender-reveal parties" to celebrate their new baby and announce, "It's a boy" or "It's a girl." But these innocent celebrations offend gender identity enforcers. In *New York Times Magazine*, Professor Kwame Anthony Appiah wrote an article which asked, "Should I Go to a Gender-Reveal Party?" Appiah's column relates his response to a correspondent who asked him whether he should go to a gender-reveal party of an expectant mother who is a close relation. The correspondent identified as "cisgender" but declared, "I am adamantly opposed to attending the gender-reveal party because it violates my moral code." These parties "violate my values because they reaffirm society's gender binarism and inadvertently perpetuate the stigma against nonbinary genders."[75]

Dr. Albert Mohler, theologian and president of Southern Baptist Theological Seminary, comments, "This question represents just one more step towards cultural insanity," because the questioner is appalled at celebrations of politically incorrect labels like "boy" and "girl." This "violates the moral code of the transgender movement." Mohler rightly notes that this type of question doesn't appear "on the leading edge of a moral revolution." The revolution must be well underway for someone to freely express such outrage in an ethics column in such a prominent publication. First, Mohler notes that the use of the term "cisgender" plays into the gender revolution. "Even adopting the vocabulary ... assumes that you accept the ideology of the transgender revolutionaries—that gender fluidity exists and that the gender assigned at one's birth *may* or *may not* be factual. 'Cisgender' signifies that you buy into the idea that all of humanity must be identified on a spectrum, with cisgender at one end and gender-non-conforming, or, transgender at the other end."[76]

I'll add that when gender activists demand that all people use their dictated terms, from "cisgender" to the other endless gender identities and pronouns, they are winning the debate and normalizing things in our culture that most people consider highly abnormal. Mohler notes the leaps in logic involved in expecting readers to share the writer's moral outrage against parents for throwing a gender-reveal party. "The question, by itself, poses enormous problems and reveals the erosion of any sane ethic," writes Mohler. He also rejects Professor Appiah's response that "biological sex has nothing to do with gender identity." "Christians operating from a biblical worldview understand Appiah's assertions as manifest nonsense," writes Mohler. "The morally important distinction between male and female is essential. Indeed, the biblical worldview clearly grounds the distinction as a vital component for true human flourishing." The assertions in Mohler's penultimate paragraph are well worth considering: "Articles like this one in the *New York Times Magazine*, and arguments like Professor Appiah's, demonstrate the unceasing desire of the LGBTQ agenda to invert civilization itself. As relentless as they might be, the moral revolutionaries aim at insanity and position arguments as reality that have no basis in any scientific court or, for that matter, common sense."[77]

"THIS ISN'T A DEBATE. THE DATA ARE IN."

Jordan Peterson flatly rejects the concept of gender ideology. He notes that schools are using cartoon characters such as a "genderbread person" or unicorn to indoctrinate students, beginning with seventh graders, to believe that one's biological sex, psychological sense of sex, manner of dress, and erotic feelings are independent of one another. The cartoons show four rows designated as "sex assigned at birth," "gender identity," "gender expression," and "sexual preference." Teachers instruct kids to place an X along the four continuums to show where they see themselves in these supposedly separate places. Yet there is overwhelming evidence that there are biological differences between men and women. "The vast majority of people who have a biological sex also claim that they are psychologically ... the same as that biological sex," says Peterson. "So the idea that they are independent is completely insane."[78] In his book *12 Rules for Life*, Peterson writes, "Boys' interests tilt towards things; girls' interests tilt towards people. Strikingly, these differences, strongly influenced by biological factors, are most pronounced in the Scandinavian societies where gender-equality has been pushed hardest: this is the opposite of what would be expected by those who insist, ever more loudly, that gender is a social construct. It isn't. This isn't a debate. The data are in."[79]

Science confirms that human beings are "sexually dimorphic"—they come in two forms, male and female.[80] One illustration of the distinct differences between men and women occurred in 2013, when the U.S. Food and Drug Administration (FDA) reduced by half the recommended dosage of the drug Ambien for women and not men. Studies showed that men and women metabolize the drug differently and the original dosage was remaining in women's bloodstreams longer, which could cause problems such as impairing their ability to drive for a longer period.[81]

Larry Cahill, a neuroscientist at the University of California, Irvine, admits that he used to believe men and women were fundamentally the same, apart from reproduction and sex hormones, but no longer.[82] "The biomedical community has long operated on what is increasingly being viewed as a false assumption: that biological sex matters little, if at all, in most areas of medicine," writes Cahill.[83] Today's biomedical research establishment, he explains, is changing but is still not properly accounting for the differences between men and women. This is partly because academia considered it distasteful to study sex differences in the brain.[84] Feminist Gloria Steinem once proclaimed that it's "anti-American, crazy thinking to *do* this kind of research."[85] Feminist attorney Gloria Allred said, "We take attacks from the media on our skills and our abilities and our talents and our dreams very seriously. This is not just entertainment. This is harmful and damaging to our daughters' lives and to our mothers' lives, and I'm very angry about it."[86]

The left has so politicized this issue that one of Cahill's colleagues warned him that pursuing this area of study could destroy his career.[87] But he survived and says that many neuroscientists have come to realize "that their deeply ingrained assumption that sex does not matter is just plain wrong."[88] There is evidence of sex differences in research involving human beings as well as in animal research, including studies on human brain structure and other human brain genetics. Researchers from the University of Pennsylvania found that women's brains show significantly stronger patterns of interconnectivity across brain regions, including across the hemispheres, than men's brains, while men's brains show greater average connectivity within local brain regions. "This means we cannot explain the sex differences in their results as simply being due to different cultural experiences between males and females," writes Cahill. "... In a comprehensive review of human-brain connectivity studies from several years ago, Gaolang Gong and colleagues concluded that 'it should be mandatory to take gender into account when designing experiments or interpreting results of brain connectivity/network in health and disease.' The data since then confirms this view." Another important study shows that sex differences exist even down to the genetic level in human beings, which means that the biological mechanisms of brain aging and disease cannot be assumed to be the same in men and women.[89]

Some other biological differences between men and women—and there are many more—are: a man's brain is about 10 percent heavier than a female's; male skin is microscopically thicker; women show more sensitivity to odors; a man's bones are heavier and his muscles bulkier, his shoulders broader, his heart and lungs larger, on average, making him physically stronger; the regions of the brain involving language and fine motor skills develop earlier in girls, but those areas involving targeting and spatial memory develop faster in boys; in adolescent girls a greater fraction of brain activity connected with negative emotion moves up to the cerebral cortex, so a seventeen-year-old girl, for example, is better able to explain in detail why she is feeling sad; and studies show that boys are more likely to engage in physically risky activities than girls are.[90]

Despite abundant evidence of the biological differences between males and females, you'd better think twice before saying it publicly. One liberal luminary, Lawrence Summers, former U.S. Treasury secretary and Harvard president, learned this the hard way. Summers, it should be noted, was never ridiculed by the liberal media for his maliciously ludicrous claim that the Trump tax cuts would kill ten thousand people.[91] But it was a different story in 2005 when he discussed various theories to explain why women hold fewer elite academic positions in science and math. One of the theories Summers mentioned was that men and women have different natural aptitudes and that married women tend to devote less time to demanding jobs than men do. The ensuing feminist uproar was fierce, with MIT biology professor Nancy Hopkins professing that Summers's comments forced her to leave the room. "I would've either blacked out or thrown up," she claimed. Predictably, multiple groveling apologies couldn't spare Summers from being ousted from Harvard in the aftermath.[92]

A few years after Summers's comments, liberal columnist Ruth Marcus grudgingly conceded his point with some caveats, citing studies that show men greatly outnumber women in scoring the highest (and lowest) aptitude test scores in math and science. Columnist Michael Barone, however, notes that Marcus nevertheless argues that Summers shouldn't have expressed his opinion because academics shouldn't utter truths that people don't want to hear.[93] Marcus's actual words were, "Summers was boneheaded to say what he said, in the way that he said it and considering the job that he held. But he probably had a legitimate point—and the continuing uproar says more about the triumph of political correctness than about Summers's supposed sexism."[94]

Irrespective of whether innate aptitudinal differences exist between men and women in the hard sciences, the object lesson is that political correctness is oppressively censorious. People should be allowed to express controversial and politically incorrect opinions, and our common goal should be the pursuit of truth—not finding evidence to confirm our biases. Regardless of whether the theory Summers discussed was correct, there are biological differences between men and women, and political correctness should not bar discussion about them.

A more recent example of the dangers of bucking the gender thought police occurred when Google employee James Damore submitted an internal memo called "Google's Ideological Echo Chamber," contending that women are biologically less suited for tech jobs. Google fired him for violating the company's code of conduct, which evidently requires employees to align their thinking with the company's minister of propaganda. Google said Damore's memo crossed "the line by advancing harmful gender stereotypes in the workplace."[95]

Diversity bean counters aren't interested in a diversity of ideas and life experiences. They are intoxicated with the exuberance of projecting moral superiority by showing they care more than others about historically disadvantaged groups—not people, but groups. They are possessed with a leftist compulsion to control people's lives, and they'll succeed until the private sector resists this bullying. While such private suppression of speech usually doesn't rise to the level of a constitutional infraction, it is nevertheless a grave concern for a free society. In the next chapter, we examine how the left's latest nostrums on gender ideology are manifesting themselves in societal insanity.

CHAPTER SIX

Weaponizing Gender

Gender-baiters are giving race-baiters a run for their money. Just as the left blames racism—instead of Obama's leftist agenda—for conservative opposition to his presidency, its members blame criticism of female politicians on sexism. CNN's Brian Stelter tweeted about AOC, "She's got a target on her back because she ticks every box that makes conservative men uncomfortable."[1] In fact, her biggest "box" upsetting conservatives is that she's a self-avowed socialist, but that's obviously not what Stelter was driving at.

Similarly, leftists claim that men find Elizabeth Warren unlikable because they're sexist—the same reason men supposedly didn't like Hillary Clinton. "Many of these voters are people who esteem themselves to be feminists or otherwise free of bias, but who will nevertheless find themselves uncomfortable with a woman in power, unable to articulate what it is that bothers them about Elizabeth Warren—except for a vague sense that they just don't like her," writes columnist Moira

Donegan. "The issue with Elizabeth Warren isn't likability. It's sexism." Likewise, liberal writer Peter Beinart insists that conservative criticism of Warren has "nothing to do with her progressive economic views or her dalliance with DNA testing," but stems from the simple fact that "she's a woman."[2]

Sorry, but these critics are overthinking it and projecting their own gender fixations. Neither Warren nor Clinton are likable, and it's not due to sexism but to their lack of any semblance of authenticity. "The truth is Warren isn't so likable.... Her full-time video team has been working since last year to capture the real Elizabeth and counter her image as a schoolmarm and a scold," writes columnist A. B. Stoddard.[3] But of course, according to leftists, if we don't support their unlikable scold then we hate women. And there's a certain irony in feminists blaming sexism when people are repelled by the phony elitists they push to the political forefront. If Warren has what it takes then she'll be competitive, but blaming voters' prejudices for her own shortcomings won't help her cause. Perhaps voters can be shamed into some things, but liking unlikable people isn't one of them.

Leftists just can't follow their own inane precepts. They insist that only women and minorities can lead their respective causes and that it's time for a woman president—but they can't get their base to comply. In April 2019, the RealClearPolitics poll average of the Democratic presidential candidates showed that four white men—Biden, Sanders, O'Rourke, and Buttigieg—had the support of 62 percent of all Democratic voters. Three white women—Senators Warren, Klobuchar, and Gillibrand—together had only 8 percent. African Americans Harris and Booker had 10 and 3 percent, respectively. Granted, this poll represented only a snapshot in time, and some of the female candidates sporadically rose in popularity. But these changes obviously had little to do with their gender or race, or support for them would have been more consistent. In August 2019 the same poll average still showed the aging white Biden far ahead of the pack, Warren (female but white) a distant second, and crazy, old, white Bernie third.[4] For all their lecturing on identity politics, white privilege, and intersectionality, Democrats can't even persuade their most loyal supporters to submit to their nonsense.[5]

LEFTIST GENDER HYPOCRISY

Leftists are just as hypocritical on gender as on race. They demand respect for females—provided they're good progressives. Leftists certainly didn't treat conservative judge Neomi Rao with feminist respect when she was nominated to replace Justice Brett Kavanaugh on the U.S. Court of Appeals for the District of Columbia. Perhaps female Indian Americans haven't secured their proper place on the intersectionality totem pole because Rao, like Nikki Haley, gets no deference from the left for her "identities." Despite her brilliant legal scholarship, the left attacked Rao based on her college writings. Some were outraged that she wrote that if a woman "drinks to the point where she can no longer choose, well, getting to that point was part of her choice." She further argued that "[a] man who rapes a drunk girl should be prosecuted. At the same time, a good way to avoid a potential date rape is to stay reasonably sober."[6] This should be uncontroversial, yet the left wildly accused Rao of blaming women for being raped.

These criticisms mask the main reason leftists oppose conservative judicial nominees. Political conservatives tend to be originalists—advocates of judicial restraint and interpreting the Constitution according to the framers' original intent. Leftists see the appellate courts as vehicles to rewriting laws when congressional legislation doesn't suit them. Originalist judges strive to keep their political opinions from influencing their judicial decisions, but the left doesn't recognize that separation. For leftists the personal is political—in fact, everything is political—and so liberal activists are the only suitable justices.

Rao's leftist critics were also incensed that in her youth Rao challenged the tenets of identity politics, an unforgivable blasphemy. She wrote, "[M]ulticulturalists...separate and classify everyone according to race, gender and sexual orientation. Those who reject their assigned categories are called names: So-called conforming blacks are called 'oreos' by members of their own community, conservatives become 'fascists.' Preaching tolerance, multiculturalists seldom practice it...."[7] Rao's observations are irrefutable. The gender-scolding left talks a good game on feminism but treats conservative women like it treats conservative minorities—with contempt—proving again that its political agenda trumps everything.

In an op-ed in *The Hill*, three women summarized leftist opposition to Rao: "Our communities count on women of color in positions of power to ensure that our fundamental and civil rights are protected, yet Rao repeatedly has shown that she will not, and cannot, fulfill that role. It is incumbent upon our senators to do their job to protect our communities and the integrity of the judiciary by refusing to confirm Neomi Rao."[8] That is, if you won't put the leftist political agenda above the Constitution, you are dead to them—so to speak.

A HODGEPODGE OF GENDER INSANITY

Inarguably, the left is on a mission to fundamentally transform our culture and browbeat Americans into submitting to its abnormal gender theories. Here is another small sampling of examples:

- ★ As the left seeks to normalize abnormal behavior, it demonizes what is normal and wholesome. A staff writer for *New York Magazine* and *Vulture* launched into a Twitter rant over a fictional character in the TV show *The Big Bang Theory* reacting happily to news of her pregnancy in the series finale. "IN THIS CLIMATE?! my mind is still boggling," tweeted Dr. Kathryn VanArendonk. "REALLY? THAT'S THE END? REALLY!? when I say that I feel sure this is an accident, what I mean is that it seems likely to have been written with no reference to current events re: abortion laws. it's clearly not an accident as far as how they decided to find an ending for that character." So the show's ending was an outrage because it didn't celebrate abortion? An intelligent human being actually posted this tweet? Sadly, I feel sure this was *not* an accident.
- ★ A video shows the ACLU, in collaboration with California school districts and Planned Parenthood, instructing public school teachers on progressive sexual education and gender theory. Teachers were allegedly told how to help students obtain abortions without parental knowledge and how to prevent parents from opting their kids out of

graphic lessons on sexuality and homosexuality. "They talk about mutual masturbation," said Murrieta School District parent John Andrews. "They discuss gender roles, the gender spectrum, and in the support materials...they take it even further. They discuss everything, topics like roleplaying for different genders, blood play, dental dams...fisting is mentioned. I mean, they mention it all.... They talk about anal and oral sex as an alternative to regular sex because you can't get pregnant."[9]

- ★ Critics blasted Taron Egerton, the straight actor who plays Elton John in the biopic *Rocketman*, insisting the role should have been given to someone from the gay community. When asked about the criticism, Elton John retorted, "That's all bulls***, I'm sorry."[10]
- ★ Similarly, in 2018 actress Scarlett Johansson was forced to drop out of the film *Rub and Tug* amidst leftist abuse for accepting a role as a transgender man. A year later, she sparked another two minutes of hate when she criticized the stifling effect of political correctness on art and asserted that as an actress, she should be allowed to play any role she wants. This was quickly followed by the obligatory self-denunciation and cringing apology. "I recognize that in reality, there is a widespread discrepancy amongst my industry that favors Caucasian, cisgendered actors and that not every actor has been given the same opportunities that I have been privileged to," groveled Johansson. "I continue to support, and always have, diversity in every industry and will continue to fight for projects where everyone is included."[11] Aside from all the nonsense about appropriation, what is it that keeps leftists from understanding that acting involves people pretending to be other people?
- ★ Social justice warriors lambasted actor William Shatner for defending the lyrics of the Christmas classic "Baby, It's Cold Outside" against feminists who claimed the tune promotes sexual harassment. When the Canadian

Broadcasting Corporation decided to ban the song, Shatner encouraged his Twitter followers to demand they reinstate it, which they eventually did. Meanwhile, Shatner responded to his critics with admirable directness: "I would think that censorship of classics because certain 'types' need to judge things through their own 2018 myopic glasses and demand they be stricken from history is important. Or is this 1984 only 34 years too late?"[12]

When an SJW accused him of not caring about sexual assault victims, Shatner countered that the lyrics shouldn't be interpreted as if they were written today, because the context in which they were written in 1949 was merely that men and women were flirting with each other on a cold winter's night. The daughter of Frank Loesser, the song's creator, agreed.[13] This incident illustrates how all considerations—including tradition, joy, and humor—must give way to social justice scolds who are on the prowl for ideological transgressions.

★ Laura Bassett, senior culture and politics reporter for *HuffPost*, womansplains that conservative men are confused by being drawn to AOC "while loathing everything she stands for.... There's an existential, panicked tinge to the behavior here—what you might call 'AOC Derangement Syndrome.' Indeed, some experts say conservative men are obsessed with Ocasio-Cortez because they're threatened by her." AOC's power and "her very existence in Congress as a young, Latina, working-class woman threatens to upend the social order that has kept white men in the ruling class for centuries."[14] Bassett cites bizarre pseudoscience from which "experts" conclude that conservatives' brains are likely to display attention biases of people with anxiety. Likewise, neuroscientist Bobby Azarian divines the real motivation underlying conservatives' opposition to AOC: "The one main cognitive difference is that conservatives are more sensitive to threat. Their fears are sometimes exaggerated. I think they fear her."

- ★ CNN host Joan Walsh called Trump "sexist" for his "appalling" off-the-cuff suggestion that Melania could make salads for the Clemson Tigers during their White House visit. "It seems to me like the president will not be happy until there is not one single female Republican voter in the country," said Walsh. "It's incredibly sexist."[15] Happy liberals.
- ★ President Obama directed public schools to allow transgender students to use bathrooms corresponding to their gender identities. President Trump rescinded this order as civil rights officials from the Justice Department and Education Department concluded that Obama's directive was improper, arbitrary, and issued "without due regard for the primary role of the states and local school districts in establishing educational policy."[16]
- ★ In 2016, North Carolina passed a bill limiting the use of men's restrooms to biological men and women's restrooms to biological women in many public facilities. This provoked a hysterical overreaction on the left, with businesses, sports leagues, and Hollywood stars alike vowing to boycott the state. The next year the provision was repealed[17] and replaced by a bill that prohibited cities from enacting nondiscrimination ordinances for workplaces, hotels, and restaurants until December 2020.[18]
- ★ There is a broader movement to pass public accommodation laws and policies that ban discrimination on the basis of gender identity in public restrooms. As of March 2017, nineteen states, the District of Columbia, and more than two hundred cities had such laws, which allow transgenders to use public facilities that correspond to their gender identities.[19] Jamie Shupe, a retired sergeant first class from the U.S. Army and a former transgender woman, argues that Obama administration policies victimize servicewomen. Despite all the effort to help men appear female to alleviate gender dysphoria, "the charade is a failure. They are and always will remain male."[20]

Similar policies in high schools are jeopardizing the health and welfare of young girls. Shupe cites examples of females feeling viscerally threatened when males enter their bathrooms. One student, Alexis Lightcap, sued the Boyertown, Pennsylvania, school district. She says she doesn't care if transgender people share a bathroom with her as long as they share her biological sex, because identity is not biology. It's patently unfair to brand those like Lightcap as bigots because they refuse to share a bathroom or locker with males who identify as females. But that's the nature of the left—demonize and stigmatize all who disagree and refuse to conform with its nonconformity.

Indeed, the leftist crusade for transgender bathrooms, like so many other leftist causes, is purportedly being pursued on behalf of the people, but, in fact, is advancing without regard for the actual concerns or wishes of children or parents. For example, a school in Alberta discovered that the gender-neutral bathrooms it ordered in 2017 didn't sit well with students. "Many students avoided them because, as any idiot knows, boys and girls generally feel uncomfortable doing their business in a stall next to a member of the opposite sex," writes pro-life activist Jonathon Van Maren.[21]

★ CNN host Chris Cuomo tweeted that if a young girl doesn't want to see male genitalia it must be either because she is the problem or her dad is overprotective and intolerant. "Teach tolerance," tweeted Cuomo. When challenged, Cuomo responded, "My point was dead clear. This isn't about a scared girl. It is about an overprotective parent who is afraid without basis. Don't twist it." Isn't it great how liberals can tell whether your feelings and opinions are legitimate and worthy of respect? One person countered, "We need to teach tolerance to 12 yr. old girls who don't want to see a penis in a locker room. Have you gone insane?" Yes, it *is* insane for leftists to paint a father's parental concerns as intolerance.

- ★ Cuomo arrogantly tweeted that there's "no proof" of a spike in sexual assaults because of gender-identity bathroom policies. How much proof does His Eminence need? How about the November 2015 incident in which a Virginia man, having entered a women's restroom in drag, was arrested for filming two women and a five-year-old?[22] Or the May 2013 affair when a Los Angeles man dressed in drag recorded hours of footage of undressed women from under bathroom stalls?[23] Or the 2012 case when a forty-five-year-old biological male identifying as a female lounged naked in a women's locker room used by girls from six to eighteen years of age?[24] Or the time when a man twice entered a changing room of a Washington swimming pool and disrobed—one time in front of a young girl's swim team—and invoked transgender policies as his authority?[25]

  It's not enough for leftists like Cuomo to label the rest of us cis-brained people as intolerant; they demand that their twisted notions of tolerance be imposed on others in derogation of their rights and well-being. To them, everything else must take a back seat to their ideology. For all the talk about protecting women and children, neither matters when their rights conflict with the latest absurd leftist theories.
- ★ The Trump Department of Defense implemented a policy allowing transgender people to continue serving in the military but mostly precluding people with gender dysphoria from joining the military. The Ninth Circuit Court of Appeals enjoined implementation of the policy, but the U.S. Supreme Court lifted the injunction and held that the policy can remain in force as the case works through the appeals process. The Court declined to review the case on the merits while it was in the appeals process in the lower courts.[26]
- ★ In August 2019, an Obama-appointed judge ruled that taxpayer-funded Medicaid must cover sex-reassignment surgery in Wisconsin.[27]

- ★ An eleven-year-old boy known as "Desmond Is Amazing" danced on stage at a New York gay bar while grown men tossed dollar bills at him. The boy was dressed in drag, imitating singer Gwen Stefani, at Brooklyn's 3 Dollar Bill, which describes itself as "queer owned & operated" and "Brooklyn's Premiere Queer Bar & Performance Venue." ABC's *Good Morning America* featured Desmond and celebrated his cross-dressing as an example of individuality, praising his parents for supporting his drag hobby. The segment included a surprise appearance of "iconic drag queens" Hedda Lettuce, Shannel, and Alyssa Edwards, who praised the boy as courageous, inspirational, and "the future of drag."[28] Conservative Matt Walsh tweeted, "The Left is applauding the sexual abuse of this child. This is why decent and rational people want nothing at all to do with Leftism. It openly promotes, advocates, and celebrates child sexual abuse."[29]
- ★ A ten-year-old girl from South London was suspended from school for a week for asking her teacher permission to be excused from participating in a "Pride Month" gay lesson.[30]
- ★ Keegan, a nine-year-old from the Austin, Texas, area, performs in drag as Kween KeeKee and spreads "a message of love and inclusiveness as he performs." When a third-grade teacher asked what her students wanted to be when they grew up, Keegan wrote, "gender creative."[31] Commentators who criticized this insane trend encountered immediate blowback from leftists. "The overt sexualization of elementary school children who don't know any better, all for the pleasure and entertainment of adults, is acceptable and shouldn't be condemned," Peter Heck observed. "I'm left wondering again why God's parameters for human sexuality aren't a better alternative for all of us?"
- ★ Activists want to change the image of sex symbol James Bond by having a transgender play him in the next installment of the movie series. British actor Dominic West was

on board, encouraging the Bond movie producers to cast Hannah Graf in the role, as she is the "highest-ranking transgender soldier in the British army." In this case, insanity did not prevail. Bond's longtime producers, the Broccoli family, have no plans to change Bond's gender. "Bond is male," said Barbara Broccoli. "He's a male character. He was written as a male and I think he'll probably stay as a male."[32] Although transgenders may have lost out, it appears feminists and intersectionality advocates will be tossed a bone, as media reports indicate the next Bond movie will depict Bond retiring from service and being replaced as 007 by a black, female agent.[33]

★ Right in time, the University of Oklahoma introduced a feminist James Bond course, called "Gender and James Bond," which "will focus and analyze the James Bond series in full, from the 'heroic masculinity' of the main character and theme of the films, to how different sexes, genders, national orientation and other forms of identity are represented in the Bond series." The course will also focus on gender and intersectionality—but of course—and explore the "problematic representation" of women in the Bond franchise.[34]

★ In 2004, designer and filmmaker Tom Ford, allegedly while drunk, commented that all men should be sexually penetrated at least once in their lifetimes, and he reportedly still stands by the statement. "I think it would help them understand women," he said. "It's such a vulnerable position to be in, and it's such a passive position to be in. And there's such an invasion, in a way, that even if it's consensual, it's just very personal." Ford has been married to his husband Richard Buckley for two years, though they've been together for thirty years and share a four-year old son.[35]

★ A federal judge ordered that twenty-seven-year-old Illinois inmate Deon Strawberry Hampton, a male who identifies as a female and is serving a ten-year sentence for burglary, be transferred to a women's prison. In court filings Hampton's lawyers explained that "she" couldn't comfortably represent herself as female in the male prison, where she couldn't wear her hair or nails long, which was psychologically devastating. "I feel inhuman," she said. Following the court order, Strawberry's attorney Vanessa del Valle hailed the ruling as a triumph for all transgender people.[36]

★ New York mayor Bill de Blasio announced that, as of late 2018, Rikers Island would begin to house transgender inmates in facilities consistent with their gender identity. This order, he said, was part of an effort to bring the Department of Corrections into compliance with an executive order requiring city agencies to allow people to use restrooms and facilities consistent with their gender identities. "It's the city's responsibility to protect the rights and safety of all New Yorkers, and that means protecting transgender individuals in city jails as well," said de Blasio.[37]

★ One can reasonably wonder whether the left's incessant vilification of men has led to misandry, such as that expressed in an open letter to "Men" published in the Jewish left-wing magazine *The Forward*. In the letter, a "straight woman" explains she is not available for dating men at this time, noting that her sexuality "dooms" her to wander the earth trying to mate with people who are the greatest statistical threat to her health. After detailing how dangerous men are, she says, "Listen, it's not that I think you're a predator—I know most of you aren't. I think you happen to have been born into a patriarchal society that you've done little to dismantle, and that's just not really lighting my fire anymore. Why would your polite supremacy endear you to anyone?"[38]

★ Stephens College, an all-girls school in Columbia, Missouri, began accepting biological men who identify as women and biological women who identify as non-binary in fall 2019. The college announced it has expanded its definition of womanhood to include both sex and gender.[39]

★ Girls sometimes get the short end of the stick as transgenderism marches on unabated. We've seen this especially in biological male transgenders entering into female sports and annihilating their competition, such as the 220-pound Australian Hannah Mousey, who transitioned to female and dominated women's handball at the Asian Championship in Japan. As recently as May 2016, Mousey played for the Australian men's handball team.[40]

★ Marathon champion Paula Radcliffe, the fastest women's marathon runner in history, was bullied when she spoke out against transgenders competing in elite women's sports. She made the unforgivable mistake of distinguishing between transgender athletes and "normal" athletes. Despite the avalanche of abuse she endured on social media, Radcliffe said she was going to continue speaking her mind because she believes her daughter should be able to participate in sports against fair competition.[41]

★ Though she's a lesbian, tennis icon Martina Navratilova outraged the left when she penned an op-ed in the *Sunday Times* on trans athletes in women's sports. "You can't just proclaim yourself a female and be able to compete against women," she wrote. "There must be some standards." After critics accused her of transphobia, she researched the issue and then doubled down. "If anything, my views have strengthened," she said. "To put the argument at its most basic: a man can decide to be female, take hormones if required by whatever sporting organization is concerned, win everything in sight and perhaps even earn a small fortune, and then reverse his decision and go back to making babies if he desires. It's insane and it's cheating. I am happy to address a transgender woman in whatever form she prefers, but I would not be happy to compete against her. It would not be fair."

Predictably, the tennis legend came under savage attack by trans activists. Athlete Ally, a New York–based gay sports advocacy group, proclaimed, "Trans women are women, period." "There is no evidence at all," they claimed, that "the average trans woman is any bigger, stronger, or faster than the average cisgender woman."[42] They are women, period? No evidence that biological males are bigger, stronger, or faster than biological females? Tell that to any girls who have finished behind transgender athletes in sports competitions.

Amidst the vilification, Navratilova apologized for the cheating remark but did not withdraw her overall concerns. Liberal Piers Morgan captured the essence of this ludicrous outrage. "It's grotesquely unfair for transgender women to compete in women's sports, and outrageous for trans people to bully and vilify LGBT heroine Martina Navratilova for stating the obvious."[43] Of course, Navratilova's apology did not appease the Stalinist activists, who likened her to Nazi propaganda minister Joseph Goebbels.[44] The irony is breathtaking.

★ Sixteen-year-old Selina Soule missed qualifying for the fifty-five-meter dash in the New England regionals by two spots, each of which were taken by biological boys. "It's very frustrating and heartbreaking when us girls are at the start of the race and we already know that these athletes are going to come out and win no matter how hard you try," said Selina. "They took away the spots of deserving girls, athletes... me being included."[45]

★ Transgender Christina Ginther, a marathon runner and second degree blackbelt in karate, won $10,000 for emotional distress and $10,000 in punitive damages when he was barred from playing on the Independent Women's Football League. This, despite the league's stated policy that "a player may not play in the IWFL, unless they are now, and always have been, legally and medically a female, as determined by their birth certificate and driver's license."[46]

★ Some South Dakota legislators proposed a bill to invalidate a policy allowing transgender students to play on the athletic team that matches their gender identity, but it failed to pass the House. The bill's sponsor, House Majority Leader Lee Qualm, noted that Texas had already passed such a law. "This is all about fair competition," said Qualm. "Boys competing against boys, girls competing against girls, based on their birth certificate." But Libby Skarin of the ACLU of South Dakota insisted that all kids should be able to play high school sports with their personal dignity respected. "No one is harmed by allowing transgender people to compete consistent with who they are," she said.[47]

★ South Dakota lawmakers also rejected measures to limit teaching about gender dysphoria in public schools and to allow parents to refuse consent to healthcare treatments for minor children if the parent thinks the treatments would induce, confirm, or promote a child's belief that his gender identity differs from his biological sex.[48] More and more we see the tyrannical nature of transgender activism as its proponents trample over parents' rights and expose kids to indoctrination based on highly dubious science. Margot Cleveland notes that the failure of this simple affirmation of parental rights to pass committee in a solidly red state should horrify parents. It exposes transgender activists' impulse to "use the government to force parents to affirm a false sex for their child, agree to hormone blockers, and accept a transition to their son or daughter's preferred gender. If parents refuse? Removal of the child from the family, due to alleged medical neglect." This strategy has come in two waves: in the context of child custody cases and in hospitals and medical professionals referring noncompliant parents to Child Protective Services.[49]

★ Poor feminists. Leftist actress Debra Messing caught holy hell when she posted on Instagram, "Happy International Women's Day! Powerful, beautiful, and sweet," along with an image of cupcakes that looked like vaginas. Unlucky Debra! She forgot that all women don't have vaginas anymore. Accusing her of transphobia, leftist critics shamed her into issuing a preposterous apology that perfectly captures the bizarre fixations of both feminists and trans activists: "I want to apologize to my trans sisters. This photo was supposed to be light, & sassy. The first thing I thought when I saw this photo was 'wow how wonderful. Each one is unique in color and shape and size. The porn industry has perpetuated this myth of what a 'beautiful' vagina looks like and as a result there are women who feel shame or insecure about the shape of the vulva. I loved that this picture said 'every single one is beautiful and unique and that's powerful.' I did not, however, think 'but there are innumerable beautiful, unique, and powerful women who don't have a vagina.' And I should have. And for that I am so sorry."[50] As Hadley Heath Manning writes in *The Federalist*, "The left pretends to champion women while actually erasing them."[51]

★ Feminists also got a comeuppance at Mount Holyoke College in Massachusetts. When they tried to create a new school logo to include the female gender symbol, students and faculty who don't identify as women were outraged. As a result, the school scrapped the idea and apologized in a statement pledging its commitment to "diversity, equity, and inclusion by assuring that what we produce supports a future that is bold, distinctive, and affirms gender variance as a core part of the human experience—and particularly at Mount Holyoke College."[52]

★ It can be argued that feminists made gains for their gender in certain areas. But just as with abortion and gay activism, many of them are not satisfied, insisting that all must agree with them or be shamed, in total disregard for *others'* choices. For leftists of all types, complete surrender and total ideological conformity is mandatory. In *The Federalist*, Stefanie Stiles describes her earlier friendship with another professionally ambitious young woman, Jane. Stiles relates that she became an academic and Jane worked as a lawyer, but Stiles eventually left academia to become a stay-at-home mom while her husband continued working.

Some years later, Stiles and Jane engaged in a social media debate, and that night Jane sent her a text saying, "It's not my fault you're bitter about being a failure. That's on you for making bad decisions." "It was an unexpected punch in the gut," writes Stiles. "My stock fell in my old friend's eyes. I had left the ranks of 'young professional women' and had descended into the sub-caste of 'stay-at-home moms.' And to Jane, a strong self-identified feminist, being a stay-at-home mom meant being a failure."

Jane, Stiles notes, is not an outlier, as many other white-collar feminists are contemptuous of women who choose full-time motherhood. The feminists' disparagement of child rearing has placed enormous pressure on women to continue working whether they want or need to.[53] Women who make their own decisions, contrary to the dogmatic dictates of the radical left, are inarguably more liberated than "liberated" feminists.

★ In *Why Women Have Better Sex under Socialism: And Other Arguments for Economic Independence*, University of Pennsylvania professor Kristen R. Ghodsee argues that women under Communist Eastern European regimes had more independence from men and better sex lives than women in other countries. Ghodsee blames the patriarchy and the oppressive capitalistic system for the abusive cycle whereby women quit their jobs to become full-time mothers, with their husbands tightly controlling their spending. Being trapped in this situation, women ostensibly finagle more money from their husbands by having sex with them.[54]

★ In 2018, Princeton Students for Gender Equality and Princeton Students for Reproductive Justice held their third annual Menstruation Celebration which, according to the *Daily Princetonian*, "aims to destigmatize conversation about periods." Signs at the event read, "You can lose a tampon in your vagina," "Period week = blow job week," and "PMS is not real." One sign urged people to stop referring to menstruation as a women's issue since transgender and non-binary people also have periods.[55]

The notion that a person with no female reproductive system can menstruate, of course, contradicts basic human biology. "Despite this social deconstruction, men who identify as women are still biologically male: transgender and non-binary individuals who menstruate are still biologically female; and regardless of thought or perception, nothing will change the immutable biological characteristics of those born with XX or XY chromosomes," writes Frank Camp of the *Daily Wire*. "Although the mainstreaming of these flagrantly anti-scientific ideas may seem quite extreme, we must accept the possibility that this is only the beginning of a long-term campaign to dismantle reality as we know it, the consequences of which could be dire."[56]

★ What with gender insanity being a global phenomenon, we see the Scottish Parliament renaming gingerbread men as "gingerbread persons" in its coffee shop in Holyrood, where staff is outright banned from saying "gingerbread man" because it's not gender neutral.[57] In Hitchin, England, a thirty-eight-year-old mother was arrested in front of her children—a ten-year-old autistic daughter and twenty-month old son—at her home and locked in a cell for seven hours for referring to a transgender woman as a man on Twitter.[58] In Spain, a transgender woman represented the country in the Miss Universe contest, declaring, "Having a vagina didn't transform me into a woman. I am a woman, already before birth, because my identity is here."[59] In this instance, feminists were again victimized by trans advocates, who ensured that the biologically male Miss Spain garnered far more attention at the pageant than Miss Philippines, the female winner.[60] Where are the anti-patriarchy activists when you need them?

A final example comes from a shopping center in Auckland, New Zealand, where a statue called "Santa Poppins," with Santa wearing fishnet stockings and carrying a carpet bag and umbrella, was erected.[61] This is in line with a burgeoning call for Santa Claus to change genders. A GraphicSprings survey of eight hundred people in the U.S. and U.K. showed that some 11 percent want Santa to switch genders, while 17 percent prefer he be gender neutral, which means that only about 70 percent want Santa to remain male.[62]

★ Notwithstanding gay activists' perpetual denunciation of the "hate" and "discrimination" they allegedly face, one gay conservative says that the stigma of being conservative today is worse than that of being gay. "To be a conservative means to be forced to choose when to speak and when to remain silent, since offending someone on the left, even mildly or by accident, is a social battle you may not be able to win," writes Chad Felix Greene. "To be a conservative means carefully regulating your speech and constructing opinions in such a way as to avoid being banned from the public square. To be a conservative means to be a marginalized voice, suppressed and dehumanized; bullied into hesitating to speak out."[63]

Leftists pilloried Greene for voicing his opinion, thus proving his point. Celebrities like Sarah Silverman denounced him on Twitter while John Cooper, chairman of the Democratic Coalition, tweeted, "Chad, you're such a snowflake! Did you know that 40% of LGBT high school students SERIOUSLY CONSIDER SUICIDE? Don't you dare compare being openly gay to being openly conservative!" Cooper also claimed religious conservatives are mostly responsible for gay teens' high suicide rates.[64] *Deadspin* sportswriter Lauren Theisen derided Green in a piece charmingly titled, "Conservative Gays Need To Shut The F*** Up."[65]

★ A Texas mother of a six-year-old boy sought to revoke the parental rights of the boy's father unless he treated their son as a female. Having dressed their son as a girl following a therapist's diagnosis of gender dysphoria, the mother accused the father of child abuse for continuing to treat him as a boy. The father, however, saw no signs of dysphoria and insisted the boy didn't identify or dress as a girl when they were together.[66] A bill has now been proposed in the Texas legislature to prohibit terminating someone's parental rights for acknowledging or refusing to acknowledge the child's gender identity or expression.[67]

★ San Francisco has created Compton's Transgender Cultural District, the world's first transgender district, to stop the alleged displacement of trans people from the area and provide a place to teach trans history. "Many of our traditions are passed down through queer bars because those are the places where our elders interact with younger generations," said Mahogany, Compton's district manager. "Drag is often seen as a way of storytelling and passing on stories of previous generations."[68]

★ A new rule proposed in Vermont would allow children and teens who claim to be transgender to have taxpayer-funded sex reassignment surgeries without having to wait until age twenty-one.[69] Similarly, Wisconsin Medicaid announced it would begin covering gender reassignment surgery following a decision by a federal judge that it's unconstitutional to exclude such surgeries from taxpayer-funded healthcare.[70] "Discrimination comes with a cost, and for the state of Wisconsin the bill has come," said Larry Dupuis, legal director of the Wisconsin ACLU.[71] In another case, a federal judge in Houston ruled that the male-only military draft is unconstitutional.[72]

- ★ The website BarbWire provides a number of disgraceful gender-related stories that occurred in 2018, including: colleges recommending that four-year-olds engage in sexual activity; sixth graders in Washington state being asked if any of them questioned their gender identity; the Macy's Thanksgiving Day parade trying to normalize teen lesbianism; numerous states and cities banning conversion therapy, thereby forbidding teens from receiving counseling to overcome homosexual feelings, even in the case of sexual abuse; a federal judge in Chicago dismissing a suit against physicians who performed female genital mutilation surgery on little girls; and more clinics opening in children's hospitals to perform gender transition treatment.[73]
- ★ As a shocking indication of the radical inversion of our societal values, the father of former porn star "Aurora Snow" told his daughter he was proud of her career. In response to critics, he asked how much money they make having sex, pointing out that his daughter made hundreds of thousands of dollars. "If I could have made hundreds of thousands of dollars having sex I would have done it too," he said.[74]
- ★ Transgender freelance writer Serena Sonoma tweeted, "We're going to stop giving attention to transphobes and start using their bones to make a bone broth. It'll be healthy for our babies when we get our womb transplants."[75] Use of the term "transphobic" is itself a form of bullying because it implies that those who don't agree with the radical trans agenda are bigots and haters.
- ★ "Januhairy" is a recently conjured feminist endeavor that encourages women to grow out their body hair. The craze was hatched by Laura Jackson, a drama student at the University of Exeter in the U.K., upon realizing how great she felt after growing her body hair for a role. "Though I felt liberated and more confident in myself, some people around me didn't understand why I didn't shave/didn't agree with it," she wrote. "I realized that there is still so much more for

us to do to be able to accept one another fully and truly. Then I thought of Januhairy and thought I would try it out. It's a start at least." An Instagram user explained she was participating in the movement to show solidarity in discussing "the importance of young women taking back ownership of how their body should look, whether that means being hairless or not, it's up to individuals to decide."[76]

★ The Cuba Libre restaurant in Washington, D.C., was fined $7,000, ordered to implement new staff training, and required to post a sign showing that D.C. law allows people to use the restroom that matches their gender identities or expressions. This was punishment for the restaurant manager having questioned a transgender activist who used the women's restroom and having insisted on seeing the person's identification. The manager said that D.C. law requires that a person must be designated as a female on her ID to use the women's restroom.[77]

★ TransKids.biz is a transgender youth website that markets gender expression gear and resources for transgender children. A few books offered are *My Dad Thinks I'm a Boy*, which features a drawing of a young girl on the cover, and *Sex Is a Funny Word*. The site recommends other books, including *Who Are You? The Kid's Guide to Gender Identity* and *Are You a Boy or a Girl?* The site, run by a person named Searah, sells garments and prosthetic penises for kids ages eight to thirteen. "Searah hopes that all parents coming here can trust that this is a safe and affirming place, where helping your kids live fully and embodied is our only goal." One prosthetic, called the extra small packer, is described as follows: "While most trans boys don't start packing until they are teens or older, sometimes young kids want to have a prosthetic and what is on the market is really just too big for most folks under 10 years old. So our friends who make our Silicone Packers came up with a mini version for young and/or smaller kids."[78]

★ Already notorious for its "toxic masculinity" ad, Gillette released a commercial that featured a father teaching his transgender son Samson how to shave. "I always knew I was different," says Samson in the commercial. "I didn't know that there was a term for the type of person that I was. I went into my transition just wanting to be happy. I'm glad I'm at the point where I'm able to shave. I'm at the point in my childhood where I'm actually happy." Sam's father encourages him as Samson brags that "everybody around me is transitioning."[79]

★ A London student has designed a kit to enable men to "chestfeed" children to overcome the gender inequality of women-only breastfeeding. The kit contains the drug progestin, which stimulates the production of milk-producing glands in males.[80] Another drug regimen causes lactation. The kit is in the planning phase, and could be available for purchase in five years.[81]

★ California representative Julia Brownley introduced a bill to rewrite federal laws using gender-neutral terms. So in all federal laws the terms "husband" and "wife," for example, would be replaced with "spouse." "While the landmark Supreme Court decision ending the ban on same-sex marriage was a historic step in the right direction, there is still more work to be done to ensure that the LGBTQ community is treated equally under the law in all respects," said Brownley. "Our words reflect our values, and every gendered reference in our federal code undermines and de-legitimizes same-sex couples."[82]

★ In a conspicuous effort to promote "gender equality," Jennifer Siebel Newsom, the wife of recently elected California governor Gavin Newsom, announced she won't use the title "First Lady." She identifies herself in her Twitter bio as the "First Partner of California." The First Partner has been a proponent of re-examining gender roles and has produced two documentary films on the subject: *Miss Representation* explores the underrepresentation of influential women by the media, and *The Mask You Live In* asserts that traditional masculinity is detrimental to boys.[83]

★ Microsoft Word has developed software to suggest edits to make your writing more "gender inclusive." It will use artificial intelligence to help people avoid gender discrimination in their writing.[84]

★ There's no end to the strangeness in the world of gender fluidity. A British lesbian couple, who identify as straight, plan to transition their five-year-old son, who likes dresses and despises "everything about being a boy," into a daughter. The couple, Greg and Jody, are both women, but Greg identifies as male and also identifies as stepdad to Jody's twenty-year-old son, Jayden.[85]

★ The ever-entertaining AOC admitted that she possesses a privilege. "I'm a cisgendered woman," she confessed. "I will never know the trauma of feeling like I'm not born in the right body. And that is a privilege that I have, no matter how poor my family was when I was born."[86]

★ Though five hundred to seven hundred people attended a pro-life rally in Virginia in early February 2019, the *Washington Post* ignored it, even though the previous week it proudly reported on a mere forty "activists calling for 'menstrual equity' at the Education Department."[87]

★ Unhappy about supposed gender disparities and the social clout and economic opportunities of fraternity members, three Yale students sued the university and certain fraternities to force the frats to gender-integrate, i.e., permit women to join. Oddly, the women wanted to join even after alleging that men groped them at fraternity parties. Ah, but there are priorities.[88]

★ On March 13, 2019, Nancy Pelosi introduced the Equality Act, which would add "sexual orientation" and "gender identity" as protected classes under federal civil rights law. The Heritage Foundation observes that while the original Civil Rights Act of 1964 advanced equality by guaranteeing African Americans equal access to public accommodations and material goods, this proposed legislation would promote inequality by penalizing Americans for their beliefs about marriage and biological sex, as similar state laws have already had that impact. The groups who would be affected include employers and workers, medical professionals, parents and children, women, and nonprofits and volunteers.[89]

★ The Equality Act would also create a federal right for biological boys to compete as girls in all sports. The mother of Selina Soule, the sixteen-year-old runner referenced above who was prevented by two biological males from qualifying for the New England regionals, said that if the act passes, "women will be completely eradicated from sports."[90] Of course she is correct, and female Olympians are coming to the same conclusion. Sharron Davies, who won a swimming silver medal in the 1980 Moscow Olympics, tweeted, "I have nothing against anyone who wishes 2be transgender. However, I believe there is a fundamental difference between the binary sex u r born with & the gender u may identify as. To protect women's sport those with a male sex advantage should not be able 2compete in women's sport." This isn't debatable, yet the transgender activists accused Davies of "fueling hate." Here again we see the left's nasty tactic of twisting the term "hate" to bully people into accepting *their* unreasonableness.[91]

★ The University of Birmingham in the U.K. assigned experienced white male professors "reverse mentors"—younger female scholars from ethnic minorities. The purpose is to teach the older professors about their biases and find ways to increase diversity in STEM (science, technology, engineering, and mathematics) fields.[92]

★ California Democrats introduced a bill that would protect pedophiles who rape children.[93] SB 145 would authorize a person convicted of certain sex offenses involving minors, including luring a minor with the intent to commit a felonious sex act, to seek discretionary relief from the duty to register as a sex offender if the person is not more than ten years older than the minor.[94]

★ Some Americans are beginning to fight back against this insane gender activism. Students in Alaska and Iowa are engaged in a pro-biology rebellion affirming that men and women (and boys and girls) are equal but different and complementary.[95] They are actively protesting the use of girls' bathrooms by "transgender" boys.[96]

Women don't monolithically support Democratic female candidates, and that's a problem for the left. In a survey, Rasmussen Reports asked respondents how important a political candidate's gender is in determining their vote, and whether they'd vote for or against candidates based solely on their gender. Seventy-six percent of likely voters said a candidate's gender is not important to their vote, with 51 percent saying it's not important at all. Only 12 percent said it was very important.[97] Independent Women's Voice similarly found that voters are less concerned with a candidate's gender than his or her qualifications and policies. A whopping 84 percent of women and 85 percent of men said gender was not a determining factor in their vote in the 2018 midterms.[98]

To surmount this problem, the left employs a scorched earth strategy on gender issues. They make an example of any woman straying from the left's identity politics—even an otherwise dependable leftist who inadvertently utters some harmless heresy—through instant, vehement shaming, magnified by the power and immediacy of social media. They insist women should show their gender solidarity by supporting female candidates for office, but there is a giant exception—conservative women are beyond the pale, just as conservative minorities and gays are. The Democratic Party is a fair-weather friend to women, minority, and gay voters. Democrats will champion these groups' unique experiences and points of view—unless they're conservatives, in which case they have nothing worthy to share, nothing useful to teach, and no inherent value worth defending.

CHAPTER SEVEN

Socialism: An Unrequited Love Affair

Socialism is making a comeback.

Nearly three decades after our nation celebrated the fall of the Soviet Union—the world's epicenter of totalitarianism—the Democratic Party has taken a big leap toward the Soviets' discredited ideology. In the 2016 presidential election, the only Democratic challenger to Hillary Clinton was the self-proclaimed socialist Bernie Sanders. After spending decades in Congress as a cranky oddball, Sanders suddenly found himself the object of a bizarre cult of personality, drawing enormous crowds to hear him tout socialism as the cure for America's capitalist ills. If Bernie mania seems to have subsided in today's Democratic primaries, it's largely because he no longer stands out the way he used to—virtually the entire slate of Democratic contenders has embraced socialist "solutions" to healthcare, taxes, and many other issues.

A February 2019 Fox News poll found that registered voters overall still have a negative view of socialism and positive view of capitalism. Fifty-nine percent view socialism unfavorably and 25 percent view it favorably, while 57 percent view capitalism favorably and 28 percent unfavorably.[1] A Rasmussen poll showed similar results. "Sixty percent of all voters believe that socialism represents a threat to America's founding ideals of freedom, equality and self-governance," writes Scott Rasmussen. "Eighty percent of GOP voters see socialism as a threat to America's founding ideals. So do 57 percent of independent voters. But a narrow majority of Democrats (55 percent) disagree."[2]

Yet other polls show that a new generation of Americans is romantically embracing socialism with a fascination bordering on idolatry. According to a 2015 YouGov poll, 43 percent of Americans between eighteen and twenty-nine years of age had a favorable opinion of socialism and preferred it to capitalism. In 2016, a Pew poll found that an astonishing 69 percent of those under age thirty would be willing to vote for a socialist to be president of the United States.[3]

Even more recently, a Gallup poll revealed that less than half of young Americans ages eighteen to twenty-nine—45 percent—have a positive view of capitalism, representing a twelve-point decline in just two years, while some 51 percent have positive views of socialism.[4] It's as if a wave of stupid has washed ashore. Likewise, a SurveyMonkey online poll of 2,777 American adults in January 2019 showed that 61 percent of Americans between the ages of eighteen and twenty-four have a positive reaction to the word "socialism," compared to 58 percent for "capitalism." All older age groups prefer capitalism and the gap increases with age, with only 27 percent of those over sixty-five having a positive view of socialism and 69 percent favoring capitalism.[5]

The news is not all bad, however. As recently as 2014, only 16 percent of millennials could define socialism, so there is hope to fill these mush-dulled minds with the truth.[6] Moreover, a 2019 poll of students aged 13–22 conducted by Young America's Foundation and Echelon found that 35 percent of respondents viewed socialism positively, but 27 percent of these students were unsure what socialism meant, while 10 percent thought it meant "free stuff."[7] The Rasmussen poll results show that young people aren't the only ones confused about socialism. A majority (54 percent) of those who have a favorable opinion of socialism prefer that government have less control of the economy. "The bottom line," notes Rasmussen, "is that growing support for the term 'socialism' does not translate into growing support for traditional socialist policies."[8]

Another significant development, however, is that membership in the Democratic Socialists of America has ballooned from just seven thousand members in 2016 to over fifty-five thousand today. There are dozens of Democratic Socialist officeholders throughout local, state, and federal governments, most notably media sensation Alexandria Ocasio-Cortez.[9]

How can we expect young people to understand the horrors of socialism with the overwhelming liberal bias of college professors? A recent study by the National Association of Scholars showed that some 40 percent of colleges in the United States have no Republican professors. "The political registration of full-time, Ph.D.-holding professors in top-tier liberal arts colleges is overwhelmingly Democratic," writes Mitchell Langbert. "Indeed, faculty political affiliations at 39 percent of the colleges in my sample are Republican free—having zero Republicans."[10] In the remaining 61 percent of these schools, with a few important exceptions, the ratio is still "absurdly skewed against Republican affiliation and in favor of Democratic affiliation. Thus, 78.2 percent of the academic departments in my sample have either zero Republicans, or so few as to make no difference."[11] In the sampling of 8,699 tenure-track, Ph.D.-holding professors from fifty-one of the sixty-six top ranked liberal arts colleges, according to a *U.S. News* 2017 report, some 60 percent of the professors are registered either Republican or Democrat. Of those, the ratio of Democrat to Republican is 10.4 to 1, but if you exclude two military colleges, West Point and Annapolis, it jumps to 12.7 to 1.[12]

Langbert notes that political homogeneity is problematic because it biases research and teaching and reduces academic credibility. He cites a recent book concluding, for example, that left-wing bias leads psychologists to study the character and evolution of individuals on the right rather than those on the left. Further, sociologists prefer not to work with "fundamentalists, evangelicals, National Rifle Association members, and Republicans." And here's the money quote: "Even though more Americans are conservative than liberal, academic psychologists' biases cause them to believe that conservatism is deviant."

To combat this academic imbalance, more than 2,500 professors, administrators, and graduate students established Heterodox Academy, "committed to enhancing the quality and impact of research—and improving education—by promoting open inquiry, viewpoint diversity, and constructive disagreement in institutions of higher learning."[13] That a group of concerned academics believes it's necessary to form such an organization speaks volumes about political bias in higher education and the illiberal mind-set and intolerance of our universities. The result of this intolerance, notes Langbert, "is that objective science becomes problematic, and where research is problematic, teaching is more so."[14] Langbert concludes with a sobering observation: any attempt to reform colleges embedded with political homogeneity by changing their cultures is "a very tall order. The solution to viewpoint homogeneity may lie in establishing new colleges from the ground up, rather than in reforming existing ones."[15] Much easier said than done.

Historical and economic literacy are among the casualties of liberal indoctrination in our public schools and universities. Hillsdale College professor Burton Folsom explains that while America was founded on the idea of protecting individual liberties through limited government, many prominent American history textbook writers are strongly biased against America's free-market tradition and believe that proactive government is the key to liberating America from predatory capitalists. The leftist influence on these textbooks has been dramatic through the years, typified by Marxist historian Howard Zinn's *A People's History of the United States*, which sold more than two million copies. Zinn freely admitted his bias as well as his political goal, saying, "I wanted my writing and my teaching of history to be part of a social struggle."

Similarly, Matthew Josephson's *The Robber Barons* demonized early American entrepreneurs such as Cornelius Vanderbilt, Andrew Carnegie, and John D. Rockefeller. Driven by Josephson's Marxist agenda, the book contained numerous errors. By his own admission, he reveled in the alleged breakdown of American business success and optimism, and he praised the Soviets' centralized system. Josephson influenced other Marxist historians such as Columbia University professor Richard Hofstadter, who at one point was an active member of the Communist Party.[16]

Though most historians are progressives rather than full-blown Marxists, notes Folsom, they nevertheless often buy into the early Marxist historians' portrayal of America's entrepreneurs as robber barons and the idea that the great American capitalists succeeded through corruption rather than by offering customers a good product at the lowest price. For example, the authors of the most popular American history book, *The American Pageant*, contend that America owes its great wealth to capitalist exploitation—"grasping railroads" and "ringmasters of rapacity." Certain organizations attempt to counter this bias by providing critiques of the textbook, but it's not clear how much impact they are making.

There can be no doubt that younger generations are being indoctrinated into socialism. To counteract this disinformation, conservatives must not only attack the appalling history and horrendous results of socialism but categorically defend the superior outcomes as well as the noble principles of free-market capitalism.

SOCIALISM: THE LONGTIME AMBITION OF THE AMERICAN LEFT

The American left has long had a love affair with socialism and its dictators and harbored a deep distrust of free markets. In the 1930s, America's radical leftists gave up hope that our capitalist system could be defeated through incremental advances of socialism and turned to militant Marxism. Their discontent, explains Marxist writer George Novack, was traceable to the Great Depression. "Many came to Communism as victims of the world crisis, cast out of jobs or faced with dim career prospects," writes Novack. "Capitalism was no longer working for them or fundamentally workable; Soviet Communism seemed the only realistic replacement."[17]

During the early years of the Cold War, the left excused the purge trials and the arrest, torture, and imprisonment of dissidents as harsh but necessary measures to protect socialist systems from "fascist" takeovers. Later, many former Stalin sympathizers came to believe Stalin had corrupted Marx's and Lenin's ideas. Their disillusionment is expressed in a 1940 book review by leftist writer Malcolm Crowley. "The question . . . that concerns . . . us is not the evolution of communism up to Lenin, but its devolution in the writings and acts of his successors," writes Crowley. "How was it that the almost selfless revolutionaries of Lenin's day were transformed into (or executed and replaced by) the present Soviet and Comintern officials, the timid and inefficient bureaucrats, the ferocious pedants, the finaglers, the fanatics and the party hacks?...Where did the original weakness lie—in Lenin, in Marx himself, or in the applications of Marx's and Lenin's theories by people who lacked their singleness of purpose and their genius?"[18]

Novack claims Marxism could have become a viable political force in America "if the major political forces on the Left had really propagated and practiced" Marx's and Lenin's ideas. Writing in the sixties, Novack urges "the oncoming generation of radicals" to understand the consequences of departing from these true teachings as they prepared to revitalize the Marxist movement in America.[19] In sum, there was nothing wrong with Marxism; it was just hijacked by people insufficiently dedicated to the cause.

In the sixties, leftists were apologists for the North Vietnamese Communists and their Soviet and Chinese benefactors. They rushed to defend Castro's Cuba, blaming the torture and firing squads on America's imperialistic opposition to the "people's revolution." After Castro was firmly in power, the left rationalized his continued tyranny as necessary to protect the revolution from the CIA.[20] Fast-forwarding to the modern era, American leftists remain infatuated with Castro and his "worker's paradise." They overlook his suppression of religious liberty and the press, his brutality, and his murders of thousands of Cubans.[21] Upon Castro's death President Obama praised "the countless ways in which [he] altered the course of individual lives, families and of the Cuban nation."[22] Leftists also supported the Communist Sandinistas in Nicaragua and the murderous, Argentine Marxist revolutionary Che Guevara.

Today, progressives defend Venezuelan dictator Nicolás Maduro. When asked directly during a CNN town hall on February 25, 2019, Bernie Sanders refused to even call Maduro a dictator despite his regime's arrest and killing of protestors, torture of political opponents, and countless other human rights abuses. This was no surprise. Sanders has boasted of his vacations in the Soviet Union, described its public transportation system as "absolutely beautiful," and glowingly praised its Communist youth program. Like his fellow travelers, Sanders also admired Cuba, declaring that Castro "solved some very important problems" and insisting Cuba was "more successful than almost any other developing country in providing healthcare for its people." In 1985 he delivered a speech for the socialist Sandinistas in Nicaragua, who had murdered thousands of their fellow citizens for dissenting from the party line.[23]

Though progressives often openly support foreign socialist regimes, they know a majority of Americans still disfavor socialism. That's why most leftists, until very recently, have been reluctant to embrace socialism at home, though their sympathies have been no secret to the discerning. To remain politically viable, they've had to conceal their ultimate political aims. Even today, after many Democrats have come out of the closet to proclaim their romance with socialism, some are still playing semantic games, insisting their fetish for big government does not make them socialists.

So what exactly is socialism? Webster's defines the term as:

1. any of various economic and political theories advocating collective or governmental ownership and administration of the means of production and distribution of goods.
2a. a system of society or group living in which there is no private property.
2b. a system or condition of society in which the means of production are owned and controlled by the state.
3. a state of society in Marxist theory transitional between capitalism and communism and distinguished by unequal distribution of goods and pay according to work done.[24]

Today there is a growing wing of the Democratic Party, led by AOC and her cohorts, that openly pledges allegiance to socialism. Most progressives, however, deny they support full government ownership of the production and distribution of goods. But can anyone dispute that most favor the centralization of power in Washington with an ever-expanding and intrusive federal government, higher and more progressive taxes, more government regulations issued by an army of unaccountable bureaucrats, delegation of government authority to administrative law judges whose decisions are subject to limited judicial review, increased domestic spending and entitlements, and federal control of healthcare?

Why quibble over the precise definition when everyone knows the left has an insatiable appetite for big government? Austrian economist Friedrich Hayek, probably a better authority than Webster's on the subject, observes that the definition of socialism evolved over time from the nationalization of the means of production and the central economic planning that accompanied it to the extensive redistribution of incomes through taxation and the institutions of the welfare state. The end result, he argues, is largely the same, but it comes about differently under the modern sense of the term.[25]

Some progressives may be content with a hybrid system, allowing limited market activities alongside confiscatory tax rates, onerous regulations, an expansive welfare state, and ever-expanding healthcare and retirement entitlements. These statist programs are destructive to the economy and individual liberties, and they are also stepping stones for socialist purists. Hayek's mentor, Ludwig von Mises, argues that socialists used the welfare state, the progressive income tax, and extensive regulation of business as tools to deconstruct the existing capitalist system.[26] Barack Obama, for example, advocated an incremental approach to a single-payer healthcare system, surmising that the public wasn't yet ready for fully socialized medicine. Even if incrementalism were not the progressives' goal, partially socialist systems tend to naturally become more socialist. This happens both organically and as a function of progressives' quest to assume greater control over people's lives. Once the government sinks its claws into something, it only tightens its clutches as dependency begets more dependency.

GOVERNMENT MOTORS

A sterling example of the left's crusade for government control of business is President Obama's assumption of control over General Motors and Chrysler during the global financial crisis. Although the bailouts began under President Bush, it was Obama who unflinchingly commandeered the firms and presided over the infusion of most of the $80.7 billion of federal funds injected into those companies. (Having already cut costs, Ford didn't need a bailout, but it sought and received large government loans anyway to avoid being destroyed by its subsidized competitors.) The Treasury Department didn't just loan money to GM and Chrysler but bought stock ownership in them, nationalizing them just as it had Fannie Mae, Freddie Mac, and the American International Group.[27]

The government invested (through loans and stock purchases) $51 billion into GM and later sold its shares for $39.7 billion, losing $11.3 billion. The government invested $17.2 billion in GM subsidiary GMAC and sold its shares for $19.6 billion, for a $2.4 billion profit. The government loaned Chrysler $12.5 billion and sold its shares for $11.2 billion, losing $1.3 billion. The total loss to American taxpayers was $10.2 billion.[28]

The stated purpose of the bailout was to save jobs, but in the end GM's production and employment were drastically reduced. As Toyota and Honda opened and expanded their U.S. plants, they provided more jobs for American auto workers. Some experts argue that but for the bailout Ford, Toyota, and Honda would have further increased their market shares and employed even more American workers.[29]

In late 2018, GM decided to shutter four U.S. plants and lay off 14,700 employees. It's hard not to conclude that this was due, in large part, to the government's takeover of the company. One of the main problems with the bailout was the government imposing its top-down will on manufacturing decisions. An elite group of government officials can't wholly manipulate consumer demand and mystically divine what consumers want and need, but the Obama administration's bailout came with that rope attached. Most notably, government planners encouraged "Government Motors" to invest in the unprofitable electric car market, one of Obama's major political priorities.[30]

Even as GM was deciding to shut down its plants and lay off its workers, its CEO Mary Barra wrote an op-ed glorifying this "collaboration by the private and public sectors, supported by comprehensive federal policies." She evidently saw her role as advancing public policy goals as much as making her company profitable for its shareholders. Sounding like one of Obama's utopian speechwriters, she underscored GM's "commitment to an all-electric future" and called for "a National Zero Emission Vehicle (NZEV) program to create a comprehensive approach to help move our country faster to an all-electric, zero emissions future."[31]

At the very time Barra was proposing an "all-electric future," GM was planning cutbacks on its hybrid plug-in Chevy Volt, which didn't seem to faze Barra. Why should it when her partner is Uncle Sam? As *Investor's Business Daily* editors quipped, "After all, who needs to please actual customers when government can compel people, either by huge subsidies or outright regulation, to buy your product?"[32] In her piece, Barra unapologetically called for certain "complementary initiatives" to "encourage widespread acceptance of electrical vehicles in this country." These initiatives included infrastructure investments to accelerate convenient electric car charging, expanding government incentives (refundable tax credits) for consumers to buy electric cars, and regulatory incentives to support U.S. battery suppliers.[33] Her vision would require 7 percent of new cars sold in 2021 to be electric and 25 percent by 2030.[34]

If this interdependent relationship between government and business doesn't illustrate the left's enchantment with socialism, what does? Barra essentially admitted her plan wouldn't work without government subsidies. It's obvious that unlike the run-of-the-mill evil capitalist CEO, Barra didn't see herself as primarily honor-bound to satisfy shareholders but to effectuate policy goals that she and her government collaborators, in their superior wisdom, deemed desirable, even if it wasn't in the best interests of her company, American consumers, or taxpayers.

"YOU NEVER WANT A SERIOUS CRISIS TO GO TO WASTE"

America has been gravitating toward socialism for years. Nobel Prize–winning economist Milton Friedman observed that late in the nineteenth century, partly due to British influence, the intellectual climate of public opinion in the U.S. began to shift from a belief in individual responsibility and trust in the markets to a belief in social responsibility and reliance on the government. Even as early as the 1920s, socialist views were held by a substantial minority of university professors who were concerned with public affairs.[35]

Friedman argued that while it was not electorally competitive, the Socialist Party was the most influential political party in the first decades of the twentieth century. With no chance of victory, it could afford to be open about its extremist goals whereas Democrats and Republicans could not. Over time both parties essentially adopted the Socialist Party agenda. "Almost every economic plank in its 1928 presidential platform has by now been enacted into law," writes Friedman.[36] Those positions included nationalization of national resources, a publicly owned giant power system, national ownership and democratic management of railroads and other means of transportation and communication, immediate government relief of the unemployed, interest-free loans to states and municipalities for public works, unemployment insurance, the nationwide extension of public employment agencies, a system of health and accident insurance and of old age pensions as well as unemployment insurance, shortening the workday and workweek, enacting a federal anti–child labor amendment, higher taxes on the wealthy, higher corporate and inheritance taxes (the proceeds to be used for old-age pensions and other forms of social insurance), and a national program for flood control, flood relief, reforestation, irrigation, and reclamation.[37]

Friedman describes the 1932 presidential election as a "political watershed for the United States."[38] The voters held President Herbert Hoover responsible for the crushing Depression and bought into Franklin Delano Roosevelt's optimistic promises to cut government waste, reduce spending, and balance the budget. But once in office, capitalizing on the public's loss of faith in our economic system, FDR launched a massive overhaul, forever transforming the role of government to levels never before contemplated. In the words of Obama chief of staff Rahm Emanuel, "You never want a serious crisis to go to waste."[39]

Before 1929, combined federal, state, and local spending never exceeded 12 percent of the national income except during major wars, and federal spending only constituted about one-third of total government spending. Federal spending, notes Friedman, was generally about 3 percent of the national income. But since 1933, government spending has never been less than 20 percent of national income and was more than 40 percent in 1980, when Friedman wrote those words. Since 1946, domestic spending has never been less than 16 percent of the national income, and in 1980 it was some one-third the national income, with federal domestic spending constituting 25 percent of the national income.

"By this measure," says Friedman, "the role of the federal government in the economy has multiplied roughly tenfold in the past half-century."[40] While the government and economists use gross domestic product (GDP) as a measure today rather than national income, total government spending as a percentage of GDP has significantly increased since 1980, and federal spending has remained at about the same level. President Clinton grossly erred in his opportunistic assurance in 1995 that the era of big government was over.[41]

Even more troublesome is the historical expansion of the federal debt as a percentage of GDP, which declined drastically after surging during World War II but has now almost returned to those wartime levels.[42] Since 2009 alone, the gross federal debt as a percentage of GDP has increased from 82.4 percent to 105 percent.[43] Thomas Sowell notes that when the national debt rose above 100 percent of GDP in 2013, Wall Street was no longer yawning. "It is one thing to have a national debt as large as the Gross Domestic Product, or larger, at the end of a major war, for the return of peace means drastic reductions in military spending, which presents an opportunity to begin paying down that national debt over the ensuing years," Sowell explains. "But to have a comparable national debt in peacetime presents more grim options, because there is no indication of the kind of reduction of government spending which occurs at the end of a war."[44]

AN EXPRESSION OF PETULANCE AND OBSTINACY FROM IDEOLOGUES

Leftists seem unconcerned about either the inevitable failures of their programs or the loss of freedoms they entail. As central planning advocates and collectivists, their goals aren't freedom and prosperity but increasing their control and advancing their redistributionist agenda.

For a while it appeared that the socialists' blind idealism would die a natural death. In fact, the worldwide failures of socialist policies sparked a general distrust of government, leading Irving Kristol to write a 1976 obituary for the very idea of socialism. "The most important event of the twentieth century is not the crisis of capitalism but the death of socialism," writes Kristol. He acknowledges that increasing numbers of people and political regimes then identified as socialist but stresses that "the socialist ideal has been voided of all meaning." Socialism had ceased to be of any interest to anyone because reality had repudiated it.

Despite true believers clinging to the fiction that socialism couldn't be judged as a failed system, history had shown otherwise. "Socialism is what socialism does," writes Kristol. "The plaintive lament of the purist that socialism...has 'never really been tried' is simply the expression of petulance and obstinacy on the part of ideologues who, convinced that they have a more profound understanding than anyone else of the world and its history, now find that they have been living a huge self-deception." It was ridiculous for self-styled socialists to decry the three-quarters of the world that actually was socialist. Kristol observes that "the most extraordinary fact of twentieth-century intellectual history is that all thinking about socialism takes place in non-socialist countries.... Not a single interesting work on Marxism—not even an authoritative biography of Karl Marx!—has issued from the Soviet Union in its sixty years of existence."[45]

Just four years later, Milton Friedman celebrated socialism's decline, noting that Britain had swept conservative Margaret Thatcher into power on a platform of reversing socialist policies. Moreover, other Western European nations were following suit, while Ronald Reagan was about to win the American presidency in a landslide. But Friedman didn't share Kristol's sanguinity about socialism's ultimate demise. He notes that this movement "may prove short-lived and be followed, after a brief interval, by a resumption of the trend toward ever bigger government."[46] While there was widespread enthusiasm for cutting taxes, it was not accompanied by support for eliminating government programs. Friedman laments that the pervasive failure of government programs did not lead to their abandonment but a demand for even bigger government. Socialism is an important tenet of the leftist, secular religion, and the adherents' faith in it does not waver in the face of empirical evidence discrediting it. They always object that true socialism has never been tried, or tried by the right people, and any failures can be remedied by a purer version or better planners.[47]

The writings of these two brilliant men and the intervening history between their writings and today demonstrate that the devoted left never accepts defeat. It still operates this way today—blaming the failures of socialism on capitalism and demanding more government intrusion. It's an ingenious strategy to introduce socialism incrementally—just enough to disrupt or financially distress a system—then demand more drastic, remedial government intervention. As noted above, in 2003, Barack Obama advocated this strategy to achieve a single-payer healthcare system.[48] And indeed, Democrats have reacted to the failure of Obamacare by calling for "Medicare for all," the abolition of private insurance, and other drastic increases in government control of the industry.

NOT SO FAST: SOCIALISM IS REBORN

Referring to Kristol's pronouncement of socialism's demise, Matthew Continetti, Kristol's grandson-in-law, laments, "If the death of the socialist idea was the most important political event of the last century, then the rebirth of this ideal must rank high in significance in the current one."[49] This is partly because utopian socialism offered what Kristol describes as "elements that were wanting in capitalist society—elements indispensable for the preservation, not to say perfection, of our humanity."[50] Elaborating, Continetti says that "socialism supplied the values, aspirations, goals, mechanisms of meaning that democratic capitalism could not;"[51] or, as Kristol puts it, "The essential point of this indictment was that liberty was not enough. A society founded solely on 'individual rights' was a society that ultimately deprived men of those virtues which could only exist in a political community which is something other than a society. Among these virtues are a sense of distributive justice, a fund of shared moral values, and a common vision of the good life sufficiently attractive and powerful to transcend the knowledge that each individual's life ends only in death."[52]

Capitalist society, notes Kristol, as imagined in the writings of John Locke and Adam Smith, is bereft of these virtues—not rejecting or scorning them but leaving them to the individual to handle privately. These "founders of capitalism" assumed the virtues would persist, because they were confident that the moral and spiritual heritage of Judaism and Christianity was unassailable and the individualism that accompanied capitalism would not liberate people from these traditions. Kristol concludes that while these virtues remained for many generations thanks to their accumulated strength, they eventually depleted over time, being replaced by a spirit of nihilism in which a "good life" had come to mean a "satisfactory life style."[53]

I would emphasize that capitalism doesn't purport to be more than an economic system; it doesn't claim to have an underlying spiritual or religious component. It is not a moral *system*, though it is perfectly moral and has produced immeasurable benefits for mankind. Socialism, despite being touted as virtuous, is immoral for reasons we'll explore further. We must challenge the claim that capitalism is flawed because it lacks a set of moral precepts. We must resist the urge to impute to capitalism the function of religion. That would be "like criticizing the U.S. Postal Service for delivering too much hate mail, but then acknowledging that 'for all its repugnant and deplorable aspects,' our postal system is better than systems that censor the mail and deliver late," writes Rev. Peter A. Speckhard.[54] "Capitalism, like the postal service, is not a religion, and so it neither can nor should measure up to the moral demands placed upon it by disillusioned Marxists seeking a new way." This is not to say that capitalism is inconsistent with biblical values. Indeed, as we shall see, it is fully compatible with Christian morality.

TURNING THE TABLES ON OUR SOCIALIST ACCUSERS

It is hardly a mark against capitalism that socialism falsely claims to be a morally grounded system that seeks to more fairly allocate economic resources. It is neither reasonable nor fair to condemn capitalism as inadequate because it fails to fulfill a promise it doesn't make. Capitalism promises greater economic efficiency, productivity, and prosperity—not an equal distribution of resources or income. There is nothing immoral in its refusal to make that promise because there is nothing morally imperative in the promise itself. Capitalism doesn't need to borrow spiritual ideas from socialism to ward off the creeping nihilism that some think is inevitable in their absence. Socialism doesn't offer true spiritual or moral ideas that survive from theory to real-world practice, so why concede that point? Socialists don't deserve credit for their allegedly good intentions and capitalists don't deserve blame for refusing to masquerade as economic high priests.

It would be healthier to acknowledge that capitalism can't provide what only biblical religion can and realize this doesn't devalue capitalism. Its sphere is limited. Likewise, the framers had no illusion that the Constitution would be a panacea for men living together in community. John Adams recognized this when he said that the Constitution was made only for a moral and religious people. He meant the Constitution couldn't supply a society's religious and moral foundations any more than an economic system could. But society must have those values for the Constitution to be able to work as intended and secure the individual rights it guarantees.

This doesn't mean free-market conservatives believe government has no role in the moral realm or that we should be indifferent to the moral quality of our culture. The Constitution most emphatically guarantees, by force of government, our religious liberties. Moreover, contrary to conventional wisdom, almost all laws are rooted in someone's notion of moral principles, and conservative Christians must seek to influence laws compatible with their moral views. In much the same way, capitalism must be undergirded by moral principles and the rule of law.

Quoting Kristol, Continetti asks, "What can a liberal-capitalist society do about the decline of religious beliefs and traditional values—a decline organically rooted in liberal capitalism's conception of this realm as an essentially 'private affair' neither needing nor meriting public sanction?" Continetti answers that at the very least we must defend religious freedom and promote religious and civic education. I agree, though I don't see the decline in religious beliefs and values as being rooted in capitalism's notion that they are a private affair. To say that capitalism doesn't address this deficiency doesn't mean the deficiency is therefore capitalism's fault. Capitalism hasn't led to nihilism, and if we are truly concerned about rampant licentiousness and an overall breakdown of our moral values, we should examine their causes and consider solutions, particularly in the spiritual realm. That is, exonerating capitalism against this unfair charge doesn't excuse or relieve us of the duty to influence society to re-cultivate our founding morals, values, and traditions.

Conservatives must respond to the socialists' attack on capitalism instead of assuming their challenge will self-destruct amidst its logical incoherence and historical failures. This new breed of socialists didn't arise in a vacuum, and we must provide answers to the younger generations who have been indoctrinated by progressive university professors on the evils of capitalism and the virtues of socialism. But we needn't overcomplicate this. The modern socialists' case is mainly a recycling of their ancestors' arguments that I encountered in college in the early seventies: that conservatives lack compassion for the poor, that capitalism is immoral because it leads to an inequitable distribution of resources, and that the rich get rich on the backs of the poor.

Conservatives have fallen short in demonstrating the compassion of our ideas. We mustn't project callousness and appear to glorify greed and selfishness as some hardcore Ayn Rand acolytes do. There's a difference between self-interest and dark-hearted selfishness. Though capitalism isn't a moral system, it facilitates man's inalienable right to liberty and produces greater prosperity for more people than any other economic system, and for those reasons alone it is morally superior.

We must address, head-on, the claim of social justice warriors that the rich don't pay their fair share and that society's resources are distributed unfairly. We must emphasize that we do care about those who fall through the cracks and that almost all conservatives believe in some form of safety net, provided it doesn't exacerbate the problems it seeks to alleviate. Jack Kemp astutely described conservatives' genuine concern for the less fortunate: "Our definition of compassion is not how many people live on the government welfare plantation, but how many of our people are liberated from government dependence."[55]

We need to turn the tables on capitalism's foes, who have a lot more to answer for than capitalism's defenders. President Trump's economic advisor Larry Kudlow wisely urges us to take the offensive in this battle against Democratic Party socialists. So, let's review capitalism in theory and in practice. Our defense of capitalism must include a comparative critique of socialism, because capitalism should not be judged against a standard of perfection but against socialism. We can't allow socialists to get away with critiquing capitalism against their unachievable utopian dreams. We must highlight the flaws and false promises of socialism as we ask if it really make sense on paper and how it has fared in history.

SOCIALISM "DOES NOT BUILD; IT DESTROYS."

Austrian economist Ludwig von Mises explains that socialist theorists believed they were advocating a rational economic system to replace the irrational, chaotic system of capitalism. In a socialist system, they argued, intelligent, knowledgeable men could plan and manage the economy. This would be far superior to capitalism, which involves "anarchy of production" and "unreasonable and self-interested individuals." The planners would rectify the unjust distribution of goods, which would eliminate "want and misery" and produce "wealth for all."[56] Socialists believed that socialism was not only more rational and produced a more just distribution of income but that "historical evolution is driving man inexorably in that direction."[57]

But at its core, von Mises explains, socialism doesn't withstand scientific scrutiny and is rooted in "petty resentments." Socialist assumptions about capitalism are false, and socialism would not only fail to make economic life more rational but "would abolish social cooperation outright." Its promise of a fairer distribution of goods is arbitrary and false, based on a misperception of the operation of capitalism. "In fact, Socialism is not in the least what it pretends to be," writes von Mises. "It is not the pioneer of a better and finer world, but the spoiler of what thousands of years of civilization have created. It does not build; it destroys. For destruction is the essence of it. It produces nothing, it only consumes what the social order based on private ownership in the means of production has created."[58] Socialism acts as a parasite on an existing capitalist system, and each incremental step toward socialism contributes to the destruction of the existing order.[59] In other words, socialism cannot produce wealth; it can only redistribute what capitalism produces. "Government can't create wealth," argues Thomas Sowell, "but it can prevent the private sector from doing so."[60]

Leftists have a much loftier view of government and its role in wealth production. Still subscribing to failed Keynesian economic theory, they believe that government stimulus spending, such as Obama's colossally wasteful trillion-dollar stimulus plan, can generate economic growth. Even when the plan failed to produce anything but more debt, Obama swore that the economy would have been much worse without it.

Likewise, FDR's revisionist defenders baselessly claim that his federal spending orgy delivered the United States from the Great Depression, while sober analysts, as noted, recognize it prolonged the Depression, which we escaped only because of the war.[61] As progressives, their faith is in government, not in free people operating in a free market. They undervalue liberty, which is the centerpiece of America's founding ideas. It is liberty—the freedom of people to create and produce—that fosters wealth creation.

Leftists reject this notion, which is why they dispute the supply-side claim that reducing marginal income tax rates can increase revenues. It is why they reject dynamic scoring of the economy, which factors in the potential effects of government taxes and regulatory policies on producers. Their refusal to consider taxpayers' and consumers' responses to positive and negative incentives also contributes to their gross miscalculations in projecting the costs of government programs.

"Wealth is created when our creative freedom is allowed to prosper in a free-market environment undergirded by the rule of law and suffused with a rich moral culture," Jay Richards observes, noting that this idea is intrinsically Christian. Christians believe that God created man in His image and that our creative freedom reflects the divine image.[62]

It should be obvious that economic pies are not finite. We often see expansions and contractions of the economy where GDP increases or decreases. Wealth isn't just a matter of accumulating material things, however. More wealth is created all the time with fewer material products—from the digital world to intellectual property.

Admittedly, with explosions of wealth in the modern era, there will probably be a greater gap between the world's richest and poorest people—not due to the rich exploiting the poor but because some places in the world are experiencing greater wealth creation than others. This disparity can widen even while the standard of living for the poor also increases, just not as much.[63] Free markets lead to a better standard of living for the most people. If they lead to greater income disparities while still greatly benefiting the most people, should we forego that greater overall prosperity just to prevent the wealthiest from getting more wealth? It is destructively covetous to advocate harming everyone—even the poor—just to prevent some from disproportionately benefiting! This is what we mean by socialists "spreading the misery."

We should strive to generate prosperity and eradicate poverty, not to equalize incomes, and the best way to do that is to unleash the power of the market at home and abroad. Leftists overlook the fact that government can't tax or redistribute income that isn't produced and that prioritizing redistribution over production stifles economic growth and generates poverty, not wealth.[64] In their compulsion to impose fairness, they strangle the goose that lays the golden egg. The only way these comatose dreamers will ever approach equal income distribution is to impoverish everyone—though under socialism a ruling elite is always excepted. Hello, Venezuela!

THE "TRICKLE-DOWN" STRAW MAN

If you believe that wealth is finite, you might think that unequal distribution is unfair—people won't get rich except at the expense of others, and as the rich get richer, the poor get poorer. But if you understand that in a free-market system the overall economic pie can be enlarged through pro-growth incentives, you might not be so preoccupied with wealth disparities, realizing that one person's gain does not necessarily result in another's loss. President Bill Clinton popularized the idea that so-called "trickle-down economics" is a myth. The wealth of the rich, he argued, doesn't trickle down to the middle class and the poor. This was partisan propaganda—a straw man to defeat President George H. W. Bush. Conservatives don't believe that wealth magically trickles down the economic ladder. We believe, and history has shown, that free markets produce wealth and that the surest way to minimize poverty is through wealth production.

Confiscatory tax rates diminish wealth. Conversely, less burdensome taxes, other things being equal, stimulate growth and income across the board. It's not a matter of wealth trickling down, as in lower-income groups gobbling up bread crumbs spilled by rich elites. "Trickle-down" is a misnomer calculated to malign supply-side economics and its conservative advocates.[65] The term is part of the left's class warfare arsenal for inflaming the poor and middle classes against upper-income groups by falsely implying the rich believe economic policy should be directed toward their own benefit while lower-income groups should be left to fight over the scraps.

Conservatives don't seek to favor the rich with tax cuts but to incentivize economic growth across the income spectrum. Indeed, contrary to leftist demagoguery, tax cuts proposed and implemented by supply-siders have been across the board, not just for the rich, and lower-income groups have usually received a proportionately greater cut than upper-income groups. The only people excluded were those paying no income taxes in the first place.

Free-market economists don't propose policies specifically to benefit the wealthy, thinking that lower-income groups will collaterally benefit. Rather, they support growth-stimulating policies to increase opportunity *directly*—for everyone. A rising tide lifts all boats. Following the Reagan tax cuts, incomes increased for all income groups, from poorest to richest.[66] Upward mobility, which had received its last rites under President Carter, roared back in 1979, as 86 percent of households in the lowest 20 percent income group graduated into higher income groups during the eighties. More people in every group moved up than down except the top 1 percent of earners.[67] Capitalists' goal isn't to transfer wealth up and down the income ladder but to create universal opportunity that will lead to widespread growth and upward mobility, as also happened with the Reagan cuts. "Wealth does not 'trickle down' from rich to poor," writes economics professor Steven Horwitz. "It is created by all of us when we develop new ideas, skills, and products as either workers or owners of capital.... And history tells us that the improving standard of living for everyone that results from more economic freedom will be more of a flood than a trickle."[68] The rich don't transfer wealth to the poor, but in a free market the rich do help provide the poor opportunities to help themselves. There is truth in the adage, "I never got a job from a poor person."

"YOU DIDN'T BUILD THAT"

Progressives believe the rich don't deserve their wealth because they don't actually produce it; the common laborers under them do, and as evil capitalists, the rich help themselves by exploiting the lower classes through excessive profits—echoing Karl Marx's theory of "surplus value." A kernel of this idea was evident in President Obama's exclamation, "If you've got a business—you didn't build that. Somebody else made that happen."[69] Obama was correct that in an interactive economy every person benefits from others along the way. We all use roads or bridges on our way to work and benefit from skilled builders who constructed the buildings in which we work. Obama was also correct that there are a lot of hardworking people who don't make as much money as other hardworking people. But there's a lot more to it than Obama's class-oriented perspective.

Marxists consider profits to be theft, or at least a gross overcharge. Marx argued that labor is the only source of value—"the labor theory of value"—and that profits are "surplus value" because they are arbitrarily added on to the costs of producing goods and services, which both drives up the costs to consumers and deprives the laborers who produce them of their just recompense. Marx taught that a product is worth the value of labor involved in producing it, and that the price should be roughly equivalent to the wages paid to the laborer. Capitalists, by contrast, believe a product is worth what one can sell it for in a free marketplace.[70]

Marxists maintain that under a government-directed economy you could eliminate those gratuitous charges, and prices would automatically decrease. That sounds fine in theory, but when socialism got a chance to prove itself in the real world it consistently failed, as production went down and prices increased. The problem is that socialist theorists don't acknowledge that competition and profit are incentives to more efficient production. The businessman's goal—to be profitable and avoid losses—motivates him to produce at the lowest possible cost and sell his products at the highest price customers are willing to pay.[71] Under socialism, where government manages and subsidizes production, there is far less incentive to produce efficiently and at lower costs. The same is true for workers. If the government gets to spend what you earn, what incentive do you have to earn it?[72] Eliminating profits in socialist countries doesn't increase the standard of living but decreases it.[73] Removing the profit motive eliminates the incentive to innovate to stay competitive with other producers, which hurts consumers who would benefit from innovation. Socialists strut their supposed moral superiority in supporting workers, but their "good intentions" actually harm both workers and consumers.

NO, COMMUNISM IS NOT BETTER IN THEORY

When I was growing up we frequently discussed Communism in our home. Our dad was a conservative's conservative, a passionate patriot, a lover of free markets, and a student of Marxism. He once gave a speech to my seventh-grade class on Marxism, and I distinctly remember him explaining Marx's distorted notion of surplus value to hundreds of kids in the school auditorium. While most people in our hometown obviously didn't discuss Marxism in depth, the ideas of Communism were on people's minds. This was a time when the Cold War was raging. People were building bomb shelters in the event of nuclear war with the Soviet Union. I remember walking out of my fourth-grade classroom after the bell rang at Franklin School and encountering a fifth grader in the hall proclaiming that World War III had started. It turned out President Kennedy had ordered the Soviets to remove their missiles from Cuba, marking the onset of the Cuban Missile Crisis.

Probably because our dad was so into politics and current events, we grew up fascinated by these subjects and thought about the relative virtues of capitalism and Communism at a young age. I remember people always mouthing the cliché that Communism is good in theory but not in practice. Maybe I was just a contrarian, but that never rang true with me. I didn't understand how everyone receiving the same amount, no matter how much effort they exerted, was fair. If it violated my sense of fairness and justice, how could it be ideal? I was sensing what I later learned to be true: Communism and socialism don't square with human nature.

I had a fortuitous opportunity to test my belief a few years later when my seventh-grade math teacher told us that on the next test he was going to give everyone an M—the equivalent of a C—regardless of our performance. I don't remember what his rationale was, but this struck me as outrageously unfair, and I told him it was Communistic. I can't remember if he was amused or annoyed, but he was serious about it—and wrongheaded. Whether you are a good, mediocre, or poor student, you innately know that such a system is unfair. If everyone were inspired to learn apart from the incentives of good grades and the deterrent of bad ones it might not be as bad, but people aren't wired that way.

Socialism appeals to naïve and well-meaning people who have a heart for the poor, which is a commendable sentiment. They want everyone to share in material prosperity, and they believe socialism ensures that. But it doesn't. And promoting an economic system that forcefully transfers some people's money to others is not a mark of personal compassion or generosity.

Research consistently shows that political conservatives make greater charitable contributions, on average, than liberals.[74] This is partly because they attend church more frequently and contribute through their congregations.[75] But their greater charitable giving extends also to other types of charities. One recent study showed that those with a religious affiliation (mostly Christian) were more than twice as generous as those without it.[76] Before the advent of the modern welfare state, American charity abounded—mostly from Christian congregations, which in 1926 donated more than $150 million to charity apart from contributions toward church maintenance. At that time state governments gave $23 million and local governments $37 million. But an economic study found that the role of churches as crucial providers of social services shrank dramatically (30 percent) with the expansion of government spending under the New Deal, and that "government relief spending can explain virtually all of the decline in charitable church activity observed between 1933 and 1939."[77]

"IF SOCIALISTS REALLY WANTED TO HELP PEOPLE, THEY'D BE CAPITALISTS"

Overburdening taxpayers with punitive taxes disincentivizes work. A familiar maxim applies—when you tax something more, you get less of it, and when you tax something less, you get more of it. Imposing onerous taxes on one's work and earnings generally results in less work and earnings, reducing growth and the overall economic pie. When you transfer people's earnings to others you reduce the incentive of the recipients to earn, thereby further stunting economic growth and the economic pie.

It's certainly not morally commendable to implement policies that reduce overall prosperity just so you can virtue signal your concern for the poor. As entrepreneur and author Andy Puzder says, "If socialists really wanted to help people, they'd be capitalists."[78] But there's another moral component involved. Discouraging able-bodied people from working, producing, and contributing to their own families and to society diminishes their self-respect. The same holds true for able-bodied people paying no income taxes when other people are. If we're going to have an income tax, then everyone needs to have some skin in the game, even if it's only a little bit, unless they are disabled or otherwise incapable of earning. When the federal income tax was instituted in 1913 only 2 percent of American households paid. But the percentage steadily increased, topping out at 85 percent with FDR's post–World War II Victory Tax. The percentage has decreased since then, with only 45 percent of households paying federal income tax today.[79] It's hardly healthy for society when fewer than half of all households pay income tax.

It's also incomprehensible that people can look at these numbers, along with the disproportionate percentage of income tax the upper-income groups pay, and conclude the rich "aren't paying their fair share," as the left insists. Most Washington politicians don't exempt more than half of American households from paying income tax out of compassion but as part of their cynical class warfare strategy to attract voters. Need proof? The famed socialist, millionaire senator, Bernie Sanders, rails against the rich for not paying their fair share but admitted in a Fox News town hall that he won't pay higher taxes until he's forced to.[80]

Socialists sometimes point to the Bible to justify their ideology, but the Bible teaches that God ordained work for man, and it is sinful for able-bodied men to disobey that ordinance. In his Second Letter to the Thessalonians, the apostle Paul writes, "For even when we were with you, we gave you this rule: 'The one who is unwilling to work shall not eat.'"[81] This was not Paul's only statement on the matter. In his First Letter to the Thessalonians, he writes, "You should mind your own business and work with your hands, just as we told you, so that your daily life may win the respect of outsiders and so that you will not be dependent on anybody."[82] He also tells them, "And we urge you, brothers and sisters, warn those who are idle and disruptive, encourage the disheartened, help the weak, be patient with everyone."[83]

Paul doesn't impart these instructions out of heartlessness; quite the opposite. He knows that idleness among capable individuals will be detrimental to them—stimulating guilt, ingratitude, and dependence—and to the group, because it causes resentment and strife. Notice his charge to help the weak and encourage the disheartened. Individual Christians and the church are morally obligated to care for the poor.[84] But unchecked welfare or transfer payments compelled by the government cause the breakdown of the nuclear family, increased crime, hopelessness, meaninglessness, and bitterness.[85]

Paul isn't the only biblical writer to condemn laziness, sloth, and idleness. The Book of Proverbs is full of such passages: "Go to the ant, you sluggard; consider its ways and be wise!" (6:6); and "The craving of a sluggard will be the death of him, because his hands refuse to work. All day long he craves for more, but the righteous give without sparing" (21:25). Here again a warning against laziness is juxtaposed with an exhortation to be generous and charitable, showing there is no inconsistency between the two. Similar proverbs abound: "As a door turns on its hinges, so a sluggard turns on his bed" (26:14); "One who is a slacker in his work is brother to one who destroys" (18:9); "A sluggard is wiser in his own eyes than seven people who answer discreetly" (26:16); "Diligent hands will rule, but laziness ends in forced labor" (12:24); and "A sluggard's appetite is never filled, but the desires of the diligent are fully satisfied" (13:4). Jesus constantly commands us to care for the poor, but there is no biblical injunction for government to undertake the task.

If sloth and laziness are sins, isn't it wrong (and unwise) to implement policies that encourage those traits? If so, then government programs that do so and thereby harm people are not as compassionate as they're portrayed. But as previously noted, conservatives support a social safety net and favor programs designed to aid the truly needy, but not to the point of fostering dependence and idleness among those capable of working. Achieving the proper balance is sometimes more difficult in practice than in theory.

Before moving on from the biblical evidence, we must note that the tenth commandment forbids covetousness: "You shall not covet your neighbor's house. You shall not covet your neighbor's wife, or his male or female servant, his ox or donkey, or anything that belongs to your neighbor" (Exodus 20:17). This admonition implicitly affirms the concept of private property—a central pillar of capitalism. It is not wrong to long for things, but it is sinful to covet that which belongs to another, and it is wrong for demagogic politicians to incite this destructive emotion in people for political gain.

When comparing capitalism and socialism, it should be enough to say that capitalism is superior because it produces greater prosperity, or even that socialism often leads to authoritarianism and enslavement of the people. But there's something more fundamental, and it is what I instinctively sensed when I first rejected the platitude that Communism is good in theory but not in practice. Why did the concept of everyone receiving the same amount of resources or the same grade bother me? On further reflection, I realized my objection was not that everyone gets the same; it's not that I wanted more than others or a better grade than them. It's that I wanted to reserve the right to earn more regardless of what others had. It was a matter of personal liberty.

It's not just that we would all receive equal amounts under pure Communism, but that the government would forcibly impose that result, depriving people of liberty to earn more and the incentive to be more productive. To deny human beings their freedom to pursue their callings—their vocational purposes—is immoral. It robs people of their dignity, value, and self-worth. It destroys the human spirit. This was at the core of my objection to this system when I was younger, even if the reasons hadn't fully crystalized for me. Capitalism allows the human spirit to breathe free. In the next chapter we'll further examine the comparative strengths and weaknesses of the two economic systems.

CHAPTER EIGHT

Socialism Kills, Capitalism Saves

"MARXISM HAS FAILED TO PROMOTE FREEDOM AND TO PRODUCE FOOD."

Milton Friedman and Friedrich Hayek underscore the interrelationship between economic and political liberty. "Economic freedom is an essential requisite for political freedom," writes Friedman. "By enabling people to cooperate with one another without coercion or central direction, it reduces the area over which political power is exercised. In addition, by dispersing power, the free market provides an offset to whatever concentration of political power may arise. The combination of economic and political power in the same hands is a sure recipe for tyranny."[1] Socialism often leads to political authoritarianism and totalitarianism. Socialist planners constrict our political liberty when they impose top-down economic dictates. Not only is economic freedom necessary for political freedom; "economic freedom," writes Hayek, "had been the undesigned and unforeseen by-product of political freedom."[2]

America's new socialists claim to offer an enlightened version of socialism; they call it "democratic socialism" because it includes democratic elections. Tell that to the people of Venezuela who "elected" Nicolás Maduro through rigged elections dominated by government-controlled media propaganda.[3] The Soviet Communists bragged about their open and fair elections too. Though America's democratic socialists tout a softer socialism they claim would not lead to tyranny, top-down control is integral to their ideas. They would centrally control the allocation of resources and most sectors of the economy—not just healthcare.

Redistributionist policies require greater administrative bureaucracies and bigger budgets. It takes enormous political power to control a modern economy. AOC's Green New Deal, examined in the next chapter, contemplates top-down control of healthcare, energy, incomes, and many other aspects of people's lives. Whether implemented through a vast web of bureaucratic administrative bodies or through a single dictator, the result is the same: the government exerts increasing control over the individual while freedom evaporates.

Socialists can only effectuate their sweeping schemes through coercion. In fact, "democratic socialism" is an oxymoron; democracy and socialism are oil and water. Meaningful democracy or representative government, in the sense of people choosing their leaders, participating in government, and holding their elected leaders accountable, isn't possible when the government controls the economy and the wide swathe of human activities and interactions encompassed by it.[4]

Leftists constantly tout their moral superiority, and it's time conservatives reclaimed the moral high ground, beginning with capitalism. While we established that capitalism is not itself a moral system, it is morally superior to socialism. It's not inherently greedy to pursue your self-interest. You couldn't stay alive if you didn't. "Only foggy moral pretense confuses legitimate self-interest with selfishness," writes Jay Richards. "In fact, proper self-interest is the basis for the Golden Rule." Adam Smith doesn't promote greed or selfishness but advocates that we pursue goals within our narrow spheres of expertise, which will lead to positive results that no group of elite geniuses could achieve.[5]

Socialism, on the other hand, destroys the incentive to produce and achieve, as evidenced by the Soviet Union and all its captive satellite nations. As President Ronald Reagan declared in 1987, "The more repressive the government, the more controlled the economy, the more confiscatory the taxation, the more likely a society is to sink into poverty and despair. John Dos Passos was so right when he observed: 'Marxism has not only failed to promote human freedom. It has failed to produce food.'"[6]

SOCIALISTS ARE MORE MATERIALISTIC THAN CAPITALISTS

Is the socialist more moral because he picks winners and losers and robs people of the fruit of their labors? Is it ethical for the government to impose equal outcomes when people contribute vastly different talents, efforts, and resources? Shouldn't government instead seek to ensure equal opportunity, in line with the framers' vision?

Human nature is full of inequalities, and we can't—and wouldn't want to—eradicate them with the stroke of a pen. Income equality is an invigorating rallying cry for virtue-signaling social justice warriors, but any credit they deserve for good intentions is outweighed by their ignorance of history, economics, and human nature. Socialism invariably leads to economic disaster and often to the government slaughter of its citizens. Even under less severe forms of socialism, regimes live off their nation's wealth that was accumulated before socialist control, until they inevitably squander it.[7]

For all their sanctimony, socialists are more materialistic than capitalists. Their passion for equalizing incomes stems from covetousness—the preoccupation with what others have. To wish to dispossess others of their property is, essentially, greed. "Greed is woven through every human heart, and it is a mistake to assume that alternatives to capitalism will render greed vanished," writes Lauren Reiff. "It doesn't go away—it merely is channeled somewhere else, into taking from others namely, and that's a dangerous game. That capitalism's most fashionable smear is that it is greedy is awfully telling but absolutely not the correct allegation to make."[8]

Professor Walter Williams argues that socialism, because of its forced redistribution of wealth, is immoral and akin to theft. "Reaching into one's pocket to assist his fellow man is noble and worthy of praise," writes Williams. "Reaching into another person's pocket to assist one's fellow man is despicable and worthy of condemnation."[9] Some may believe it's not theft when the duly elected representatives of the people legislate income redistributions. But Dr. Williams's use of the term "theft" is far more appropriate than Nancy Pelosi's use of the same word to describe the Trump income tax cuts. "This tax cut for corporate America is theft. It's theft from the future," asserted Pelosi. "Their flagship issue is to give tax breaks to the wealthiest people in the country at the expense of our children's future."[10]

Progressives like Pelosi believe all taxpayer-produced income is the government's, and only the amount the government allows you to keep is yours. Few things better illustrate their socialist mind-set. In reality, government doesn't create wealth, and it only derives revenue by taxing those who produce it. The government doesn't bestow income on people any more than it gives them their God-given rights. It legally protects our freedom to earn and preserve our own income and wealth. But it doesn't create them, and to claim otherwise is to contradict America's founding ideas. If progressives were concerned about robbing from our children, they would quit demagoguing efforts to reform entitlements—whose skyrocketing costs will break the federal budget for future generations—and join with Republicans (whose recent record on this is also deficient) to ensure their long-term solvency.

We must be mindful of the proper role of government. The framers didn't idealize the state but believed the government's purpose is to protect its citizens from domestic and foreign threats, to enforce the rule of law, and to preserve order to maximize citizens' freedoms. They cherished liberty and considered it a virtuous end in itself. Today, we have lost sight of the value of liberty, as we have increasingly traded it for the illusory promise of economic security. As history has consistently shown, when you engage in this Faustian bargain you end up losing both freedom and security.[11]

We must rekindle our spirit of liberty, especially among the younger generations. "The unbridled energy of free people is the most powerful, creative, and moral force on this planet," President Reagan affirmed. He described freedom and prosperity as "two mutually reinforcing goals."[12] We must realize that every expansion of government entails a reduction of our liberties and consider whether it's worth it. Of course, certain voluntary surrenders of liberty are part of our social compact, but we must strive to limit them wherever possible.

Despite abundant evidence that capitalism produces greater prosperity and liberty, many people still associate capitalism with evil corporations, robber barons, heartless entrepreneurs, and rampant selfishness and greed. This misperception cannot be blamed solely on leftist propagandists. Adam Smith wrote, "It is not from the benevolence of the butcher, the brewer, or the baker that we expect our dinner, but from their regard to their own interest." Misunderstanding Smith's point, even some defenders of capitalism unduly emphasize the idea that benevolence has no place in a free market. But Smith's point is that we can rely on the free market to work its magic apart from individual benevolence, not that capitalists aren't benevolent. In the real world, greed has very little to do with the prices sellers set for their products. In a market economy, a seller can't set an arbitrary price and expect buyers to pay it. Market competition, not greed, governs prices. "A seller's feelings—whether 'greedy' or not—tell us nothing about what the buyer will be willing to pay," writes Dr. Sowell.[13]

"AT ITS CORE, SOCIALISM CALLS EVIL SOMETHING THAT GOD CALLS GOOD"

Unfortunately, some libertarian purists, inspired by atheist objectivist Ayn Rand, have perversely glorified Adam Smith's statement as an endorsement of greed and a repudiation of selflessness. Conservatives, especially Christians, must reject this pernicious argument. Christians are taught not only that they must not covet but that the love of money is the root of all evil (1 Tim. 6:10). Jesus tells us we can't serve two masters (Matt. 6:24)—if we idolize money, we cannot properly worship and trust God. Notice that the problem isn't money itself but the undue focus on it—the love of money. There is nothing wrong with wanting to prosper if we keep it in proper perspective and don't idolize wealth or the pursuit of wealth.

Unquestionably socialism has a seductive appeal. On the surface it sounds compassionate for a presumably benevolent government to ensure that every citizen has what he needs to live comfortably. Why shouldn't the government go further and ensure "fairness" so that everyone gets the same amount? But as we've seen, that wouldn't actually be fair, and efforts to equalize incomes have caused untold damage. Although socialism has been thoroughly discredited in practice, people have short memories and little insulation from progressive media and academic indoctrination. Consequently, in some quarters, socialism has escaped history's devastating verdict against it and been resurrected in the dreams of new generations of naïve, historically obtuse Americans.

Social justice warriors are not confined to the secular realm. The modern Christian church, both in Catholic and evangelical circles, is filled with misguided utopian dreamers. After all, didn't the early Christian church model a Marxist society for us? Shouldn't Christians follow that pattern and reorder their political system accordingly? As described in the Book of Acts, "No one claimed that any of their possessions was their own, but they shared everything they had," and "there were no needy persons among them." Moreover, "From time to time those who owned land or houses sold them" and gave the proceeds to the apostles to distribute among the needy (4:32, 34–35).

These early Christian brothers certainly shared everything they had with one another, but this was hardly Marxism. It was a church-inspired arrangement of *voluntary* sharing. There was no hint of a class struggle pitting one group against another,[14] and the state wasn't involved—there was no taxation, confiscation of property, or redistribution of wealth by a governmental entity. People owned their property, and government didn't compel them to sell it and surrender the proceeds. Yes, Ananias and Sapphira were punished for failing to deliver all the proceeds from their land sale, but their sin was lying to the Holy Spirit, not withholding money. The Bible even acknowledges that they owned the property, and it was their prerogative to sell it or not to sell it.[15] "The early church was able to share possessions and property as a result of the unity brought by the Holy Spirit working in and through the believers' lives," writes Bruce Barton. "This way of living is different from communism because the sharing was voluntary, didn't involve all private property but only as much as was needed, and was not a membership requirement in order to be a part of the church."[16]

The believers willingly participated out of a shared love and shared goal—glorifying God and living for Jesus Christ. Under Communism, people are forced to give, so their "giving" doesn't proceed from a charitable heart and says nothing about their character or spirit. "Under communism, the cheerful, generous giver and the stingy man are both required to give exactly the same amount."[17] Scripture is clear that "each [person] should give what [he has] decided in [his] heart to give, not reluctantly or under compulsion, for God loves a cheerful giver" (2 Cor. 9:7).

There is no directive in Acts for Christians to model this early communal practice, which ended before the apostolic age.[18] "The description, 'having all things in common,' never appears in the New Testament with any other church," says biblical scholar Michael Heiser. "That's important because if this was a norm for all churches—this is the way Christianity en masse is supposed to operate, like a socialistic or communistic system—you would think that this would be a pattern that we would read about in the New Testament, but we don't. It's never presented as a norm for the believing community, so how could we say it's a norm for all society now?"[19]

The passages describing this communal arrangement, argue Norman Geisler and Thomas Howe, are not prescriptive but descriptive. It's not a command for all believers but a description of what those early believers were doing.[20] The communal arrangement by the early church was not for the entire community of mankind but only for the church, and it was not intended to be permanent but rather to avert a temporary crisis.[21] The Book of Acts tells of other early believers who didn't sell their possessions. Mark's mother Mary, for example, held on to her house (12:12). Simon, the tanner, did the same (10:32).

Other passages in both the Old and New Testaments implicitly affirm the right of individuals to own private property. "At its core, socialism calls evil something that God calls good," writes Mark Ward, and that is "[t]he right to private property."[22] Ward notes that many of the laws God gave to Israel protected property rights (Exodus 21:33–33:14). The right to private property is implicit in the eighth commandment—"Thou shall not steal"—as well as in the tenth commandment, as noted earlier. In theory, pure socialism or Communism involves the abolition of private property, but in practice property is commandeered by the state—an elite, tyrannical few. To avoid misunderstanding, we should note that while Christianity doesn't ordain socialism, it does command that we voluntarily and with a loving spirit give freely and otherwise support the poor and others in need. There are few things clearer in scripture.[23] As Robert Morey argues, however, "[A]ny government that violates the dignity and freedom of human beings is not ordained of God."[24]

Far from mandating socialism, Christianity is incompatible with it. Socialism and Communism are in conflict with biblical teaching on the depravity of mankind. They are utopian systems that cannot work, among other reasons, because they are based on the belief in man's perfectibility.[25] The leftist pursuit of earthly utopia is a humanist conceit—a form of idolatry that contradicts biblical teaching and is grounded in the fantastical notion that if we try hard enough, through our unaided human wisdom and scientific knowledge, we'll be able to achieve heaven on earth.

"Voluntary socialism" is another oxymoron. All forms of socialism entail centralized control of the economy and substantial encroachments on liberty.[26] The government's coercive redistribution of people's property is vastly different from individual philanthropy. When people act under coercion they aren't proceeding from a charitable spirit. Thus, socialism is directly antithetical to economic freedom. "The so-called economic freedom which the planners promise us means precisely that we are to be relieved of the necessity of solving our own economic problems and that the bitter choices which this often involves are to be made for us," writes Hayek. "Since under modern conditions we are for almost everything dependent on means which our fellow men provide, economic planning would involve direction of almost the whole of our life. There is hardly an aspect of it, from our primary needs to our relations with our family and friends, from the nature of our work to the use of our leisure, over which the planner would not exercise his 'conscious control.'"[27]

Christian theologian Augustus Hopkins Strong addressed Christianity, socialism, and freedom in his 1907 book on systematic theology. He concluded, "Socialism abolishes freedom, which the church cultivates and insists upon as the principle of its life. Tertullian (wrote), 'It is not the business of religion to compel religion.' . . . By abolishing freedom, socialism destroys all possibility of economical progress. The economical principle of socialism is that, relative to the enjoyment of commodities, the individual shall be taken care of by the community, to the effect of his being relieved of the care of himself."[28]

SOCIALISM'S RECORD OF BRUTALITY AND DEVASTATION

The historical record is unambiguous and indisputable—socialism has consistently devastated human lives and entire nations. In the name of progress, it has brought poverty, misery, despair, and often dictatorship and death. The twentieth century stands as a permanent indictment of socialism. The socialist states and regimes of the Soviet Union, Red China, Nazi Germany, North Korea, Cambodia, Africa, Afghanistan, Vietnam, Eastern Europe, and Latin America are responsible for murdering more than 100 million people.[29] Indulging the convenient fiction that fascism is right-wing, leftists pretend that Nazism was not socialist, even though socialism was in its title and platform. Walter Williams observes that no such record of brutality has occurred in countries with free-market economies.[30]

Socialism has failed—not because the perfect group of geniuses hasn't come along to correctly administer it but because it is inherently flawed. Socialism has been disastrous everywhere.[31] Consider Chile's horrendous experience in the early 1970s, when the government's imposition of socialism flatlined the economy. The cost of living rose by 746 percent, unemployment soared, and the chaos finally sparked a coup, which substituted one repressive regime for another.[32] Argentina tried socialism in the late 1940s under Juan Perón, who enacted wage and price controls, nationalized many industries, took over private property, and radically increased government spending. This led to an economic catastrophe and hyperinflation that once again ended in a coup. The new regime retained the socialist model, leading to economic stagnation. After further forcible regime changes, by the late 1980s the nation was reeling from 12,000 percent inflation.[33]

A few short years ago Venezuela was the wealthiest nation in South America—before socialism brought about abject poverty.[34] A UN report revealed that the army's death squads have executed thousands of young men.[35] Yet the American left couldn't praise this socialist nightmare enough. When Trump declared solidarity with the Venezuelan people in their noble quest for freedom and condemned the brutality of the Maduro regime, few Democrats responded receptively.

Many of them want to take us down that Venezuelan road, to a place where three million people have fled their own country (and the UN expects that number to top five million by the end of 2019),[36] 93 percent of those remaining live in poverty, and roughly that percentage say they don't have enough to eat.[37] The nation's health system has disintegrated, with more than one hundred private and public hospitals found to be in deplorable condition. Seventy-nine percent of these facilities have no access to water, 14 percent of their intensive care units have been shut down, and more than 80 percent can't perform ultrasounds, X-rays, or CT scans. Between a third and half of all doctors in public hospitals have left. There is a shortage of 85 percent of medicines, so patients have to bring their own medications, along with their own bandages and surgical gloves.[38] Seven million people suffer from malnutrition, and the hunger rate has tripled since 2010.[39] All this in a nation rich with oil, gold, and other natural resources.[40] Meanwhile, the family of the late despot who led the nation's socialist "revolution," Hugo Chavez, owns seventeen country estates over more than 100,000 acres and has liquid assets of $550 million. Chavez's daughter Maria has a net worth of $4.2 billion.[41] So much for the equitable distribution of resources in socialist nations!

"BUT SWEDEN"

Grasping socialist apologists desperately cite Sweden as the one exceptional oasis that proves socialism works. Even some free-marketeers grudgingly acknowledge Sweden's success, which they attribute to its homogenous culture. But the evidence isn't so clear. Some argue that socialism nearly destroyed the Swedish economy and that free-market reforms revived it.[42] Furthermore, it was not Sweden's socialist decades but its years of economic freedom in the late nineteenth and early twentieth centuries—coupled with its avoidance of war and consequent preservation of resources—that initially ignited its entrepreneurship and prosperity.

Prior to the second half of the nineteenth century, argues Stefan Karlsson, Sweden was mostly poor, and it escaped this fate through sweeping market reforms in the 1860s, which enabled it to benefit from the spreading Industrial Revolution. Sweden had the world's highest per-capita income from 1870 to 1950, but this was because of its freedom tradition, which started to erode in the 1930s under the Social Democrats who came to power in 1932. Piggybacking on its previous decades of success, the government still presided over one of the freest economies in the world in the early 1950s. But from 1950 to 1976, Swedish government spending spiked, the number of government employees jumped, the welfare state rapidly expanded, and taxes and government transfer payments sharply increased. Under the cumulative weight of these socialist programs, the economy weakened in the late 1970s and 1980s, culminating in a deep recession in the early 1990s as Sweden fell to between fifteenth and twentieth place in international income rankings.[43]

During that period, unemployment rose alongside government programs disincentivizing work, increasing disability payments, and subsidizing sick days. "The growth of taxes and benefits punished hard work and encouraged absenteeism," writes Kevin Williamson. Swedish economist Johan Norberg maintains that the onset of socialism changed the national psychology so that it became acceptable to game the system and defraud one's taxpaying neighbors.[44] Williamson notes that one reason Swedes have tolerated high levels of taxation and an expansive welfare state is that the country's programs involve less redistribution and operate more as government-imposed forced savings, such that people are largely the beneficiaries of their own taxes, especially compared to the United States.

Following its downturn, Sweden's economy began to perform better following another round of free-market reforms, though socialists credit the turnaround to lingering high taxes and welfare programs. "Yet as should be clear, the relative improvement of performance is due not to high taxes (lower now than previously), but to free-market reforms," writes Karlsson. "The reason Sweden no longer trails the rest of Europe is that these reforms, which have not been implemented in most continental European countries, have made the Swedish economy relatively freer."[45]

"AN EQUALITY OF POVERTY"

Contrary to leftist dogma, mankind has experienced poverty throughout history, but capitalism has greatly reduced it in the past two centuries, creating unprecedented prosperity.[46] Great accumulations of wealth and inequality preceded capitalism and have been with us throughout history. Today, people operating in a free-market environment voluntarily give money and participate in enterprises owned by the wealthiest people. No law requires us to buy products from Amazon, Apple, or Microsoft, and their owners are not elected officials. "By contrast, most of history is a tale of economic and political power held by the very few," writes Thomas Del Beccaro. "If you lived in the Middle Ages, you lived in a system where those in political power, i.e., the kings, nobles, gentry, and churches, also owned the greatest accumulations of land—the wealth of the age. Your service to them was required and you were often tied to their land."[47]

That general condition, with little opportunity for social mobility, prevailed until a few centuries ago, when capitalism and the Industrial Revolution changed everything. In *The Lessons of History*, Will Durant explains that capitalists gathered the people's savings into productive capital by promising dividends and interest, then financed the mechanization of industry and agriculture as well as the rationalization of distribution. Consequently, goods flowed from producer to consumer as never before. The capitalist "put the gospel of liberty to his use by arguing that businessmen left relatively free from transportation tolls and legislative regulation can give the public a greater abundance of food, homes, comfort, and leisure than has ever come from industries managed by politicians, manned by government employees, and supposedly immune to the laws of supply and demand," writes Durant. Free enterprise spurs competition and "the zeal and zest of ownership arouse the productiveness and inventiveness of men.... Competition compels the capitalist to exhaustive labor, and his products to ever-rising excellence."[48]

Economics professor Deirdre McCloskey argues that the Industrial Revolution led to a worldwide economic transformation marked by "poor people who are rich by historical standards, ordinary people in charge of their own politics, women with jobs outside the home, children educated into their 20s, retirees living into their 80s, universal literacy, and the flowering of the arts and sciences."[49] Likewise, Luke Muehlhauser researched the condition of mankind over the sweep of history by examining six metrics of human well-being: life expectancy, GDP per capita, the percentage of people living in extreme poverty, war-making capacity, energy capture (people's access to food, livestock, firewood, and in modern times, electricity), and the percentage of people living in a democracy. His data, spanning from 1000 BC to the present, show that for most of human history there was simply no progress in any of these six areas. Living in extreme poverty, people were close to starvation most of their lives. Economic historian Joel Mokyr says that life expectancy in 1750 was about thirty-eight at most and much lower in some places.[50]

Most significant historical events actually had little effect on people's longevity, freedom, economic productivity, and prosperity. But the advent of the Industrial Revolution in the late 1700s dramatically improved human lives in all these categories.[51] There's a reason the Industrial Revolution occurred in Europe and not in China: though China had previously experienced faster scientific progress, Europe developed a culture of competitive scientific and intellectual advancement. "Europe creates a competitive world that encourages intellectual innovation," writes Mokyr.[52]

One major difference between capitalists and socialists, as noted, is that capitalists believe in wealth creation. They understand that economies are dynamic—that economic output is not a zero-sum game with a finite pie of output. They consider economic decisions in terms of incentives they create, focusing more on results than supposedly good intentions.[53] Having a heart for the poor, by itself, doesn't put food on anyone's table. But, as noted, an economic system that incorporates incentives and other mechanisms to maximize production is more likely to lead to broad-based prosperity, whereas command-control economies are guaranteed, in the long run, to spread the misery, in part because incentives don't operate in such systems. "Unfortunately, true socialists are pushing for a government that would drive Americans into a society in which everyone is guaranteed an equality of poverty," writes Jeff Charles. "No system of government can ensure that inequality doesn't exist. Under socialist and communist governments that strive to provide equality of outcome, citizens are still grouped into the haves and have-nots.... There are two separate classes: those who rule, and those who are ruled."[54]

Dr. Sowell notes that when India and China introduced market forces in the late twentieth century, they each began to experience dramatic economic growth. Within a decade an estimated 20 million people in India rose out of poverty. The number of people in China living on a dollar a day or less fell from 374 million in 1990 to 128 million in 2004.

Clinging to the false perception that economic output is fixed, socialists have diminished their expectations accordingly. This has been true, albeit on a lesser scale, in the United States. Presidents Jimmy Carter and Barack Obama each indicated that Americans should expect anemic economic growth rates in perpetuity—no more than 1 or 2 percent.[55] They inspired pessimism about the future, which is especially ironic in Obama's case, since he ran on a platform of "hope and change." They called for economic sacrifice rather than assuring Americans that a rekindling of their entrepreneurial spirit would revive growth.[56] But in each case, their successors, Presidents Reagan and Trump, reignited the economy through pro-growth policies of cutting taxes and regulations, thus shattering their predecessors' predictions of permanent malaise.

THE INVISIBLE HAND OF THE MARKET

I remember asking my dad when I was a young boy what would happen if no one wanted to do certain jobs. "What if no one wanted to be a policeman or fireman?" I asked him. I confess not remembering his precise answer, but he assured me that it would always work out. Despite my naïveté then, it really is a basic question. In a free economy with no central planners, something has to ensure that essential jobs do not go unfilled. This is where the metaphorical "invisible hand of the free market" comes into play. The concept originated with Adam Smith in his *Wealth of Nations*:

> Every individual necessarily labors to render the annual revenue of the society as great as he can. He generally, indeed, neither intends to promote the public interest, nor knows how much he is promoting it. By preferring the support of domestic to that of foreign industry, he intends only his own security; and by directing that industry in such a manner as its produce

> may be of the greatest value, he intends only his own gain, and he is in this, as in many other cases, led by an invisible hand to promote an end which was no part of his intention. Nor is it always the worse for the society that it was no part of it. By pursuing his own interest he frequently promotes that of the society more effectually than when he really intends to promote it. I have never known much good done by those who affected to trade for the public good. It is an affectation, indeed, not very common among merchants, and very few words need be employed in dissuading them from it.[57]

Smith wasn't advocating greed but merely pointing out that when individuals act out of their own self-interest in a free market, greater benefits accrue both to the individual and to society at large. How likely is it that government bureaucrats, far removed from the people whose lives they attempt to control, could make spending choices for people as beneficial as if the individuals made those choices themselves? The planners would have to be omniscient to do so, and no one ever accused bureaucrats of omniscience. "Adam Smith's key insight was that both parties to an exchange can benefit and that, so long as cooperation is strictly voluntary, no exchange will take place unless both parties do benefit," writes Milton Friedman. "No external force, no coercion, no violation of freedom is necessary to produce cooperation among individuals all of whom can benefit."[58]

Perhaps it is counterintuitive that so much order springs from a system involving millions of transactions by individuals cooperating voluntarily without any organized planning. But Friedman observes that human language and scientific knowledge also developed under similar circumstances.[59]

The "miracle" of the free market, due to the crucial role of prices, profits, and private property, ensures that societies' economic needs will be met. "In a capitalist economy, incentives are of the utmost importance," writes AEI scholar Mark Perry. "Market prices, the profit-and-loss system of accounting, and private property rights provide an efficient, interrelated system of incentives to guide and direct economic behavior. Capitalism is based on the theory that incentives matter!"

When you remove incentives, you act contrary to human nature and dampen the human spirit.

The success of the free market subverts the cult of planning that underlies all socialist theories. "How an incredibly complex, high-tech economy can operate without any central direction is baffling to many," writes Thomas Sowell. "The last president of the Soviet Union, Mikhail Gorbachev, is said to have asked British Prime Minister Margaret Thatcher: 'How do you see to it that people get food?'" Sowell explains that Thatcher had nothing to do with it. Prices served that function—and despite no central planning and Britain having not been self-sufficient in food for more than a century at that point, the British people were better fed than the people of the Soviet Union. "Prices bring them food from other countries." If prices didn't do their magic it would take an unimaginably large bureaucracy to meet the food needs of London alone each day. But in a free-market economy there is no need for such a bureaucracy, and the people who would fill it are free to produce elsewhere in the economy "because the simple mechanism of prices does the same job faster, cheaper, and better."[60]

None of this means that economic activity in a market economy is completely random. Individuals and entities enter into transactions throughout the economy on mutually agreed terms that are conveyed by prices throughout the system. This happens more efficiently than if planners were to accomplish the same tasks, since they would have no way of knowing all the goods being produced and how much of each resource should be allocated to the production of millions of products. This is where prices come in, which play "a crucial role in determining how much of each resource gets used where and how the resulting products get transferred to millions of people," explains Sowell. "Yet this role is seldom understood by the public and it is often disregarded entirely by politicians."[61]

It's not only prices that are emasculated under socialism. When a central government controls the means of production and distribution, there's also no competition, profits, or losses. In a market economy, profits, losses, and prices steer scarce resources to meet their most highly valued means, which are determined by countless people acting freely and making their decisions in the marketplace.[62] Socialism's failures, by contrast, can be largely attributed to its neglect of three incentive-promoting components: prices, profits, and private property rights.[63]

Central planners couldn't possibly get access to this much information, and in the real world, they don't care to know it. Planners issue decrees based on their presumed superior knowledge and goals. In their view, they know better than you what is best for you. But they don't. They can't. Planning an entire economy efficiently is impossible. The planners would have to set prices and production levels for all goods and services, and countless wrong decisions would reverberate throughout the economy, creating surpluses and shortages.[64]

Hayek elegantly describes the market's ability to produce order out of chaos:

> We are led—for example by the pricing system in market exchange—to do things by circumstances of which we are largely unaware, and which produce results that we do not intend. In our economic activities we do not know the needs which we satisfy nor the sources of the things which we get. Almost all of us serve people whom we do not know, and even of whose existence we are ignorant; and we in turn constantly live on the services of other people of whom we know nothing.... Modern economics explains how such an extended order can come into being, and how it itself constitutes an information-gathering process, able to call up, and to put to use, widely dispersed information that no central planning agency, let alone any individual, could know as a whole, possess, or control.[65]

Sowell points out, however, that prices themselves do not keep people from having all the luxuries they want, such as a beach house—as if a planner could merely lower the price and everyone who wanted it could have it.[66] It's a matter of scarcity; there aren't enough beach houses for everyone to have one, and prices, which are established by supply and demand (many people bidding on a smaller number of beach houses), reflect that scarcity. Scarcity would exist irrespective of the type of economy, so that in a centrally planned economy the planners would have to handle access to the scarce homes through a different mechanism than price, such as rationing. Despite their unchecked political power, they wouldn't be able to make enough houses available even if they declared access or ownership to them a basic right.

The concept of scarcity applies to all goods and services in the economy. Healthcare is no exception—planners can issue a fiat that healthcare services are a fundamental right until they're blue in the face, but their decrees will not alter the scarcities involved, and they will inevitably be reflected in the quantity and quality of care, waiting times, and the like.

As noted, profits and losses also play a crucial role in economic efficiency and in promoting prosperity because they lead companies and industries to use scarce resources efficiently.[67] Preening socialist theorists misapprehend profits, believing them to be a greedy surcharge that robs from labor and overcharges consumers. But in the real world, socialism makes goods less affordable. This is because, as mentioned before, in a free-market economy the business owner's desire to make profits and avoid losses motivates him to produce at the lowest cost and sell at a price customers are willing to pay. Socialism offers no such incentives for efficiency.[68]

Leftists decry profits, but the pursuit of profits not only helps the entrepreneur pursuing them but also satisfies the needs of others. He can only make a profit if he meets the consumers' demands on quality and price. In other words, the businessman will succeed in direct proportion to the extent that he satisfies his customers. Unlike in a command-control economy, if you fail to provide customers what they want, your business will fail. The socialists' problem is that they believe they know better than their "customers" what is good for them. To paraphrase Andy Puzder again, if they trusted the people to make the right decisions, they'd no longer be socialists but capitalists.[69]

It is difficult to reach generations of people indoctrinated by universities and a culture hostile to free-market capitalism. Socialism sounds so good to their itching ears and to their admirable desire to eradicate poverty and economic hardship. "The idea of socialism is at once grandiose and simple," writes Ludwig von Mises. "We may say, in fact, that it is one of the most ambitious creations of the human spirit...so magnificent, so daring, that it has rightly aroused the greatest admiration. If we wish to save the world from barbarism we have to refute socialism, but we cannot thrust it carelessly aside."[70]

We must try to reach these misguided people whose idealism will lead them—and us—into the abyss of poverty and possibly totalitarianism. "The dispute between the market order and socialism is no less than a matter of survival," writes Hayek. "To follow socialist morality would destroy much of present mankind and impoverish much of the rest."[71] On this score there is some cause for optimism. A Fox News poll reveals that a strong majority of Americans still embrace the American dream, with 38 percent saying they've achieved it and 40 percent saying they're "on the way" to achieving it.[72] Similarly, 63 percent say they're optimistic about the U.S. economy, and only 33 percent are negative. These polls should be encouraging to supporters of free markets and the American dream. Though polling also shows that younger generations are more negative on capitalism and positive on socialism, as mentioned previously many of them clearly misunderstand what socialism really entails. This should not be grounds for despair but rather a challenge to educate future generations on the true history and actual principles underlying this noxious ideology.

We've now compared free-market and socialistic economies, in moral, political, and economic terms. In the next chapter we'll take an in-depth look at the left's infatuation with socialism today.

CHAPTER NINE

The Green New Deal and Other Socialist Schemes

THE GREEN NEW DEAL IS A RAW DEAL

Conservatives should thank Alexandria Ocasio-Cortez for one thing—by devising the Green New Deal (GND), she has provided Americans with a textbook example of socialists' pathological ambition to seize control of the economy.

You may have thought the GND is primarily a product of environmental hysteria—the kind of embarrassing, reckless scheme that naturally springs from someone who believes life on earth will end in an environmental cataclysm in about a decade. AOC made this prediction, and ridiculed anyone who would question her plan's exorbitant price tag, in her trademark linguistic style: "Millennials and people, you know, Gen Z and all these folks that will come after us are looking up and we're like: 'The world is going to end in twelve years if we don't address climate change and your biggest issue is how are we gonna pay for it?' And, like, this is the war—this is our World War II."[1]

As we'll see, the GND's scope is breathtaking and utopian. It envisions a vast restructuring of the U.S. economy according to government decrees. What you may not know is that this economic transformation—not any environmental concern—is the true impetus for the GND. In what the *Washington Post* described as a "surprising disclosure," AOC's then–chief of staff, Saikat Chakrabarti, told a *Post* reporter during an interview, "The interesting thing about the Green New Deal is it wasn't originally a climate thing at all. Do you guys think of it as a climate thing? Because we really think of it as a how-do-you-change-the-entire-economy thing."[2]

And indeed, the GND would surely change the entire economy. The plan, as originally outlined in draft legislation to establish a congressional committee to pursue it, calls for totally eliminating fossil fuels and transitioning national power to 100 percent renewable resources in ten years. AOC would thus summarily scrap America's entire oil and gas drilling industry and its hundreds of thousands of employees just when the shale revolution has made us a net exporter of oil for the first time in seventy-five years. To grasp the magnitude of this fairy tale, consider that renewable resources now constitute just 11 percent of the nation's total energy, with wind and solar providing only 3 percent, despite decades of federal and state subsidies and mandates.[3]

The proposal also calls for phasing out all nuclear power plants, though that was one of numerous elements AOC later walked back following widespread ridicule.[4] Most notably, AOC disavowed a GND information sheet released by her office and posted on her own website that called for eliminating air travel and "farting cows" as well as providing "economic security" for people "unwilling to work."[5]

The sudden, forced, and total transformation of our energy supply is just the beginning. The bill would also create a new energy-efficient grid, compel transition to electric cars and hydrogen-powered plants by abolishing transportation emissions, eliminate industry emissions, and upgrade *every single one* of America's 136 million homes and all industrial buildings for energy efficiency.[6] The grandiose scheme would guarantee a living wage and possibly basic income programs and universal healthcare. It would supposedly "mitigate deeply entrenched racial, regional, and gender-based inequalities in income and wealth" while "virtually eliminat(ing) poverty in the U.S. and... "mak(ing) prosperity, wealth and economic security available to everyone participating in the transformation...to be driven by the federal government."[7] The GND included no estimated cost for its grandiose initiatives, but AOC later suggested a price tag of $10 trillion,[8] while an analysis by the conservative American Action Forum put the price much higher, between $51.1 trillion and $92.9 trillion, or $316,010 to $419,010 per household.[9]

AOC is not merely posturing; she is a deadly serious vanguard of today's Democratic Party. And she makes her contempt for capitalism quite clear: "We should be scared right now because corporations have taken over our government.... Capitalism is an ideology of capital—the most important thing is the concentration of capital and to seek and maximize profit.... To me, capitalism is irredeemable."[10]

Many observers understandably focus on AOC's economic witlessness, but the real culprit is her ignorance of history and the demonstrable failure of the socialist ideology she champions. She has now effectively endorsed the startling goal of Christiana Figueres, former head of the UN's climate program, "to change the economic development model that has been reigning for at least 150 years, since the Industrial Revolution." This should alert the slumbering among us that climate change activism is grounded in its ambition to transform the world's economy through international government coercion—national sovereignty be damned—to socialism.[11]

Some GND supporters have touted a survey by the Yale Program on Climate Change Communication and the George Mason University Center for Climate Change Communication showing that 92 percent of Democrats and 64 percent of Republicans support the GND.[12] Apart from propaganda purposes, the poll is meaningless, if for no other reason than it failed to present the plan's astronomical projected costs. In fact, polls show "climate change" remains a low priority for Americans.[13] A survey by the Energy Policy Institute at the University of Chicago and the AP-NORC Center found that 71 percent of Americans say climate change is real and most of them believe that human activity is primarily responsible, while only 9 percent disagree. The believers, however, are unwilling to put their money where their fears are, which suggests the fears aren't that serious. The poll shows 57 percent of Americans would pay a one-dollar monthly fee to combat climate change and 23 percent would pay forty dollars per month.[14] This paltry commitment wouldn't even give AOC a down payment for her plan.

It is inconceivable that more than a handful of extremists would support the GND if Americans understood the sweeping changes it demands. As always, theoretical socialism gets annihilated in the real world. This could serve as a template for fighting socialism on a grander scale. Once people realize the costs and other consequences of socialist projects, they reject them out of hand. Had President Obama been forthright about the costs and consequences of Obamacare, for example, there's little doubt more Americans would have opposed it.

Even if you accept the false assumptions on which the GND is based, its projected costs are prohibitive. But if its draconian initiatives *were* affordable and people were willing to sacrifice the modern luxuries of conventional energy, they still would only have a minimal environmental impact. According to a Heritage Foundation study, if the United States were to entirely eliminate all its carbon dioxide emissions, the earth's temperature would decrease less than 0.2 degrees Celsius by the year 2100. If the entire industrialized world cut carbon emissions to zero, which is a howling pipe dream, global temperatures would be reduced by less than 0.4 degrees Celsius by 2100.[15]

Not only would the GND be ineffective and fiscally ruinous, but it would hurt the poor and minorities the most. Craig Richardson, president of the Energy and Environmental Legal Institute, calls the GND a reckless prescription for poverty that "will most certainly harm those already living in poverty and do nothing to improve the environment.... Behind the rhetorical smokescreen, the ugly truth is that a mandatory shift to higher-cost solar and wind energy before the market is ready to support those, as the GND does, would serve as a regressive tax on the poor."[16] Richardson points to Europe for a preview of the GND's likely results. Far less stringent energy mandates in Germany caused an enormous hike in electricity rates, with people paying an average of $400 a month. In France, ambitious environmental measures have rendered electricity unaffordable for eight million households, some 12 percent of the population. And one-third of British families are struggling to pay their energy bills and are not using their heaters even during colder months. Since it's even more radical than these European measures, the GND would impact America's middle class and the poor even harder.[17]

Other experts concur with these dire predictions. Philip Rossetti, director of energy at the American Action Forum, estimates the costs per household of transitioning entirely to renewable energy: "Simply, a 100 percent renewable electricity grid would require Americans to pay between 43 and 286 percent more on their electric bills. In 2017, the average monthly electric bill was $111, so a 43–286 percent increase would translate to an average of between $576 and $3,882 more spent on electricity per year per residence."[18]

Heritage Foundation energy and environmental policy expert Nicolas Loris provides a succinct summary of the GND's predictable effects:

> The so-called Green New Deal would make energy unaffordable and devastate the economy, hitting working-class Americans the hardest. Not only would [it] be fiscally and economically catastrophic for American families and business—there would be no meaningful climate benefit, so this is nothing but a raw deal for America.... If the Left was serious about anything other than amassing power for itself, it would offer a real new deal that included removing barriers to technology innovation, permitting new projects and energy trade, providing efficient pathways to commercialize research at America's national laboratories, and promoting competitive electricity market policies that empower consumers to choose what type of energy is best for their needs.[19]

In sum, the GND is a socialist initiative disguised as an environmental one—an increasingly common phenomenon. And it's noteworthy how often these sorts of pie-in-the-sky proposals fail spectacularly notwithstanding enormous government funding. Though President Obama pushed through 500 percent increases in federal subsidies for solar energy—from $1.1 billion to $5.3 billion between 2010 and 2013—this "didn't stop the largest U.S. solar panel manufacturer, SolarWorld, from filing bankruptcy [in 2017] despite $115 million in federal and state grants and tax subsidies since 2012, along with $91 million in federal loan guarantees," writes Veronique de Rugy of George Mason University's Mercatus Center.[20] And recall that a $535 million federal loan guarantee wasn't enough to keep solar panel manufacturer Solyndra from filing for bankruptcy. And Obama fell short—by 600,000 cars—of his pledge to get a million plug-in electric cars on the road by 2015.[21] And the list goes on.

Despite all this absurdity, as of February 2019, sixty-seven House Democrats had signed onto AOC's resolution to recognize the duty to create a Green New Deal and pushed for a vote on the House floor.[22] Sentiment in the Senate seems much different, however. When Senate Majority Leader Mitch McConnell forced a procedural vote on the GND, not a single Democrat supported the motion—forty-three voted "present," and four voted against it.[23]

THE FALLACY OF SOAKING THE RICH

AOC also supports a wacky progressive economic idea known as Modern Monetary Theory (MMT). MMT holds that a country that controls its own currency can't go broke; it can continue to pay down its debt as long as it is denominated in that currency. Since the U.S. prints its own currency and issues debt in dollars, its debt isn't like household debt—it can ostensibly pay it down without relying on taxes to fund the debt issuance.[24] What could better represent socialists' warped view of economics? Who says there's no such thing as a free lunch, as long as you have a magical money printer? In a survey of forty-two top economists by the University of Chicago Booth School of Business, respondents overwhelmingly opposed the basic tenets of MMT. Thirty-six percent disagreed and 52 percent strongly disagreed with the statement, "Countries that borrow in their own currency should not worry about government deficits because they can always create money to finance their debt." Likewise, 26 percent disagreed and 57 percent strongly disagreed with the statement, "Countries that borrow in their own currency can finance as much real government spending as they want by creating money."[25]

AOC unveiled another socialist initiative during an interview with Anderson Cooper on CBS's *60 Minutes*, floating the idea of a 70 percent marginal tax rate on people earning more than $10 million a year. Shockingly, even the arch-liberal Cooper called the proposal "radical." Some Democrats brushed aside her idea, but former Senate majority leader Harry Reid showed at least some of the objections were a matter of political strategy, not principle. "When you talk about 70 percent and all that," said Reid, "we have to be careful because the American people are very conservative in the sense of not wanting radical change quickly."[26]

Alarmingly, one poll showed that 59 percent of registered voters support the plan, including 71 percent of Democrats, 60 percent of independents, and 45 percent of Republicans.[27] If the poll is accurate, it indicates the Democrats' class warfare tactics are working. Even with evidence pouring in that the Trump tax cuts greatly stimulated economic growth and reduced unemployment to its lowest level in fifty years, including for minorities, the left is undeterred.[28] Substantial increases in the standard of living of all groups, including those Democrats purport to care most about, don't satisfy them. Their appetite for government spending and class conflict is insatiable, and their contempt for Trump precludes their support for his policies regardless of how effective they are. Indeed, the Trump presidency is playing out according to a rule stipulated by conservative economist Stephen More: "The better the economy performs under President Trump and the more successes he racks up, the more unhinged the left becomes. It's a near linear relationship. And it goes for the media as well."[29]

To downplay the novelty of sky-high tax rates, advocates of "soaking the rich" often note that from the mid-1940s to the mid-1960s, the top federal marginal income tax rate was 91 percent, and prior to President Reagan's 1981 tax cut it was 70 percent. Phillip Magness of the American Institute for Economic Research, however, explains the crucial difference between the statutory tax rate (the percentage the statute requires taxpayers to pay) in those years and the effective rate (what taxpayers actually pay after deductions and exemptions). "Although statutory tax rates were extremely high between World War II and the Reagan-era tax cuts, practically nobody actually paid the taxman's full sticker price on their earnings," writes Magness. "Instead, a plethora of intentional tax exemptions, deductions, and legal income shelters ensured that wealthy individuals paid a much lower effective tax rate."[30] The effective average tax rate for people earning $1 million in 1963 was actually around 40 percent.[31]

Common sense dictates that no free person will work hard just so the government can confiscate 91 percent of his earnings. "The takeaway from the history lesson of the 1950s is not the golden age of high taxes and prosperity that supporters of the Green New Deal imagine it to be," writes Magness. "Rather, the tax policy of this period strongly suggests that high statutory rates are only sustainable when they are accompanied by massive legal tax shelters that are written into the tax code by design.... What this implies for Ocasio-Cortez and her supporters is that a return to 70 percent-plus top marginal rates would likely trigger a disastrous fiscal contraction for the United States" unless large loopholes are restored.[32]

Recognizing that these marginal rates were stifling economic growth, Democratic icon President John F. Kennedy proposed a major tax cut that his successor, President Lyndon Baines Johnson, steered through Congress. Both the Kennedy and Reagan tax cuts, like the current Trump cuts, dramatically stimulated economic growth and increased tax revenues. The same holds true for the tax cuts of President Warren Harding in 1921 and the further cuts implemented by his successor, Calvin Coolidge.[33] With these cuts, the economy grew 59 percent from 1921 to 1929.[34] Sadly, the days of pro-growth Democratic leaders like JFK are long gone.

Even drastic increases in marginal tax rates will not suffice to finance the Democrats' spending wish list. Brian Riedl of the Manhattan Institute estimates that the costs of the GND and the Democrats' other big-item spending proposals could double federal spending from its already horrific levels. Democrats are proposing an astronomical *$42 trillion* of additional socialist programs including the single-payer healthcare plan "Medicare for All" ($32 trillion), a federal jobs guarantee ($6.8 trillion), student loan forgiveness ($1.4 trillion), free public college ($800 billion), infrastructure ($1 trillion), family leave ($270 billion), and Social

Security expansion ($188 billion).[35] Note that these figures don't even include the extravagant costs of all elements of the Green New Deal.

Proposed new taxes on the rich couldn't pay for a fraction of these programs. The spending hikes would yield an annual budget deficit of $5 trillion in today's dollars, which would be borne by the middle class. Riedl further calculates that even if Democrats realized all the spending cuts and offsetting savings they claim are possible, they'd still need to collect $34 trillion from American taxpayers, possibly requiring a European-style value-added tax of 87 percent.[36]

Such prohibitive foolishness illustrates the hypocrisy in the leftists' professed heart for the poor. Equally dishonest is their claim that their programs could be funded by stingy rich people who don't pay their fair share in taxes. In fact, if you confiscated all income above $1 million, you couldn't balance the current fiscal budget, let alone finance a new spending spree. And if you doubled the highest tax rates from 35 percent and 37 percent to 70 percent and 74 percent, even if people's incomes remained constant and they didn't devise new tax avoidance ploys, you still couldn't raise enough to pay *half* the current budget deficit. AOC's 70 percent tax plan, again assuming no adverse impact on income production, would only raise about $50 billion annually.[37] The plan's purpose is clearly not to raise adequate revenue to pay for the GND but to virtue signal that AOC wants to punish the rich villains who supposedly blight our nation.

THE VERY ANTITHESIS OF LIBERTY

When it comes to spending, it's clear socialism's advocates aren't operating in the real world—this is monopoly money to them. But their ideas can't be dismissed out of hand because influential people are proposing their ideas and defending them. *New York Times* columnist Paul Krugman argues that AOC's plan aligns with enlightened economic thought. "When taxing the rich, all we should care about is how much revenue we raise," writes Krugman. "The optimal tax rate on people with very high incomes is the rate that raises the maximum possible revenue."[38] Let's set aside, for a moment, the obvious moral objections to the notion that the government has the natural right to confiscate as much income from people as it wants. Krugman approvingly cites economists who argue that the optimum tax rates for raising revenue on the rich are from 73 to 80-plus percent.[39] As AOC's plan tracks with these recommendations, Krugman maintains she's not the buffoon conservatives claim she is.

But Krugman ignores historical evidence demonstrating the correlation between lower marginal rates, increased growth, and often, increased revenues. He's willfully blind to the devastating impact of large tax increases on the economy.[40] One needn't be an expert in human behavior to understand that the rich aren't indifferent to additional earnings, if for no other reason than their desire to transfer their estates to their heirs. Studies show they employ tax avoidance strategies to circumvent rate increases and that they pay more in taxes when incentives to hide income are reduced.[41]

Krugman also omits the gap between AOC's tax hike proposals and the cost of her spending plans. He disregards the reality that raising tax rates to these exorbitant levels wouldn't make a dent in our current budget deficit, even assuming it wouldn't impair productivity. Leftists like Krugman are cavalier about private property and the rights of people to earn in a free market. They are more inclined to villainize and punish the wealthy than afford them legal protection. Krugman's argument that the government should tax at whatever rate yields the most revenue—apart from any other considerations—contradicts America's founding principles. Why should maximizing revenue be the only goal?[42] Why not devise a fair rate that finances essential government functions rather than extracting every last dollar from income producers to punish them and to finance progressive wish lists? As you see, leftists no longer champion civil liberties. Their priority is to maximize their power to achieve goals *they*, not the people, believe are best, which is the very antithesis of liberty.

It'd be bad enough to deprive people of fundamental liberties in exchange for government benefits. But the socialists' promised benefits will not—and cannot—be delivered. AOC might believe the government can magically decree jobs for everyone, but that's impossible. "This idea reflects a complete ignorance of the fact that wealth is created, not something that exists in stagnant perpetuity, and that jobs exist to generate that wealth," writes Christine Goss. "No one, not even the rich, can pay for something if they don't create the revenue to do so."[43] Simply put, the government doesn't create wealth; people and businesses do.

The same magical thinking underlies socialist healthcare proposals. There's no way to guarantee free healthcare to all without a drastic drop in quality, access, and choice, along with increased costs and waiting times. Fantasists can make these promises and memorialize them in legislation, but what good is the promise of universal healthcare if, as in many socialist countries, the quality is so bad that people are forced to travel to capitalist countries to get treated?

This disconnect between theory and reality now permeates the Democratic primaries, where AOC's proposed 70 percent tax triggered a bidding war. Senator Elizabeth Warren suggested a "wealth tax" on the super-rich that would target their assets rather than income. Thus, households with more than $50 million in assets would pay a 2 percent tax on their net worth each year and those with over $1 billion would pay 3 percent.[44] Good luck enforcing that—the rich are experts at devising methods to reduce their taxable net worth by saving less and concealing their assets or moving them to foreign countries. According to an OECD study, "[C]ountries with wealth taxes have tended to collect relatively similar amounts of revenue over time even as the overall wealth in their countries increased at much faster rates. This suggests taxpayers either found new ways to get around them or that legislators and tax collectors weren't keeping pace with annual growth." Anticipating such avoidance schemes, Warren proposes to expand the IRS—as if it's not big enough already—to conduct wealth tax audits and devise ways to indirectly value certain assets.[45]

Warren also presented a plan for universal childcare in which families with income below 200 percent of the poverty line would pay nothing, and no family would spend more than 7 percent of its income on such care. Creeping childcare costs can surely be an obstacle to employment for some parents, but as usual, leftists like Warren go too far, ensuring that these vast government subsidies will increase childcare prices. Such programs should be limited to the needy and those for whom childcare costs would deter employment. Existing programs provide support through the earned income tax credit, the child tax credit, and the child and dependent care tax credit. AEI experts suggest it's better to expand existing programs targeted to the neediest rather than establish a new universal program. Warren's program would cost $700 billion over ten years,[46] supposedly to be financed by her wealth tax. Some leftists consider her plan too modest and advocate publicly financed childcare from kindergarten through high school, on the public education model.[47]

Obviously not wanting to be bested in the socialist sweepstakes, Senator Bernie Sanders proposed a highly progressive estate tax, which would apply a 45 percent tax on estates valued from $3.5 million to $10 million, 50 percent on those from $10 million to $50 million, 55 percent from $50 million to $1 billion, and 77 percent on those above $1 billion. By contrast, Republicans propose to eliminate the estate tax, which has always been a socialist redistribution scheme that involves double taxation and makes death a taxable event. It is an assault on private property that deprives property owners of assets on which they've already paid taxes and impedes their ability to transfer them freely upon death. It discourages savings and investment by incentivizing people to spend money to keep the government from confiscating it. It imperils family-owned businesses, restricting their ability to add jobs and forcing some 28 percent of them to sell or close upon the taxpayer's death. It also generates needless administrative waste and legal and accounting fees.[48] One study in 2017 found that only 27 percent of those required to file an estate tax return ended up with any estate tax liability.[49] Sanders also proposed to eliminate all $1.6 trillion in student debt held by Americans by levying a tax on Wall Street banks.[50]

"GOD FORBID THE RICH LEAVE"

One high-profile liberal belatedly discovered that soaking the rich can deter economic growth and revenue collection. New York governor Andrew Cuomo said he was "serious as a heart attack" about stopping the slide in the state's revenues. While he didn't concede that the rich pay more than their fair share, he acknowledged that the top 1 percent of tax filers pay 46 percent of the state's personal income taxes. Then he said something fairly shocking for a New York liberal: "Tax the rich. Tax the rich. Tax the rich. We did that. God forbid the rich leave."[51] Cuomo admitted the prospective loss of these taxpayers would substantially reduce state revenues, which is as close as a liberal ideologue can get to admitting the rich are overtaxed. "I don't believe raising taxes on the rich," declared Cuomo. "That would be the worst thing to do. You would just expand the shortfall."[52]

New York is not the only state precariously dependent on a small percentage of rich taxpayers. Less than 1 percent of California's taxpayers pay almost half of the state's income tax revenues. "California cannot afford to lose even a few thousand of its wealthiest individual taxpayers," writes Victor Davis Hanson. But new federal tax laws that limit state and local deductions—meant to eliminate the phenomenon in which taxpayers from low-tax states effectively subsidize those in high-tax states—will cost wealthy Californians substantially. "If even a few thousand of the state's one-percent flee to nearby no-tax states such as Nevada or Texas, California could face a devastating shortfall in annual income," notes Hanson. "A California reckoning is on the horizon, and it may not be pretty."[53]

Democrats are also pushing a $15 minimum wage law, again placing their quest to look compassionate ahead of the interests of the people they claim to protect. As with other proposed government expansions, Democrats are going big. Rep. Bobby Scott and other Democrats introduced the Raise the Wage Act, which would more than double the current federal minimum wage of $7.25 per hour by 2024.

Studies show that minimum wage increases are not an effective antipoverty tool, according to Employment Policies Institute.[54] Only 4 percent of hourly wage workers make the minimum wage or less.[55] In 2016, Heritage Foundation experts estimated that a minimum wage hike of this magnitude would destroy seven million jobs and particularly harm workers, businesses, and economies in areas with low costs of living.[56] Younger and less-educated workers and small businesses would be harmed most.[57] The labor costs for a small business with ten minimum-wage employees would increase by $170,000 per year. If it were making 5 percent annual profits, it would have to increase sales by $3.5 million per year—an extra $67,000 every week.[58] But as the Heritage

Foundation's Rachel Greszler notes, this is not a realistic scenario, and such businesses would either have to cut back working hours or fire some workers altogether, which would render many employees worse off than before.[59] Some 150 businesses have already had to lay off workers, reduce hours, increase prices, or go out of business because of local and state minimum wage increases.[60]

Minimum wage hike advocates willfully ignore that minimum wage jobs are low-skill, entry-level positions that help employees transition to higher-earning jobs once they get more experience. Additionally, most minimum wage employees receive a raise within a year. Artificially high minimum wages hurt the people Democrats claim to champion, as they make it difficult for low-skilled workers to enter the workforce.[61] It's misleading to suggest that these jobs, by and large, are for heads of households whose families will starve unless their wages rise.

Progressives have no excuse for their indifference to the likely consequences of their proposals or the economic realities involved. What right do they have to force businesses to lay off workers or cut their hours so they can afford to pay employees more than the economic value they provide? Someone has to subsidize their largesse and, as usual, the American consumers and taxpayers will ultimately bear the cost through increased prices and/or government subsidies.

"I'M GOING TO DO TO YOU WHAT YOU DID TO US"

In their ongoing war against evil capitalists, some vengeful Democrats have their eyes on banks, which they blame for making millions of loans that resulted in foreclosures and the 2008 financial crisis. Never mind that it was progressives who forced the government to make these loans to low-income borrowers with poor credit ratings through the Community Reinvestment Act and anti-discrimination laws. They promoted minority home ownership without regard to the owners' ability to repay, and the result was catastrophic. But being a leftist means never having to say you're sorry—just pass a misguided policy and blame everyone else when it predictably fails.

Democratic Rep. Maxine Waters, emboldened by Democrats recapturing control of the House, issued a stern warning to bankers before the 2019 session began. "I have not forgotten" that "you foreclosed on our houses," she said, and "had us sign on the line for junk and for mess that we could not afford. I'm going to do to you what you did to us."[62] How's that for good governance—using her newfound power as incoming chairwoman of the House Financial Services Committee to punish bank executives for the disaster she and her fellow Democrats caused? Waters is also targeting corporations for allegedly excluding minorities and women from executive positions. Forming a new subcommittee on diversity and inclusion, she immediately held a hearing to discuss the importance of examining the systematic exclusion of women, people of color, persons with disabilities, gays, veterans, and other disadvantaged groups.[63] Why concentrate on policies to stimulate economic growth and improve people's standards of living when you can employ identity politics to demonize your opponents?

With the subprime mortgage meltdown, we see the same pattern evident with Obamacare: if some socialist or partially socialist program fails, blame it on capitalism and demand more government, just like when the *Washington Post* risibly blamed the problems of leftist-run San Francisco on capitalism.[64] The left's latest cockamamie healthcare scheme is even more extreme. The Medicare for All Act of 2019, part of the GND package, had 117 Democratic cosponsors as of August 2019. "The bill—which resembles Medicaid more than it does Medicare—would transform our entire health-care system into an iron-fisted centralized technocracy, with government bureaucrats and bioethicists controlling virtually every aspect of American health care from the delivery of medical treatment, to the payment of doctors, to even, perhaps, the building of hospitals," writes Wesley J. Smith, senior fellow at the Discovery Institute's Center on Human Exceptionalism. "It would obliterate the health-insurance industry and legalize government seizure of pharmaceutical manufacturers' patents if they refuse to yield to government drug-price controls."[65] The plan would provide "free," comprehensive healthcare for everyone. Comprehensive means just that; the list of services, which would make Karl Marx blush, includes primary care, hospital and outpatient services, dental, vision, audiology, women's "reproductive health" services, long-term care, prescription drugs, mental health and substance abuse treatment, laboratory and diagnostic services, ambulatory services, and more. The estimated cost, as noted, would be $32 trillion over ten years. Meanwhile the current Medicare fund, which is far less ambitious, is scheduled to go insolvent by 2026.

This boondoggle would create a "Physician Practice Review Board 'to assure quality, cost effectiveness, and fair reimbursements for physician-delivered items and services.'"[66] Smith notes that the term "cost effectiveness" is simply code for rationing. The measure would prohibit out-of-pocket costs to patients, meaning there would be no private fees allowed for doctors, hospitals, or other service providers, which even the *New York Times* admits would mostly eliminate health insurance companies.[67] That's the thanks insurance companies get for rolling over for President Obama and his party, whose loyalty lasted only so long as they were useful.

While the bill would not directly make doctors government employees, it would force them to sign a "participation agreement" to be eligible to receive government payments. This agreement, says Smith, would require the doctors to accept the government fee as full compensation for their services, allow the government to inspect their books, and accept government regulations in the future. With no bargaining leverage, doctors would have to comply to continue in their profession. Such is the world of a government-imposed monopoly.

Further, as if the bill's drafters are trying to showcase their fundamental ignorance of economics and the role of prices, profits, and competition, the bill aims to remove profit in healthcare. It states that "tens of millions of people in the United States do not receive healthcare services while billions of dollars that could be spent on providing health care are diverted to profit. There is a moral imperative to correct the massive deficiencies in our current health system and to eliminate profit from the provision of health care."[68] Under the bill, the government could coopt pharmaceutical patents; illegal aliens would receive free healthcare; and women would receive free abortions.[69] As to the funding of abortions, the bill states, "Any other provision of law in effect on the date of enactment of this Act restricting use of Federal funds for any reproductive health service shall not apply to monies in the Trust Fund."[70] Is there any limit to how far Democrats will go to fundamentally transform America?

"ADDRESS THESE FINANCIAL CHALLENGES AS SOON AS POSSIBLE"

President Trump didn't campaign on entitlement reform, but I trust he realizes major reform will have to occur soon because of the imminent insolvency of both Medicare and Social Security and because these and other entitlements are eating up an increasing portion of our budget. The Social Security and Medicare trustee's report of 2018 projected that the Medicare trust fund would be entirely depleted by 2026 absent congressional reform of the program.[71] Trump and his economic advisers understand that while tax cuts stimulate growth, they must be coupled with spending cuts to ensure long-term fiscal solvency and stability. Mindful of this, Trump's 2020 budget sought cuts in non-defense discretionary spending by 5 percent across the board, for a total of $2.7 trillion in savings over ten years, and, according to OMB projections, would balance the budget by 2034—obviously not soon enough, which further proves the indispensability of entitlement reform to bringing the budget and debt under control. The proposal would also limit the co-pay for high-priced prescription drugs, which would hopefully result in some Medicare savings, though the budget contains no structural reforms to Medicare.[72]

Senator Bernie Sanders's pointed questions to OMB acting director Russ Vought during a Senate Budget Committee hearing exemplify how Democrats demagogue entitlement reform and other responsible efforts to reduce spending. "How many thousands do you think will die because of massive cuts to Medicare and Medicaid?" asked Sanders. Other Senate Democrats also accused the Trump administration of trying to cut Medicare. Vought told them that no cuts were being made but that they were trying to reduce drug prices enough to extend the solvency of Medicare for eight years.

Senator Debbie Stabenow was equally accusatory. "We have this outrageous budget in front of us," said Stabenow. "The administration may claim to care about women and children. There is no way that's true, obviously.... I don't even know where to begin with all this. I would suggest that we just throw [the proposed budget] out the window."[73] Republican senator David Perdue countered that posturing Democrats need to look at the reality instead of exploiting people's emotions, noting that our national debt has increased from $6 trillion in 2000 to more than $20 trillion today and that by 2024 interest payments on the debt would exceed military spending. Contrary to Democratic fearmongering, noted Vought, federal tax cuts are not responsible for the government's fiscal crisis, as "revenues are increasing and are in line with 50-year historic averages. The problem is not that Americans are taxed too little; it is that Washington spends too much."[74]

If Democrats accuse Republicans of killing people for trying to lower drug prices, just imagine their hysteria if Republicans propose meaningful entitlement reforms. Nevertheless, despite the inevitable charges of throwing Grandma down the stairs, Republicans must plead the case for structural entitlement reform to the American people or the nation will experience a severe financial reckoning—in the not-too-distant future. From the leftist perspective this may not be bad news, for the collapse of existing systems often leads to radical change. But for liberty lovers the situation is ominous, for the longer a solution is postponed, the more financial pain will ensue. As the Social Security and Medicare Board of Trustees concluded, "Lawmakers have many policy options that would reduce or eliminate the long-term financing shortfalls in Social Security and Medicare. Lawmakers should address these financial challenges as soon as possible. Taking action sooner rather than later will permit consideration of a broader range of solutions and provide more time to phase in changes so that the public has adequate time to prepare."[75]

TRUMP'S ECONOMIC BOOM

Under President Obama, Democrats gave up on substantial economic growth, saying we'd have to resign ourselves to feeble increases. The idea of a new normal of economic stagnation, recurring recessions, and anemic economic growth was invoked by Obama White House economist Larry Summers.[76] Federal Reserve officials under Obama told us that 2 percent real GDP growth is "the most likely scenario" for the U.S. economy.[77] These declarations were meant as apologias for Obama, who was the first president to fail to deliver a year of 3 percent economic growth.[78] His average GDP growth was 1.64 percent.[79] The Congressional Budget Office forecasted in 2016 that America would never see 3 percent growth again.[80]

"High rates of growth, and the productivity that drives it, are likely distant memories from a bygone era," said bond expert Bill Gross. Similarly, Northwestern University economist Robert J. Gordon stated that the best years are already gone for U.S. GDP. Under the progressives' vision of government, with increased taxes and spending, increasing regulations and expanding bureaucracy, and more redistributionist schemes, it's no wonder the economic experts were pessimistic. Hillary Clinton was promising a third Obama term on steroids and had she been elected, she would have imposed further obstacles to growth, resulting in more stagnation.[81]

But not everyone was prepared to settle for such a dismal economic fate—to accept a future of an America hell-bent on socialism. Rejecting this gloom and doom, Trump took office vowing to reignite the economy, earning condescending ridicule from the mainstream media. "In fact, the only place one can find confidence about a growth rate of 3%-plus is inside the Trump administration, where Treasury Secretary Steven Mnuchin says it's 'very achievable,'" wrote the *Los Angeles Times*' Michael Hiltzik. "But he would say that, wouldn't he? After all, Trump's economic doctrine is dependent on it. Without such growth, Mnuchin's promise that the Trump-backed tax cut would 'pay for itself' is a fantasy."[82] Hiltzik should have quit when he was behind, but he dug himself a deeper hole, insisting that Trump's optimistic forecast could only be realized through growth in labor and productivity. "But unemployment statistics suggest instead that there isn't much slack in the workforce," Hiltzik smugly wrote. "At 4.4%, the unemployment rate is at about the point economists judge to be full employment."[83] Hiltzik was just as confident Trump would have no success turning productivity around.

Thankfully, the naysayers lost. Under Trump, wages rose for the first time in two decades.[84] In November 2018, unemployment dropped to its lowest rate in a half century. Black unemployment reached its lowest recorded level in May 2018, at 5.9 percent, and unemployment rates for Latino, young, and low-skilled workers are lower than they've been in years. Unemployment for Americans with disabilities also reached an all-time low.[85] In the same year women's unemployment reached its lowest rate in sixty-five years. By the close of 2018 there were more job openings in America than unemployed people for the first time in this nation's history. More than five million jobs had been created since Trump took office.

Most notably, manufacturing industries are booming again, having added 284,000 jobs in 2018, though skeptics had predicted these industries were dead and never coming back. David Urban notes that the elites never seemed to particularly care as the U.S. manufacturing base hollowed out under previous administrations. "It didn't matter that we strangled our own coal and steel industries with unworkable regulations, the globalists insisted, because we could just import goods from far-flung places," says Urban. "The underlying message was that there was no point in fighting back and that American industrial decline was irreversible." By cutting regulations and taxes and confronting international trade cheaters, however, Trump has created a manufacturing renaissance. Urban concludes, "The political establishment initially laughed at Trump when he promised to revive American manufacturing, but now, less than three years later, it's clear that Trump, and American workers, are getting the last laugh."[86]

Our economic freedom has dramatically increased, with America moving from eighteenth place to twelfth in the world on the Heritage Foundation's 2019 Index of Economic Freedom.[87] Progressives absurdly credit Obama for this amazing growth, though his economy was in perpetual stagnation and his experts had resigned themselves to more of the same. Trump, not Obama, is the one who slashed regulations at a record pace and implemented a major tax cut that reduced corporate rates, included a substantial cut for middle-class families, and raised the estate tax threshold to assets exceeding $11.2 million.[88] Trump slashed regulations and issued executive orders to improve the regulatory process, including a requirement that two old regulations be removed for every new one. Diane Katz of the Institute for Economic Freedom and Opportunity said the Trump administration "issued 65 percent fewer 'economically significant' rules—those with costs to the private sector that exceed $100 million a year—than the Obama administration, and 51 percent fewer than the Bush administration, after 22 months in office."[89]

The labor participation rate, which had fallen to the lowest rates since the 1970s under President Obama as people gave up on searching for a job, had created falsely optimistic unemployment numbers at the time. While unemployment continued to plummet to record lows under Trump, as noted, the labor participation rate began to rise and continued to stay at substantially higher levels.[90]

LEFTIST ANTI-SEMITISM

Leftism and socialism worldwide have a long association with anti-Semitism, and we increasingly see this phenomenon in America today. For example, AOC has established a comradery with Jeremy Corbyn, the leader of Britain's Labour Party, whose never-ending anti-Semitic statements and associations have sparked a full-blown anti-Semitism crisis in his own party. Corbyn and AOC met and broke bread after which AOC tweeted, "It was an honor to share such a lovely and wide-reaching conversation with you, @jeremycorbyn! Also honored to share a great hope in the peace, prosperity, + justice that everyday people can create when we uplift one another across class, race, + identity both at home & abroad."[91] Dominic Green asks why AOC can get away with endorsing Corbyn with so little blowback. "Corbyn is a career communist, a supporter of Castro, Chavez, and Maduro," writes Green. "He is a supporter of Hamas and the IRA. He hates the United States, but he never has a bad word to say about Russia.... He refuses to accept Israel's right to exist and endorses conspiracy theories about Israeli subversion in Arab states," and he shares platforms with Holocaust deniers.[92]

Corbyn returned a fawning tweet to AOC: "Great to speak to @ AOC on the phone this evening and hear firsthand how she's challenging the status quo. Let's build a movement across borders to take on the billionaires, polluters and migrant baiters, and support a happier, freer and cleaner planet." Green reports that one of AOC's Jewish Twitter followers tweeted his distress at AOC's joining hands with Corbyn, whose reference to "billionaires" could be code for, as Green puts it, "Judeo-American capitalism, whose tentacular global empire uses Israel to forestall the inevitable workers' revolution in the Arab states." AOC was quick to respond that she wouldn't move forward "without deep fellowship and leadership with the Jewish community. I'll have my team reach out." Green notes that AOC was "a little wounded" by the suggestion that she could be in league with anti-Semites. "Of course, she couldn't be," Green remarked. "She's far too young and perky for that. It's just that the company she keeps is that of 'everyday people' like Ilhan Omar and Rashida Tlaib—and now Jeremy Corbyn."[93]

Like AOC, Bernie Sanders has also cultivated links with Corbyn, with both men's campaigns reportedly advising and supporting each other in elections.[94] Embracing comparisons with Sanders, Corbyn confessed in an interview with writer Naomi Klein that his Labour Party borrowed ideas from Sanders's presidential campaign. Corbyn also admitted that to Sanders when Sanders called to congratulate him on his campaign. Sanders, in turn, has often cited Corbyn's campaign as an example of how leftist politics can win. In an interview with the *Washington Post*, Sanders marveled at Corbyn's ability to get younger voters to turn out and praised that model as a formula for a Democratic landslide victory. As long as young voters continue to identify with socialism, Sanders is doubtlessly correct.[95]

Green is adamant that the Democrats are building the same political coalitions as Britain's Labour Party and Europe's other left-wing parties, and he sees a connection between their anti-capitalism and anti-Semitism. "The hatred of Jews is foundational to the anti-liberalism and anti-capitalism of the radical left," writes Green. "This is why the Democrats have developed what used to be called a 'Jewish problem'—which is to say, representatives and voters who have a problem with Jews, and a DNC unwilling to do anything about it because that would cost votes."[96]

Undeniably, a disturbing number of leftists seem to regard Jews as greedy super-capitalists. There is so much anti-Semitic smoke on the left, in fact, one must look for fire. It's easy to find it, for example, with fervent Israel-hater Linda Sarsour, a leader of the Women's March who is an admirer of Imam Siraj Wahhaj. Sarsour calls him her "mentor, motivator, and encourager," even though Wahhaj is an unindicted coconspirator in the 1993 World Trade Center bombing.[97] Sarsour also warned that Israelis should not be "humanized" because they are "oppressors." Unsurprisingly, AOC praised Sarsour after she was arrested for disrupting the Supreme Court confirmation hearing of Judge Brett Kavanaugh. She tweeted, "Our future is a shared responsibility. This woman putting it all on the line for healthcare, women & LGBT + rights is @lsarsour. The far right constantly maligns her with false attacks + threats of violence. Yet, there she is, as always, fighting for everything our flag represents."[98]

We've already discussed anti-Semitic controversies stoked by Sarsour and other Women's March leaders. Yet there are more disturbing instances. Evvie Harmon, the Women's March co-global coordinator, described one such incident that occurred at a January 2017 Women's March meeting.[99] Harmon said co-chair Tamika Mallory told them the problem was that only three of the eight women in the room were women of color, and she didn't trust white women. Harmon said Mallory and Carmen Perez then began berating Venessa Wruble—not because Wruble is white but because she's Jewish. They allegedly declared, "Your people hold all the wealth."

Mallory also attended a Saviors' Day event that featured a three-hour speech by Louis Farrahkan in which he blamed Jews for "degenerate behavior in Hollywood, turning men into women and women into men." Mallory and Perez allegedly defended Farrakhan in a conference call of some forty women, refusing to denounce anything he had said. Asked whether she believes the co-chairs are anti-Semitic, Mercy Morganfield, a former spokesperson for the Women's March, told *Tablet* magazine that they refuse to put Jewish women on the board. She further noted, "They refused to even put anti-Semitism in the unity principles."[100]

Far-left Democratic congresswoman Ilhan Omar has richly earned her reputation for anti-Semitism. In 2012 she tweeted, "Israel has hypnotized the world, may Allah awaken the people and help them see the evil doings of Israel."[101] Another time she downplayed the Holocaust on Holocaust Remembrance Day by equating the Nazis' genocidal slaughter of Jews with other casualties of war.[102] Omar's partner in normalizing anti-Semitism in Congress is Rep. Rashida Tlaib, who criticized Senator Marco Rubio for opposing boycotts of Israel, tweeting, "They forgot what country they represent." Tlaib never apologized for accusing Rubio of dual loyalty.[103]

In February 2018, Omar got herself into hot water again with a series of tweets in response to a piece by Glenn Greenwald in which he noted that Rep. Kevin McCarthy was "threatening punishment" of Omar and Tlaib "over their criticisms of Israel." Omar brazenly responded, "It's all about the Benjamins baby," indicating that

McCarthy is in the pocket of Jewish interests. When a person tweeted, "Would love to know who Omar thinks is paying American politicians to be pro-Israel," Omar responded, "AIPAC," referring to the American Israel Public Affairs Committee, which does not contribute to politicians.[104] Omar also retweeted, and later deleted, a tweet saying that Omar was basically calling all Jews "hooked nose." Jewish advocacy groups condemned Omar's tweets, with the American Jewish Committee describing her comments as "stunningly anti-Semitic."[105]

House Majority Leader Nancy Pelosi issued a statement "condemning anti-Semitic comments made over Twitter by Congresswoman Omar," but other Democrats and progressives rushed to Omar's defense.[106] Omar later apologized for these slurs. Columnist David Harsanyi notes the disingenuousness of Omar's defenders, who say that she and Tlaib are merely criticizing Israel. No one equates mere criticism of Israel with anti-Semitism, argues Harsanyi. What is anti-Semitic is advocating the extinction of the world's only Jewish state. The best way to determine whether they favor the abolition of Israel, says Harsanyi, is to see if they seek to delegitimize Israel—as do supporters of Boycott, Divestment, and Sanctions (BDS); if they demonize Israel—as in suggesting Israel hypnotizes the world for evil; and if they engage in "double standards"—reflexively condemning Israel while defending the Palestinians and the rest of the Muslim world for far worse actions.[107] For both Omar and Tlaib, the answer is yes to all three questions.[108]

President Trump called Omar's apology "lame," as she reaffirmed her position that Congress supports Israel because it is paid to do so.[109] Vice President Mike Pence also condemned Omar, tweeting, ".@IlhanMN tweets were a disgrace & her apology was inadequate. Anti-Semitism has no place in the United States Congress, much less the Foreign Affairs Committee. Those who engage in anti-Semitic tropes should not just be denounced, they should face consequences for their words." Other Republicans called for Omar to resign or be removed from the Foreign Affairs Committee.[110]

House Majority Whip James Clyburn defended Omar, calling her "an incredible young lady" and urging his colleagues to let the controversy go. He said he believed her apology was sincere and she just misspoke. But Omar left no doubt that her remarks were intentional. She engaged in an exchange with Rep. Nita Lowey, who condemned the anti-Semitic practice of accusing Jews of dual loyalty, saying that throughout history these accusations had led to discrimination and violence against Jews. Omar countered that she "should not be expected to have allegiance/pledge support to a foreign country."[111] Critics observed that she was peddling the Palestinian cause to sneak in her bigoted talking points.[112]

In the wake of Omar's slurs, House members proposed a resolution condemning anti-Semitism. But Democrats could not bring themselves to approve even this simple message—it would have been too offensive to the left. Rep. Alexandria Ocasio-Cortez said it was unfair to single out Omar, even though the resolution did not mention her name. House progressives delayed a vote to include condemnation of anti-Muslim bias.[113] And members of the Congressional Black Caucus opposed the resolution because lawmakers didn't denounce Republicans and Trump. "We need to have equity in our outrage," said Rep. Ayanna Pressley, explaining that she was focused on "the occupant of the White House who is seeding every form of hate, emboldening it with racist rhetoric and policies. That is who we all need to be focused on and this is a distraction."[114] The rabid loathing for Trump is a singular obsession that obscures everything else.[115]

Eventually the Democrats passed a largely meaningless resolution denouncing numerous forms of bigotry, with an emphasis on "white supremacists," and condemning some of Omar's anti-Semitic tropes without mentioning that she was the one spreading them. The inclusion of anti-Muslim bigotry in the resolution was a shameful attempt at moral equivalency. It legitimizes Omar and Tlaib's tactic of portraying themselves as victims of anti-Muslim bias as a means to deflect and excuse their flagrant anti-Semitism.[116] In a stunning display of the rising power of the radical left over the old-guard Democrats, House Foreign Affairs Committee Chairman Eliot Engel, a strong Israel supporter, also denounced Omar's comments but said he didn't want to "exacerbate the situation" by punishing Omar, who sits on his committee, and expressed hope that she would grow and change. Republican Rep. Dan Crenshaw tweeted the obvious response: "At some point Dems just need to accept that @IlhanMN has deeply held prejudices about the Jewish people. Stop explaining her comments away and 'asking for dialogue.'"[117]

After the House passed its toothless resolution, Nancy Pelosi and three Democratic presidential candidates publicly stated that Omar is not anti-Semitic—though she made the precise claims the resolution condemned. Omar, Tlaib, and Democratic Rep. Andrew Carson brazenly released a statement praising the resolution, saying, "We are tremendously proud to be part of a body that has put forth a condemnation of all forms of bigotry including anti-Semitism, racism and white supremacy. Our nation is having a difficult conversation and we believe that is great progress."[118] It is remarkable, and only possible in the upside-down world of progressivism, that an initiative aimed at condemning anti-Semitic slurs uttered by a specific congresswoman could be twisted into a resolution defending that very offender.

Yet that was not even the most ludicrous statement of the affair. Democratic congressman James Clyburn suggested that Omar's experience in fleeing Somalia and spending time in a Kenyan refugee camp was more personal and powerful than that of the families of Holocaust survivors. "I'm serious about that," said Clyburn. "There are people who tell me, 'Well my parents are Holocaust survivors.' 'My parents did this.' It's more personal with her. I've talked to her, and I can tell you she is living through a lot of pain."[119] So there you have it—Omar has apparently suffered more than the children of any Holocaust victims. After all, what person could possibly feel as much anguish as Omar just because his mom and dad were forced into Nazi concentration camps?

It is mystifying that American Jews overwhelmingly vote Democrat in light of the party's attitude and policies toward Israel and its feckless handling of this issue. It is not "a coincidence that the Democratic Party is increasingly both the anti-Israel party and home to a growing number of anti-Semites," writes columnist Michael Goodwin. "To be clear, the two things are not always the same, but something is going on when both are defining elements of a political organization."[120]

THE ROAD AHEAD

The AOC branch of the Democratic Party is unabashedly confident that it can sell socialism to the American voters largely by villainizing capitalism. As a practical matter there are only two different types of economic systems. We're either going to have a mostly free-market system or one that is largely socialist. Leftist activists realize that while socialism doesn't currently sell well with middle-aged and older Americans, capitalism isn't that popular either, so if they can continue to denigrate it and demonize its proponents as Wall Street predators, they'll be more likely to sell socialism by default.

In the *New Republic*, Alex Shephard takes this tack, attributing socialism's revival in America to the 2008 financial crisis, which he believes Americans blame on the banking industry and America's wealth inequality. These stir the type of outrage that drove the Occupy Wall Street movement in New York City in 2011 and fueled Bernie Sanders's 2016 presidential effort. The major "flaw in Trump's anti-socialism strategy ... is that it's forcing him to be staunchly pro-capitalism at a time when its popularity is severely ebbing," writes Shephard.[121] Shephard apparently believes Trump's admittedly "hot" economy won't help him much because the top 20 percent have benefited most from it. This is how leftists think—it doesn't matter that conditions for the poor, women, and minorities are improving if the wealthiest people are getting wealthier. Their contempt for the wealthy blinds them to the progress of middle- and lower-income groups. But you can't gut the wealthy through transfer payments and exorbitant taxes and expect the economy to continue to grow to the benefit of lower-income groups.

Sadly, Democrats will continue their class warfare attacks, which are based on envy and resentment and bring out the worst in people. Republicans must seize this opportunity to counter the Democrats' hopeless message with one of optimism, hope, and an earnest desire to improve the economic plight of all people. The GOP must emphasize the stark contrast between the two approaches and cogently present their uplifting message.

CHAPTER TEN

Leftist Intolerance and Hate

The left and the Democratic Party paint conservatives as intolerant, haters, and bigots. Remember when Joe Biden told an African-American audience that, if elected president, Mitt Romney would "put you all back in chains?"[1] Remember the Democrats' repeated, baseless charge that Republicans suppress black votes? Their claim that Mississippi Republican Senator Cindy Hyde-Smith is racist?[2] Viewed in the most favorable light, they are projecting their own intolerance and hate—toward anyone who opposes their agenda, particularly conservatives.

"I DON'T HAVE TIME FOR POLITICAL CORRECTNESS"

Leftists demonize Christians, suppress their religious liberty, and muzzle their speech, even portraying some biblical teachings as hate speech. Their outlook is pessimistic and their humor is gone—all that remains is an unlimited capacity for political warfare and a rapacious appetite for control over people's lives. With people waiting to be offended, comics are now afraid of their own shadow. Some have stopped performing on college campuses altogether because young people claim to be infuriated by ideas, statements, or even jokes that stray outside the leftist narrative. The only acceptable topic of humor today, increasingly, is what we see in leftist late-night talk shows—mean-spirited "jokes" about greedy, stupid, racist Republicans. "It's okay not to hurt feelings of various tribes and groups," said Hollywood comedy legend Mel Brooks. "However, it's not good for comedy. Comedy has to walk a thin line, take risks." Brooks says because of the stifling atmosphere of political correctness, he wouldn't be able to make his classic comedy *Blazing Saddles* today.[3]

A growing number of people, however, are tiring of the left's politically correct straitjacket. An NPR/PBS NewsHour/Marist poll shows that 52 percent of Americans, including a majority of independents, oppose America becoming more politically correct, which was doubtlessly a factor in Trump's election. Many appreciate that Trump refuses to be hamstrung by the left's artificial constraints on our thoughts and speech. "I think the big problem this country has is being politically correct," said candidate Trump during a GOP primary debate. "And I don't, frankly, have time for political correctness, and to be honest with you, this country doesn't have time, either."[4]

Since Trump's election, leftists have grown increasingly intolerant and uncivil toward conservatives. Sure, there's some of this on both sides, but the left is noticeably angrier, less forgiving, and more violent. You won't find many places in society where liberals hesitate to identify themselves as liberals for fear of shunning, incivility, or violence from conservatives, but just see what happens when someone wears a MAGA hat in a venue full of liberals. In fact, the campaign of presidential candidate Corey Booker suggested Trump rallies should be banned altogether.[5] It's not that conservatives are morally superior, but most, especially those who follow the biblical ethic, at least aspire to treat people civilly.

There is no self-policing among the left. To the contrary, leftists' hateful actions are applauded by their peers. Rather than encouraging people to appeal to the better angels of their nature, they invite them to summon their demons and join the mob mentality. How often do leftists condemn Hollywood narcissists like Robert De Niro for his vile public outbursts or Jim Carrey for his deranged hate-art? They have dehumanized conservatives, believing that we have forfeited any expectation of civility and must rightly be disrespected, boycotted, and suppressed. Even children are not exempt. When seven-year-old Benton Stevens of Austin opened a hot chocolate stand near a strip mall to raise money for President Trump's border wall, leftists labeled him "little Hitler."[6]

There are enough examples of liberal intolerance, hatred, and incivility to fill volumes—in this chapter, I provide just a fractional sampling. The left has become a giant outrage mob, bullying everyone who refuses to submit to its ideas. Leftists are everything they say they are not, and they embody what they rail against. They talk diversity and inclusiveness and claim to champion gays, minorities, and women, but as noted, they'll viciously turn on any member of these groups whenever they deviate from leftist orthodoxy.

On a daily basis, leftists get away with statements that any conservative would be flayed alive for saying. Former *Saturday Night Live* star Jane Curtin, for example, announced on CNN, "My New Year's resolution is to make sure the Republican Party dies."[7] *Washington Post* columnist Jennifer Rubin went even further, proclaiming, "It's not only that Trump has to lose, but that all his enablers have to lose. We have to collectively, in essence, burn down the Republican Party. We have to level them because if there are survivors—if there are people who weather this storm, they will do it again."[8] Predictably, there was no uproar on the left about the casual heartlessness of these comments, which were made around two years after a Bernie Sanders supporter shot up a congressional Republican baseball practice, wounding four people including Republican Rep. Steve Scalise. If a Republican comedian had mused on CNN about ensuring the death of the Democratic Party, she'd be subject to a nationwide boycott to this day. Then again, it's hard to imagine a Republican comedian being invited on a mainstream media platform at all—because for the left, everything is political.

By "everything" I mean *everything*, as when students at the University of California, Davis, protested a photo of a heroic slain female police officer holding a Thin Blue Line flag because they regarded it as "anti-black" and "disrespectful."[9] This was an apolitical tribute to an officer killed in the line of duty. But for many leftists, supporting police officers is, by definition, racist.

While no slander of conservatives or Republicans is beyond the pale for the left and the media, they cannot abide even the most innocuous show of support for President Trump. CNN was outraged when American soldiers stationed in Iraq asked the president to sign their MAGA caps and their embroidered patches reading "Trump 2020." In denouncing these troops, CNN cherry-picked Department of Defense guidelines to suggest they had violated prohibitions against partisan political activities, omitting the express provision: "Active duty members may, however, express their personal opinions on political candidates and issues, make monetary contributions to a political campaign or organization, and attend political events as a spectator when not in uniform." White House press secretary Sarah Huckabee Sanders observed, "CNN will attack anyone who supports President Trump, including the brave men and women of our military who fight every day to protect our freedom."[10]

"A WANNABE DICTATOR'S BUTTBOY"

It is rich that the left and the media blame President Trump for the destruction of public discourse when they have pummeled him with a daily barrage of obscene lies and vulgar hate since he first launched his primary campaign. They wring their hands over Trump's supposed lack of decorum, his bad manners, and his offensive tweets but exempt themselves for worse behavior and don't report that Trump is often responding to Democratic and leftist provocations.

The *Washington Post* helped drive the left into a frenzy when one of the paper's contributors, Saudi citizen Jamal Khashoggi, was murdered by Saudi agents in Turkey. Upon his death, Khashoggi was widely hailed as an honest, independent, crusading journalist—until the *Post* itself revealed he was essentially an agent of the Qatari government who cooperated with Qatari representatives to devise his *Post* contributions so they would achieve maximum propaganda value.[11] Willfully ignoring that inconvenience, the media uniformly tried to exploit Khashoggi's death to bash Trump for not reacting strongly enough to the incident.

MSNBC host Joe Scarborough asserted, despicably, that President Trump didn't care about the murder because of his financial interests. He didn't offer this as an opinion but as a naked statement of fact. Co-host Mika Brzezinski venomously lashed out at Secretary of State Mike Pompeo as a "wannabe dictator's buttboy" for his apparently inadequate response to Khashoggi's death. Brzezinski later apologized—not to Pompeo but for her choice of words—and said she should have said "water boy."[12] Needless to say, had a right-wing commentator uttered that gay slur there would have been hell to pay.

This double standard is not lost on columnist Michelangelo Signorile, a gay man who asks why liberal comics keep using "homophobia" in their routines if they are defenders of gay rights. He cites a comedian who portrayed Maricopa County, Arizona, sheriff Joe Arpaio saying he'd accept an "amazing bl** job" from President Trump. "The absurdity of it draws a laugh, even from many of us who are queer," writes Signorile. "But the joke nonetheless rests on the tired premise that gay sex is one of the most grotesque things anyone could possibly do." Among other examples, Signorile hits Jimmy Kimmel, Stephen Colbert, and the *New York Times* editorial page for implying that Trump and Russian president Vladimir Putin are sex partners.[13] One might fairly ask why the left was outraged at Kevin Hart, a black man, for decade-old jokes about gays while Brzezinski, Scarborough, Kimmel, Colbert, and the *Times* were given a pass. Thus, we see that leftists excoriate homophobia and other outrages only when politically convenient, not because they are actually crusaders against these outrages. It's about power, not principle.

Bill Moyers is a perfect example of an intolerant, rage-filled liberal who projects his own attitudes onto conservatives. Several years ago he argued that conservative talk radio incites domestic terrorism and hate. Now consider whether that could describe his own comments during the 2016 presidential campaign: "Trump and his ilk would sweep the promise of America into the dustbin of history unless they are exposed now to the disinfectant of sunlight, the cleansing torch of truth. Nothing else can save us from the dark age of unreason that would arrive with the triumph of Donald Trump."[14]

In a dramatic reversal of the sixties free-speech movement, leftists openly proclaim that their political opponents have no right to participate in politics or even walk the streets. At a rally in Los Angeles, Congresswoman Maxine Waters declared, "If you see anybody from that Cabinet in a restaurant, in a department store, at a gasoline station, you get out and you create a crowd and you push back on them, and you tell them they're not welcome anymore, anywhere." This was no misstatement, as Waters reiterated her sentiments in a television interview.[15] Speaker Nancy Pelosi called Waters's remarks unacceptable but immediately blamed them on President Trump's "daily lack of civility."[16]

Leftist bullies drove White House press secretary Sarah Huckabee Sanders out of the Red Hen restaurant in Lexington, Virginia, and it was easier to find liberals applauding the incident than condemning it.[17] Similarly, a restaurant owner in California tweeted that he would refuse service to MAGA hat–wearing customers. "It hasn't happened yet, but if you come to my restaurant wearing a MAGA cap, you aren't getting served, same as if you come in wearing a swastika, white hood, or any other symbol of intolerance and hate," tweeted J. Kenji López-Alt, a chef-partner of the restaurant Wursthall in San Mateo. The tweet received 2,100 likes and 200 retweets. In other tweets he again compared Trump supporters to KKK members: "MAGA hats are like white hoods except stupider because you can see exactly who is wearing them."[18]

CNN host Chris Cuomo unsurprisingly sympathized with López-Alt, claiming that MAGA hats "triggered" people and wearing them is equivalent to wearing a shirt that says, "I hate black people." Cuomo's CNN colleague Don Lemon agreed, saying, "If you're going to wear that hat…maybe that hat means the Central Park five to people. Maybe it means birtherism to people. Maybe it means Mexicans are rapists to people. And so you cannot erase those things from the story of that hat…."[19] So, in Lemon's view, Trump supporters shouldn't wear the hats because they know Trump haters will assume they're racist. It's not the fault of Trump haters, you see, but those who dare to publicly show support for Trump—a president supported by half the American people.

Lemon knows his fellow leftists. A forty-one-year old woman attacked twenty-three-year-old Bryton Turner in a Mexican restaurant in Falmouth, Massachusetts, and knocked his MAGA hat off. Like a good progressive, the attacker said *she* was the victim because Turner's hat upset her. "He's not a victim. I am the victim," she claimed, though witnesses said Turner was minding his own business when she assaulted him without provocation.[20]

Similar examples of leftist intolerance abound:

- ★ After Senator Susan Collins supported Judge Brett Kavanaugh at his Supreme Court nomination hearing, she received a slew of belligerent voice messages and a threatening letter that the writer falsely claimed contained ricin.[21]
- ★ Sam Lavigne, a New York University professor, created a database of 1,595 Immigration and Customs Enforcement employees from LinkedIn, including their full names, locations, and their roles at ICE. Leftist group Antifa spread the database to their Twitter followers, and the list circulated to one of its subgroups on Reddit, which encourages spreading personal information about people they consider "Nazis" or "alt-right," including ICE and NSA employees. "Doxing ICE agents is good and moral," said one Reddit user.[22] Unsurprisingly, New York University representatives were silent about its professor's outrageous action.[23] The *Daily Caller* reported that Twitter had not suspended Professor Lavigne.[24]
- ★ Antifa has become an extremely violent terror group. Its members move in large packs and attack their outnumbered targets with clubs, steel pipes, and bear spray. They've repeatedly terrorized entire sections of Portland, Oregon, harassing and chasing utterly innocent motorists, not even sparing the elderly or the handicapped.[25] In Philadelphia, an Antifa gang attacked U.S. Marine Corps reservists Alejandro Godinez and Luis Torres, mistakenly believing they had attended a nearby right-wing rally. The Marines were touring city landmarks when about ten Antifa members swarmed them, punched and kicked them, and sprayed them with mace, calling them "white supremacists" and "Nazis." One of the Marines testified later that the attack was so brutal they could have died.[26]

★ In response to reports of the separation of families at the border, the late actor Peter Fonda tweeted that President Trump's son Barron should be taken from his mother and caged. Fonda had previously tweeted about White House press secretary Sarah Huckabee Sanders, "Maybe we should take her children away and deport her to Arkansas, and give her children to Stephen Goebbels Miller for safe keeping." The Secret Service investigated the matter, as it had when comedian Kathy Griffin posed for a photo while holding a mock decapitated head of President Trump.[27]

A half century ago, at the Democratic National Convention in Chicago in 1968, the radical left unleashed its rage on the Democratic Party. Today, the radicals control the party, with leftist Alexandria Ocasio-Cortez dominating the headlines, socialist Bernie Sanders achieving enormous popularity among the party's base, and the Democratic National Committee being chaired by radical leftist Tom Perez, who previously had his fellow radical Keith Ellison working as his deputy.[28] At best, these agitators offer sympathetic silence as their acolytes harass, intimidate, and attack conservatives in every conceivable public venue.

"SOME WHITE PEOPLE MAY HAVE TO DIE"

Iram Osei-Frimpong, a leftist teaching assistant at the University of Georgia, posted on the university's Facebook page, "Some white people may have to die for Black communities to be made whole in this struggle to advance to freedom. To pretend that's not the case is ahistorical and dangerously naïve." So he advocates murder while accusing others of being "dangerous"? In a later-deleted post on *Medium* he allegedly said, "Killing some white people isn't genocide; it's killing some white people.... We had to kill some white people to get out of slavery. Maybe if we'd killed more during the twentieth century we still wouldn't talk about racialized voter disenfranchisement and housing, education, and employment discrimination. This should not be controversial."[29]

While not all leftists are violent, it's hard to deny that compared to conservatives, leftists are not a happy lot, which is ironic since they're the ones with utopian dreams. Too many leftists are consumed with rage, believe most of their own countrymen are inveterate racists, and await some kind of environmental cataclysm. Instead of investing confidence in Americans' ability to succeed through their ingenuity and work ethic, they burden people with victimhood in the name of protecting them. AOC is billed as the party's fresh new face of optimism, but in reality she has an extremely low opinion of America today. Here's how she describes her policy proposals: "I think all of these things sound radical compared to where we are, but where we are is not a good thing. And this idea of like, ten percent better than garbage, it shouldn't be what we settle for."[30] So there you have it. America is just a smidgeon better than garbage—a fitting Democratic Party slogan.

Unfortunately, it's virtually impossible now for Republicans to reach across the aisle and work with Democrats. First, Democrats have no interest in compromising with Republicans, and anyone who did would be attacked by other leftists. And second, it's hard to compromise with people who slander you daily as a bigot. You can't compromise with people who claim you're the root of all evil and will condemn any of their own who even reach out to you in friendship, let alone compromise.

Filmmaker and actor Mark Duplass, as part of a challenge to "do a good deed every day," tweeted, "Fellow Liberals: If you are interested at all in 'crossing the aisle' you should consider following @benshapiro. I don't agree with him on much but he's a genuine person who once helped me for no other reason than to be nice. He doesn't bend the truth. His intentions are good."

From the progressives' reaction, you'd think Duplass had cursed their families. Swarming on him as an irredeemable traitor, one exclaimed, "F*** Mark Duplass. Why do liberals always have to cede EVERYTHING for the sake of bipartisanship?" Another declared, "I will bet money mark duplass either has sexual assault in his past or bodies in his basement." And another: "The privilege of being able to look past someone's sh*tty opinions because they were nice to you once is staggering, as staggeringly dull and overrated [as] mark duplass' films are I'd wager." Finally, "For Posterity, @MarkDuplass is a racist monster." Duly chastened, Duplass deleted the tweet and stated, "Genuinely appreciate all of your comments. My goal is to create further understanding of each other's positions. If we 'vote them out' without any attempt to understand, they'll likely just vote us out next time the same way. That said, I hear your points. Best to all of you."[31]

Sorry, I'm not buying this. Are we to believe Duplass genuinely appreciated being denounced for encouraging people to follow a single conservative on Twitter? If so, it doesn't speak well of him. Out of decency alone, he should instinctively reject such bile. At any rate, his apology didn't work. It just triggered more vitriol from "tolerant" leftists who revile conservatives for their alleged intolerance. One lovely leftist writer commented, "In addition, letting 'good' white guys slide on bullsh*t like this where they make an uneducated statement and aren't held accountable for it are part of why we are where we are today in lots of different parts of Hell."[32] One wonders how many Hollywood denizens actually buy into liberalism of their free will as opposed to oppressive peer pressure—clearly, people are not free to dissent from the liberal line. Indeed, the left has cultivated a mania for blacklisting that you simply don't find among conservatives.

Former vice president Joe Biden is another liberal who has been forced to apologize for saying something nice about a conservative. During a speech in Omaha, Biden casually alluded to Vice President Mike Pence's speech at the Munich Security Conference in February 2019. "The fact of the matter is it was followed on by a guy who's a decent guy, our vice president, who stood before this group of allies and leaders and said, 'I'm here on behalf of President Trump,' and there was dead silence." Calling Pence "a decent guy" was more than leftists could stomach. Liberal activist and actress Cynthia Nixon delivered the obligatory smackdown. "You've just called America's most anti-LGBT elected leader 'a decent guy,'" she tweeted. "Please consider how this falls on the ears of our community."

Realizing he'd committed an unpardonable sin, especially for a Democratic presidential aspirant, Biden immediately genuflected to the gender gods. "You're right, Cynthia," Biden tweeted. "I was making a point in a foreign policy context, that under normal circumstances a Vice President wouldn't be given a silent reaction on the world stage. But there is nothing decent about being anti-LGBTQ rights, and that includes the Vice President."[33]

Even a Democratic luminary like Biden is not allowed to be gracious toward the left's political foes, and this goes double for social conservatives and triple for unapologetic Christian conservatives. Mike Pence is one of those guys whose decency is undeniable, yet he is vilified by the McCarthyite left. Pence is among that special breed of individuals who walk the Christian walk and remain true to their principles even under the most intense pressure to disown politically incorrect convictions. Though many Americans probably still believe in the biblical principle that marriage is between one man and one woman, few have the courage to admit that in public for fear of scorn from the secular left. Pence's innate decency is particularly galling to the left because it exposes their contrasting gracelessness, intolerance, and mean-spiritedness.

The left has become a closed-minded mega-cult that arbitrarily declares issues beyond debate and opponents unworthy of respect or civil treatment. Those who don't agree are not just wrong but evil, and openly embracing this noxious idea is now part of the rite of passage among leftists' ranks.

"THEIR CONCERNS ARE IRRELEVANT"

When people criticized Jimmy Kimmel for implying that surgeries for newborn infants weren't covered by insurance before Obamacare, he sarcastically commented, "I would like to apologize for saying that children in America should have health care. It was insensitive, it was offensive, and I hope you can find it in your heart to forgive me."[34] In typical leftist fashion, Kimmel wasn't merely expressing disagreement with conservatives on healthcare policy but suggesting that anyone who disagrees with him is immoral and indifferent to children's health.

It's commonplace for leftists to argue that people who oppose same-sex marriage hate gays, those who support border enforcement are racist xenophobes, those who support welfare reform despise the poor, those who favor entitlement reform are indifferent to the elderly, and those who oppose abortion want to rob women of their autonomy. And with greater frequency, leftists violently protest and block conservatives from speaking on university campuses or in the streets of liberal cities. "Liberals are creating an America, where it's natural to hate people of differing political views," writes columnist John Hawkins. "Not disagree with, hate.... It's the liberal mentality that says, 'People who disagree with us on anything are racist, sexist, homophobic and evil. Therefore, we don't have to treat them fairly. Therefore, their concerns are irrelevant. Therefore, it's acceptable to lie about them, take away their rights or even use the IRS or legal system to mistreat them.'"[35]

Leftist closed-mindedness also pervades American journalism. The mainstream media are monolithically liberal, mostly atheist, Democratic, and cloistered in their own echo chamber. On his podcast, outspoken atheist Sam Harris noted that surveys show few leftist journalists follow their conservative counterparts on Twitter, while many right-wing journalists follow their counterparts on the left.[36] Mainstream media figures insist they are unbiased, objective reporters, but researchers from Arizona State University and Texas A&M University found the opposite when they conducted a survey of some 462 financial journalists around the country. The results surprised the researchers, as even the supposedly hard-nosed financial reporters were overwhelmingly liberal. Some 58 percent admitted to being left of center and 37 percent said they were moderate. Only 0.46 percent said they were "very conservative" and 3.94 percent said they were somewhat conservative—a combined total of 4.4 percent, then, lean right of center.[37] This bias is not lost on the American people. Rasmussen Reports found that 45 percent of all likely voters in the 2018 midterm elections believed that most reporters tried to help Democratic candidates whereas only 11 percent said they tried to help Republicans.[38]

"THIS CASE IS ABOUT CRUSHING DISSENT"

A textbook example of leftist intolerance is the campaign to vilify Chick-fil-A. The attack is aimed at the franchise owner, Dan Cathy, who supports traditional marriage, which the left wrongly characterizes as anti-gay hate. In 2016 Mayor Bill de Blasio called for a boycott of New York City's Chick-fil-A restaurants, declaring, "I'm certainly not going to patronize them, and I wouldn't urge any other New Yorkers to patronize them." But his officious intermeddling failed and possibly backfired. Three years later, Chick-fil-A now has twenty stores in the city, including the largest store in the franchise, which opened in 2018 in the city's financial district. Chick-fil-A, in fact, is a good corporate citizen. All the company's New York City restaurants contribute to the New York Common Pantry to provide meals for the poor.[39]

Recently, San Antonio City councilman Roberto Treviño, boasting of the city's efforts "to become a champion of equality and inclusion," proposed removing the Chick-fil-A from the San Antonio airport.[40] "San Antonio is a city full of compassion, and we do not have room in our public facilities for a business with a legacy of anti-LGBTQ behavior," he said. In other words, we'll show our inclusiveness by excluding Chick-fil-A and show our compassion by being uncompassionate toward the restaurant and its patrons. Can anyone point to one instance in which Chick-fil-A refused to serve a gay person or mistreated one in any way? Why not let customers make their own decisions about their dining instead of punishing restaurants and their customers because of their owners' opinions?

Leftists have targeted and boycotted Chick-fil-A throughout the nation. Thankfully, their efforts have mostly failed, as Chick-fil-A was already flourishing just a year after the boycott began in 2012.[41] But this doesn't discourage gay activists, who demand that companies fulfill a slate of demands or risk losing their ranking in the annual Corporate Equality Index published by the Human Rights Campaign, a gay advocacy group. Companies, despite no government coercion, are changing their policies to meet these demands, which include ensuring that sex-reassignment surgery is covered by every health insurance plan a company offers.[42]

The left's assault on Christian religious liberty goes far beyond Chick-fil-A. In 2006 Elane Photography of Albuquerque, New Mexico, declined to photograph a "commitment ceremony" for two women in a same-sex relationship due to the religious beliefs of its owners, the Huguenins. One of the women, Vanessa Willock, filed a complaint with the New Mexico Human Rights Commission, which ruled the Huguenins had violated state anti-discrimination laws.[43] The decision was affirmed by the Second Judicial District Court, the New Mexico Court of Appeals, and the New Mexico Supreme Court, after which the U.S. Supreme Court declined to hear the case. New Mexico Supreme Court justice Richard C. Bosson, in his concurring opinion, wrote, "In the smaller, more focused world of the marketplace, of commerce, of public accommodation, the Huguenins have to channel their conduct, not their beliefs, so as to leave space for other Americans who believe something different. That compromise is part of the glue that holds us together as a nation, the tolerance that lubricates the varied moving parts of us as a people. In short, I would say to the Huguenins, with the utmost respect: it is the price of citizenship."[44]

But the price of citizenship shouldn't include being forced to accept others' beliefs. Justice Bosson is twisting the definition of liberty to include ideas antithetical to liberty. Jordan Lorence, senior counsel for the Alliance Defending Freedom, a Christian liberties law firm that represented the Huguenins, commented, "The core of what's happening to the Huguenins is basically a government action to suppress dissent and force affirmation to a specific set of beliefs. This is a threat to basic First Amendment freedoms."

Lorence is correct. It was not Ms. Willock's and her partner's liberty that was at stake. Their rights weren't violated by one photographer who, it's important to note, didn't deny them service in general but only for this specific ceremony, for religious reasons. This cannot be fairly described as a balancing of competing rights or freedoms. Only the Huguenins' freedom was infringed, not that of the same-sex couple. But in our politically correct culture, certain activities are accorded quasi-holy status as courts and other decision-making bodies contort themselves into logical incoherence to justify their decisions. Consequently, they greatly diminish civil liberties and turn the victimizers into victims.

In a similar case, Barronelle Stutzman, proprietor of Arlene's Flowers in Washington state and a devout Christian, had no problem serving and employing homosexual people during her career. She served one such person, Robert Ingersoll, for more than eleven years before he asked if she would prepare an arrangement for his same-sex marriage ceremony. She declined based on her religious beliefs, and he sued her. Washington is not among the twenty-plus states that have enacted Religious Freedom Restoration Acts (RFRAs), which allow defendants to assert their religious faith as an affirmative defense in such actions. Stutzman lovingly serves everyone, including gays, but her conscience doesn't permit her to use her talents in support of a ceremony she believes contradicts her faith.

The Washington State Supreme Court ruled against her. Her attorney, Kristen Waggoner, who works with Alliance Defending Freedom, observed, "This case is about crushing dissent. In a free America, people with different beliefs must have room to coexist. It's wrong for the state to force any citizen to support a particular view about marriage or anything else against their will. Freedom of speech and religion aren't subject to the whim of a majority; they are constitutional guarantees."[45] In our leftist culture, which dominates the judiciaries of too many states, some people are more equal than others, and certain liberties must yield to the gods of political correctness.

In perhaps the most well-known such incident, Jack Phillips, owner of Masterpiece Cakeshop in Colorado, refused, because of his religious convictions, to make a wedding cake for a gay couple. Once again, he didn't deny them service in general but would not prepare a cake to celebrate a same-sex wedding. The complaining couple wasn't harmed. They could have gone anywhere else to buy a custom-made wedding cake. But they refused to allow this baker to exercise his religious liberty, and the Colorado Civil Rights Commission ruled against Phillips. This surely was a deliberate targeting of a Christian baker to force him to conform to their values and thought edicts. The U.S. Supreme Court held that the commission violated Phillips's First Amendment liberties, on the narrow grounds that the commission displayed "anti-religious bias."

But the relentless left never quits.[46] It went after Phillips again. Denver attorney Autumn Scardina won a ruling from the commission against Phillips for discrimination because he refused to bake a custom-ordered cake to celebrate her transition from male to female. After Phillips sued the state, claiming that he was being persecuted for his Christian beliefs, he and the commission agreed to drop their respective cases. But Scardina wouldn't let it go. She filed a civil suit against Phillips in federal district court.[47] Please tell us again who the true haters are?

It's noteworthy that conservatives don't tend to react to inconveniences by declaring all-out political war the way the left does. A photographer refused to photograph the family of Alan Sears, the president and CEO of Alliance Defending Freedom, the Christian religious liberties law firm. "While I appreciate your inquiry," the photographer said, "I oppose the goals and interests of your organization and have no interest in working on its behalf." Objecting to Sears's beliefs on gender issues, the photographer refused him service for an innocuous shoot having nothing to do with those issues. Note that no leftists were outraged over this denial of service, and unlike leftist bullies, Sears did not sue the photographer or stoke an angry online mob against him. He simply found another photographer, like most other people would do in a free society.[48]

SUBMIT OR BE BULLIED INTO SUBMISSION

Unforgiving activists savagely attacked Brendan Eich, cofounder of Mozilla, leading to his resignation from his position as CEO of the company just days after being appointed in 2014. His sin was having contributed $1,000 to Proposition 8, a California state measure to codify that marriage is between one man and one woman, six years earlier. Leftist groups also boycotted Mozilla's internet browser, Firefox. Mozilla chairwoman Mitchell Baker said, "Mozilla believes both in equality and freedom of speech. And you need free speech to fight for equality. Figuring out how to stand for both at the same time can be hard."[49]

But Mozilla did not vindicate free speech or balance the interests of free speech and equality. To the contrary, by capitulating to pressure to oust Eich, the company sacrificed free speech at the altar of political correctness. Some rationalized that free speech wasn't the issue, claiming Eich wasn't fired for his views but instead resigned. In fact, he was forced out because a large part of the Mozilla community refused to follow his leadership after he voiced opposition to same-sex marriage and wouldn't retract it. Employees and volunteers were threatening to quit the company, users were switching browsers, and donors were announcing they would no longer contribute to the firm.

While he had a right to free speech, some said, so did the Mozilla community and its supporters and consumers, so free speech wasn't compromised.[50] This is sophistry. The salient issue is the intolerance of the left and its insistence on hyper-politicizing everything. It's not as if Eich was looking for soapboxes to denounce same-sex marriage. Yes, he stood by his views when challenged, but that was a matter of his personal integrity. Why couldn't leftists just accept one person having a different opinion than theirs? Why couldn't they let Eich's personal views remain personal? This is the way the left operates. You either support its agenda, get bullied into submission, or get forced out.

Leftists have successfully targeted other groups for their views, statements, and practices on same-sex marriage and other gender issues. They effectively shut down Pure Passion Ministries and their videos on Vimeo about people who abandoned homosexuality or transgenderism. The videos featured a Christian perspective of sexuality and relationships, which is now anathema to the left. Vimeo also blacklisted an announcement for the "Hope Conference" featuring Christian speakers Janet Mefferd and Joe Dallas. Its message opposing same-sex marriage was deemed offensive and inappropriate, as the conference proclaimed there is hope in Jesus Christ for change and transformation.[51] Vimeo spokesperson Melissa B. explained, "It seems that a number of your videos go against the Vimeo Guidelines of: 'We also forbid content that displays a demeaning attitude toward specific groups, including: Videos that promote Sexual Orientation Change Efforts (SOCE).'"

Dr. Michael Brown highlights the hypocrisy, noting that by this logic Alcoholics Anonymous, weight loss, and debt reduction videos would be censored, as they each arguably demean certain groups. "In reality, all these videos are welcome on Vimeo, because none of them cross the forbidden line of saying: If you're not happy being gay (or bisexual or transgender), God has a better way," writes Brown. "This is absolutely forbidden!"[52] Brown says those who have come out of the closet now want to put dissenters into the closet. The contradiction in such thinking is worth repeating: they insist on gender fluidity, almost as an article of faith, yet they forbid expression of the opinion that fluidity can operate from gay to straight. Brown also observes that Vimeo is full of videos of terrorists and pornographers, two groups not blacklisted by the high priests of political correctness.

Dr. Brown's own videos on cultural issues, including sexuality, marriage, and male-female distinctions, were removed from YouTube's "AdSense" program because they allegedly contained "controversial religious" ideas and were marked "not suitable for advertisers." Similarly,

AmazonSmile removed videos of Christian legal defense firm Liberty Counsel and D. James Kennedy Ministries because the notoriously leftist Southern Poverty Law Center wrongly labels both organizations as "hate groups."[53] Of course, the SPLC's definition of hate is, essentially, "politically conservative."

"APOLOGIZING IS LIKE A MATH PROBLEM"

Don't ever doubt that leftists enforce conformity among themselves, ensuring that few register dissent from their dogma. Like Mark Duplass and Joe Biden, mainstream media icon Tom Brokaw learned the hard way that his liberal bona fides don't immunize him from violating leftist speech codes. During a *Meet the Press* panel on NBC, Brokaw portrayed Republicans as racist, claiming that when he asks them about immigration they say they "don't know whether [they] want brown grandbabies." So far, so good, as far as the left is concerned. Then he stepped in it. "I also happen to believe that the Hispanics should work harder at assimilation," Brokaw said. "That's one of the things that I've been saying for a long time, that they ought not to be codified in their communities but make sure that all of their kids are learning to speak English and they feel comfortable in the communities. And that's going to take outreach on both sides, frankly."[54]

Brokaw apparently did not know the broad, bipartisan consensus on the value of assimilation has collapsed—the left now views assimilation as just another racist ploy. The blowback was predictably intense. Investigative journalist Aura Bogado accused Brokaw of "arguing classic white supremacist talking points in a deeply racist rant on national television." Julio Ricardo Varela of LatinoRebels.com said, "It really was a punch in the gut to a lot of people. It was not only factually incorrect; it was also xenophobia in action." An alliance of Latino advocacy groups demanded that NBC issue an apology, increase diversity among *Meet the Press* guests, produce a series on American Hispanics, and cough up money for the National Association of Hispanic Journalists. "Mr. Brokaw's comments are more than just out-of-touch musings," the groups decalared. "Mr. Brokaw's comments are part of a legacy of anti-Latino sentiment that is spreading freely in 2019."

Naturally Brokaw profusely apologized, declaring, "I feel terrible if part of my comments on Hispanics offended some members of that proud culture," and noting that he has "worked hard to knock down false stereotypes." He later added that he was "very sorry" for comments that were "offensive to many.... I never intended to disparage any segment of our rich, diverse society which defines who we are."[55] The outrage at Brokaw's remarks reveals both the left's malicious redefinition of racism and its rejection of assimilation in general. The alternative to assimilation, of course, is balkanization—and that's precisely what the left wants.

One common thread in the left's speech policing is that an apology no longer suffices. The offender must repeatedly grovel and then do some form of penance, either publicly paying homage to the cause he offended or making significant financial contributions. In some cases, offenders cannot earn forgiveness, no matter how much they prostrate themselves before the altar of left-wing orthodoxy. Self-appointed leftist elitists are the sole and final arbiters of whether sufficient contrition has been displayed. Kevin Hart got a taste of this when he was bullied into stepping down from hosting the Academy Awards. When he was selected, leftists decried allegedly homophobic tweets he'd made almost a decade before and a statement he had made during a 2010 special, "Seriously Funny," indicating he would prevent his son from being gay if he could.

Hart initially refused to apologize, saying his remarks were jokes and he had matured since then. But when the condemnations piled up, he withdrew from the Academy Awards and apologized "to the LGBTQ community for [his] insensitive words from [his] past." This still wasn't enough. Brandi Miller, in *HuffPost*, argued Hart "still misses the point.... A true apology, a true acknowledgment of harm done from Hart would involve talking about the implications of his words, not just apologizing for who he used to be.... Apologizing is like a math problem. To get the credit, you have to show your work.... Let's be honest, tweeting 'I apologize' isn't that hard and doesn't really involve much internal reckoning, but with his actions, he can show a changed life." Hart could "show his work," she said, by donating money to gay groups or requesting a gay cohost for the Academy Awards.[56] *USA Today* opinion contributor Rich Kiamco suggested Hart should "make a 20-minute killer set about his homophobic fears."[57]

You see, it's not enough to apologize. You must fully adopt and crusade on behalf of their viewpoint or be permanently banished. On a steady march to control our thoughts and behavior, the left will mow down anyone in its way.

CANADA—"A COUNTRY FILLED MOSTLY WITH WHITE PEOPLE"

The left uses accusations of racism as an effective political weapon against Trump supporters. They especially enjoy employing this smear against border hawks because immigration is Trump's signature issue. Democrats insist they aren't for open borders, and yet they slander anyone who supports border enforcement as a bigot.[58]

Race actually has nothing to do with border enforcement, which is the right and obligation of every sovereign government. But since Democrats have successfully demonized Republicans as racists with African Americans, they are using the same tactic with other minorities. Leftists know that illegal immigrants are potential beneficiaries of future amnesties, so alienating those future voters from Republicans is just good politics for them—no matter how despicable and destructive. Democratic politicians know the racism charge sticks. It has with their own constituents, as a recent SurveyMonkey online poll shows that a whopping 61 percent of Democrats believe Republicans are racist, bigoted, or sexist.[59]

Defining the very idea of border enforcement as racist is a major priority of the left. Democratic senator Chris Murphy blasted Republicans for favoring a wall with Mexico but not Canada—a "country filled mostly with white people."[60] The senator, however, must know that illegal crossings from Canada are a fraction of those from Mexico. Likewise, before she began denouncing Trump for running "concentration camps" on the border, AOC denied there was any border crisis at all, telling *60 Minutes* there is "no question" that Trump is a racist, as "he manufactures crises like immigrants seeking legal refuge on our borders."[61] Senator Kamala Harris made the same claim.[62] Senator Sherrod Brown said there are no divisions in the Republican Party because "they've followed [Trump's] racist actions... like lemmings off the cliff."[63]

Sunny Hostin, cohost of *The View*, asked if Republicans would "step up to the plate with Donald Trump" on his border wall, which she claimed he was using as a "dog whistle for racism."[64]

In an attempt to make Trump associates permanent outcasts from society, a coalition of progressive groups called Restore Public Trust circulated a petition urging corporate CEOs to refuse to employ former members of the Trump administration. "The cruelty of the [separation] policy was matched only by the incompetence of its execution," they wrote in an open letter.[65]

"EVERYONE LOOKS DIFFERENT BUT THINKS EXACTLY THE SAME"

The left's attempt to punish, humiliate, and ostracize its opponents is particularly apparent in universities. Students at the Savannah College of Art and Design began a petition demanding the removal of the name of Savannah native Justice Clarence Thomas from one of the campus buildings, preposterously claiming he is "anti-woman."[66] Across the pond, Cambridge University rescinded its invitation for a visiting fellowship from Professor Jordan Peterson after students protested Peterson's skepticism of white privilege and global warming, among various heresies.[67] Laughably, they say Peterson isn't welcome on their campus because they promote an "inclusive environment." Only leftists could speak such Orwellian pap with a straight face. As the *Spectator*'s Toby Young observed, inclusiveness means an environment where "everyone looks different but thinks exactly the same."[68] Indeed, how can liberal academics think they are training young minds to think for themselves when they censor ideas not in lockstep with their own?

In this environment, it is surreal to see liberal professors and students pretend to promote open inquiry and tolerate dissenting opinion. Charlotte Townsend, a sophomore at the College of Charleston in South Carolina, says she'd heard the school had a tough political climate for conservatives, but she didn't realize how bad it was until she experienced it herself. "I live in a world where many of my peers are too afraid to support conservatism in front of their friends," she contends. Charlotte herself refuses to be censored and regularly engages in "battles," but she doesn't blame conservative friends who are afraid to join the fight. "The stigma against being a conservative on campus is a lot to handle," she says. "I've been frustrated by how conservatives are treated here."

Charlotte tells of three nasty encounters she's had with campus liberals, both faculty and students. In one, strangers destroyed flyers she posted promoting a conservative workshop. In another, a female student told her that as a conservative she was "against" her own sex. Finally, she's had professors who teach that conservatives have been corrupted by "rich, white men."[69] Isn't it ironic that it is liberals who are always complaining about bullying and demanding safe spaces, while they bully and make spaces unsafe for conservatives?

Senator Ted Cruz took the dramatic step of opening an investigation into a Yale Law School policy that allegedly targets Christian groups. The policy provides that students who work for "discriminatory" organizations will not have access to certain funds, such as summer and post-graduate public interest fellowships and loan forgiveness for public interest careers. The affair began when the Yale Federalist Society invited an attorney with Alliance Defending Freedom, the Christian civil liberties law firm, to speak on campus, which triggered a campus gay organization called "Outlaws." Denouncing ADF as a "hate group," Outlaws demanded that the law school expand its nondiscrimination policy to Christian groups because of their position on gay rights, which of course they characterized as discrimination against gays. Shortly thereafter, Yale Law School dean Heather Gerken announced that the school would indeed expand its nondiscrimination policy, noting that nondiscrimination "based on sexual orientation and gender identity and expression is a key component of the Law School's discrimination policy."

Cruz then sent a letter to Gerken asserting, "[It] appears that the policy arose from unconstitutional animus and a specific discriminatory intent both to blacklist Christian organizations like the Alliance Defending Freedom and to punish Yale students whose values or religious faith lead them to work there." Senator Josh Hawley, a graduate of Yale Law School, sent a letter to Attorney General William Barr asking that the Justice Department closely monitor Yale and strip the school's funding if its law school continues to "target religious students for special disfavor."

Denying that they discriminate against Christians and insisting that the school "enthusiastically supports the efforts of Jewish, Catholic,

Muslim, liberal, and conservative groups to hire our students," Yale announced they would exempt religious organizations from their policy.[70] Hawley subsequently wrote to Barr saying he'd need more details to confirm whether Yale's statement was meaningful, noting that the initial policy change was a direct response to student protesters. Hawley asked Barr to closely monitor the school going forward.[71]

THE "OPPRESSION OLYMPICS"

The left's intolerance and censorship have grown so severe that even some leftists are objecting. Atheist author Sam Harris announced he would delete his account from the crowdfunding site Patreon to protest the company's banning of several content creators from its platform. The company claimed they'd targeted the accounts for violating service terms, but Harris insisted it was clearly due to political bias by leftists.[72] Not long after, psychologist Jordan Peterson and comedian and podcaster Dave Rubin deleted their Patreon accounts as well, citing political censorship.[73] Rubin called out "progressives" for abandoning the principles of tolerance and liberty, including religious liberty, arguing that much of the left is no longer progressive but regressive. "If you're black, or female, or Muslim, or Hispanic, or a member of any other minority group," Rubin declared, "you're judged differently than the most evil of all things: a white, Christian male. The regressive left ranks minority groups in a pecking order to compete in a kind of 'Oppression Olympics.' Gold medal goes to the most offended."

Rubin shared that though he is a married gay man, he strongly opposes the government forcing Christian bakers, photographers, and florists to act against their religious beliefs. He is pro-choice but opposes the government forcing Catholic nuns to violate their faith and pay for abortion. "Today's progressivism has become a faux-moral movement, hurling charges of racism, bigotry, xenophobia, homophobia, Islamophobia and a slew of other meaningless buzzwords at anyone they disagree with," said Rubin. ". . . This isn't the recipe for a free society, it's a recipe for authoritarianism."[74] We'll examine the authoritarianism of the left, which goes hand in hand with its intolerance, in the next chapter.

CHAPTER ELEVEN

Leftist Authoritarianism: Assaults on the System

A LOGICAL LINE

The left's authoritarian impulse goes hand in hand with its dogmatic ideology. Leftists are so certain their philosophy is the sole correct moral viewpoint that no other views are accorded the slightest respect. With this outlook, it doesn't take much to rationalize the use of force to foist their beliefs on the entire country.

Take "climate change" for instance. Progressives claim there is a scientific consensus on man-made global warming—the science is settled. They manipulate facts, data, statistics, computer models, and surveys to support that conclusion, disseminate it with the fervor of Soviet propagandists, and label dissenters "climate deniers," thus likening them to neo-Nazi Holocaust deniers. Though they claim to be the sentinels of science, which they've elevated to an idol, they bastardize the scientific method by declaring that their views are irreversibly established.

Their arrogance blinds them to the possibility of human error and reversals in so-called "settled science." Just consider how the scientific experts tell us one year to avoid drinking coffee and promote it virtually as an elixir the next. They tell us for decades the proper food pyramid is etched in stone, then wake up one day and declare, "Never mind." One day we can't use enough sunscreen, then we're told that overuse can cause vitamin D deficiency. Top authorities touted the enormous health benefits of drinking red wine, then pointed to new studies showing health risks in any alcohol consumption at all. There are countless other examples, from eggs, to red meats, to fatty foods in general, to the physical activities of walking and standing. Settled science just can't make up its mind.[1]

As they indoctrinate and intimidate people into believing their "climate science," leftists seek to impose rules so comprehensive and draconian that the full force of the federal government is needed to enforce compliance. Ultimately, only a consolidated world government is adequate for the task, but until that is more feasible, they concentrate their efforts on top-down federal controls. As previously discussed, the Green New Deal is a textbook example of their *modus operandi*—work the public into a frenzy about a supposed crisis, then demand that the government exert control over vast, new areas of our lives in exchange for saving us from ourselves.

There is a logical connection between the leftists' absolute moral certainty on climate change, gender ideology, socialism, and other issues and their quest for absolute governmental power to effectuate remedial action—extremism begets extremism. It is no exaggeration to call it "absolute moral certainty," because nothing short of that explains their intolerance of opposing views and their mania for suppressing the free speech and religious freedoms of dissenters—from college campuses, to federal funding of abortion, to the bullying of bakers and florists.

As we've seen, the left is particularly vicious in attacking women and minorities who stray from its ideological reservation. In a surreal twist, these dissidents are de facto stripped of their minority status. Since black conservatives reject the left's patronizing approach to African-American issues, they are virtually cast out of their race by arrogant white leftists. Nary a leftist will defend the "Uncle Toms," though their skin color remains the same hue it always was.

The leftists' passion is not for minorities, women, or the downtrodden, but for their ideology, which seeks radical transformation of the existing order. Women, minorities, and the poor are convenient props, ripe for exploitation to advance their cause. Sometimes they are willing to be patient and play the long game, working for decades to achieve their goal, if necessary, such as their systematic infiltration of academia or the federal government's control over public education. Other times, they operate with revolutionary fervor—manufacturing a crisis and moving with dizzying speed to force complete and immediate transformation.

They approach most issues with equal certainty and zeal. Theirs is the only legitimate position, so all opposition must be silenced in proceeding to the mandated, top-down solution. Often superficially appealing, their causes are always billed as urgent. Remember their passion for the homeless? Why do we hear so little from Democrats on the issue now, when homelessness is rising sharply in deep-blue states like California and in other major cities under Democratic control?[2]

How about healthcare? The Clintons started the modern drumbeat for socialized medicine by repeating the misleading statistic that there were 40 million medically uninsured Americans, who they falsely depicted as having no access to healthcare. They left unmentioned, of course, that it was governmental intermeddling that caused skyrocketing healthcare costs and associated problems in the first place. Obama eventually took the baton from the Clintons, with their failed healthcare proposal, and proceeded at warp speed to further socialize medicine through Obamacare with the thinly disguised goal of achieving a single-payer system as soon as practicable.

Abortion is another example. The left created a perceived crisis of back-alley abortions until the Supreme Court legislated federal abortion rights. Using clever semantics, abortion advocates pretended to be proponents of "choice" when politically expedient, but many have come out of the closet to support outright infanticide today, as we'll discuss in a later chapter. Same with same-sex marriage—as we will discuss in chapter thirteen, after dozens of states banned same-sex marriage through state constitutional amendments, activists turned to the Supreme Court to mandate the recognition of same-sex marriage everywhere. In an instant, the American people were deprived of any say in the issue. And immediately thereafter, the left turned the heat up on their gender identity agenda. These are such front-burner issues today that others must take a back seat until the culture has been sufficiently bludgeoned into submission.

Political liberty diminishes when economic liberty shrinks—and the left understands that. Their drive to establish federal control over the economy necessitates a smaller sphere of personal freedom. With healthcare, for example, it would be impossible for the government to commandeer one-sixth of the economy without exercising enormous control over people's everyday lives. The Medicare for All Act, as previously noted, would afford them that control, as it would abolish almost all private healthcare plans, including employer-based plans, and impose complete federal control over Americans' healthcare.[3]

SWEATING THE SMALL STUFF

Leftists in local governments are every bit as authoritarian as those in federal government. They are forever trying to force their values on people and control their lifestyles, from what size sodas we can drink to the types of foods we eat. As one of a thousand examples, New York City mayor Bill de Blasio announced in March 2019 that "Meatless Monday," a program serving only vegetarian menus, would be expanded to all New York City public schools beginning in the 2019–2020 school year. "Cutting back on meat a little will improve New Yorkers' health and reduce greenhouse gas emissions," said de Blasio. "We're expanding Meatless Mondays to all public schools to keep our lunch and planet green for generations to come."[4]

You have to wonder if these progressives really believe their own bilge or are just intoxicated by the rush of virtue-signaling euphoria. Being forced to eat a vegetarian lunch on Mondays would not improve the health of a single student or have any effect whatsoever on the earth's climate. The only impact it would have is to deny liberty to those affected. Apparently, the sanctimonious mayor learned nothing from his predecessor Michael Bloomberg's boneheaded and unconstitutional crusade to limit sales of sugary drinks.[5]

One of the latest existential threats to society, apparently, is the menace of plastic straws. California enacted a law that prohibits full-service restaurants from giving them to customers unless they request them. But the biggest offenders—fast-food restaurants—are exempt. Of course they are. Meanwhile Seattle, Washington, D.C., and other cities have outright banned the use of plastic straws, a move that was also proposed by Britain's supposedly conservative former prime minister, Theresa May.[6] This is painfully ridiculous. Once again, the law creates no actual benefit—the *New York Post* reports there is no serious research warranting these bans, and even the bans' proponents admit they're more about making a statement than reducing plastic usage.[7] It's also curious that plastic straws are now a worldwide threat, considering not long ago plastic bags were touted as an environmentally sensitive alternative to paper bags. It seems the bottom line is that both paper and plastic are bad, and the left will limit your access to both.

A SEDUCTIVE MORAL CAUSE OOZING WITH URGENCY

Conservatives often say the left is unpatriotic because of its constant harping against the United States as founded and its push to cede greater control to global entities. The leftist ideology is antithetical to our founding principles, at the core of which is liberty. There is no trace left today of the civil libertarianism leftists once claimed to champion. Yet they falsely paint conservatives as authoritarian, especially during the Trump presidency, despite realizing that conservatives favor smaller, less intrusive government and greater individual liberties. The left invokes abortion as an example of conservatives' authoritarian tendencies, though that's an Orwellian argument that overlooks the government's proper, constitutional role to protect lives and our animating motivation of protecting the innocent unborn.

Trump has the persona of a business executive, but he's no authoritarian president. He champions the free market and presided over criminal justice reform. Even his occasional implementation of tariffs on international trade is more a tactic for rectifying unfair trade deals than a function of some philosophical opposition to free trade. The left, by contrast, is dedicated to expanding government to impose their ideas on the people, though they always find a seductive moral cause oozing with sufficient urgency to justify government encroachments on our liberties.

It's not that a majority of rank-and-file Democrats are part of a sophisticated conspiracy to upend the established order in the United States, though leading activists, academics, and many Democratic Party leaders do have such intentions. Many left-leaning Americans, especially younger ones, don't remotely understand some of the ideas they support, such as socialism, and what their implementation would really mean. They are simply caught up in promoting a "noble" cause. They serve as foot soldiers for policies that produce results exactly opposite of their stated intention and ultimately lead to impoverishment, slavery, and tyranny. Imbued with a sanctimonious sense of self-worth, they look down on their political opponents and are stubbornly impervious to reason.

Sometimes Democratic officials grossly abuse their power to advance their agendas and chill dissent. When a piece in the *New Yorker* accused former Fox executive Ken LaCorte of spiking the Stormy Daniels story to protect Trump, some House Democrats demanded to know why Fox News didn't rat out Trump prior to the 2016 election. LaCorte adamantly denied the story, insisting it lacked corroboration and that Fox was just exercising responsible journalistic practices, as did other outlets. But House Oversight Committee chairman Elijah Cummings demanded that a former Fox reporter produce documents about Trump's alleged affairs, reportedly seeking information that could be used to review Fox's editorial decisions.[8] What's almost as ominous about Cummings's attempt to oversee the conservative media is the left's myopic fantasy that Fox is more a threat to political liberty than the cadre of leftist mainstream media outlets.

"THE ADMINISTRATIVE STATE IS NOT SIMPLY UNCONSTITUTIONAL; IT IS ANTI-CONSTITUTIONAL"

The left seeks to undermine freedom as understood by the framers, who sought to establish a government that maximizes personal liberties. The government was to be just powerful enough to establish and maintain civil society under the rule of law and to protect the people from domestic and foreign threats, but not strong enough to quash the people's liberty.

The left's increasingly authoritarian bent, however, threatens our founding principles. To protect individual liberties, the framers incorporated limitations on government power in our constitutional framework. They divided power between the national, state, and local governments pursuant to the doctrine of federalism; adopted the Bill of Rights to guarantee specific individual liberties; and granted Congress enumerated powers. They separated federal power among three branches of government, each of which would operate as a check on the overreaches and usurpations of the others. In *The Federalist* No. 47, James Madison wrote, "The accumulation of all powers, legislative, executive, and judiciary, in the same hands, whether of one, a few, or many, and whether hereditary, selfappointed, or elective, may justly be pronounced the very definition of tyranny."

The age-old doctrine that prohibits undue delegation of powers by the legislative branch—based on the framers' vision of government by consent of the governed—has eroded with the expansion of the administrative state. Congress has increasingly abdicated its authority to administrative agencies, often by enacting skeletal laws with the meat to be provided by agencies, such as with Obamacare. The agencies frequently overreach, as when the U.S. Department of Health and Human Services seeks to compel religious organizations to provide and subsidize birth control or when the Environmental Protection Agency exerts authority over private land under the Clean Water Act.[9]

Leftists, despite their professed fealty to "democracy," have long advocated delegating enormous powers to the vast administrative state. One major reason the people elected Trump was to wrest control from this unaccountable "branch" of government and return it to the people. Trump has honored his mandate by repealing administrative regulations at a record pace, bit by bit restoring the sovereignty of the American people—the exact opposite of the actions of a tyrannical dictator.

The separation-of-powers doctrine has steadily eroded, with certain branches usurping the power of others or delegating power they should retain. The proliferation of the administrative state has also greatly diminished the separation of powers. "The administrative state is not simply unconstitutional; it is anti-constitutional," writes William Turton. "In its structure and operation, it represents a system of government that cannot be reconciled with constitutional government. In effect, the modern administrative state destroys the separation of powers by uniting all the powers of government in its hands."[10]

This directly contradicts the Constitution's design. Article I, Section 1 of the Constitution provides, "All legislative powers herein granted shall be vested in a Congress of the United States, which shall consist of a Senate and House of Representatives." Article II, Section 1 provides, "The executive power shall be vested in a President of the United States of America." Article III, Section 1 provides, "The judicial power of the United States, shall be vested in one supreme Court, and in such inferior Courts as the Congress may from time to time ordain and establish."

America's administrative state was spawned by the Administrative Procedure Act of 1946 (APA), which resulted in major delegations of legislative powers to executive agencies manned by unelected and unaccountable bureaucrats. The APA established guidelines for the rulemaking power of administrative agencies. The courts' review of actions and rulemaking by the agencies is limited. Only if an agency acts arbitrarily and capriciously or beyond the scope of its authority can the courts strike down the offending rules or regulations.

Over time, through legislative negligence or apathy and the power-grabbing nature of these agencies, power has increasingly shifted from the legislative branch to administrative agencies. Though they are in the executive branch, they have often crippled the president's executive authority. When conservatives refer to the "deep state" today, they are not just referring to the coordinated effort of establishment politicians to take down President Trump but also to the entrenched bureaucracy in the plethora of administrative agencies, which are often led and staffed by career leftists hell-bent on advancing their agenda with as little oversight or accountability as possible.

Most administrative rules are never challenged, and even when they are the courts will often defer to the agency's discretion under the "arbitrary and capricious" standard, which means that increasing power is wielded by this unelected bureaucracy instead of by the people's duly elected representatives in Congress. The EPA's issuance of carbon emission standards is another example, as they dramatically impact consumers, contrary to the will of the people. This vast administrative state is eroding America's constitutional order by replacing representative democracy with rule by unelected "experts."[11]

WINNING AT ANY COST

The framers believed in natural rights—that our rights derive from God, not government, and are therefore unalienable. The Constitution and Bill of Rights codify this foundational principle. Progressives effectively reject the notion of natural rights, believing our rights derive from the state—a principle that underlies their efforts to make citizens dependent on government. Just as progressives believe that all revenues are the property of the government and income producers are entitled only to that portion the government, in its beneficence, decides not to tax, they believe the people have only those rights that government confers on them. It's a radical inversion of the social compact the framers envisioned and established. Over the years, this shift in understanding has resulted in an assault on limited government and the expansion of the state.

Above all, progressives intend to advance their agenda and nothing, including the Constitution, shall impede their efforts. If they can't get a majority in Congress to enact their policies, they turn to activist courts, lawless executive orders, or administrative rules and regulations. If these don't work, they'll seek to circumvent constitutional provisions with end-around remedies in the various states, such as efforts to neuter the Electoral College indirectly which we will examine below.

On a more basic level—elections—they'll interfere with the voting process by suppressing votes, enabling voter fraud, and divining favorable votes from hanging chads—all while accusing Republicans of doing the very things they're doing. They oppose voter ID laws on the specious and patronizing ground that it's racist to require African Americans to furnish identification at polling places. Yet a recent study by the National Bureau of Economic Research confirms that voter ID laws don't suppress election turnout.[12] Upon losing the 2000 presidential election,

Democrats employed an army of lawyers to confuse the system and reverse the results through an intricate scheme of deceit. When the Supreme Court put an end to their charade, they accused Republicans of stealing the election that they had tried, unsuccessfully, to steal themselves. Similarly, when gobsmacked by Trump's election, Democrats tried to force him from office through false allegations that he colluded with Russia to steal the election. All the while, they were trying to steal the election themselves.

Opposing voter ID laws was just the beginning of the left's ongoing assault against the integrity of ballots. "A lot of you know about voter ID," said former Justice Department lawyer J. Christian Adams. "But that's yesterday's issue and it is 10 years old. Voter ID is not the solution; the left has moved on.... The next battle space is alien registration," which involves illegal immigrants acquiring driver's licenses that enable them to become registered voters.[13] This concern about noncitizens voting is no mere theoretical problem. For example, Texas attorney general Ken Paxton announced that some 95,000 non–U.S. citizens were registered to vote in his state and almost 58,000 of them had voted in one or more Texas elections. The *New York Times* spuriously downplayed this, saying that even if all these noncitizens had voted they would have represented only 0.69 percent of the total votes cast. "That's one way to put it—if you want to obscure the significance of 58,000 fraudulent votes!" writes Margot Cleveland. "After all, George W. Bush defeated Al Gore in Florida by a mere 537 votes to become our 43rd president."[14]

A CONSTITUTIONAL REPUBLIC OR MOB RULE?

In January 2019, Democratic congressman Steve Cohen introduced a bill to eliminate the Electoral College and provide for the direct election of the president and vice president. It's certainly any congressman's prerogative to propose a bill to start the constitutional amendment process, but Cohen knew he couldn't pull that off, so he attempted an end run with a National Popular Vote (NPV) bill. This pernicious measure would call upon states to sign a contract agreeing to pledge their presidential electors to the winner of the national popular vote rather than the winner of their state's popular vote. If all states honored this dubious commitment, all presidential elections would be unanimous because every state would have to pledge its electors to the winner of the national popular vote, meaning all 535 electors would go to the winner. In addition to this being a shameless fraud on the constitutional system, does anyone believe that deep-blue states would honor their "contractual" obligations if a Republican—let's say, Donald Trump—won the national popular vote?

Such an arrangement would diminish the sovereignty of the states under the current, decentralized system of fifty-one separate elections (including the District of Columbia, which is governed by its own separate laws). Under the present system, only the voters of a certain state can choose the electors for that state. Under the NPV, that would change. The NPV could also lead to the centralization of voting rules, reducing safeguards that protect the integrity of the election process, such as laws concerning voter registration, early voting, absentee ballots, the voting of felons, election contests, and recounts—most or all of which are governed by state law. Obviously, the NPV would also result in candidates prioritizing urban areas over rural ones—a primary concern that led the founders to devise the Electoral College.[15]

The clear impetus behind the NPV is that Democrats believe it would help them win more elections than they do with the Electoral College. They're showing contempt for the fundamental structure of our government, which no longer serves their political interests. The Electoral College system has effectuated the framers' intent to check the potential tyranny of the majority by rejecting the election of presidents by direct or popular vote. The system has reduced voter fraud, promoted coalition building, and empowered small as well as large states.

As opponents of direct democracy, the framers created a constitutional republic—and their wisdom has been vindicated, especially if one compares the American Revolution to the French Revolution, which led to frenzied mob rule and eventually the guillotine, a device that was ultimately used on some of the revolutionaries themselves.

The framers believed that a constitutional republic would provide greater stability by insulating the government from mob rule by passion-inflamed citizens. Today's Democratic leadership seeks to weaken those safeguards through a seductive message that appeals to voters' emotions. "Most of the Founding Fathers believed that a diffuse democracy would weaken the ability of politicians to scaremonger and rely on emotional appeals to take power," writes columnist David Harsanyi. ". . . Democrats agree, which is why they want to scrap the system.... Democrats prefer a system in which politicians who promise the most free stuff to the largest number of people win. Because they can't admit it, we have to wrestle with preposterous arguments in favor of overturning the Electoral College. The most absurd is the notion that in a direct democracy, every vote 'counts.'"[16]

The left, with its *1984*-style penchant for erasing history, is distorting the legacy of the Electoral College. For example, CNN fraudulently intimated that James Madison, the Father of the Constitution, opposed the system when he was instrumental in creating it. CNN has also suggested that the Electoral College was created to perpetuate slavery, a notion that has been thoroughly discredited by history professor Allen Guelzo. Among other points, Guelzo notes that the Electoral College played a crucial role in *ending* slavery, since it allowed Abraham Lincoln to become president after winning 40 percent of the popular vote. Guelzo further offers this ringing defense of the founders' brilliant presidential election system:

> The Electoral College was designed by the framers deliberately, like the rest of the Constitution, to counteract the worst human impulses and protect the nation from the dangers inherent in democracy. The Electoral College is neither antiquated nor toxic; it is an underappreciated institution that helps preserve our constitutional system, and it deserves a full-throated defense.... This is, after all, a constitutional republic, and even the most casual reader of the Constitution cannot fail to notice that the Electoral College is the only method specified by that document for selecting the president of the United States. For all the reverence paid to the popular vote in presidential elections, the Constitution says not a word about holding a popular vote for presidents.[17]

Though the system is not purely democratic, it ensures that the government reflects the will of the people, who determine the states' electoral votes.

OTHER DEMOCRATIC SCHEMES TO STEAL POWER

Democrats are also looking at extra-constitutional gambits to reduce the voting age and pack the Supreme Court. In March 2019, a majority of House Democrats voted to lower the federal voting age from eighteen to sixteen. House Speaker Nancy Pelosi said that the measure would stimulate voter engagement and students' interest in politics. "I myself have always been for lowering the voting age to 16," said Pelosi. "I think it's really important to capture kids when they're in high school, when they're interested in all of this, when they're learning about government, to be able to vote."[18]

Pelosi's offhand remark about capturing kids has an ominous ring. Prudent adults surely don't believe children of that age possess the wisdom to vote, but calculating adults realize they can be manipulated. After all, the utopian, compassionate-sounding Democratic message seductively appeals to immature minds ripe for indoctrination. This illustrates the stark difference between knowledge and wisdom.

The sudden embrace of this proposal by the Democratic Speaker of the House is jarring. Just a few years ago only one member of Congress expressed serious interest in this idea. But Massachusetts congresswoman Ayanna Pressley then took up the cause, citing teenage activists who pushed gun control and making spurious comparisons with driver's licenses. When Pressley introduced it in 2019 as an amendment to the For the People Act,[19] lowering the voting age to sixteen garnered 126 votes, including 125 Democrats.[20] It is inconceivable that even liberal Democrats truly believe it is prudent to let sixteen-year-old kids vote—unless you define as prudent anything that increases Democrats' chances of winning. Yet a majority of them supported the amendment. The common thread in all these system-altering proposals is that they are calculated to enhance Democrats' election prospects. They reject timeworn wisdom in pursuit of political power—a choice with ominous consequences.

The For the People Act is Nancy Pelosi's signature bill. It would overhaul federal election laws to micromanage the election process now administered by the states and centralize the process to favor Democrats. The Heritage Foundation says the bill would interfere "with the ability of states and their citizens to determine qualifications for voters, to ensure the accuracy of voter registration rolls, to secure the integrity of elections, to participate in the political process, and to determine the district boundary lines for electing their representatives."

The law would allow people to vote without an ID if they sign a statement averring their identity. It would expand regulation and government censorship of campaigns and political activity and speech, and it would require states to allow felons to vote—a proposal several pandering Democratic presidential candidates, such as Kamala Harris, have said they would support.[21] It would prevent election officials from checking the eligibility and qualifications of voters and removing ineligible voters. It would degrade the accuracy of registration lists by automatically registering people from state databases, including large numbers of ineligible voters and noncitizens. It would facilitate voter fraud by mandating same-day voter registration, giving election officials insufficient time to verify the accuracy of the registration information.[22]

Despite all this, the bill passed the House 234 to 193. The website American Commitment explains in lay terms what the bill would do if passed into law. It would:

- ★ use YOUR tax dollars to support political candidates you don't agree with;
- ★ regulate speech that mentions a federal candidate or elected official at any time;
- ★ regulate the online speech of American citizens;
- ★ end the long-standing parity in the campaign finance law between corporations and unions;
- ★ turn the Federal Election Commission from a balanced board of three Republicans and three Democrats into a partisan commission with a 3-2 majority;
- ★ mandate that all states adopt same day voter registration, automatic voter registration, no-excuse absentee voting, and other provisions that undermine election integrity;
- ★ mandate that all states adopt redistricting commissions that take the power to draw congressional districts away from our elected state officials and give it to unelected bureaucrats;
- ★ declare that Congress supports DC statehood.[23]

In short, it's a glorified Democratic power grab. "The Democrats intend to save 'democracy' by putting themselves in charge of elections," writes Jarrett Stepman of the *Daily Signal*.[24] Even the left-leaning ACLU has slammed the bill as unconstitutional, saying it would gravely damage the First Amendment. "[It] will have the effect of harming our public discourse by silencing necessary voices that would otherwise speak out about the public issues of the day," writes the ACLU's national political director and legislative counsel.[25]

On court-packing, three current or former Democratic presidential candidates—Kamala Harris, Kirsten Gillibrand, and Elizabeth Warren—say they'd be open to adding judges to the Supreme Court, while Senator Cory Booker says he supports term limits for Supreme Court justices.[26] South Bend, Indiana, mayor Pete Buttigieg, another Democratic presidential candidate, favors expanding the bench from nine to fifteen justices. The current proposal is that each party would pick five justices and those ten justices would pick the remaining five. This would blatantly violate the Constitution, which provides that the president nominates the justices with the advice and consent of the Senate. But once again, constitutional niceties have to take a back seat to the Democrats' political calculations—they are advancing this proposal in fear of a sustained conservative majority on the Court.

Another proposal, which has been endorsed by all Democratic presidential candidates, is statehood for Washington, D.C. As the Constitution requires a separate capital district, which could not be changed absent a constitutional amendment, this proposal is another clever plot to circumvent the system by shrinking the district to the small area surrounding the White House, the Capitol Building, and the National Mall, with the remaining area constituting a new, heavily Democratic state.

Yet another Democratic attempt to game the vote is evident in the census controversy mentioned earlier. When President Trump requested that the 2020 U.S. Census include a citizenship question, Democrats objected, saying it would make immigrants less likely to respond. They also raised privacy concerns—as if any U.S. citizen would have a reasonable expectation of privacy about his citizenship status. Democrats hope to have illegals and noncitizens counted because states' electoral votes and some federal funding are determined by their population, and they believe counting illegal aliens would mean more electoral votes apportioned to blue states and those trending blue. But with a citizenship question included, illegal immigrants may not respond, which would have the opposite effect.[27]

"This is a craven attack on our democracy and a transparent attempt to intimidate immigrant communities," said DNC chairman Tom Perez. "The census is a constitutionally-mandated count of all U.S. residents, not a political tool for Donald Trump to push his agenda and disempower Latinos and other people of color."[28] There you have it in plain prose. The leader of the Democratic Party wants to empower illegal immigrants in the name of "our democracy."

Some other left-wing proposals are bizarre and, if taken seriously, disturbing. Professor Eric W. Orts of the Wharton School of the University of Pennsylvania has suggested thwarting the ironclad provision in the Constitution guaranteeing that each state shall have two senators. Instead, states would be given a number of senators equal to their percentage of the nation's population, so that California, for example, would have twelve.[29] How convenient. It's a stunning coincidence, no doubt, that it would make the Senate dramatically bluer overnight.

JUDICIAL ACTIVISM

For decades, the left has displayed its authoritarian impulse in supporting and practicing judicial activism to advance policies it cannot secure through legislation. In the Trump era, judicial activism occurs as it has under previous presidents. For example, a federal judge in New York struck down President Trump's above referenced attempt to place a citizenship question on the census form, holding it was an arbitrary and capricious rule.[30]

But judicial activism during the Trump presidency has sometimes occurred in an alarmingly more expansive form. When courts thwarted Trump's lawfully issued administrative rules allowing employers and universities to cease providing insurance coverage for birth control, a federal court in Pennsylvania didn't just block the rule locally but applied its injunction nationally. This was after another ambitious injunction from a California judge blocked the rules in thirteen states and the District of Columbia. As usual, the left characterized the courts' rulings as a vindication of people's rights—without expressing the slightest concern about the courts' overreach. "It is a good day when a court stops this administration from sanctioning discrimination under the guise of religion or morality," said the ACLU. "We applaud the order to enjoin the enforcement of these discriminatory rules."[31] So a rule exempting entities from being compelled to violate their consciences is discriminatory and a fraudulent invocation of religion or morality? There's no end to the left's distortions—not to mention its assaults on the Constitution.

This Pennsylvania example is not an isolated case. The left has essentially weaponized universal injunctions to empower just one of the nation's six hundred federal district judges hearing a case involving specific litigants to block the president from enforcing or implementing a law, regulation, or executive policy nationwide. This is a monumental usurpation of power by a tiny fraction of the judiciary that can cripple action by the executive or legislative branches. It has been employed from the travel ban to DACA to the issue of transgenders serving in the military. Observers note this could have especially dangerous foreign policy implications, as a single judge could substitute his judgment for that of the commander in chief.

Unheard of for the first 175 years of the Republic, such nationwide injunctions were used twenty-two times in the first two years of the Trump administration, though Trump's predecessors were not stymied so frequently. Congressman Bob Goodlatte introduced the Injunctive Authority Clarification Act of 2018 to prohibit the issuance of national injunctions except in certain specified situations, but the bill did not advance through Congress.[32]

Judicial activism is almost exclusively the province of the left, though leftists have distorted the term to argue that conservatives are equally guilty of the practice. Judicial invalidation of a law on constitutional grounds is not judicial activism. That judicial prerogative has been enshrined in constitutional jurisprudence since *Marbury v. Madison* in 1803, which held, "It is emphatically the province and duty of the judicial department to say what the law is."[33] Judicial activism occurs when judges rewrite laws based on their policy preferences rather than on constitutional grounds, often twisting the plain meaning of constitutional provisions to pretend there is a constitutional basis for their decisions. It happens when judges overturn or uphold laws on specious constitutional grounds in order to achieve a desired policy result.[34]

If the Supreme Court eventually strikes down the landmark abortion case of *Roe v. Wade*, for example, the Orwellian left will decry "conservative judicial activism." But while *Roe* has been the law of the land for almost fifty years, it was never good law because the court manufactured constitutional provisions (emanations and penumbras). If the court finally invalidated the law, it would restore sound constitutional principles—a reversal of a former court's judicial activism, not judicial activism itself. Yes, the principle of *stare decisis* requires deference to long-established precedent, but it doesn't bind future courts to legal fictions. That means nothing to leftists, however. Senator Kirsten Gillibrand flatly said that pro-life supporters should not be judges and compared their beliefs to "racism,"[35] accusing them of being "too backward looking."[36]

FAIR-WEATHER RESPECTERS OF THE CONSTITUTION

One creative scheme to tilt the elections to the Democrats involved New Jersey legislators attempting to remove President Trump's name from their state's ballot through legislation requiring presidential and vice-presidential candidates to disclose their federal income tax returns.[37] California governor Gavin Newsom signed into law a similar bill, though it would only keep Trump's name off the primary ballot, not the general election ballot. Although Newsom's predecessor, Jerry Brown, was one of America's most liberal governors, even he had denounced the antidemocratic nature of such laws when he rejected one in 2017. Noting the measure's likely political intent and questionable constitutionality, he declared, "A qualified candidate's ability to appear on the ballot is fundamental to our democratic system. For that reason, I hesitate to start down a road that well might lead to an ever-escalating set of differing state requirements for presidential candidates."[38]

All these ploys would diminish the electoral power of law-respecting adult voters, thus showing the left's willingness to subordinate anything to its political agenda. Leftists' efforts to scrap the Electoral College disrespect the framers' healthy skepticism of pure democracy. Their comprehensive scheme to relax voting requirements on age, citizenship, criminal record, and proof of voter identification demonstrates their contempt for the rule of law. If illegal immigrants from the southern border tilted Republican, Democrats would likely be rabid border enforcement fanatics.[39] Nothing is sacred for the tradition-scoffing Democratic Party, so structural changes to our constitutional and electoral systems are just another day at the office.

If Democrats were champions of democracy as they would have us believe, they wouldn't support measures designed to undermine it by relaxing basic voting requirements. They wouldn't be such staunch advocates of an activist judiciary, which constitutes an ongoing assault on the will of the people through their duly elected representatives. They also wouldn't support delegating vast powers to unelected, unaccountable administrative agencies. Democrats favor the Constitution's prescribed democratic features when they serve their political agenda and oppose them when they do not.

In an interview with the *Washington Post*, presidential candidate Beto O'Rourke admitted his cynical ambivalence about the Constitution. He asked whether "an empire like ours" with its expansive military presence and trade and security agreements around the world could "still be managed by the same principles that were set down 230-plus years ago."[40] It always amazes me that leftists don't seem to grasp that the Constitution is a document that establishes the structure of government rather than a super-code of detailed legislation governing every specific problem. Leftists resent that the Constitution restricts their ability to make sweeping changes that would shrink our liberties and so, like O'Rourke, they'll sometimes voice their frustration at its structural limitations.

What O'Rourke is really saying, as President Obama sometimes did in his candid moments, is that he wishes this annoying piece of paper didn't hinder the advancement of the glorious, utopian leftist agenda. If he had his druthers, he'd eliminate those parts of it that impede leftist social planners from acquiring further power. The framers provided methods for amending the Constitution, which are deliberately cumbersome. We should be grateful for this. Otherwise the individual liberties the Constitution guarantees would be even less secure. In the next chapter we'll see more proof of the left's authoritarian proclivities and its disturbing trend of censoring speech through private sector action and intimidation.

CHAPTER TWELVE

Leftist Authoritarianism Goes Private

"I'D LOVE TO BE ABLE TO REGULATE SPEECH"

Democratic congressman Ted Lieu, a leftist's leftist, conceded he'd like to suppress Americans' free speech. "I would love to be able to regulate the content of speech," Lieu told CNN after denying claims that Google does just that. "The First Amendment prevents me from doing so. And that's simply a function of the First Amendment. But I think over the long run, it's better that government does not regulate the content of speech." So, in his heart of hearts, he would like to suppress speech but accepts the constitutional prohibition against it. That's a lot different from saying, "I wish everyone would agree with my political beliefs." This is wishing he could force them to agree or shut up.

But Lieu went further, saying he'd have no problem with the private sector acting as a speech censor, which is troubling given the power and reach of social media megafirms. Having just defended Google against the charge of censorship, he proclaimed, "I would urge these private sector companies to regulate it themselves. But it's really nothing I believe government can do. And so that's been my position all along."[1] Lieu seems totally oblivious to the horrors of his authoritarian impulse.

HATE-FILLED LEFTIST FLASH MOBS

The day after the press first reported the manufactured scandal against the MAGA hat–wearing Covington Catholic students, Democratic congressman John Yarmuth tweeted, "I am calling for a total and complete shutdown of teenagers wearing MAGA hats until we can figure out what is going on. They seem to be poisoning young minds. The conduct we saw in this video is beyond appalling, but it didn't happen in a vacuum. This is a direct result of the racist hatred displayed by the President of the United States who, sadly, some mistake for a role model."[2]

This is another chilling illustration of the tyrannical leftist mind-set. Denouncing Trump supporters—half of all Americans—as hateful racists, a congressman advocates forcibly muzzling them due to false reports that a group of them acted improperly. How often do conservatives propose banning liberal speech or dress because they find it offensive? It is leftists who seek to suppress conservative speech, spuriously claiming it is hate speech that leads to violence. We saw this clearly when President Trump, on Twitter, juxtaposed an image of Congresswoman Ilhan Omar dismissively referring to the tragic events of 9/11 as "some people did something" with an image of the actual 9/11 attack. Posturing Democrats claimed Trump was inciting violence against Omar—and of course, they claimed it was racist.

AOC said Trump's criticism of Omar was "incitement of violence against a progressive woman of color." MSNBC's Chris Hayes tweeted, "The president is actively and willfully endangering the life of a member of Congress." Democratic presidential hopefuls Elizabeth Warren and Beto O'Rourke piled on with the same inflammatory message, as did Congressman Joe Kennedy III.[3] If this is considered an incitement to violence, Democrats have incited violence against Trump every day of his presidency. But it's absurd. This is how the left forms choruses—like flash mobs—to intimidate opponents and quash their free speech.

Omar's comment was ghastly, and it was perfectly appropriate for the president to expose the outrage.

For a real-life example of hateful speech, as opposed to the expression of an idea the left disputes, consider the left's vicious attack on Congressman Dan Crenshaw, a decorated Navy Seal who lost an eye in Afghanistan, for posting a video in which he criticized Omar's callousness. "It's terrorists who killed almost 3,000 Americans, we should talk about it that way. We should talk about it with deference," said Crenshaw. His comments unleashed a storm of vulgar abuse from the left. Talia Lavin, a former New York University journalism professor, called Crenshaw "captain sh*thead." Freelance writer Rob Rousseau wrote to Crenshaw, "You're deliberately lying about what [Omar] said you eyeless f*ck." Political cartoonist Eli Valley chimed in, "Wow, it's GOP-Nazi Party Terrorist Incitement Night on NBC." And Ryan Cooper of *The Week* called Crenshaw's comments "fascist propaganda."[4] Note that despite their vile condemnations of Crenshaw's innocuous comments, no one is suggesting these crude loudmouths be denied *their* First Amendment freedoms.

The thrust of the First Amendment's free-expression guarantees is to protect political speech, which wouldn't need protection if it were never controversial. Leftists' efforts to censor speech they dislike, carried to its logical conclusion, would mean that only one political ideology would be protected. It's a bit rich for the left to complain about the poisoning of young minds as leftists in academia, our public schools, the media, and Hollywood endlessly disseminate leftist bile.

There is no moral equivalence here. It is members of the left, not people in MAGA hats, who are threatening and attacking those who disagree with them. If they were intellectually honest, they would admit that liberals don't fear voicing their opinions in a college classroom or any other public place. Notice that Congressman Yarmuth is not the least bit reluctant to call President Trump a racist and hater because he knows he will suffer no consequences. Contrary to conventional wisdom, Trump exercises restraint by not reacting even more aggressively to the constant, baseless attacks leveled against him.

"THE VOICE OF RAW POWER... IS WHAT WE SHOULD FEAR THE MOST"

In December 2018, the Anti-Defamation League (ADL) bestowed its first "Courage Against Hate" award to Apple CEO Tim Cook because he had "championed inclusion and diversity at Apple, investing in educational opportunities for students of all ages and backgrounds, and ensuring Apple offices and stores are open and welcoming to everyone." This was an interesting tribute considering that Cook quickly declared, "We only have one message for those who seek to push hate, division, and violence: you have no place on our platforms, you have no home here."[5] Every person listening to Cook knew exactly what he meant, since the left defines "hate" as "positions the left disagrees with." And his statement squarely contradicts the lofty sentiments of the award presenters—because Apple isn't welcoming to everyone, only those who share its social and political views.

The First Amendment protects even noxious opinions, so Cook was on thin ice. Apple, like other social media entities, comes under the protective umbrella of Section 230 of the Communications Decency Act. This law exempts social media companies from liability for the content that users post on their platforms. Like phone companies, they are open to all contributors regardless of their views. Social media companies are not content providers—but when they censor participants' political views, that's precisely what they become. Despite warnings from Republicans that they risk losing their exemption if they continue in this mode, the tech giants arrogantly persist and deny discriminating against conservatives.

Leftists regard their views as sacrosanct and opposing ones as aberrant. They confuse their subjective notions of morality with objective truth. Cook displayed this attitude in accepting the ADL award. "My friends, if we can't be clear on moral questions like these, then we've got big problems," intoned Cook. "...I believe the most sacred thing that each of us is given is our judgment, our morality, our own innate desire to separate right from wrong. Choosing to set that responsibility aside at a moment of trial is a sin." Andrew Klavan finds these comments "chilling." "Only a man worth over 600-million dollars could spout such simplistic horse manure without someone telling him he's a chucklehead," writes Klavan. "Of course we all have an inner moral voice. Throughout the centuries, people in the sure and certain faith in that voice have set each other on fire for disagreeing with religious doctrines, loosed dogs on them for the color of their skin and gassed them to death because of their religious heritage. Each of these killers thought he was doing good." Klavan further notes that the question isn't whether people support "hate" but who gets to decide what constitutes hate and when it should be silenced.

That's exactly right. Cook was purportedly referring to anti-Semitism and white nationalism—repulsive sentiments, but the left often finds them where they don't exist and ignores them where they really are. The left believes "fascism" is a right-wing ideology, though it is decidedly left-wing, so when Cook self-righteously denounces fascism, he is clearly referring to the mainstream political views of Trump supporters. Leftists often set themselves up as ultimate moral arbiters whose judgment obviates First Amendment protections, which is arguably more dangerous to the fabric of society and our liberties than whatever tiny pockets of "white nationalism" exist. Klavan trenchantly summarizes the danger: "Tim Cook's is not the voice of morality, but the voice of raw power. It's that voice—not the voice of 'hate'—we should fear the most."[6]

Apple displayed its bias by reportedly removing from its platform the app "Inconvenient Facts," which countered climate alarmism. The app's content was based on the book *Inconvenient Facts: The Science That Al Gore Doesn't Want You to Know* by geologist Gregory Wrightstone. Noting that Al Gore is an Apple board member, Wrightstone claims many inferior pro–climate change apps are available on the app store, and that other apps are only rarely approved and later removed, as his was. "A key takeaway here is that Apple has a monopoly over iPhone apps and the Apple App Store is the only place to get them," said Wrightstone. "It appears that Apple has chosen to weaponize its control over purchasing apps to stifle science that doesn't conform to its politically correct notions."[7]

HUGE TEAMS ADJUST SEARCH RESULTS

Conservatives have good cause to complain about the liberal bias of social media giants Facebook, Google, Twitter, YouTube, and even Pinterest. For example, Twitter temporarily suspended the investigative journalism team Project Veritas for tweeting Pinterest internal communications in which an employee called Ben Shapiro a "white supremacist." Project Veritas also found that Pinterest removed Christian-related terms from auto-fill search functions and that it banned pro-life group Live Action's posts for a day because they may have "detrimental effects on health and public safety." Live Action's Lila Rose notes that they did not ban posts from abortion clinics, including ads for the abortion pill RU-486.[8]

One reporter's encounter with YouTube is also instructive. *Slate*'s April Glaser contacted YouTube to complain that too many anti-abortion videos surfaced when she used the search term "abortion." Afterward, she noticed a marked change. "Anti-abortion content meant to enrage or provoke viewers was no longer purely dominating the results," she said, "though they still looked very different from the generally more sober Google results."[9]

There is plenty of anecdotal evidence that YouTube, which is run by Google, manipulates search results. This contradicts the sworn congressional testimony of Google CEO Sundar Pichai that Google does not "manually intervene" on any particular search result. A leak from an anonymous Google engineer alleging that the term "abortion" was added to a "blacklist" file for "controversial YouTube queries" also casts doubt on Pichai's testimony. The engineer reportedly called the manipulation of search results on abortion a "smoking gun," confirming that the change occurred after the *Slate* reporter's inquiry.[10]

One Google employee in a leaked discussion thread said it "seems like we are pretty eager to cater our search results to the social and political agenda of left-wing journalists." While a Google spokesperson adamantly maintained that Google has never manipulated search results or content to promote a particular ideology, one participant in the leaked discussion confirmed Google maintains "huge teams" to adjust search results for subjects that are "prone to hyperbolic content, misleading information, and offensive content."[11] It is unsettling that Google's spokesperson actually believes banning or limiting "offensive content," which to leftists means conservative views, is not promoting a particular ideology. This is the same type of self-deception that induces mainstream media figures to believe they are unbiased journalists.

When the YouTube community posted its 2018 YouTube "Rewind" video, which was full of social justice messages, it received a record number of dislikes. The Gillette ad on toxic masculinity also racked up an enormous number of dislikes—some 1.3 million at one point, compared to 700,000 likes. As a result of these incidents and others, YouTube considered deleting its dislike button, claiming that "dislike mobs" descend on the platform to spread negativity.[12]

Google's skewed political climate has reached a comical extreme. When a company executive used the term "family" in a company-wide presentation about a children's product, employees objected that the statement implied families have children and was therefore homophobic. One female employee said, "It smacks of the 'family values' agenda by the right wing, which is absolutely homophobic by its very definition. It's important that we fix our charged language when we become aware of how exclusionary it actually is. As a straight person in a relationship, I find the term 'family' offensive because it excludes me and my boyfriend, having no children of our own."[13]

In light of these examples, it's unsurprising that Google worked hard to elect Hillary Clinton and that her loss to Trump caused a large-scale meltdown at the company. A leaked video showed Google was involved in targeted turnout operations designed to increase voter participation in Democratic areas in the 2016 election. One top Google employee referred to the operation as a "silent donation" to the Hillary Clinton campaign.[14] When Trump won, the company convened an all-hands meeting with despondent employees and executives. A video leaked to *Breitbart* showed Google's VP for Global Affairs Kent Walker trying to buck up his demoralized troops, insisting history was on their side and that they must work to ensure that populism and nationalism were just a historical "blip" and a "hiccup."[15] The *Daily Caller* further reports that Google employees debated whether to suppress *Daily Caller* articles and other conservative media in Google's search function after Trump's victory. Employees also allegedly sought to interfere with search results to help thwart Trump's travel ban.[16]

In another Project Veritas sting, a senior Google executive was caught on video apparently suggesting that Google try to prevent "the next Trump situation" in the 2020 election. "We all got screwed over in

2016, again it wasn't just us, it was, the people got screwed over, the news media got screwed over, like, everybody got screwed over so we've rapidly been like, what happened there and how do we prevent it from happening again," said Jen Gennai, Google's head of "responsible innovation."[17] Senator Ted Cruz grilled Google's UX director Maggie Stanphill about the Project Veritas revelations. Stanphill claimed she was aware of them but was too busy to review the matter. She said she didn't believe it is Google's job to ensure that someone like Trump never comes to power again. "Conservatives aren't stupid," comments Beth Baumann at *Townhall*. "We *know* our content is being suppressed. We *know* our thoughts and values threaten the Left's agenda. If it wasn't, they wouldn't feel the need to keep us from spreading our message."[18]

In a particularly alarming development, Dr. Robert Epstein, a psychologist and liberal Democrat who supported Hillary Clinton, testified to the Senate Judiciary Committee that Google generated a minimum of 2.6 million votes for Hillary Clinton in the 2016 election through deceptive manipulation of search results. He claimed that if big tech companies like Google and Facebook coordinate behind a certain candidate, they could influence up to 15 million votes.[19] Epstein's warnings should cause all Americans great concern.

A growing part of our political debate today occurs on Twitter, which conservatives have long believed discriminates against conservatives and conservative opinion. It's not much of an open question—*Vice News* reported in July 2018 that the platform had shadow banned (that is, limited the appearance in search results) numerous conservatives, including "[t]he Republican Party chair Ronna McDaniel, several conservative Republican congressmen, and Donald Trump Jr.'s spokesman."[20] After that story became public Twitter removed those shadow bans, but it has also outright ejected a number of conservatives from the platform, including Houston radio host Jesse Kelly. Senator Ben Sasse likened Kelly's expulsion to the de-platforming common on many college campuses.[21]

Other conservatives have abandoned Twitter amidst this pressure, including prominent columnist and blogger Glenn Reynolds, a.k.a. "Instapundit," who deactivated his account to protest the "crappy SJW types" who, he argued, are stifling free speech.[22] Likewise, conservative actor James Woods, who had amassed more than two million followers, left Twitter after being repeatedly suspended and censored. "The irony is, Twitter accused me of affecting the political process, when in fact, their banning of me is the truly egregious interference," Woods declared. "Because now, having your voice smothered is much more disturbing than having your vocal cords slit. If you want to kill my free speech, man up and slit my throat with a knife, don't smother me with a pillow."[23]

Twitter CEO Jack Dorsey denies that political ideology affects Twitter's decision-making process, "whether related to ranking content on our service or how we enforce our rules. We believe strongly in being impartial, and we strive to enforce our rules impartially." People aren't buying it. A Pew poll in June 2018 found that 72 percent of Americans believe social media firms censor certain views, and four times as many respondents believe such firms favor liberals over conservatives rather than the reverse.

Richard Hanania, a postdoctoral research fellow at Columbia University, researched the issue, and his findings "make it difficult to take claims of political neutrality seriously. Of twenty-two prominent, politically active individuals who are known to have been suspended since 2005 and who expressed a preference in the 2016 U.S. presidential election, twenty-one supported Donald Trump." Hanania argues that leftists' abusive internet behavior is unsurprising considering their uncivil and violent behavior off-line. "It is unthinkable that we would allow a telephone or electricity company to prevent those on one side of the political aisle from using its services. Why would we allow social media companies to do the same?"[24]

Senator Ted Cruz and other Republican lawmakers have blasted the bias of social media companies. At a Senate Judiciary Committee hearing on social media censorship, Cruz said he'd considered whether some big tech companies had committed antitrust violations, and he suggested removing their immunity from liability under the Communications Decency Act. "What makes the threat of political censorship so problematic is the lack of transparency, the invisibility, the ability for a handful of giant tech companies to decide if a particular speaker is disfavored," Cruz said.[25]

Indeed, the pushback against online censorship seems to be gaining steam. In late July 2019, the Department of Justice announced it would investigate "market-leading online platforms" for anticompetitive conduct and federal antitrust violations. The DOJ said it would address "widespread concerns" of "consumers, businesses, and entrepreneurs" concerning the practices of "search, social media, and some retail services." The *Washington Free Beacon* reports this investigation will run in addition to an existing antitrust investigation into Google.[26]

COLD CASE PC DETECTIVES

Sanctimonious leftists treat their own pronouncements as holy writ. No matter the cause, their message is righteous and compelling. All must align with their viewpoint or be chastised. In December 2018, the Monterey Bay Aquarium posted a photo of a sea otter and tweeted, "Abby is a thicc girl. What an absolute unit. She chonk. Look at the size of this lady. OH LAWD SHE COMIN. Another Internetism!" Responses were favorable to the humorous tweet, which provoked a lively discussion about otters. A group of pseudo-pious academics, however, was insulted that the aquarium fat-shamed the otter with "appropriative language." One person called the tweet "digital blackface." Another said it contributed to a "hostile environment" for minorities because organizations that are not run by blacks or focused on black audiences have no right to do such things.

The aquarium eventually surrendered and apologized. When some Twitter users insisted the apology was unnecessary, it replied, "As an organization that seeks to educate, we absolutely welcomed the perspective, information and open discussion. If we want people to listen to us, we have to be willing to listen to them."[27] Sounds wonderful, but this was pure bullying, and the aquarium obviously decided it wasn't worth the risk of resisting and getting into further PC hot water.

A willingness to listen is not the same as a duty to capitulate. The aquarium staff could have listened instead to the majority of people who scoffed at the manufactured controversy, but they knew there was no risk in bucking *them*. In the leftist PC world, the frequent call for "dialogue" and "national conversations," as we've observed, is loaded with PC meaning. These terms are code for, "You will be made to embrace the social justice warriors' message. If you don't, it's because you didn't listen." To disagree with leftists is, by definition, being unreasonable, as there is only one reasonable position on a given issue—theirs.

Fat-shaming seems to be the next faddish offense. British actress Jameela Jamil of *The Good Place* is on a crusade against this insidious malfeasance. When Avon released an ad saying, "Dimples are cute on your face (not on your thighs)," Jamil went ballistic. "And yet EVERYONE has dimples on their thighs, I do, you do, and the CLOWNS at @Avon_UK certainly do," she exclaimed. "Stop shaming women about age, gravity, and cellulite. They're inevitable, completely normal things. To make us fear them and try to 'fix' them, is to literally set us up for failure." Of course, Avon groveled with the mandatory, profusely apologetic tweet: "Hi Jameela, we intended this to be lighthearted and fun, but we realize we missed the mark. We've removed this messaging from all marketing materials. We support our community in loving their bodies and feeling confident in their own skin."[28]

Isn't Jamil taking this a bit too far by likening "fat-shaming" to hate speech? Jamil obviously doesn't think so, considering she launched an entire new company based on the idea. "I'm turning 'I Weigh' into a company, and one of our main goals is to work towards a policy change that means this way of talking about people's bodies is considered hate speech. Fat-phobia is real, it is pervasive and prevalent and is damaging the mental health of millions," she tweeted.[29]

The left is also now combing through history in search of people whose reputations and careers they can destroy for offensive statements they made years ago, even ones made in private. There is no such thing as a youthful indiscretion anymore. Conservative activist Kyle Kashuv learned this when Harvard University rescinded his admission because of racist posts he made on a private Google document when he was sixteen years old, even though Kashuv apologized and has never made any similar public comments.[30] It's clear that the left doesn't believe in forgiveness and redemption.

Leftists cannot even relax and enjoy a TV sitcom without hunting for some politically incorrect transgression. Some millennials watching *Friends* on Netflix are shocked by the storylines, which they regard as "transphobic," "homophobic," and "sexist," the *Independent* reports.[31] Similarly, writer Angelica Florio dissects thirteen jokes from the nineties

Seinfeld series that she now deems "super offensive." "Hopefully most people can agree that comedy, even 'edgy' comedy, doesn't need to alienate marginalized groups in order to make people laugh, though," writes Florio. "Thanks to more modern understandings of what political correctness entails—and why being PC is important—it's less common these days to find jokes like the offensive ones that often played out on *Seinfeld*."[32]

Here we go. The joy of being offended, like so many other privileges in the leftist world, is exclusive to certain groups. The implication is that all other groups can be freely offended and have no right to complain about it. Thus leftist late-night talk shows stridently target conservatives and routinely ridicule Christians with impunity. And, no, we don't all agree that political correctness is helpful. It is a weapon to intimidate people into silence for fear of saying the wrong thing and triggering the wrath of leftist speech enforcers.

Citing the popular *Seinfeld* episode "The Soup Nazi," which centers on an irritable soup salesman, Florio claims that because "groups of Neo-Nazis have become noticeably emboldened," it's no longer acceptable to use the term "Nazi." So humorless leftist scolds won't let us joke about Nazis, but they'll use the word freely to describe Trump supporters. Florio is also aghast at another episode in which a journalist believes Jerry and George are in a same-sex relationship. "Even if this same joke recurred in *Friends* years later, it's really not funny now," she writes. In another episode Jerry's neighbor has visiting Japanese businessmen sleeping in dresser drawers. "That just wouldn't fly now," chides Florio.

The lesson is that everyone must be uptight these days, lying in wait for the next offense. Even if you believe that most stereotypical humor is offensive, is it constructive for progressives to dredge up alleged past infractions as if they are cold case detectives? If leftists seek societal harmony as they claim, wouldn't it be better to let sleeping dogs lie? Or must everyone be made a social felon for past sins that may not have even been regarded as offensive at the time?

CLOSING YOUNG AMERICAN MINDS

Refreshingly, Dwayne "The Rock" Johnson is weary of the "snowflake generation." "So many good people fought for freedom and equality," he said, "but this generation are looking for reasons to be offended.... I don't have to agree with what somebody thinks, who they vote for, what they voted for, what they think, but I will back their right to say or believe it. That's democracy."[33]

The Rock better not utter something like that on university campuses, which have become ground zero for political intolerance. Egged on by leftist administrators and professors, radical students howl like wounded animals when exposed to any views outside the left-wing narrative. This humorless, oppressive mentality explains why Jerry Seinfeld no longer performs at colleges.[34] He says kids don't even understand the politically correct terms they throw around. "They just want to use these words: 'That's racist,' 'That's sexist,' 'That's prejudice,'" says Seinfeld. "They don't know what the hell they're talking about." Indeed, they project themselves as morally superior and glorify themselves as champions of persecuted people by harshly condemning others for alleged offenses against protected groups. This quest for public praise, far more than any desire to help disadvantaged people, explains the sanctimonious zealotry underlying the PC craze.

Progressive administrators, faculty, and students alike often work to silence conservative women in particular on campus. Congresswoman Donna Shalala, when president of the University of Miami, rejected the application of four female students to organize a campus conservative group. Having claimed the group was redundant, the school reversed its decision after receiving public criticism.

Karin Agness, writing for *Campus Reform*, describes five ways colleges silence conservative women. The first is requiring that student clubs be sponsored by a faculty member, which hampers conservative groups since the overwhelming majority of university professors are liberal. (Though the gross ideological imbalance of professors is undeniable, Education Secretary Betsy DeVos still came under attack from liberal professors for criticizing the disparity.)[35] Other methods used to intimidate and muzzle conservative women, according to Agness, are operating departments and women's centers that exclude conservative women, reporting on conservative groups unfairly in campus newspapers, attacking conservative women on social media, and protesting conservative speakers on campus.[36]

University campuses are supposed to be bastions of free and open academic inquiry. But leftists believe they are justified in denying conservatives a platform because, as noted, they deem conservative speech hate speech that leads to violence—a clever but deceptive tactic. In anticipation of Ben Shapiro's speech at Loyola Marymount University, Professor Nina Lozano tweeted, "Ben Shapiro espouses hate speech, and is linked to numerous hate groups. As an LMU Professor, I will be organizing protests, and alerting the media of LMU's decision to support hate speech—which is completely antithetical to our University Mission."[37] It is especially ironic that Lozano is a communications professor, while her tweet is riddled with misinformation. Shapiro doesn't espouse hate speech and is certainly linked to no hate groups. One can't say the same for the Berkeley radicals and local Antifa members who "protested" former *Breitbart* writer Milo Yiannopoulos's "hate speech" during his February 2017 campus appearance by setting fires, beating attendees, and vandalizing buildings.[38]

To prevent "hateful" speech, campus leftists establish speech codes, which are tools for suppressing dissent and ensuring that the monolithic liberal message is unchallenged. Some colleges have created free-speech zones for dissenting views—that they are deemed necessary illustrates the severity of the problem. Unless the entire campus is a free-speech zone, the university is assaulting the First Amendment. Other devices used to silence campus conservatives are safe spaces, which are areas where students are insulated from hearing speech that offends them; trigger warnings, which involve professors alerting students that subject matter the class is about to discuss might upset them; and warnings to avoid microaggressions, which are minor, perceived slights or insults that make students uncomfortable.[39]

Isn't it obvious that these concepts foster suspicion and distrust—the very things they are purportedly designed to prevent? Such hand-wringing discourages students' intellectual development and maturation process. Why should a university encourage kids to believe they're so vulnerable that they can't risk exposure to ideas that vary from the university's monolithically leftist message? This insanity has led to such incidents as Colorado State University students objecting to the use of student fees to bring conservative Dennis Prager to campus,[40] though students never seem to protest the funding of left-wing speakers. It's devastatingly ironic that universities are closing—and locking—young American minds.

The Foundation for Individual Rights in Education estimates that some 90 percent of colleges and universities restrict speech.[41] To combat this gross offense, in March 2019 President Trump signed an executive order requiring universities to certify they are protecting free speech as a condition to receiving federal grants through the Departments of Education, Health and Human Services, Defense, and others.[42]

"HE DOESN'T DESERVE TO BE LISTENED TO"

Sometimes even liberal professors are subject to PC wrath. Yale professors Nicholas and Erika Christakis presided over one of the school's undergraduate colleges, living among students and providing them residential guidance. When students complained that Yale administrators were advising them to avoid certain Halloween costumes, Erika emailed students encouraging everyone to lighten up. "This year, we seem afraid that college students are unable to decide how to dress themselves on Halloween," Erika wrote. "I don't wish to trivialize genuine concerns about cultural and personal representation, and other challenges to our lived experience in a plural community.... But...I wonder if we should reflect more transparently, as a community, on the consequences of an institutional (bureaucratic and administrative) exercise of implied control over college students." She noted the inequity and absurdity of imputing to students the intent to culturally appropriate—as opposed to simply fantasizing about a character whose outfit they were wearing. Faculty should trust students to work things out for themselves, she said—in other words, they should not treat students like a bunch of snowflakes.

If you've read this book up to this point, you can guess the reaction to Erika's advice—a group of disgruntled students tried to remove the couple from their residential positions and expel them from campus residency.[43] When Nicholas tried to explain their position, student radicals screamed and cursed at him.[44] One student told another, "Walk away, he doesn't deserve to be listened to." Another told Nicholas, "In your position as master, it is your job to create a place of comfort and home for the students who live in Silliman. You have not done that. By sending out that email, that goes against your position as master. Do you understand that?" Nicholas said he disagreed, at which point the student shouted, "Then why the f*** did you accept the position? Who the f*** hired you? You should step down!… It is not about creating an intellectual space.… It is about creating a home. Here. You are not doing that.… You should not sleep at night. You are disgusting."[45] It is amazing that students who feel so free to disrespect and insult a professor could claim they feel uncomfortable or threatened in that environment. Leftists are encouraging a generation of navel-gazing narcissists manifestly unconcerned about the feelings of anyone who rejects any part of their dogma or demands.

In a similar incident, Harvard University surrendered to a mob of student activists and fired law professor Ronald Sullivan from his position as faculty dean of Winthrop House, an undergraduate residence, because of his "trauma-inducing" decision to assist Harvey Weinstein's legal defense team.[46] Even this man with pristine liberal bona fides was crushed under the unforgiving torrent of political correctness. "Too bad Ivy League elitist bubbles have purged themselves of people with the backbone, integrity, and courage to end the madness," commented columnist Michelle Malkin.[47]

Speaking of charlatan snowflakes, Princeton University's American Whig-Cliosophic Society—touted as the university's elite debate club and the oldest debating union in the United States—withdrew a speaking invitation to conservative law professor Amy Wax one day before her scheduled appearance. Professor Wax thought the cancellation might be a hoax, given that she was to speak at a free-speech event and she was being disinvited for stating her opinion. Among the "controversial statements" leading to the cancellation was Wax's remark, "I've never seen a black person graduate at the top quarter of my class." Wax explained that she believed the black students in her classes were at a disadvantage because they had been admitted due to affirmative action policies at the University of Pennsylvania Law School where she taught.[48] How can a debate society produce the best debaters with such cowardice? Debate clubs often force students to argue positions they find contemptible. It is the nature of the beast. Shouldn't controversial statements motivate sharp students to challenge her views rather than censor them? It's a sad testament to the state of free speech on campuses that even debate societies can't handle a free exchange of ideas.

If debate clubs formed to promote debating skills can censor speech, why can't book festivals as well? We are, after all, in an era of leftist metaphorical book burning. The Tucson Festival of Books hosts panels of authors to discuss various subjects in their areas of expertise. According to a *RedState* report, no panel touching on political issues had any Trump-supporting (or even marginally Trump-supporting) participants.[49] This one-sided arrangement doesn't faze leftists. They expect it, and in fact, will protest if even one conservative appears. This disgrace is commonplace on university campuses.

According to leftists' twisted reasoning, activists are justified in suppressing speech and even engaging in violence to prohibit conservative discussions they contend could suppress speech or lead to violence. Let that sink in.

SACRIFICING EMPLOYEES AT THE PC ALTAR

The left also routinely attempts to censor conservative opinions and generate boycotts of conservative shows to discredit hosts and destroy their careers. "There is . . . pervasive evidence showing that left-wing activists are quite content using every tool at their disposal to silence influential voices on the right," writes Mark Hemingway.[50] Fellow leftists are happy to pile on, encouraging their brethren to join boycotts. "The Tucker Carlson advertiser boycott continues, and what's wrong with that?" asks columnist Michael Hiltzik. "Those unhappy with Carlson's brand of exclusionary white male power should keep the boycott threat alive—and they should be considering themselves to be operating in the American mainstream." Do you see? Because Carlson highlights the problems caused by illegal immigration, he's a racist.

Once again, liberals themselves are not necessarily immune to the left's attacks. Bill Maher is a reliably left-wing voice on HBO and a scathing critic of Republicans and President Trump. Yet Maher champions free speech and often denounces political boycotts, which sometimes puts him at odds with left-wing activists. When Maher criticized the anti-Israel Boycott, Divestment, and Sanctions movement endorsed by Rep. Rashida Tlaib, the congresswoman responded by suggesting her supporters boycott Maher's show.[51] So criticizing a boycott is now an egregious act that will get you boycotted.

Such Stalinist behavior pervades our society, including corporations, where employees are often assigned to sensitivity training for proper leftist indoctrination. For example, Starbucks closed more than 8,000 stores in May 2018 to train 175,000 employees and address implicit bias, promote inclusion, and help prevent discrimination—because an employee called the police on two black men who'd been denied permission to use the restroom in a franchise store in Philadelphia.[52] Apparently the men were not customers, and the employee believed the store did not allow people to remain in the store without ordering something.

Though some identified the employee as an "SJW feminist of the highest order," Starbucks CEO Howard Schultz threw her under the bus and implied she acted with racist motives. It always has to be about race. It's noteworthy that employees of Starbucks, whose founder is decidedly leftist, would need to be trained in proper racial behaviors. If leftist outlets don't understand the strictures of political correctness after dousing us in this thinking for years, how can anyone ever learn it? And if racism was actually involved in this case at all, why couldn't Starbucks discipline the one employee rather than subjecting all employees to an indoctrination session?

One particularly egregious example of censorship involved administrative law judge Salvatore Davi, who worked for New York's Office of Temporary and Disability Assistance. Though he was considered an exemplary employee, the employer accused him of seven counts of professional misconduct for statements he made off the job on Facebook. Davi's offense was disagreeing with a friend's post that lauded the effectiveness of food stamps. Davi offered an oft-articulated conservative position that welfare programs should be temporary and designed to help people return to the workforce. After someone shared Davi's post with his superiors, they said that someone with such views couldn't adjudicate disability cases impartially. For this, they charged him with professional misconduct and sought his termination. Failing that, they suspended him for six months and placed him in a position in which he couldn't decide cases. They punished him without presenting a scintilla of evidence of his bias on the job or complaints from colleagues or claimants. His record revealed that he recommended benefits in 95 percent of the cases he handled.[53]

DIRTY TRICKS

Democrats habitually accuse Republicans of the type of dirty tricks they themselves commonly practice in elections. One glaring example occurred in the 2018 congressional election campaign, when Democratic operatives purchased deceitful ads on Facebook designed to suppress Republican turnout. Funded by leftist billionaire Reid Hoffman, the ads were produced and bought by American Engagement Technologies, a firm launched by Mikey Dickerson, a former Obama administration official. Crafted to look like they were sponsored by disgruntled conservatives, the ads encouraged GOP voters to stay home on election day because Republicans hadn't governed conservatively enough.[54]

In the 2016 presidential election, Project Veritas revealed that Democratic groups ran an extensive dirty-tricks operation for the Hillary Clinton campaign. Their tactics included infiltrating Trump rallies to incite violence and sending mentally ill and homeless people to do "crazy stuff." Operatives were caught on tape explaining how coordination and payments were run through myriad organizations to subvert campaign laws and regulations. "It doesn't matter what the friggin' legal and ethics people say, we need to win this motherf*cker," declared one of the chief organizers of the effort, Scott Foval.[55]

Another dirty trick arose in an unlikely context. Citing two unnamed sources, a May 2018 McClatchy article reported that investigators were looking into a scheme in which the Russians laundered money through the NRA to help the Trump campaign. The report claimed an NRA lawyer named Cleta Mitchell was aware of the ploy, but Mitchell denied any knowledge of it. She noted that she wasn't even working for the NRA anymore, which forced McClatchy to issue a correction to the bogus story.[56] Through congressional testimony by former associate deputy attorney general Bruce Ohr, it later became clear that the source of the false report was Glenn Simpson, head of Fusion GPS, the firm that drafted the discredited Steele dossier claiming Donald Trump conspired with the Kremlin.[57] Although the entire story fell apart, in August 2019 the Federal Election Commission's Democratic chairwoman advocated investigating the supposed money laundering scheme based solely on allegations reported by McClatchy.[58]

When the Senate Select Committee on Intelligence contacted Mitchell about her contacts with Russian entities, she told them the story was "completely fabricated and concocted by Glenn Simpson & Co. You should be pursuing them for perjury and for making false statements to congressional investigators." Mitchell told *The Federalist* that she heard nothing further from the committee after that. "So some scumbag like Glenn Simpson can get the FBI to open an investigation by just making things up?" Mitchell exclaimed. "It is appalling. And frightening." "Mitchell is right," wrote *The Federalist* contributor Margot Cleveland. "Simpson and others who pushed false claims of Russia collusion to the FBI and DOJ should be prosecuted. The failure to do so will only embolden political operatives and establish that there is no downside to reporting fraudulent information to the FBI."[59] It is indeed horrifying that political operatives can fabricate stories out of whole cloth and launch investigations into political opponents.

In the next chapter, we'll examine how extreme and morally bankrupt the left has become on the issue of abortion and its continuing pattern of discrimination against Christians.

CHAPTER THIRTEEN

Shouting Your Abortion While Attacking Christians

It's horrifying that we are rapidly approaching the kind of culture that God ordered the Israelites to wipe out when he finally allowed them to enter the Promised Land—a culture of rampant immorality, idolatry, and child sacrifice.

The left used to concede that abortion was an unpleasant affair, even if their denial that an unborn baby is a human life made that illogical. If an unborn baby is merely a clump of cells, an abortion is just a clinical procedure with no moral component. With such a low opinion of unborn babies there is no reason to make abortion rare, yet that was the position of Democrats until recently—abortion should be "safe, legal, and rare."

So if they didn't believe an unborn baby is a human life worthy of protection, why *did* they insist abortion should be rare? Perhaps it was cognitive dissonance—they subconsciously knew an unborn baby is a human life and were trying to mitigate the evil while still preserving a woman's unfettered autonomy to terminate the child. Or maybe they just cynically pretended, for political purposes, that they sought to minimize abortion to deceive those who might be uncomfortable with it.

Despite their protests, pro-abortionists did nothing to make abortion rare. Furthermore, abortions are never safe for the aborted baby and often harm the mother, psychologically and emotionally if not physically. The left has always been pro-abortion, not pro-choice. They resist any restrictions on abortion, operating with a paranoid fear that any concession would be a slippery slope leading to the outlawing of abortion and forcing women to return to back alleys.

So jealously did leftists safeguard abortion that it served as a sacrament of their secular ideology. They conspired with the multi-million-dollar abortion industry to expand the number of abortions. Since the Supreme Court's *Roe v. Wade* decision in 1973, there have been an estimated 60 million abortions in America[1] (the vast majority being for nonmedical reasons),[2] which would have been impossible if one political party opposed the procedure and the other was trying to make it rare. If they were truly pro-choice, they would inform pregnant women contemplating abortions about all the risks of the procedure, including psychological and emotional harm, and advise them on adoption as an alternative. To make responsible choices people must be fully informed of all their options.

"WHEN DOES HUMAN LIFE REALLY BEGIN TO MATTER?"

Advancements in ultrasound technology have produced real-time 4D images of babies in the early phases of pregnancy, making it even more difficult to deny unborn babies are human beings. Upon watching them, some pro-abortionists have been converted on the spot. A short video posted by Jonathon Van Maren of the Canadian Centre for Bio-Ethical Reform shows a perfectly formed eight-week-old baby arching his back and moving his arms and legs in his mother's womb. It begins with this statement: "This 8-second video of a first-trimester baby tells you everything you need to know about how wrong abortion is."[3]

A baby's heart is beating at six weeks post-conception and fetal movement of the limbs begins at about 7.5 weeks, with more complex movements like thumb-sucking and yawning occurring around fourteen weeks.[4] Maureen Condic, an associate professor of neurobiology and anatomy at the University of Utah, testified to a congressional committee that unborn babies have the capacity to feel pain as early as eight weeks.[5] At seven weeks the preborn baby is 10,000 times bigger than at conception and has developed tiny buds for arms and legs. At eight weeks, not only does the baby have limb movement but all her major organs have begun developing and she's the size of a raspberry. At nine weeks her toes are visible, and all the essential organs are formed. At ten weeks tooth buds are formed, and the baby can flex from her elbows. Preborn babies between eleven and thirteen weeks are the size of a lime, begin to grow fingernails, and have tongues, ears, and nasal passages. They are sometimes already capable of stretching and doing somersaults.[6] Hearing can occur within twenty-three weeks of gestation.[7]

These are human beings, not clusters of cells. Gallup polling shows that 60 percent of Americans support the legality of abortion during the first trimester.[8] But how many in that 60 percent would hold fast to their position if they could see these images and videos—and if they were aware of the scientific facts?[9] Admittedly, some people have the opposite reaction, which further proves the effectiveness of these kinds of images—a pro-abortion feminist college student at the University of North Carolina at Chapel Hill was arrested for assaulting a member of Created Equal, a pro-life group, for showing graphic photos of aborted children.[10] I believe pro-life advocates should continue showing such images despite the fear of offending people. If these images are offensive, how much more so is the reality they depict? We shouldn't elevate people's sensitivity above the right of the innocent unborn to life, and if graphic pictures awaken people to the horror of abortion, then we should use them to save lives.

For decades pro-abortionists have lived their contradictions and masqueraded as equal-opportunity dispensers of compassion, with empathy toward women and love and concern for the unviable tissue mass. Today, apparently emboldened by its overall Trump-era onslaught, the left has become less circumspect and started aggressively embracing the culture of death, with some leftists brazenly defending abortion even while conceding it involves killing a human being. They now champion abortion as something in which women should take pride. This is a stunning development. Self-congratulation for killing one's innocent offspring is a level of spiritual evil too horrific to contemplate, and yet that's where much of the left currently resides, as witnessed by activists wearing T-shirts boasting of their abortions and book authors glorifying the practice. One Reddit user proclaimed she had an abortion the previous week just "because I wanted to." "I have never been pregnant and consider myself a fairly responsible person," she wrote. "...I also don't want to have something control my life that I have made every considerable effort to avoid."[11]

The pro-life organization Live Action cites a number of abortion proponents who have publicly admitted that abortion ends human lives. Ann Furedi chillingly writes, "We can accept that the embryo is a living thing in the fact that it has a beating heart, that it has its own genetic system within it. It's clearly human in the sense that it's not a gerbil, and we can recognize that it is human life.... [T]he point is not when does human life begin, but when does it really begin to matter?"[12] Yes, when, indeed?

Writer Naomi Wolf once described her agitated response, when pregnant, to a person challenging her about whether she was carrying a baby. She responded, "Of course it's a baby. And if I found myself in circumstances in which I had to make the terrible decision to end this life, then that would be between myself and God." Likewise, Judith Arcana said, "I performed abortions, I have had an abortion and I am in favor of women having abortions when we choose to do so. But we should never disregard the fact that being pregnant means there is a baby growing inside of a woman, a baby whose life is ended. We ought not to pretend this is not happening."[13]

In a sex-ed video, even Planned Parenthood admits that an unborn child is a baby.[14] The narrator instructs parents how to respond to their children if they ask where babies come from. "You can say 'A baby grows in a parent's belly and comes out of their vagina," responds the narrator. Later, he says, "Most men have very tiny seeds, called sperm. If sperm and egg meet, they can grow into a baby."[15] It's surprising that the nation's premier abortion provider could bring itself to admit this simple biological fact. But what exactly happens to that "baby" during an abortion? A separate Planned Parenthood video on the abortion procedure describes it briefly and vaguely: "During an in-clinic abortion, a doctor, nurse, or other health care provider empties your uterus using gentle suction and sometimes other medical tools." What precisely is being emptied from the uterus is left unsaid, and viewers get little hint from the video's graphics, which depict a straw-like device inside a sketch of a uterus removing two wavy red lines while soothing elevator-style music plays in the background.[16] When the horror of what an organization is doing is so intense that it can't even fully describe it, it may be time for the group to rethink its actions.

"THE MUSIC OF MURDER"

There are many other instances of abortion activists or clinical workers admitting an unborn baby is a human life and, in some instances, that abortion is actually murder.[17] Yet the left is moving us ever closer to a death culture, as exemplified by an Ohio mother singing a lullaby her baby "gave" her in the waiting room before she aborted her. She later sang the lullaby at a ceremony blessing an abortion clinic. Pro-life witnesses of the creepy event commented, "Watching this mother sing the lullaby to those gathered is haunting. This tune became the music of murder for one baby, and those assembled celebrated in hopes it would become the same for countless other children."[18]

The pro-abortionists' exclusive focus on the mother's rights, which stems in part from their militant feminism, allows them to rationalize the killing of innocent babies including, of course, female babies. Any encroachment on the mother's unfettered right to murder her unborn baby is seen as an assault on women's rights. From a spiritual perspective it is a stunning outworking of pride, a self-absorbed focus that wholly ignores the baby's life. Because they are promoting a lie, they have to marshal other lies to support their indefensible position, such as claiming they are protecting the mother's health—though late-term abortions are almost never necessary for that purpose because delivering a baby by C-section is faster and safer than killing her in a two-day late-term abortion.[19] They also define "mother's health" expansively, to include situations that involve no physical threat to the mother.

Abortion advocates employ other euphemisms to package their advocacy in more palatable terms. NPR issued a "guidance reminder" directing journalists to use (and avoid) certain terminology when reporting on abortion, including: use "intact dilation and extraction," not "partial-birth abortion"; use "medical or health clinic," not "abortion clinic"; use "doctor who operates clinics where abortion is performed," not "abortion doctor"; use "fetus," not "unborn baby"; and use "abortion rights opponents," not "pro-lifers." The goal is to sanitize and depersonalize the language.[20] Whoopi Goldberg's response to comments from former U.N. ambassador Nikki Haley illustrates the unreality of pro-abortionist thinking. When Haley said that pro-choice advocates demand uniformity and that's not real feminism, Goldberg took offense. "See to me, you taking choice from people is anti-human.... I don't say that everybody has to believe, but I say you want to have choice, I don't want you in my coochie...and you don't want me in yours either."[21]

Activist judges employed word fictions in *Roe v. Wade* to manufacture a federal limit on the states' right to regulate abortion by divining a right to privacy in the so-called "emanations" and "penumbras" of the Constitution. Abortion advocates couch the debate in terms of the mother's autonomy over her own body, wholly ignoring the other human being involved. They describe abortion as involving the mother's "reproductive health," though it has nothing to do with reproduction, which has already occurred, except to terminate it; it rarely relates to "health," as by definition it destroys the baby's health; and as noted, it is rarely done to protect the mother's health, as honestly defined. And while some on the left grudgingly acknowledge an unborn baby's humanity, others still describe the unborn human life as an unviable tissue mass or clump or cluster of cells, in a conscious effort to dehumanize the baby.[22]

The abortion industry also plays word games to paint pro-life advocates in a negative light. Consider these comments by the former head of Planned Parenthood, Dr. Leana Wen: "It's insulting when people describe their anti-choice stance as pro-life. What I do, is promote life and the well-being of women, and families, and communities.... I'm a physician. I went to medical school. Everything I've ever done is to save lives." Dr. Albert Mohler, president of Southern Baptism University and a cultural commentator, was aghast at this declaration. "Now, just consider the evil of that statement, the evil in the fact that she made the statement, the evil frankly, in the fact that it was published in the mainstream media without any acknowledgement of the horror of what she had just said," said Dr. Mohler.[23]

In response to congressional efforts to defund Planned Parenthood in 2015, Amelia Bonow defended the organization on Facebook. "I had an abortion at Planned Parenthood and it was an overwhelmingly positive experience, I felt nothing but relief...and I'm a good person," said Bonow. "My abortion made me happy." Lindy West supported Bonow with a tweet using the hashtag #ShoutYourAbortion. West and Bonow, along with Emily Nokes, published *Shout Your Abortion*, a book of personal essays in which women describe their abortion experiences. In an eight-minute video promoting the book, Bonow is shown promoting abortion to children. "You go to the doctor, and they put this little straw inside of your cervix, and then inside of your uterus, and then they just suck the pregnancy out," said Bonow. "It was just like a crappy dentist appointment or something. It was just like, 'Ah, this is like a body thing that's kind of uncomfortable,' but then it was over, and I felt really just grateful that I wasn't pregnant anymore."[24] The magnitude of this lie is staggering. From a Christian perspective, lying to children about the gravity of abortion is especially troubling for the same reason abortion is troubling: we are to protect the innocent. As Jesus taught, "It would be better for him if a millstone were hung around his neck and he were cast into the sea than that he should cause one of these little ones to sin" (Luke 17:2).

In an exchange with a boy who asks why not choose adoption instead of abortion, Bonow says, "I feel like if I am forced to create life, I have lost the right to my own life. I should be the one to decide if my body creates a life. Even if you give a kid up for adoption, you still like have a kid out there somewhere." She isn't forced to "create life"—the life has already been created when a decision to abort is made. And terminating the child is not deciding not to create; it's ending an already-created human being. The notion that she should be entitled to end her child's life because she doesn't want to be bothered by the thought of having "a kid out there somewhere" reveals, in stark terms, how twisted pro-abortion thinking is. It takes the idea of a mother's convenience to stratospheric levels. When the boy asks Bonow what she believes God thinks about abortion, she replies, "I think it's all part of God's plan"[25]—reminiscent of the serpent telling Eve to go ahead and eat of the tree in the middle of the garden because "You will not surely die. For God knows that in the day you eat of it, your eyes will be opened and you will be like God, knowing good and evil" (Gen. 3:4–5).

"WHAT IS BORN IS HER OWN CONFIDENT AGENCY OVER LIFE"

Lindy West appeared on *The Daily Show* to discuss *Shout Your Abortion* and her efforts to remove the abortion stigma. She described the book as "just people telling the truth about their experiences, experiences we've been taught to feel shame about and apologize for, which has really been engineered by the evangelical right." West explains that the writers share their stories about various abortions, including those by women who desperately wanted to be pregnant and some by women who'd had multiple abortions. "Anti-choice people are not trying to stop abortion," said West. "They're trying to legislate who can and cannot have abortions. Because conservative politicians—their wives, and mistresses, and daughters are always going to be able to go get an abortion somewhere. Really, all anti-choice rhetoric does...is keep people trapped in poverty and drowning in poverty for generations. That's the goal. If it wasn't the goal, they'd spend their time and money on comprehensive sex education, free birth control, free contraception, and all the things that pro-choice people do spend their time on that actually do affect the abortion rate."[26] You see, even abortion is a function of the Marxist class struggle.

One woman's story related in the book confirms the movement's arrogance, even acknowledging that abortion involves terminating human life. The account reads, "The simple truth is this: if a sperm and egg come together when a child is desired, a human being is born. But if a sperm and egg come together when a woman knows in her bones that it is not the right time for her to be a mother, then perhaps what is born is her own confident agency over life."

Another woman betrays a hint of narcissistic callousness, writing, "I'm telling you my story plainly, proudly, flippantly even, because we've all been brainwashed to believe that the absence of negative emotions around having an abortion is the mark of an emotionally bankrupt person. It's not. I'm a good person and my abortion made me happy. It's perfectly reasonable to feel happy that you were not forced to become a mother."[27] Again, we see the unapologetic elevation of a woman's prerogative to decide whether to carry her baby to term over the innocent baby's right to life. But it's an abominable lie to suggest that the life of an unborn baby is any less sacred because the mother carrying the baby doesn't want it to be born. How does a woman's confidence in her own "agency over life" or her bizarre happiness over terminating her own offspring justify her decision to have an abortion? These stories and the language the women use may make women feel better about their decisions temporarily, but they certainly don't advance their moral argument that unborn babies don't deserve to live.

One of the most dramatic illustrations of pro-abortionist brazenness was the public admission of Planned Parenthood president Dr. Wen that the core mission of her organization is abortion. Adamantly insisting that the media had misconstrued comments she made about expanding non-abortion services, she declared that Planned Parenthood's "core mission is to provide, protect, and expand access to abortion." She continued, "We will never back down from the fight. It's a fundamental human right, and women's lives are at stake."

This was a stunning admission by an organization that typically tries to present itself as a women's healthcare provider, not an abortion provider. According to Live Action, Planned Parenthood even manipulates its data to conceal that the overwhelming part of its business is abortion, not healthcare services for women. The group claims that abortion accounts for only 3 percent of its services, but abortion accounts for more than 90 percent of its services for pregnant women, and one in eight Planned Parenthood patients gets an abortion.[28] Dr. Mohler captured the significance of Wen's reversal. "This is an absolute contradiction of what she had been trying to say with media complicity in the early days of her leadership of Planned Parenthood in the fall," said Mohler. "What she has now done is to reveal the fact that under pressure, Planned Parenthood is ready to say aggressively it's really about the core mission of abortion." In the end, Wen's emphatic defense of abortion was insufficient—in July 2019 Planned Parenthood removed her as president. According to the *New York Times*, the group wanted a president who would be even more political and aggressive in advocating for abortion.[29]

Mohler trenchantly notes that to characterize abortion as a fundamental human right is "a particularly alarming argument, and one that wouldn't have been offered with a straight face until quite recently, at least on those terms.... What we're seeing there...is a renewed, very aggressive liberal defense of abortion that comes down to suggesting that any kind of reluctance to talk about abortion is a form of cowardice, or caving in to the pro-life movement."[30] The same type of pro-abortion belligerence was on display in Congresswoman Norma Torres's insulting remarks about her GOP colleagues during an abortion debate in the House. "Mr. Speaker, it is tiring to hear from so many sex-starved males on this floor talk about a woman's right to choose," said Torres.[31]

"ABORTION AS A MORAL GOOD"

Renowned feminist Gloria Steinem compared the modern pro-life movement to Nazism. "On a more serious note, to put it mildly, is why Hitler was actually elected, and he was elected and he campaigned against abortion," said Steinem. "I mean, that was—he padlocked the family planning clinics. Okay, so that is still relevant in the terms of the right wing." Dinesh D'Souza tweeted in response, "Just saw a strange clip on @IngrahamAngle of Gloria Steinem insisting Hitler was anti-abortion. A big lie! Hitler was vehemently anti-abortion for Nordic Germans, and vehemently pro-abortion for the so-called inferior races. This can hardly be called a pro-life position!"[32]

The left gets more extreme and militant on abortion every day. In February 2019, Georgia's Emory University hosted a lecture by a speaker positing that abortion is a moral good. The lecture, titled "Reframing Choice: Abortion as a Moral Good," was presented by feminist professor Dr. Rebecca Todd Peters of Elon University. Peters contends that racism and patriarchy are behind the culture's shaming of women for having abortions. So pro-abortionists, like good leftist wind-up dolls, are blaming everything on the evil triumvirate of racism, sexism, and classism. "The starting point of our ethical conversation should be women's lives," writes Peters, "[yet] the problem that we face in this country is our failure to trust women to act as rational, capable, responsible moral agents."[33]

So Peters is arguing that rational, capable, responsible, and moral agents will decide to terminate their children, and that patriarchy and racism are hamstringing them from exercising their eminently moral and rational choices? Peters, an ordained minister in the Presbyterian Church (USA), perversely believes her faith requires that she be pro-abortion. "There is nothing Christian about requiring women to 'justify' their reasons for abortion," Peters writes. "And there is certainly nothing Christian about forcing women to continue pregnancies against their will."[34] "If we truly value women and healthy families," she continues, "we must accept that 'I do not want to have a baby' is an imminently appropriate reason to end a pregnancy. And we must trust that pregnant women are the only ones who are capable of making these decisions."[35] One wonders where terminated babies fit into Peters's definition of a healthy family.

The culture of death has sunk its claws into the most seemingly innocuous places. The Girl Scouts of Southern Arizona bestowed its highest honor, the Gold Award, on teenage scout Meghna Gopalan for her project on "reproductive health justice," a term that includes support for abortion on demand. The project involved working with the pro-abortion Women's March. Gopalan said she wanted to "educate people about and destigmatize access to women's healthcare," i.e., abortion. The left politicizes everything it touches, and it has certainly touched the Girl Scouts, though the organization maintains it takes "no position" on abortion. Former Girl Scouts CEO Kathy Cloninger let the cat out of the bag, however, when she admitted the Girl Scouts partner with Planned Parenthood organizations throughout the country.[36]

SIDELINING, OUSTING, AND HANDICAPPING PREGNANT EMPLOYEES

Planned Parenthood is inaptly named, as abortion ends the possibility of parenthood for the aborted baby every bit as much as it ends the baby's life. Thus, planning an abortion is not planning for parenthood but the precise opposite. Planned Parenthood also uses the euphemism "abortion care"[37] to mask the horror of the procedure, and some abortion proponents brazenly refer to abortion as a "family value."[38]

Indeed, the hypocrisy of the abortion rights movement is clearly revealed in the corporate climate of Planned Parenthood. The *New York Times* reports that the group's employees accused it of mistreating pregnant workers. "Employers that champion women face accusations of discrimination against their pregnant workers, showing how widespread the problem is in American workplaces," reports the *Times*.[39] When one pregnant employee told the HR department for Planned Parenthood's clinic in White Plains, New York, that high blood pressure was threatening her pregnancy and that her nurse recommended frequent breaks, her managers ignored her. "Discrimination against pregnant women and new mothers remains widespread in the American workplace," says the *Times*. "It is so pervasive that even organizations that define themselves as champions of women are struggling with the problem. That includes Planned Parenthood, which has been accused of sidelining, ousting or otherwise handicapping pregnant employees, according to interviews with more than a dozen current and former employees."[40]

Commentator Michael Knowles points out that while the *Times* seems to be shocked that an ostensibly pro-women organization would treat pregnant women disrespectfully, reasonable people understand it's no contradiction at all. "You've got an organization that exists singularly, simply to end pregnancies and kill babies, and the *New York Times* is shocked that that agency, that organization would not treat pregnant women with respect," writes Knowles.[41]

"A HISTORIC VICTORY FOR PROGRESSIVE VALUES"

Conservative commentators attribute the Democratic Party's rapid leftward shift to the rise of radicals such as Alexandria Ocasio-Cortez and the extremist nature of their base, whose approval is required for any presidential hopeful. I think both are true, but politicians wouldn't move left if their consciences prevented them from doing so, and the entire party has demonstrated itself to be comfortable with this radicalism. Democrats aren't becoming more openly leftist as part of a strategic calculation but because it represents what they actually believe.

On no issue has this been more apparent than abortion. On both the state and federal levels, Democrats are promoting increasingly extreme abortion-related legislation. In January 2019 Democratic senators blocked a bill that would have permanently banned the use of taxpayer funds for abortion, despite a Marist poll showing that 54 percent of Americans oppose the practice. The Hyde Amendment, which is still in effect, is an annual appropriations rider that bans taxpayer-funded abortion, but this newly proposed bill would have codified it.[42]

During one of the Democratic presidential debates, each candidate vied to prove he or she was the most extreme abortion proponent. Washington governor Jay Inslee boasted that he passed a law forcing insurance companies to pay for abortions. Senator Amy Klobuchar noted that she was one of the three women on stage who "have fought pretty hard for a woman's right to choose." Former HUD secretary Julian Castro bragged, "I don't believe only in reproductive freedom, I believe in reproductive justice." In the end, it was apparent that all ten candidates on stage support taxpayer-funded abortion throughout the term of pregnancy for any reason.[43]

Earlier, Democrats had promoted legislation to expand taxpayer funding of abortion overseas as part of their package to end the government shutdown. This is remarkable, considering the same Marist poll found that 75 percent of Americans oppose taxpayer funding of abortion abroad and only 19 percent approve of it. The results of this poll on other abortion-related questions are complex. While the survey found that 55 percent of respondents say they are pro-choice compared to 38 percent who are pro-life, a full 75 percent believe abortion should only be allowed—if at all—in the first trimester. Even 61 percent of those who identify as pro-choice and 60 percent of Democrats favor abortion only in the first trimester.[44] Given that the Democratic Party favors abortion virtually on demand throughout pregnancy,[45] it is clear the party is not in sync with public opinion. Democrats have additional cause for concern, as the poll found that only 35 percent believe an unborn child is "part of a woman's body," while 56 percent believe it is "a unique life."[46]

On the state level, Democrats have been even more extreme. New York passed the Reproductive Health Act (RHA) on the forty-sixth anniversary of *Roe v. Wade*. The RHA legalizes abortion at any time within the first twenty-four weeks of pregnancy and at any time after that when it is necessary to protect a woman's life or health. The exception for the mother's health is so expansively interpreted that the bill essentially allows abortion on demand to the point of birth.[47] The sanctioning of late-term abortions is especially cynical considering—as noted above—such abortions are rarely necessary for a mother's health. Shockingly, this law even removes protections for babies who survive an abortion procedure, meaning the babies could be left to die after birth.[48]

Democrats jubilantly celebrated the bill's passage, with New York governor Andrew Cuomo obscenely lighting the One World Trade Center spire in ghoulish pink to commemorate the event. Cuomo giddily stated, "The Reproductive Health Act is a historic victory for New Yorkers and for our progressive values. In the face of a federal government intent on rolling back *Roe v. Wade* and women's reproductive rights, I promised that we would enact this critical legislation within the first thirty days of the new session—and we got it done. I am directing that New York's landmarks be lit in pink to celebrate this achievement and shine a bright light forward for the rest of the nation to follow."[49] Comedy Central's *Broad City* creator Ilana Glazer was equally elated, praising Democratic legislators and Planned Parenthood supporters. "Your work is making the world a better place, in real time," said Glazer. "It is chiller in New York state because of your work."[50]

Following passage of the bill, Illinois considered a bill that would make it the most "abortion friendly" state in the nation. The proposed legislation, also called the Reproductive Health Act, would legalize abortion through all nine months of pregnancy, for any reason. The state's Catholic bishops strongly condemned the proposal. "As Illinois faces so many pressing issues involving human life and dignity, it is incomprehensible that our elected officials have decided the pressing issue of the day is to enhance the chances that the lives of the most vulnerable and voiceless will be taken," said the Catholic Conference of Illinois. "Their efforts, similar to recent actions in New York and Virginia, focus on corrupting our God-given right to life and sowing unnecessary division."[51]

The Vermont legislature is prepared to pass H.57, a radical measure that would amend the state's constitution to provide that the unborn "shall not have independent rights under the law." This would further enshrine its existing law which states that there is no criminal liability for the murder of an unborn baby (such as when a criminal kills a pregnant mother and her unborn child). The bill would also remove civil liability for the negligent killing of an unborn baby.[52]

Democrats in Virginia introduced the Repeal Act to permit the outsourcing of second-trimester abortions to non-doctors and to permit abortion during the mother's labor or, according to Virginia governor Ralph Northam, even after the baby's birth, in some cases.[53] "If a mother is in labor, I can tell you exactly what would happen," said Northam. "The infant would be delivered. The infant would be kept comfortable. The infant would be resuscitated if that's what the mother and the family desired, and then a discussion would ensue between the physicians and the mother."[54]

Following an uproar over these comments, Northam unconvincingly attempted to walk back his statement, blaming his callous utterance on political opponents misconstruing his intent. "No woman seeks a third-trimester abortion except in the case of tragic or difficult circumstances, such as a nonviable pregnancy or in the event of severe fetal abnormalities, and the governor's comments were limited to actions physicians would take in the event that a woman in those circumstances went into labor," his office said in a statement. "Attempts to extrapolate these comments otherwise is in bad faith and underscores exactly why the governor believes physicians and women, not legislators, should make these difficult and deeply personal medical decisions."[55] However, the bill's sponsor, Virginia delegate Kathy Tran, admitted the legislation would allow doctors to kill a baby even when the mother "has physical signs that she's about to give birth," including when she's dilating.[56] All that would be required for a legal abortion just before birth would be a certification by a single doctor that the pregnancy would likely impair the physical *or mental* health of the mother, with no standards provided for what would qualify as such an impairment.

The left's militant abortion advocacy reveals another gaping contradiction in its ideology. A dirty little secret is that abortion disproportionately impacts the black community—black women are far more likely than non-black women to get an abortion.[57] This appalling reality exposes the pathetic folly and irony in actress Anne Hathaway's scolding pro-life "white women" for promoting restrictions on abortion. "Let us call out the complicity of the white women," urged Hathaway, "who made this awful moment possible, and which—make no mistake—WILL lead to the unnecessary and avoidable deaths of women, a disproportionate number of whom will be poor and/or black."[58]

"ABORTION IS SO 1973. WELCOME TO 2019."

The Democrats' extremism and militancy may be backfiring, as pro-life advocacy is making headway and the abortion industry is experiencing significant setbacks. Planned Parenthood and the Guttmacher Institute released a report stating that forty-one states have enacted more than 250 bills restricting abortion since the beginning of 2019, and state legislatures have passed more than 400 pro-life bills since 2011.[59] These developments, coupled with President Trump's appointment of originalist judges, have unnerved the left about the future of abortion law.

Some conservative states have recently pushed back against abortion radicalism. Georgia legislators proposed HB 481, the Living Infants Fairness and Equality (LIFE) Act, which bans abortions if the baby's heartbeat is detected. In response, Hollywood went ballistic, with some fifty celebrities signing a letter by Alyssa Milano to Georgia House speaker David Ralston and Georgia governor Brian Kemp threatening to boycott the state if the bill passed. Milano appeared at the Georgia statehouse to protest in person.

Georgia resident Ashley Bratcher, star of the pro-life movie *Unplanned*, responded to Milano's letter in *Deadline*. "For the latter part of a year I've watched as women I've admired, like you, spoke out in regards to women's rights, more specifically women's reproductive rights," Bratcher wrote. "With radical laws like the ones in New York and Vermont being passed, it's more critical than ever that we are using our voices to fight for the rights of women. One problem, you're forgetting about the rights of women within the womb. If feminism is all about equal rights, then where are her rights?" Bratcher also responded eloquently and defiantly to Milano's boycott threat:

> In Georgia, we care just as much about being pro-life as being pro-film. We don't believe in putting a price tag on the value

> of a human life. Our brave leaders have stepped up to say enough is enough, we will no longer sit idly by as innocent lives are taken by the thousands each day. If you fault Georgia for choosing to be morally correct over politically correct, then that says more of your personal agenda than the goal of our governor to protect life, liberty and the pursuit of happiness for all. You claim that the HB 481 "Heartbeat Bill" would make Georgia the most regressive state in the country; I couldn't disagree more. Abortion is so 1973. Welcome to 2019, a time in which medical advances preserve the life of babies born as early as 21 weeks. In case you didn't know, that's three weeks earlier than what most states in the U.S. consider "viable" in their abortion legislation.[60]

TV networks joined Hollywood to try to sabotage the Georgia bill. Marketers for *Unplanned* told the *Hollywood Reporter* that numerous networks refused to accept their advertising money, including the Travel Channel, Cooking Channel, HGTV, Lifetime, Food Network, Hallmark Channel, and USA Network. Some networks declined due to the "sensitive nature" of the movie's content, while others said they didn't want to get involved in the political nature of the topic.[61]

The Hollywood threats failed to deter the Georgia legislature, which passed the bill on March 29, 2019. Mississippi and Kentucky already had similar laws, and other states are considering following suit. After the Georgia bill passed, entertainment giants Disney, Netflix, and WarnerMedia threatened to stop producing movies and TV shows in Georgia. Comcast's NBC Universal hinted at doing the same. Disney CEO Bob Iger said Disney would find it "very difficult" to film in Georgia if the new law takes effect. "I think many people who work for us will not want to work there, and we will have to heed their wishes in that regard," said Iger.[62] He didn't express concern over Disney's millions of pro-life patrons. Nor did he address the inconsistency in his company's willingness to film in foreign nations that have stricter abortion laws than Georgia's, such as Bolivia, Croatia, and the United Arab Emirates.

At the federal level, Senator Ben Sasse introduced the Born-Alive Abortion Survivors Protection Act, providing that babies who survive attempted abortions must receive medical care. "You're either for babies or you're defending infanticide," says Sasse. "That's literally what this bill is about."[63] Callous Democrats blocked the bill, with Senator Patty Murray accusing Sasse of misrepresenting the bill's purpose, claiming laws already prohibit infanticide.[64] As of August 2019, Democrats had blocked a vote on the House version of the bill eighty times.[65]

The Trump administration has revised Title X funding programs to ban abortions from being referred or provided by participating health clinics, a change that caused Planned Parenthood to abandon the programs. Predictably, Hollywood liberals from Elizabeth Banks to Alyssa Milano have come out in droves to lobby against these changes, warning that "reproductive health care" is at risk.[66]

While these are positive signs, we must also be aware that dark forces are ever at work to undermine life. In January 2019, the Supreme Court delayed its decision on whether to accept review of a Seventh Circuit Court of Appeals decision striking down two Indiana abortion statutes, one of which outlawed abortions due to the child's race, sex, or disability. The bill was meant to address the indisputable fact that abortion facilitates eugenics. If an unborn child is a human being then disabled unborn children are human beings as well, and we have no more moral justification to terminate their lives than if they had already been born. "It is morally unacceptable to claim that either women or people with Down Syndrome are less valuable than men or people without Down," writes Seth Newkirk. "...Reintroducing genetic 'purification' to modern society reveals the inherent problems with abortion: abortion dehumanizes the most vulnerable and pretends we can judge the unborn as unworthy of life based on arbitrary parameters. Parameters such as genetic makeup, sex, disability, even convenience have become legitimate measures of worth in the age of abortion."[67]

THE LEFT'S WAR ON CHRISTIANITY MARCHES ON

The left's attacks on the pro-life community are part of its wider assault on Christians and their religious liberty. I chronicled the left's war on Christianity in my 2003 book *Persecution*, and matters have only deteriorated since. Many liberals deny the left targets Christianity and routinely demonizes Christians, but the evidence doesn't lie. You can barely watch a television show without Christians being portrayed as kooks, bigots, racists, sexists, or homophobes, or scripture being treated as hate speech. In countless movies and television dramas fanatical white Christians are depicted as terrorists. Leftist politicians interrogate Christian judicial nominees about their faith as if it's inherently dangerous, while on social media Christians are assumed to be enemies of science and reason. Examples of the left's crusade against Christianity are too numerous to thoroughly detail here, but the following instances amply illustrate the point:

★ During the confirmation hearing for judicial nominee Neomi Rao to replace Justice Brett Kavanaugh on the U.S. Court of Appeals for the District of Columbia Circuit, Democratic senators grilled Rao on her religious beliefs. Senator Cory Booker homed in on Rao's personal convictions about marriage, implying that if she holds the traditional, biblical view that marriage is between one man and one woman, she is unfit to hold public office. "Are gay relationships in your opinion immoral?" Booker demanded to know.[68]

★ In a Senate Judiciary Committee hearing for the Seventh Circuit Court of Appeals, Senator Dianne Feinstein interrogated nominee Amy Coney Barrett on her Catholic faith. "When you read your speeches, the conclusion one draws is that the dogma lives loudly within you," intoned Feinstein. "And that's of concern when you come to big issues that large numbers of people have fought for for years in this country."[69] Feinstein denied she was invoking a religious test for the nominee, but she obviously was, since she implied Barrett's Christian beliefs would impede her objectivity on the bench.

Many liberals have a distorted view of the First Amendment's Establishment Clause, thinking that Christian officeholders in all branches of government must erect a sort of Chinese wall between their religious faith and their policy positions. But no person, from Christian to Buddhist to atheist, can escape the influence of her worldview on her policy preferences. It's preposterous to suggest that only Christians should operate in such a vacuum.

Judges, of course, are required to put aside their predispositions and review cases impartially in light of the facts and the applicable statutes and precedents. Unlike legislators, they are not advocates. But they are not required to be spiritual cyphers under some baseless concern over church-state separation. Christian judges are no less capable than secular ones of putting aside their biases to decide a case based on the law and facts. Indeed, Barrett has argued that Catholic judges (and presumably all other Christians) must not impose their faith on others, and if they determine they can't avoid doing so in a particular case, they must recuse themselves.[70]

★ Christian soccer player Jaelene Hinkle refused to wear a rainbow pride jersey celebrating the gay lifestyle in several games because of her religious beliefs. Though she is considered one of the best players in the National Women's Soccer League, the United States Women's National Soccer Team omitted her from its twenty-three-woman roster for the 2019 World Cup.[71]

★ The left is on a mission to eradicate Christianity from foster care and adoption. The Anti-Defamation League (ADL) claimed that South Carolina's Miracle Hill foster care agency was guilty of discrimination and of "immoral" and "deeply disturbing" practices because it recruited only Christian parents. The ADL has attacked Catholic social services and charities in major American cities such as Philadelphia and Buffalo for operating in accordance with their principles—for example, by preferring to place foster children with families that have both a mother and father.

Leftists are willing to shut down adoption agencies that won't surrender to their demands, even if it leads to a shortage of homes for adoptive children. The left's motivation here is clearly not to secure adoptive homes for non-Christian couples but to purge the adoption industry of Christian influences. How's that for tolerance? There are other options for non-Christian parents, as there are secular agencies in all states. But just as with same-sex couples or transgenders who can get any number of bakers or photographers to perform services for them, they are not satisfied unless every knee bows to their will.

What is presented as discrimination by Christians is actually discrimination *against* Christians who are forced to comply, which directly violates their free exercise of religion.[72] This is the same phenomenon we saw earlier with "non-discrimination" ordinances that force Christians to involuntarily provide services for gay wedding ceremonies.

★ Similarly, New York state threatened to shut down Christian adoption agency New Hope Family Services unless it agreed to change its long-standing practice of placing children only in homes with a married mother and father. Though no formal complaints were lodged against New Hope, the state sent it a letter saying its policy was "discriminatory and impermissible."[73]

★ A Catholic senior living center in Chehalis, Washington, prohibits residents from saying "Merry Christmas" or displaying religious-themed Christmas cards or decorations in common areas, supposedly because the center receives funds from the U.S. Department of Housing and Urban Development.[74]

★ Harvard University's Faculty of Arts & Sciences invited Tim Wise, an "anti-racism writer, educator and activist," to speak at its annual diversity conference. He has demeaned Christians as "Jeezoids" and "fascists" and tweeted that "people who believe in a God of hell/damnation deserved to be mocked viciously and run out of the public square." In 2015, he said that people who base their morality on the Hebrew scriptures "deserve to be locked up," adding he was "sorta kidding but not by much."[75] It is inconceivable that such bigotry against any non-Christian or non-Jewish group would be tolerated on this campus.

★ The city of Upper Arlington, Ohio, denied a permit to Tree of Life Christian Schools to operate in a vacant building it had purchased in the city, though the facility would provide the city tax revenues and 150 jobs. The zoning code permits secular day cares to operate in the area but not this Christian school.

★ Senate Democrats attacked Brian C. Buescher, President Trump's nominee for the United States District Court for the District of Nebraska, because of his membership in the Catholic-connected Knights of Columbus. They asked whether belonging to this Catholic charitable organization would inhibit his fairness and impartiality in cases. Buescher's defenders denounced this religious bigotry and lamented the current trend of excluding Christians from public service based solely on their faith.

★ In a series of articles titled, "12 Days of Chris-Mas," which featured different actors named Chris, *TV Guide* magazine warned its readers about actor Chris Pratt. "When you take a deeper look at Pratt the man and not necessarily Pratt the actor, some of the shine wears off," writes Kaitlyn Thomas. "Although he can be as funny offscreen as he is on—his recurring 'What's My Snack' videos on Instagram are almost always delightful—it's impossible to ignore some problematic aspects of his life offscreen." Some of his "problematic aspects" are his love of hunting and his mocking of our outrage culture. Perhaps the fact that Pratt had recently read from the Gospel of Luke at Disneyland and confessed his Christian faith might have influenced Thomas's view of him and her assessment that he "remains the most complicated and divisive of the Chrises." To self-styled tolerant liberals, only conservatives and Christians are divisive.

- ★ Comedian Jenny Hagel, a writer for *Late Night with Seth Meyers*, ripped into Pope Francis for saying that gays should not be priests. Pointing to his picture, Hagel said, "Here's the thing: This guy's not cool. This guy is homophobic. We should all care about this because the Pope is a world leader who is giving people permission to be prejudiced. This dude may seem harmless because he's shuffling around in a white robe, but remember: White robes are the official uniform of people with bad ideas"[76]—presumably a reference to the Ku Klux Klan. Does it occur to Hagel that she is smearing all Catholics who believe the Church's doctrine on homosexuality?
- ★ To avoid offending students who don't celebrate Christmas, Manchester Elementary School principal Jennifer Sinclair warned teachers not to adorn their classrooms with candy canes because their "J" shape stands for Jesus. Thankfully, the Nebraska school district placed the principal on administrative leave.[77]
- ★ Outraged that Vice President Mike Pence's wife Karen had taken a job at a Christian school, Lady Gaga lashed out at him during a concert in Las Vegas. "To Mike Pence who thinks that it's OK that his wife works at a school that bans LGBTQ, you're wrong," she exclaimed. "You're the worst representation of what it means to be a Christian. I am a Christian woman, and what I do know about Christianity is that we bear no prejudice, and everybody is welcome. So you can take all that disgrace, Mr. Pence, and look yourself in the mirror and you'll find it right there."[78]

Sure, Lady Gaga bears no prejudice against anyone—except practicing Christians who embrace the biblical view of marriage. Other like-minded progressives, such as the Human Rights Campaign, the ACLU, and a writer for *HuffPost*, joined Lady Gaga in trashing Karen Spence. CNN anchor John King questioned whether she should be denied Secret Service protection and government housing during the government shutdown because she works at a Christian school.[79] One Pence basher tweeted, "Karen Pence is a terrible human being." Another said, "Mike Pence is an extremist bigot, Karen Pence is an extremist bigot. She's unfit to even be around kids, let alone teach them. Anyone willing to allow their kid to be taught by a dangerous monster like Karen Pence is unfit to be a parent. Ask me how I really feel."[80] During this controversy, a *New York Times* reporter solicited help from Twitter users for an article he planned to write on Christian schools. He included the hashtag #ExposeChristianSchools, whose creator said it was intended to expose the "trauma" induced by "those bastions of bigotry."[81]

It's pretty clear who the extremists, haters, and bigots are—who is tolerant, kind, and loving, and who isn't. Just being a Bible-believing Christian makes you subhuman to these belligerents. Almost all religious schools, Christian and otherwise, have codes of conduct and voluntary acceptance of a specific belief system. This attack on Karen Spence and the Christian school for which she works is an ominous sign for what Christian schools may be facing from the militant left in the near future. The left's goal is not to preserve the church-state separation as they claim but to ban Christian expression and practices from the public square and even from private life, as they demand utter uniformity of thought and seek to stigmatize the Christian faith and punish its adherents.

★ Sheridan School, a progressive private school in Virginia, refused to play sports with Christian kids from Immanuel Christian School, the school where Karen Pence teaches, because playing basketball at a Christian school supposedly makes children feel "unsafe." Sheridan principal Jessica Donovan said that when Immanuel kids come to play at Sheridan, her students plaster images from the gay community on their clothing and wave celebratory signs during the games.[82] Who is the aggressor here?

- ★ On *The View*, Joy Behar said of Vice President Mike Pence, "It's one thing to talk to Jesus. It's another thing when Jesus talks to you. That's called mental illness, if I'm not correct."[83]
- ★ The annual comic book convention Comicon banned actor Kevin Sorbo due to his conservative political leanings and, some believe, his Christian faith.[84]
- ★ U.S. district judge Haywood Gilliam Jr. blocked a Trump administration rule change designed to expand the Obamacare exemption to include more employers who, because of their religious or moral convictions, can refuse to cover employees' contraception. "No American should be forced to violate his or her own conscience in order to abide by the laws and regulations governing our health care system," said Caitlin Oakley, spokeswoman for Health and Human Services. "The final rules affirm the Trump Administration's commitment to upholding the freedoms afforded all Americans under our Constitution."[85]
- ★ James Wesolek, a writer at *The Federalist*, argues that leftist legislators in Texas are promising a "transformative agenda, which includes a number of "sexual orientation and gender identity" laws that Wesolek says "would attack people of faith so aggressively that they can justifiably be described as 'Ban the Bible' bills."

Under the guise of anti-discrimination advocacy, the bills would authorize the government to ban the free expression of biblically grounded beliefs, says Wesolek. They would force religious homeless shelters, colleges, and universities—even shelters for abused women and small dormitories—to allow biological men to sleep next to women. They would force private business owners to allow men into intimate spaces intended for women—showers, locker rooms, and public bathrooms. They "would force *all* businesses to adopt these radical LGBT policies, even those owned by people who oppose them for religious or safety reasons," writes Wesolek. Another bill would permit the government to discipline counselors, marriage and family therapists, psychologists, and other mental health providers licensed by Texas if they discourage homosexual behavior or the desire for a "gender transition."[86]

- ★ Democrats on the House Committee on Natural Resources moved to eliminate God from the oath for witnesses who testify before the committee. Ultimately, after criticism and debate, the committee decided to retain the phrase, "So help me God."[87] When House Judiciary Committee chairman Jerrold Nadler omitted the phrase while swearing in a witness, he was called out by Republican congressman Mike Johnson and forced to repeat the oath including the reference to God.[88] These small successes should encourage Christians to fight back and defend God in the culture.
- ★ A major exhibition of J.R.R. Tolkien's artwork at the Morgan Library in New York conspicuously omitted references to his deeply held Christian faith.[89]
- ★ A federal court ruled that the University of Iowa illegally targeted religious groups, such as Business Leaders in Christ (BLC), by disallowing them from requiring their leaders to follow principles of their faith. Under the guise of "anti-discrimination," the school had expelled BLC from campus because of its expressions of faith and had placed thirty-one other student groups—exclusively religious ones—on a watch list. The court held that the university must end its unequal treatment of religious student groups.[90]
- ★ Leftists attacked Judge Brian Hagedorn, a candidate for Wisconsin's Supreme Court, for opinions he expressed in blog posts during law school about litigation involving abortion and gay sex, and because he was on the board of a small Christian school. "I expected to be attacked here because that's what's happening all across the country—you know, 'Are you now or have you ever been associated with the Knights of Columbus?'" said Hagedorn.

"Interrogating people [nominated for office] if they went to a Bible study or the Knights of Columbus, that's where we are as a country."[91]

★ America's university campuses are inarguably hostile to Christian students. Many of the actions targeting campus Christians stem from the Supreme Court opinion in *Christian Legal Society v. Martinez*, in which the majority ruled that public institutions such as university law schools can mandate that all student organizations, even if formed on the basis of shared beliefs such as religious and political groups, admit members and leaders irrespective of their beliefs.

The case arose from students at Hastings College of Law at the University of California who applied to register as a chapter of the Christian Legal Society (CLS). The group requires all members to sign a statement of faith affirming their belief in certain fundamental Christian doctrines, including that the Bible is the inspired word of God. The national organization had adopted a resolution that unrepentant participation in or advocacy of a sexually immoral lifestyle is inconsistent with an affirmation of the statement of faith and would disqualify students from CLS membership. A sexually immoral lifestyle under the resolution included "acts of sexual conduct outside of God's design for marriage between one man and one woman." Claiming these injunctions violated the school's nondiscrimination policy, Hastings refused to register CLS, which is the first time in its history it has denied registration to any applying group. CLS then sued the school for violating its members' freedom of speech.

The school later changed its position, claiming CLS was rejected because the school requires clubs to have an accept-all-comers policy. The Supreme Court sided with Hastings, provoking a dissent in which Justice Samuel Alito argued, "The Court arms public educational institutions with a handy weapon for suppressing the speech of unpopular groups—groups to which, as Hastings candidly puts it, these institutions 'do not wish to ... lend their name[s]'.... I do not think it is an exaggeration to say that today's decision is a serious setback for freedom of expression in this country."[92]

Justice Alito was prescient, as the decision emboldened universities throughout America to target Christian student groups. For example, a Christian singing group at the University of North Carolina was prohibited from expelling a member who advocates a homosexual lifestyle. San Diego State University permits campus groups to exclude students who disagree with messages advocated by the groups—except for religious groups, based on the *Martinez* decision. Countless other examples abound.[93]

★ A New Jersey school suspended a substitute teacher for giving a student a copy of the Bible and talking about a scripture verse with the student.[94]

★ A Seattle-area assistant high school football coach was placed on paid leave for continuing to pray on the field following games after his school warned him against the dastardly practice.[95]

★ An Atlanta fire chief was suspended, sent to sensitivity training, and ultimately fired because of a passage about homosexuality in a book he wrote for a Bible study group at his church.[96]

★ A Marine was court-martialed for pasting a Bible verse above her desk.[97]

★ The left demonizes homeschooling (and homeschoolers), with some, such as Richard Dawkins, likening it to child abuse.[98]

★ A high school student in Ohio was threatened with suspension for posting Bible verses at school in response to gay pride flags being displayed in school hallways. The principal asked the student why she posted the verses and she responded that she wanted to spread the word of God. When the principal asked whether she had received permission to do so, she said she didn't know it was necessary, as students often post notes on lockers.[99]

★ Leftist intolerance, of course, emanates from liberal Christians as well, as demonstrated by a group of snowflake students at the small Christian school Taylor University who were mortified that Vice President Mike Pence was invited to deliver the school's commencement address. More than 3,300 people signed a petition for the school to rescind the invitation because Trump-Pence policies are "not consistent with the Christian ethic of love we hold dear." One student said the school "should be ashamed.... I am physically shaking.... I feel personally attacked." Consider the hypocrisy of this student—and the other objecting students—complaining about an ethic of love while behaving like this.[100]

In the next chapter, we'll see just how devoid of the love ethic the anti-Trump left has become.

CHAPTER FOURTEEN

Trump Derangement Syndrome: Politicians and Entertainers

"HE PINCHED THE EDGE OF A SCAB"

Nowhere is the left's collective insanity more prominently displayed than in its fanatical hatred of President Trump. Leftists hated Presidents Nixon, Reagan, and the Bushes, and you might be surprised to review the level of vitriol they leveled at each of them, but their antipathy for Trump is radically more intense. He is their worst enemy, but they hide behind their disdain for his "crudeness" and tweets to disguise their greater outrage at his conservative policies and his counterpunching. If Trump would do their bidding, I guarantee you they wouldn't have the slightest problem with his manners.

The left particularly loathes Trump's unapologetic bullishness on America. "Trump rides a populist nationalist wave to make explicit a fundamental clash of narratives between the left and the right," writes *Forbes* contributor Ralph Benko. "The hard left holds America to be Evil while the 'globalist' elites hold America to be an atavistic, irrelevant artifact. Trump, his followers, and the right, take an unflinching stand that America is Beautiful. Not perfect. But Beautiful. This is a clash of worldviews and a kind of civil war."[1]

As if to prove Benko's point, *New York Times* columnist Frank Bruni, in a piece titled, "Donald Trump's Phony America," vents his contempt for America under Trump and for Trump's supporters. "This isn't just the land of the fraud but the home of the knave," writes Bruni. "...I sometimes think that when Trump came down the escalator at Trump Tower, he didn't just begin a presidential campaign. He pinched the edge of a scab on our body politic and began to tug, revealing all the racism, resentments and partisan fury beneath it. He gave us a fresh, jolting glimpse of just how much depravity and even criminality exists among the powerful (and the power-mad).... Trump's amorality play contradicts our paeans to the Puritan work ethic. It's not the script that we teach our children. But with Trump in the White House, validated by millions of votes, it may well be what some of them are learning."[2] In light of leftist policies discouraging work, it's unclear why Bruni would fret about the work ethic.

Trump doesn't just vigorously pursue a conservative political agenda; he flouts political correctness and dishes back to the left in direct proportion to its attacks. A perpetual outsider despite his billionaire status, Trump openly rejects leftists' smug elitism and defies their moral authority to condemn him. Unused to this insubordination, his opponents are reacting with malicious indignation. Trump doesn't usually initiate attacks—he's a counterpuncher who mostly leaves his opponents alone if they treat him fairly. But that rarely happens. They viciously and relentlessly attack him, his family, and his supporters, and their shrillness and incivility expose their hypocrisy in attacking him for his alleged rudeness and vulgarity.

As always, leftists exempt themselves from the standards they impose on others, and so they—Democratic politicians, narcissistic Hollywood scolds, and the liberal media—feel free to savage Trump in ways we never see from him. Even if Trump devoted his entire presidency to denouncing his detractors, he could never approach the quantity and nastiness of attacks they hurl at him on a daily basis.

"BADASS GLEE"

Trump Derangement Syndrome is acute among Democratic politicians. From the leadership down, Democrats show contempt for Trump, according him—and the office of the presidency—zero respect. They depict him as the personification of evil and an enemy of democracy, even though there is nothing remotely extreme about his policies.

Their opposition goes beyond mere personal insults—it's an orchestrated attempt to obstruct every aspect of his agenda. In the first two years of the Trump presidency, Trump's district court appointees got 64 percent more negative confirmation votes than such appointees during the first two terms of all newly elected presidents combined. Leftists were incensed over the "vacancy crisis" in federal courts during Obama's presidency. But under Trump, the vacancies are some 80 percent higher, while leftist groups such as Alliance for Justice lead the obstruction rather than sound more alarm bells over the "crisis."

Another telling statistic involves Senate Rule 22, which details a formal process to end debate. The Heritage Foundation's Thomas Jipping notes that from 1949 to 2016, the Senate used Rule 22 to end debate only six times during newly elected presidents' first two years. Democrats used it forty-eight times in Trump's first two years.[3]

The left simply doesn't care about any harm that befalls everyday Americans as a consequence of its attempts to paralyze the government. HBO's Bill Maher declared he's "been hoping for a recession" because it would help "get rid of Trump." When a guest noted that people lose their jobs and homes during a recession, Maher replied, "I know. It's worth it."[4] There is the left's compassion in a nutshell.

After discussing government spending with Trump at the White House, then–House Minority Leader Nancy Pelosi told her aides, "I was trying to be the mom. It goes to show you: You get into a tinkle contest with a skunk, you get tinkle all over you. It's like a manhood thing with him—as if manhood can be associated with him." Well, if anyone supports one gender over the other, it's not Trump but Pelosi. In an interview with CNN, she said, "I take some, for lack of a better term, badass glee, in just saying, 'Women, you know how to get it done. Know your power.'... I want women to see that you do not get pushed around." She said her pursuit of the speakership was partially inspired to empower women who felt dejected after Hillary Clinton's loss in 2016.[5] Incoming congresswoman Veronica Escobar also trashed Trump on gender grounds, labeling him "a misogynist, a president who has been antagonistic to women's issues."[6]

Congresswoman Maxine Waters has a particularly acute case of Trump Derangement Syndrome, discouraging people from even listening to him. "I don't even know why he wants to come and give the State of the Union," she complained. "The state of the union under him is not good. And he has been divisive, and I think he's putting us all in harm's way. And so he is not worthy of being listened to.... And so, I'm not looking forward to his State of the Union, and I hope people will turn the television off!"[7] A month later Waters launched a bizarre Twitter tirade against Trump. "Lying Trump came away from the fake summit with terrorist & killer Kim Jong-un with nothing because Kim never intended to offer anything," she exclaimed. "Don the con man got conned! Hey number 45, are you still in love w/ Kim?" Another Waters tweet informed Trump that "God will never forgive you" for allegedly supporting Saudi crown prince Mohammad bin Salman following the murder of Saudi writer Jamal Khashoggi. Yet another Waters outburst tried to advance the Russia collusion hoax: "Trump, you have screamed no collusion and no obstruction of justice so many times, trying to influence others, that I think you really believe your own lies. Just stop it. No honesty. No truth. No trust. No patriotism."[8]

Attempting to leverage her prosecutorial experience and her party's raw hatred for Trump, Democratic presidential hopeful Senator Kamala Harris argued that the next president should be capable of prosecuting Trump. "We're gonna need a fighter, and we're going to need somebody who knows how to prosecute the case against this president," said Harris.[9]

Not to be outdone, Congresswoman Ilhan Omar described Trump as subhuman. Asked to compare Presidents Obama and Trump, Omar replied, "That is silly to even think and even equate to. One is human, the other is really not."[10] Similarly, Alabama state representative John Rogers said Trump's mother "should have aborted him."[11] And for anyone who thought Trump Derangement Syndrome stops at our borders, former Canadian prime minister Kim Campbell will prove you wrong.

As Hurricane Dorian bore down on Florida, Campbell tweeted gleefully, "I'm rooting for a direct hit on Mar-a-Lago!"[12]

"THEY DIDN'T WANT TRUMP TO HAVE A VICTORY"

When DHS secretary Kirstjen Nielsen testified before the House Judiciary Committee, Congressman Luis Gutierrez denounced her, the entire Trump administration, and American Christians *en masse.* "It is repugnant to me, and astonishing to me, that during Christmas ... a time in which we celebrate the birth of Jesus Christ, a Jesus Christ who had to flee for his life with Mary and Joseph, thank God there wasn't a wall that stopped him from seeking refuge in Egypt," said Gutierrez. "Thank God that wall wasn't there, thank God there wasn't any administration like this, or he would have to have perished on the 28th, on the Day of the Innocents, when Herod ordered the murder of every child under two years of age." Condemning the separation of illegal immigrant families at the border, he proclaimed, "Shame on us for wearing a badge of Christianity during Christmas and allow the secretary to come here and lie." In response, Nielsen calmly reiterated that the administration had no separation policy independent of what was mandated by Congress.[13]

Several commentators note how embarrassingly wrong Gutierrez was in his biblical analogy. "No—baby Jesus is not comparable to the illegal migrants being trafficked by globalists," writes Bethany Blankley. "No—the biblical story of Jesus's birth, which Christians celebrate at Christmas and year round, has nothing to do with the Border Wall. (By the way, the Roman Empire built walls—many of which are still standing today.)"[14] Even more pointedly, Blankley observed, "This is coming from a man who advocates that federal dollars be used to kill babies in the exact same way King Herod ordered. They killed live babies, either with a knife, sword, chopped their heads off or crushed their heads with stones. The Clintons, Obamas, and Democrats like Gutierrez have publicly supported the similar procedure called partial-birth abortion. This is why the procedure is called partial-birth—because a living baby is killed."[15]

At the World Economic Forum in Davos, CNBC's Tania Bryer interviewed former secretary of state John Kerry, who slammed Trump for pulling out of the Paris Climate Agreement that Kerry helped negotiate for the Obama administration. When Bryer asked Kerry what advice he would give Trump, he said that Trump "doesn't have an ability to have that kind of conversation." Bryer then pressed, "What would your message be?" "Resign," demanded Kerry, earning loud applause from the Davos mandarins.[16]

The Democrats' antipathy to Trump is so all-consuming that they even oppose him when he's advancing policies they support. When Trump proposed the First Step Act in an effort at criminal justice reform, some Democrats couldn't bring themselves to back it, even though they had long advocated such legislation. Senators Kamala Harris, Cory Booker, and Dick Durbin and Representatives John Lewis and Sheila Jackson Lee sent a letter to their colleagues in May 2017 opposing the reform. CNN liberal commentator Van Jones observed, "I think publicly they were saying it doesn't go far enough. I think privately, they just didn't want Trump to have a victory."[17]

"ROMNEY DIDN'T WIN, DID HE?"

In an interview with *New York Times Magazine*, retired Nevada senator Harry Reid oddly compared Trump with organized crime, which does "not do well with chaos. And that's what we have going with Trump. Trump is an interesting person. He is not immoral but is amoral. Amoral is when you shoot someone in the head, it doesn't make a difference. No conscience."[18] Speaking of amoral, remember when Reid falsely claimed, on the Senate floor, that GOP presidential nominee Mitt Romney had paid no taxes over the past decade? When later asked if he regretted that lie, he responded cynically, "Romney didn't win, did he?" Consider also Reid's response to the *Washington Post*'s Ben Terris, who asked him whether there is a line he wouldn't cross when it comes to political warfare. "I don't know what that line would be," Reid admitted.[19]

Former Clinton secretary of labor Robert Reich was none too pleased with President Trump's planned 2019 State of the Union address, claiming Trump uses "divisive" language to appeal to his base. "There's another reason Trump aims to divide," Reich added, "and why he pours salt into the nation's deepest wounds over ethnicity, immigration, race and gender. He wants to distract attention from the biggest and most threatening divide of all: the widening imbalance of wealth and power between the vast majority, who have little or none, and a tiny minority who are accumulating just about all."[20] Well, that covers nearly all the major themes of this book. Leftists consciously divide us while falsely accusing us of racial, gender, and class divisiveness. Reich is saying that Trump and his supporters are racist, and so Trump ingratiates himself to them by fueling their bigotry. This is sick stuff. The last thing Trump supporters want is to divide the nation along racial, gender, and economic lines. We do wish, however, that leftists would quit pouring salt into wounds they themselves have inflicted.

Democrats and the media constantly paint Trump as a racist, which is their lazy, fallback attack on every Republican president at least going back to Reagan. There's no evidence whatsoever that it's true—notwithstanding widespread but utterly false reports that Trump praised neo-Nazis who rallied at Charlottesville[21]—but they hope to make it conventional wisdom through sheer repetition. AOC tweeted, "The President is a racist. And that should make you uncomfortable."[22] Discussing Trump's border wall proposal on CNN, journalist Carl Bernstein declared, "We have had in this country situations where maybe half the country hates the president of the United States at one time or another. We've never had a president that hates half the country.... We're talking about a wall here that is a symbol that says, 'brown people, we don't want you.'"[23] MSNBC's Chris Hayes alleged that Trump's base wants "an ethnically pure America in the sense of not having immigrants, not having folks of color here." He added, "The wall originated as a device to jog the President's memory, to make sure to remind him to cater to the most xenophobic part of the base of the Republican Party because there is a cluster of people in the Republican Party who catapulted Trump to his win in the primaries who hate and/or fear immigrants and not only that, these are people who define their political life by stemming and stopping the invasion of people who do not look like them."[24] Racism is one of the most damning smears that can be leveled against people, and it says something about leftists that they freely sling the bogus charge without evidence not only against Trump but his millions of supporters as well.

AOC also accused Trump of anti-Semitism, which is rich, considering her alignment with anti-Semitic progressives. When asked about the anti-Semitism of the Women's March, she tried to turn the tables. "First of all, right now in this moment, in the United States we have to center this conversation, I think that concerns of anti-Semitism with the current administration in the White House are absolutely valid and we need to make sure we are protecting the Jewish community and all those who feel vulnerable in this moment," said AOC.[25] Is this blind projection or cynically strategic? If she were truly concerned about anti-Semitism, she'd stop defending the constant anti-Semitic eruptions from her close colleagues, Reps. Omar and Tlaib, instead of lobbing baseless charges against Trump, who has been a stalwart friend of the Jewish people and of Israel. But such inconsistencies give leftists no pause because what truly animates them is their animus against conservatives and their agenda. Being a raging anti-Semite is easily excused among fellow leftists for the good of the cause. "The enemy of my enemy is my friend," as they say.

UNLEASHING INVESTIGATORY HELL

Progressives fantasized that Special Counsel Robert Mueller would produce a report resulting in Trump being frog-marched out of the Oval Office in handcuffs. Mueller's failure to deliver such a report—or find any Russian collusion at all—didn't deter them, much less move them to contrition. Even before the report bombed, the House Democratic majority began unleashing investigatory hell on the president. Democrats had long been chomping at the bit to impeach the president—Rep. Cedric Richmond is clearly not the only congressman who views impeachment as his "sole focus."[26]

In early 2018, sixty-six Democratic House members voted to move impeachment proceedings forward. Congressman Brad Sherman even filed a resolution of impeachment on the very first day the Democrats took control of the House in January 2019. The *Washington Examiner*'s Byron York noted that these efforts were not based on a detailed bill of particulars against Trump. Sherman's resolution was based solely on Trump's firing of FBI director James Comey—which Trump had full authority to do, as Comey himself admitted[27]—and the Comey memos. Meanwhile, impeachment articles filed by Rep. Al Green sought to oust Trump for "sowing discord among the people of the United States" because of his comments on Charlottesville, transgender troops, and Muslim immigration.[28] Witlessly admitting his purely partisan motive, Green confessed he was "concerned if we don't impeach this president, he will get re-elected."[29] That's rich, coming from a party that routinely accuses Trump of being anti-democratic.

Speaking to MoveOn.org activists on the same day Sherman introduced his bill, incoming freshman Democrat Rashida Tlaib vowed, "[W]e're going to go in there and we're going to impeach the mother****er."[30] When a video of her remarks became public, instead of apologizing for her profanity Tlaib denounced Trump for being "completely unfit to serve as president" and tweeted, "I will always speak truth to power. #unapologeticallyMe."[31]

Hypocritical leftists who are always harping about Trump's alleged crudeness constantly ignore vulgarity from their own leaders. Indeed, they often applaud it, as was the case here. "I identify with [Tlaib] because I'm capable of saying something like that off the top of my head at a rally," said *The View*'s Joy Behar.[32]

"WE'RE DESPERATE TO GET TRUMP OUT OF OFFICE"

America's left-wing entertainers are among Trump's greatest haters. When the Supreme Court refused to set aside President Trump's ban on transgender military members, singer Cher tweeted, "No One Is Really Safe in trump's America Unless They're MEMBER OF MAR-A-LAGO, LIVE IN trump TOWER, WHITE, OR WEARS MAGA HAT. My amazing Trans Son is Kind, Smart, Strong, Loving, Talented, & Patriotic American. Trump 'Judges NO ONE By the Content Of Their Character.'" Earlier in the month, Cher tweeted about Trump's cabinet members, "These White Men Sat Around a Table, & Stared Breathlessly at trump like he was going To Donate a Kidney To One Of Them. I CAN'T WAIT TILL THEY ALL GO 2 JAIL."

Joy Behar unwittingly conceded the left's blinding bias when discussing why the media happily prejudged the Covington Catholic High

School students. Cohost Whoopi Goldberg asked, "Why do we keep making the same mistake?" Behar replied, "Because we're desperate to get Trump out of office.... I think that's the reason. The press jumps the gun a lot.... We are basically hoping that [Trump lawyer Michael] Cohen's got the goods, so it's wishful thinking."[33]

Behar is a one-woman army of anti-Trump venom. She asserted that Trump could start a war to avoid having his sons go to prison, that he needs to be "medicated and hospitalized ... or he is going to just kill all of us," and that he is less sane (or moral) than Kim Jong-un and Vladimir Putin. She claimed participants of the annual Conservative Political Action Conference have a "penchant for Nazis." On MSNBC's *The Beat*, Behar called Trump a "psycho" and an "anarchist." On another show, she castigated the CMA Awards hosts for failing to inject politics into their event, since "democracy is at risk, and everybody should be speaking up, everybody." (Notice, however, that she only wants to hear from Trump haters.) On yet another show, she attacked retiring senator Orrin Hatch. "He is going out of office. He has nothing to lose by speaking, against, truth to power about Trump. Maybe he needs to go to jail, too."[34]

Behar is no fan of the First Lady either. She once suggested that a body double was standing in for Melania Trump during her public appearances.[35] She also belittled Melania's immigrant background, declaring, "OK, she was a model, now she's the First Lady. I mean, come on. She is now enjoying the fruits of the American country. . . . You know, she was in Slovenia doing nothing. I don't know what she was doing there."

Actor Robert De Niro has long been an enraged critic of President Trump. When Trump was the Republican presidential nominee De Niro proclaimed, "I'd like to punch him in the face."[36] At the same event he called Trump a "punk," "a dog," a "bullsh*t artist," "a mutt who doesn't know what he's talking about," an "idiot," an "embarrassment to this country," a "fool," and a "bozo."[37] At the Tony Awards, De Niro continued in the same vein. "I'm going to say one thing, F*** Trump," he declared while pumping his fists in the air. "It's no longer 'Down with Trump.' It's f*** Trump." The leftist crowd gave De Niro a standing ovation.[38] "We're at a point with all of this where it's beyond trying to see another point of view," the tolerant, open-minded actor has further stated.[39]

Trump Derangement Syndrome has also spilled into the arts. "Ivanka Vacuuming" is a performance art exhibit on display at CulturalDC's former Flashpoint Gallery in Washington, D.C. The exhibit features an Ivanka Trump look-alike with a pink dress and stiletto shoes vacuuming crumbs off a luxurious pink carpet. Viewers are encouraged to interact by taking crumbs from a pedestal and tossing them at her to vacuum up. In *The Federalist*, Kelsey Harkness notes the irony in the exhibit's reflecting "every stereotype feminists claim to stand against, oversexualizing Ivanka's body and ignoring her hard work. (One can only imagine the feminist rage if it were, say, Michelle Obama on display.)" Harkness points out that the exhibit not only mocks Ivanka's looks but also demeans her success as a businesswoman and White House advisor. "Worse, in the process of shaming stay-at-home mothers, 'Ivanka Vacuuming' encourages onlookers to throw trash at her."[40]

Trump hatred seeps into sports as well. So thoroughly have the Democrats and media smeared President Trump as a racist that some members of the champion New England Patriots team stated they would refuse to visit the White House if President Trump invited them.[41] Harry Potter actor Daniel Radcliffe showed that athletes will be called out if they don't adhere to the proper political viewpoints; he denounced Tom Brady because a MAGA hat could be seen in his locker during a post-game interview.[42]

Sportswriter Natalie Weiner had an even more extreme reaction to a MAGA hat. Triggered at a jazz festival she attended, she took to Twitter to unburden herself. "Just yelled at a pr*ck with the audacity to wear a f*cking make america great again hat in the middle of a jazz festival," she tweeted. "He was walking to see [singer] irma thomas and he doesn't deserve to be within a 10 mile radius of irma thomas." Oblivious to her own hypocrisy, she said, "I don't understand how people can be so hateful I really don't."[43]

"HIS SUPPORTERS KNOW HE'S A CRIMINAL. THEY JUST DON'T CARE."

Actor Jim Carrey has taken to political art, drawing sketches to express his uncontainable angst. He directs his hostility at Trump and his millions of supporters. He also has a strange fixation on Republican women, particularly those who serve in the Trump administration. He drew an image of Alabama's pro-life governor, Kay Ivey, in the shape of an unborn baby, being aborted by having her brains sucked out.[44] He posted a sketch of former White House press secretary Sarah Huckabee Sanders as "the Gorgon," a creature who will "turn your heart to stone." He drew a picture of Department of Homeland Security secretary Kirstjen Nielsen after calling her a kidnapper and a murderer. He drew Mississippi senator Cindy Hyde-Smith as a ghoulish figure holding a noose while standing with Trump in front of a burning cross. "Nothing comforts a federally-abducted refugee child like a photo op with a Slovenian model wearing a coat that says she doesn't give two craps about your misery," wrote Carrey within a drawing depicting Melania Trump. "Smile for me darlink [sic]. I came very long way." How many strictures of political correctness did Carrey violate there? But who cares? Certainly not hypocritical leftists.

Carrey also mocked Sarah Huckabee Sanders's faith. "This is the portrait of a so-called Christian whose only purpose in life is to lie for the wicked. Monstrous!" he wrote on a drawing of her. When Sanders's father, conservative commentator and former Arkansas governor Mike Huckabee, defended his daughter and called Carrey a "pathetic bully, sexist, hater, bigot & Christaphobe," Carrey doubled down, boasting that he had incurred the disapproval of Sanders's defenders. "I am so gratified by the reaction to my little drawings. It is the job of a political cartoon to vex those who abuse power or enable those abuses," said the self-important Carrey. "This administration has been lying to the American people from day one while plundering the country and debasing our values. And those who cover for this shameful mobster of a President are putting makeup on a melanoma and telling the cancer patient that everything's fine. Monstrous? You bet!"[45]

Carrey also sketched a picture of a chimpanzee wearing blue glasses and thinking about the evolutionary process in reverse, with a red-capped Trump supporter at the beginning of the chain ultimately devolving into an ape. In his Twitter post of the sketch, Carrey said, "Let's remember this year that according to very sound scientific evidence, human beings evolved from apes and not the other way around."[46]

Actor Mark Hamill, who played Luke Skywalker in *Star Wars*, claimed Darth Vader is morally superior to Trump and former vice president Dick Cheney because Vader repented for his sins. "He saw the error of his ways," said Hamill. "I don't see either one of them doing that." Hamill also tweeted a parody advertisement for "Trump tear gas," saying, "NEW: TRUMP TEAR GAS FOR TODDLERS!!! '1st of all, the tear gas is a very minor form of the tear gas itself—It's very safe. The ones that were suffering, to a certain extent, were the ones putting it out there. But it's very safe!'"[47]

Comedian Chelsea Handler tweeted, "Everyone in the president's inner circle is a criminal because they all work for one." Handler also ripped Trump supporters. "It's not whether or not Trump is criminal," she tweeted. "He cheats, lies, steals, any time he talks. His supporters know he's a criminal. They just don't care. But, what about Republicans in govt. who know and do nothing at the expense of everyone in our country? That is criminal, too."[48] Where would we be without Chelsea Handler's criminal law and political expertise? At least she seems to be adjusting well after she claimed Trump's election drove her to therapy. "I had a midlife identity crisis once Trump won, because I had never had my world feel so unhinged, I think," she told HBO host Bill Maher.[49] Somehow that is not difficult to believe.

Actress Meryl Streep has repeatedly shown her animus for Trump, as when she turned her Golden Globes acceptance speech in January 2017 into a tirade against the president-elect. She did the same in an interview with Stephen Colbert, who contributed his own barbs as well. Colbert said, "What's it like for you to see somebody who is the President of the United States who is the top politician who is indifferent to the idea of empathy? I'm not sure he knows what you mean when you say it." It's telling that so many leftist Trump bashers are indignant about his supposed callousness while demonstrating a pathological hatred for him. Streep's bizarre response was revealing. "I'm scared. I'm scared by him, by his possibility," said Streep. "And I do empathize with him. I can't imagine what his 3 a.m. is like. There's a gathering storm—everyone feels it, he feels it. His children are in jeopardy, and I feel that. I think, 'What if my children were in jeopardy?' I would do anything—anything—to get them out of trouble. So we should be afraid. That's what I think."[50] So Trump may act recklessly to keep his kids out of jeopardy—a strange action for a guy supposedly lacking empathy.

A MANUFACTURED CRISIS—THAT HAPPENED TO BE REAL

The left ramped up the attacks on Trump during the partial government shutdown of December 2018 and January 2019, which stemmed from congressional Democrats' refusal to fund a border wall. Denouncing Trump as a "dangerous menace," HBO *Real Time* host Bill Maher urged Democrats not to cave. "Trump is holding this country hostage," Maher exclaimed. "You don't deal with terrorists."[51] Nancy Pelosi also accused Trump of holding the American people hostage and insisted he stop manufacturing a border crisis.[52] Likewise, referring to Trump's border security speech, MSNBC's Nicolle Wallace said, "But the big scam of the whole address was that there is a crisis. There is not a crisis."[53]

Speaking about the border, Congressman Robert Menendez said, "I hate to say this about the president of the United States, but he lies, and he is, you know, fast with the ... half-truths at the end of the day."[54] NBC's Chuck Todd attempted a similar attack. "The President has manufactured one heck of a political crisis for himself," he claimed, implying Trump's "manufactured" border crisis had turned into a political crisis for him.[55] The liberal media echo chamber enthusiastically repeated the Democrats' mantra that Trump was "manufacturing" a border crisis and lying about conditions there—though eventually even they were forced to acknowledge the emergency, at which point they effortlessly switched from denying a crisis existed to blaming the entire situation on Trump's racism.

On the House floor, Congresswoman Yvette Clarke unleashed a tirade tying together many of the Democrats' disparate insults—Trump was a despot, a plutocrat, a tormentor, a thief, and a grifter, all rolled into one:

> Let's be clear, this government shutdown is not a—about a border wall. Our country is in the midst of a government shutdown because a man who has fashioned himself after a Banana Republic dictator, a con man engaging in the

> proverbial bait and switch, has decided to pickpocket the American people for an immoral border wall policy that the American people do not support. This billionaire bully is intentionally imposing pain, anguish, and anxiety on 800,000 federal workers, including over 14,000 New Yorkers holding them and their families hostage in order to extort billions of dollars from the American taxpayer to satisfy a broken promise to his supporters that Mexico would pay for his wall.[56]

TOOTHLESS GARBAGE PEOPLE

The left's unhinged hatred for Trump extends to the president's associates as well as his everyday supporters. Disgraced FBI agent Peter Strzok—the lead investigator of the Russia collusion hoax until he was removed and later fired for exchanging profane anti-Trump text messages with his paramour, FBI lawyer Lisa Page—complained to Page about a trip he took to Walmart where he said he "could SMELL the Trump support."[57] Along the same lines, after watching a video of rowdy Trump supporters at a rally in Tampa, *Politico* reporter Marc Caputo referred to them as toothless "garbage people."[58]

Jimmy Kimmel also has a low opinion of Trump supporters, ridiculing those who raised private funds for a border wall as "dopey people." "People, this is what people do with their disposable income when they don't have loans from college to pay off," explained Kimmel. "Donating money for a wall that will never exist. It's like starting a college fund for Harry Potter.... A more useful thing to do with your money would be to go outside and feed it to a bird but you do have to admire the sacrifice they're making. I mean, a lot of these people are dipping into their meth money for this."[59]

Trump haters play for keeps. They want to make Trump administration officials permanent outcasts from mainstream culture and the workplace. When *Dancing with the Stars* announced former Trump White House press secretary Sean Spicer would compete on the show, the left was thrown into spasms of rage. "The apoplexy was immediate," noted Kevin Williamson in the *New York Post*, "calls for ABC-Disney boycotts by Democratic activists, the *Independent* demanded Spicer be put on a 'permanent blacklist'—even *Variety*, which still exists, got in on that hot outrage action."[60] *Dancing with the Stars*' famed integrity, you see, cannot be sullied by the appearance of a former Trump official.

In their trademark thuggish style, leftists want to ensure everyone understands that working for Trump will impede their future job prospects. So a coalition of leftist groups is pressuring companies not to hire former Trump administration officials. When DHS secretary Kirstjen Nielsen resigned from her post, *Bloomberg* reporter Jennifer Epstein tweeted, "Nielsen's next stop will be carefully watched. If any major companies hire her, pay her to speak, etc., expect to see major outcry from immigration and civil rights groups and beyond." In a *Bloomberg* piece Epstein referred to an open letter signed by forty-one groups and sent to CEOs of all Fortune 500 companies, warning companies against hiring Trump officials. "They should not be allowed to seek refuge in your boardrooms or corner offices," the letter cautioned. "Allowing them to step off of the revolving door and into your welcoming arms should be a non starter." The letter names thirty current and former officials including Nielsen, John Kelly, Sarah Huckabee Sanders, and others. The groups purchased an ad in the *New York Times* warning corporate America not to "let hate into your boardroom" and featuring a photo of a MAGA-looking hat that reads "Put Kids in Cages."[61]

SATAN HATES TRUMP TOO

Satan worshippers are apparently not big fans of President Trump—then again, satanists are generally on the political left. Lucien Greaves, cofounder of the Satanic Temple, said, "For me, it seems kind of obvious that there's been a complete reversal in the roles of who's ostensibly the good guys and who are the bad guys. Right now, we have evangelical nationalists pushing a theocratic agenda in the United States and making great headway to take away people's reproductive rights, endorse corporal punishment in schools, spread pseudoscience of or otherwise reject the scientific point of view, and really undermining liberal democracy." Penny Lane, director of the film *Hail Satan?*, shares these views. Speaking of Trump, she says, "You know, the evangelical Right really did a lot of work to elect him. So he's repaid them in various ways. And so I feel like the work the Satanic Temple is doing is particularly resonant now. I also think that we're in *such* dark political times that people who—maybe typically—wouldn't care what the satanists have to say might be a little more open-minded in their desperation for answers."[62] You have to love satanists complaining about "dark" times.

In the next chapter we'll see how Trump Derangement Syndrome has infected and largely destroyed the mainstream media.

CHAPTER FIFTEEN

Trump Derangement Syndrome: The Media

"GETCHO HAND OUT MY POCKET"

The mainstream networks are openly hostile to Trump. Having monitored and analyzed every moment of coverage of President Trump on ABC, CBS, and NBC evening newscasts in 2017 and 2018, the Media Research Center found that an astounding 90 percent of their coverage was negative, with the Russia collusion hoax rating as the most-covered topic.[1] Furthermore, after NBC reported in February 2019 that the Senate Intelligence Committee had found no material evidence of collusion between the Trump campaign and Russia, none of the three major news networks gave it one second of coverage in their evening newscasts over the next two days. This compares to 2,202 minutes of airtime the Russia probe received from January 21, 2017 to February 19, 2019.[2]

The networks' anti-Trump bias transcends their newscasts. On ABC's *The View*, cohost Ana Navarro encouraged furloughed federal workers to steal meals from Trump hotels. "Listen…there are 800,000 federal workers," said Navarro. "I have a suggestion for these federal workers. Since Donald Trump says that people will know them and will work with them, I think federal workers should show up at Trump properties, eat and eat and eat and eat and then say to the people when the bill comes, you know, the President said he'd work with me. I'm here to eat for free and get room and board for free!"[3] A *Boston Globe* columnist went even further, calling for waiters to contaminate the food of Trump administration officials.[4]

During Trump's 2019 State of the Union speech, *The Atlantic* sportswriter Jemele Hill expressed a Trump assassination fantasy, tweeting that AOC should yell, "Getcho hand out my pocket"—the words used to distract the audience in the Manhattan Audubon Ballroom in 1965 to facilitate the assassination of Malcolm X. Hill later said she was joking, but imagine the uproar if someone had "joked" about assassinating President Obama. Donald Trump Jr. condemned the tweet and challenged *The Atlantic* to take action.[5]

The Trump-loathing media are far nastier in their shots at Trump and his family than Trump has ever been in a locker room among friends. They castigated him for not meeting with U.S. troops in a war zone, and then when he and the First Lady met with soldiers in Iraq during Christmas, they denounced him for signing their MAGA hats. Trump shot back on Twitter, exposing their pettiness: "CNN & others within the Fake News Universe were going wild about my signing MAGA hats for our military in Iraq and Germany. If these brave young people ask me to sign their hat, I will sign. Can you imagine my saying NO? We brought or gave NO hats as the Fake News first reported!" Oozing hypocrisy, the media also mocked Melania for wearing "out of touch" Timberlands, when just six days earlier they swooned over Michelle Obama's $3,900 thigh-high designer glitter boots.[6]

Former First Lady Michelle Obama responded to a photo of Melania at the prompting of NBC's Jimmy Fallon, who asked her what she was thinking when she and former President Barack Obama were departing from the White House after Trump's inauguration in 2017. "Bye, Felicia!" she said, invoking a phrase from Ice Cube's 1995 movie *Friday*, which means to smugly dismiss a person or situation. Michelle Obama said elsewhere that at some point during that day she "stopped even trying to smile."[7] I thought Trump was the ungracious one!

Indeed, the left is strikingly vicious toward Melania, blasting her over the most trivial details imaginable. In *Vogue*, Bridget Read mocked her White House Christmas decorations, sarcastically noting that they were pointedly designated "Christmas" rather than the generic "holiday" decorations. "It seems that FLOTUS has chosen a theme more inspired by hell than a holly, jolly Christmas," writes Read.... "This year's decorations have taken a different dystopian tack: Walking through a strange assemblage of bloodred trees, Trump looks to be channeling *The Handmaid's Tale*. All they're missing are the bonnets worn by the handmaidens in Margaret Atwood's patriarchy-cum-totalitarian Gilead."[8]

Could leftists be any more spiteful—while attacking the Trumps for their alleged maliciousness? A few weeks later, as if to prove its mean-spiritedness was no one-off fluke, *Vogue* bitingly panned the White House Christmas portrait as "surreal." "The photo, which was reportedly snapped before the first couple headed to the Congressional Ball last Saturday, shows FLOTUS and POTUS looking almost like cardboard cutout versions of themselves. And they are very, *very* smiley—despite this season of indictments, and the dissolution of their flagrantly fraudulent charity organization. They are also holding hands, a move that is famously out of character for them."[9]

Late-night host Jimmy Kimmel went further into the gutter in attacking Trump's family, ridiculing President Trump's son-in-law and adviser Jared Kushner, and throwing in a sexual slur against Ivanka. "I guess the thinking of [Trump] is: if he's good enough to screw my daughter, he's good enough to screw the country," said Kimmel.[10]

The media's bias against Trump comes in all shapes and sizes, all colors and flavors. It's not just their direct barbs at him on their opinion shows but also in their "news" reports, which are thinly veiled opinion shows. The print media incorporate their biases throughout their reporting—in headlines, the placement of pieces, and the structure of stories, such as omitting facts that reflect well on Trump or burying them deep in a piece.

Broadcast media use similar tactics. Columnist Quin Hillyer, no fan of President Trump, showcases CNN's practice of dressing opinions as facts, calling such presentations "fake news." After criticizing Trump for hyperbole in calling the news media the "enemy of the people," Hillyer writes, "[I]t would surely help matters if the media maintained at least a modicum of objectivity and fairness. Day after day, CNN's bottom-of-screen chyrons during its supposedly straight-news shows make that network one of the worst violators of the journalistic ethic that once mandated separating news from opinion." Hillyer cites CNN's on-screen graphics on the morning of January 8, 2019, before Trump's scheduled address to the nation that evening on the border crisis. One chyron read, "Trump faces credibility crisis in prime-time address tonight"—an obvious editorial comment by CNN. "Who decided it's a 'credibility crisis'?" asks Hillyer. "Is that a universally, or even widely, agreed-upon analysis? Even if so, if it's analysis at all, why is it a news headline—and if it is a headline, shouldn't the source of the judgment somehow be named?"[11] We see similar examples each day on cable and broadcast news networks as they deviously cloak opinions with a veneer of factuality.

The media's hostility to Trump should be no surprise in light of the uniformity of thought in today's newsrooms. Former CBS News reporter Lara Logan noted that 85 percent of America's reporters are registered Democrats and have largely lost all objectivity, which leads to propaganda. Logan explained to Fox News' Sean Hannity that the major players at the liberal news and cable outlets prefer to *make* news rather than report it. As Beth Baumann observes at *Townhall*, many so-called "journalists" despise President Trump because he has called them out on their "fake news" and more of the American public is on to their game.[12]

"STOP FACT-CHECKING NORMATIVE CLAIMS"

Another sleazy tactic the media use to discredit Trump is their meticulous yet utterly bogus "fact-checking" critiques of his statements and speeches. Being in cahoots with the Democrats, the mainstream press showed no interest in fact-checking their ridiculous denial that a border crisis existed. But once the White House announced Trump would give an Oval Office speech on the subject, they geared up for battle. CNN's Alisyn Camerota warned, "Fact-checkers are eating their Wheaties and getting extra rest since they will be working overtime tonight to separate fact from fiction on this border situation." Afterward, CNN barking Chihuahua Jim Acosta said that Trump's speech "should have come with a Surgeon General's warning that it was hazardous to the truth."

As *The Federalist*'s Mollie Hemingway observed, however, most of the alleged "fact" checks were actually critiques of opinions. Many critiqued topics Trump didn't even discuss, and sometimes they dinged him for completely truthful statements. One egregious example was *Politico*'s Ted Hesson declaring "not true" Trump's claim that there is a border crisis. Hemingway responded with a simple request: "Stop fact-checking normative claims and subjective, value-based assertions! It degrades the entire enterprise of fact-checking!"[13]

It's ludicrous for the liberal media to conduct fact checks when they are obviously agenda-driven, not facts-driven. They are in lockstep with Democrats against border enforcement and diligently slant the "news" to promote their opposition to a border wall and other enforcement proposals. KUSI, a local TV station in San Diego, California, reported that CNN declined an interview with its reporter Dan Plante because he was prepared to say the San Diego border wall is effective. While CNN unconvincingly denied this, the channel heavily relied on reporting from Jim Acosta, who naturally disputed the wall's effectiveness—an opinion CNN knew wasn't shared by at least some informed locals.[14]

Along the same lines, two of the foremost border security experts in the nation, former acting ICE director Tom Homan and National Border Patrol Council president Brandon Judd, told the *Daily Caller* that Fox News was the only cable news network that offered to interview them during the government shutdown over border wall funding. "I don't think that aligns with the stories [the other networks] are trying to tell," said Homan. "You know, the president being a racist and anti-immigrant, and I give facts about what's happening at the border that just don't fall within their talking points because I think immigration enforcement should be colorblind." Judd said, "All I want to do is, I want to get a truthful conversation out. I just want people to have all of the facts and then they can make their opinion based upon the facts and if their opinion is disagreeing with me, that's perfectly fine. But disagree with me on the facts.... Normally, when we're on CNN, we don't fit [its] narrative and we're able to express from a law enforcement standpoint what's really happening on the border and... because we're going to challenge the people to think differently I think that's why you don't see us on those networks."[15]

Tax cuts are another issue the media grossly distort. They often deny that Trump even cut taxes at all for the middle and lower classes, which echoes a Democratic narrative. For example, Senator Kamala Harris claimed that the average American's tax refunds have decreased, so Trump's tax cuts are actually a "middle-class tax hike." To the contrary, the Heritage Foundation's Adam Michel says that some of the biggest cuts are benefiting the lowest-income Americans—at least those of them who still pay income taxes. A typical family of four, said Michel, got a $2,917 tax cut in 2019. Besides, one's refund may have nothing to do with the amount of one's tax cut. Heritage projected that the average household could expect about $26,000 additional take-home pay over the next ten years from the Trump cuts.[16]

"THE ONLY GROUP WHO CAN'T PUT THEIR RAGE AND BILE AWAY FOR A SINGLE DAY"

Like a Pavlovian dog, the media reflexively convert every story into an opportunity to bash Trump, even when he has no connection to the topic whatsoever. While monitoring a livestream of President George H. W. Bush's funeral, ABC News' Terry Moran turned his attention to the current president. "Probably a different tone in that funeral," Moran said, speaking of Trump's future funeral. "First, he's going to choreograph it, so there might be more trumpets and fanfare. Yes, he would do it bigger, one would imagine," ABC correspondent Devin Dwyer added. "It will be the best presidential funeral ever," said Moran. "No one will ever have seen anything like that funeral."[17] This is news? Do these frustrated comics not see the irony in displaying their own classlessness while trashing Trump for his?

Commentator Andrew Klavan captures this trenchantly. "There's this narrative going around that the funeral and the tributes to the grace and dignity of President George H. W. Bush were an inherent rebuke to Trump, who obviously is a rough neck and has this boorish style," said

Klavan. "But I think the true narrative is exactly the opposite of that. I think that the Bushes had a very graceful funeral in which they included President Trump, President Trump behaved very well, and in doing that, it isolated the only group of people in the country who cannot put their rage and bile away for even a single day. Namely, the media."[18]

Not a "single day" is right. *Daily Beast* writer Corbin Smith denounced the New England Patriots as "Team MAGA," "MAGA scum," and "the preferred team of white nationalists." Bizarrely, Smith attacked quarterback Tom Brady for leading Patriot fans in a chant of "We're still here." While most sane Americans would view that as a fun but unremarkable event, Smith perceived nefarious political meaning, comparing Brady to a "square-jawed grifter throwing red meat to the hogs at an alt-right rally, screaming at the libs who thought Nancy Pelosi and her gender warriors were gonna keep DECENT AMERICAN FOLKS from BEING HERE."[19]

Showing public support for Trump with MAGA hats, lawn signs, or bumper stickers is risky. "Having to feel so afraid to express our political views is outrageous," writes Lloyd Marcus. "Democrats and fake news media have so twisted the meaning of 'MAGA' and generated such hatred for Trump that citizens are afraid to publicly support the president of the United States. This is still America. Thugs who physically attack us for expressing our First Amendment right to free speech must be prosecuted."[20]

"IT REINFORCES EVERY BAD STEREOTYPE ABOUT THE MEDIA"

Leftists routinely blame Trump for things he has nothing to do with, such as Chicago mayor Rahm Emanuel implying Trump was responsible for the Jussie Smollett hoax. "The only reason Jussie Smollett thought he could take advantage of a hoax about a hate crime is because of the environment, the toxic environment that Donald Trump created," argued Emanuel.[21]

Similarly, Megan Garber of *The Atlantic* blamed the 2019 college admissions bribery scandal on Trump. Why were the sins of actress Lori Loughlin, who was indicted for a scheme in which her daughters' athletic backgrounds were falsified to get them into college, Trump's fault?

Simple—because "the logic of the con—the perversity of it—is becoming normalized," writes Garber. ". . . People talk about, and financially depend on, side hustles. An alleged grifter sits in the Oval Office, near a bust of Andrew Jackson and the nuclear codes." When Fox News' Ed Henry asked Republican senator John Kennedy to respond to the article, Kennedy replied, "Someone needs to tell whoever wrote that article that the voices [s]he's hearing in h[er] head aren't real. That is, to try to turn this into Trump's fault, is to say it's a bridge too far, is a gross understatement. It's absurd."[22]

When Virginia governor Ralph Northam got himself in hot water over wearing blackface while in college, *Today* cohost Craig Melvin asked his panel why blackface seems "all of a sudden front and center in America again?"—as if leftists haven't obviously turned everything into a race issue today. "I think it has something to do with what Donald Trump has unleashed," replied Princeton professor Eddie Glaude Jr. "It has something to do with the reservoir that's underneath our politics that can always be activated at any moment. So it's not like it's something new has happened. It's always underneath. It's the undertow." MSNBC political analyst Zerlina Maxwell concurred, saying, "You know, young children of color are dealing with kids saying, 'Build the wall.' Donald Trump has normalized this overt display of racism."[23]

Likewise, Congressman Al Green tried to corral support for his impeachment motion by blaming Trump for the racial controversies involving Virginia's Democratic politicians. Congress, said Green, needs to fight bigotry "starting at the top." He described the refusal of Ralph Northam and Virginia attorney general Mark Herring to resign despite wearing blackface in the past as "a symptom of a greater syndrome that currently plagues our country as a result of not acting on President Trump's bigotry."[24]

Sometimes the Trump-scapegoating is more sinister, such as when *BuzzFeed* reported, based on two anonymous sources, that Trump suborned perjury from his attorney Michael Cohen. But one of the story's reporters told CNN that neither he nor his colleague had personally seen the evidence to back up their "bombshell."[25] Despite having no idea whether it was true, CNN and MSNBC ran with the story all day before later admitting they were uncertain. So the entire liberal media were gobsmacked when Mueller's team, after witnessing this breathless coverage, pulled the rug out from under them and said it wasn't true.[26] "BuzzFeed's description of specific statements to the special counsel's office, and characterization of documents and testimony obtained by this office, regarding Michael Cohen's congressional testimony are not accurate," said Peter Carr, a Mueller spokesman.[27]

CNN chief legal analyst Jeffrey Toobin was concerned by the story's collapse. "The larger message that a lot of people are going to take from this story," said Toobin, "is that the news media are a bunch of leftist liars who are dying to get the president, and they're willing to lie to do it. I don't think that's true, but...I just think this is a bad day for us.... It reinforces every bad stereotype about the news media."[28] Everything Toobin says here is accurate except his denial that the media is as dishonest and biased as the public believes—which it is.

The media also deliberately distort Trump's words to villainize him. When a reporter told Trump that British princess Meghan Markle had referred to him as "divisive" and a "misogynist," Trump responded, "I didn't know that. What can I say? I didn't know that she was nasty." Anyone who listened to the exchange knew that Trump meant, "I didn't know she had said those nasty things about me." Yet the liberal media seized on Trump's comment and in unison, dishonestly and maliciously, accused him of calling Markle a nasty person, which is an entirely different thing.[29]

"JUST LIKE THE NAZIS?"

The media can't even give Trump his due where his record is clear. It's hard to deny that as president, Trump has been a stalwart supporter of the pro-life cause. Yet *Slate*'s William Saletan accuses Trump of devaluing life. Apparently triggered by Trump's call during his State of the Union address for legislation to outlaw abortion after twenty weeks of pregnancy, Saletan writes, "Abortion is a serious matter. People may disagree on when life begins, but everyone agrees, at least in principle, on the sanctity of human life. Everyone, that is, except Trump. He treats human life as expendable, not just in the womb or infancy, but in childhood and adulthood. He condones killing people in every context:

capital punishment, counterterrorism, assassination, and crushing political dissent. He's the least pro-life president in American history." While acknowledging that other presidents have started or fought bloodier wars, what distinguishes Trump "is his malicious intent."[30]

Given the left's authoritarian disposition and actions, it's striking that it postures over Trump's alleged authoritarianism, especially considering that his policies focus on decentralizing government power. As noted, the left confuses Trump's strong leadership, decisiveness, and his background as head of his own business empire with political authoritarianism and tyranny. Unlike President Obama, Trump has shown no tendency to act lawlessly through executive orders or otherwise.

In the summer of 2018, when the left was losing its mind over Trump supposedly persecuting the children of illegal immigrants, MSNBC's Joe Scarborough said, "Children are being marched away to showers, just like the Nazis said they were taking people to the showers, and then they never came back. You'd think they would use another trick."

"Just like the Nazis?" asks media watchdog Brent Bozell. "Where was PolitiFact to calmly explain that Mexican and Guatemalan kids were not in fact being marched to poison gas chambers?"[31] MSNBC's Mika Brzezinski declared Trump "will be forever remembered as the president who traumatized little children. That's his brand now. He's the president who purposefully traumatized babies and children, and he traumatized them for his political gain…or to look like Kim Jong-un." Brzezinkski's network colleague Joy Reid said, "The Republicans will fall in line…[T]hey're the North Korean army marching behind the Dear Leader." "Trump creates a mass sense of victimization amongst his base," said Steve Schmidt on MSNBC. "And then he asserts extraordinary claims of power to protect the victims from the scapegoated populations and the nefarious conspiracy. That is fundamentally illiberal, deeply un-American, and, frankly, could be straight out of Munich circa 1928." It's noteworthy that these overwrought accusers never cite any authoritarian act that Trump has actually done to support their claims.

The media wouldn't quit carping about Trump's "evil" actions on the border. During Christmas season 2018, Felipe Gomez Alonzo, an eight-year-old-immigrant boy from Guatemala, died while in the Border Patrol's custody. The media went berserk, feeding off each other's false claims that immigration authorities were responsible for the boy's death. The DHS reported that the child's father was offered but rejected medical treatment after the boy threw up. Far from being neglected, he was taken to the hospital twice and given prescriptions to treat his illness. There was no evidence that border officials did anything wrong, yet the media continued to portray them essentially as murderers.[32]

CBS anchor Dana Jacobson indignantly asked U.S. Customs and Border Protection commissioner Kevin McAleenan why officials let the sick immigrant child out of the hospital. "That's a call made by the medical professionals," said McAleenan.[33] *Townhall*'s Matt Vespa aptly noted that the media's phony outrage was selective. They were silent when the Obama administration shot tear gas at migrants and separated children from adults at the border. Though eighteen migrants died under his watch, they never called Obama a Nazi.[34]

SiriusXM talk radio host and MSNBC guest Mark Thompson found biblical inspiration for denouncing Trump, suggesting that Jesus might not have survived Trump's rule. "If Jesus were today or Trump was back then, He would have been separated from his parents," said Thompson to MSNBC host Stephanie Ruhle. "Joseph and Mary would have been put in a separate detention center—He would have been put in a separate detention center, and He might likely have died in custody like another child did over the holidays."[35]

"THE *TIMES* IS WIDELY KNOWN TO BE LEFT-LEANING"

The media also blamed Trump for illegal immigrants breaking the law. "More now than ever, these families are going to remote areas because it's harder and harder to get in the legal way," said MSNBC's Julia Ainsley. "They're having to wait weeks and months in some cases." MSNBC contributor Maria Teresa Kumar said, "When they decided that they were going to start closing ports of entry—when they were going to teargas families trying to go through the legal channels, she (DHS Secretary Kirstjen Nielsen) and the President forced individuals to go and make more dangerous areas to cross the border."[36] So it's Trump's fault for *forcing* migrants to approach this country and seek illegal entry?

The media dwell on Trump's alleged mistreatment of illegal immigrants but studiously ignore reports of illegal immigrants killing Americans, as if it's their duty to protect the murderers. When the left exalts any group as a protected class, it allows nothing to interfere with the narrative. The media also cover up the many incidents of criminal alien DUIs in America, though every year, ICE takes thousands of illegals into custody. Illegals commit some 80,000 DUIs, 76,000 other traffic offenses, 76,000 drug offenses, and 50,000 assaults annually. Outrageously, leftists provide many of these criminals safe harbor in sanctuary cities.[37]

The media's scapegoating of Trump for every imaginable problem is particularly acute on the race issue. "Killing black people is an old American tradition, but it is experiencing a revival in the Trump era," writes *New York Times* columnist Paul Krugman.

One constant source of irritation for conservatives is the media's denial of its bias. CNN's Don Lemon suggested that his network should add a delay to Trump's prime-time address on border security to prevent the network from "promoting propaganda." "People will believe it whether the facts are true or not," reasoned Lemon. "I guess that's the chance you take with any president. But this one is different. And then by the time the rebuttals come on, we've already promoted propaganda possibly, unless he gets up there and tells the truth."[38] How can you deny being biased when you're openly suggesting tactics to ensure people don't believe what the president says?

The conservative claim of liberal media bias was confirmed by an unlikely source when Jill Abramson, executive editor of the *New York Times* from 2011 to 2014, admitted the paper's news pages are "unmistakably anti-Trump." She said the same holds for the *Washington Post*. "Some headlines contained raw opinion, as did some of the stories that were labeled as news analysis," said Abramson. ". . . Given its mostly liberal audience, there was an implicit financial reward for the *Times* in running lots of Trump stories, almost all of them negative: they drove big traffic numbers and, despite the blip of cancellations after the election, inflated subscription orders to levels no one anticipated." But it's more than just a matter of financial incentive. The younger *Times* employees—many in digital jobs—believe "urgent" times call for "urgent measures: the dangers of Trump's presidency obviated the old standards," says Abramson. Abramson's admission was hardly unique, as Project Veritas caught *Times* senior home page editor Des Shoe on video admitting that the paper is "widely, widely understood to be left-leaning. Our main stories are supposed to be objective. It's very difficult in this day and age to do that."[39]

"RUSSIA HYSTERIA SPRUNG FROM ONE PREDETERMINED OUTCOME"

The media's most shocking display of anti-Trump bias was its despicable conspiracy with the Democrats to overturn the 2016 election by advancing the false narrative that Trump colluded with Russia to steal the election.

As the left hungrily anticipated the release of the Mueller report, MSNBC host Elie Mystal was elated in thinking that Ivanka Trump could be in legal jeopardy, which could spell the end for President Trump. "Look, we've talked a lot about Don Jr., we know now he was at the Trump Tower meeting," he said, "we talked a lot about Eric, because he seems to be Fredo—this is the first time that we have Ivanka, which is like the only kid [Trump] likes, in the crosshairs." Chris Matthews fantasized that President Trump could resign as part of a deal with Special Counsel Mueller. "But what if the prosecutor were to offer the president an alternative? What if he were to say he would let the children walk if the old man does the same? That would mean giving up the presidency in exchange for acquittals all around—not just for himself, but for all his kids."[40]

The Trump-hating media mob indisputably put all their hopes and dreams in Special Counsel Robert Mueller, fully expecting he would deliver the coup de grace and end the Trump nightmare. Nothing made the leftists salivate more than speculating about the long-awaited Mueller report, which they believed would lead to Trump's demise and their salvation. Whether in conspiratorially inventing stories or deluding themselves with false expectations, they were out over their skis. Most of these reporters surely knew—and the rest should have known—that they were pushing a false narrative largely based on laughably asinine allegations funded by the Democrats and compiled by Fusion GPS in the Steele dossier. These collusion claims were expanded upon in an endless parade of reports quoting anonymous intelligence officials spinning stories about classified information, the veracity of which could not be independently confirmed.

CNN contributor and security analyst Juliette Kayyem argued the entire Trump clan was in Russia's pocket. "I personally think that what Mueller is heading to, is not only the indictments... but also a report that discloses the extent to which Trump and his family are compromised by the Russians," said Kayyem.[41]

Journalist Carl Bernstein asserted that Trump's collusion with Russia was a provable certainty. He insisted that Trump's "lies" all concerned Russia and that lawyers working with the White House informed him that Trump hadn't told the truth on multiple issues concerning Russia. "Part of what I know comes from lawyers of some of the other defendants in this matter who have appeared before Mueller, including members of the joint defense team which collaborates with the White House, and those lawyers believe the president has been lying at every turn about his relationship with Russia," Bernstein said. "Look, let us look at all of the lies, follow the money, follow the lies. They are all mostly and most vehemently about Russia."

Bernstein baldly asserted that Mueller already had the goods on Trump. "He has helped Putin destabilize the United States and interfere in the election, no matter whether it was purposeful or not, and that is part of what the draft of Mueller's report, I'm told, is to be about," Bernstein claimed.[42] Since the report showed no such thing, one wonders who, if anyone, told Bernstein these lies. Of course, that goes for every reporter who knowingly advanced the false collusion narrative.

When presidential historian Jon Meacham discussed the Trump-Russia investigation with MSNBC's Brian Williams, he told Williams we've never had "a President of the United States who is considered to be possibly an asset of a foreign government."[43] That may be true, but we've also never had a press corps that spent years conspiring to falsely portray a president as a foreign asset.

After this years-long hype, Mueller's inability to find any collusion was a devastating blow to the media. "Now that Special Counsel Robert Mueller has delivered his report on Russian collusion, it's clear that political journalists did the bidding of those who wanted to delegitimize and overturn Trump's election," writes columnist David Harsanyi. "While bad behavior from partisan sources should be expected, the lack of skepticism from self-appointed unbiased journalists has been unprecedented. Any critical observer could see early on that Trump-era partisan newsroom culture had made journalists susceptible to the deception of those peddling expedient stories. Our weekly bouts of Russia hysteria all sprung from one predetermined outcome: the president was in bed with Vlad Putin." Harsanyi correctly notes that the default position of true journalists should be skepticism, but there was none of that on the Russian collusion yarn.[44]

During the investigation countless liberal media figures baselessly accused Trump of outright sedition. Cable network ratings rose in direct proportion to their sensationalism. Despite being humiliated by their errors, they never apologized. Some of them simply changed their allegation from collusion to the equally preposterous accusation of obstruction—that Trump illegally tried to thwart an investigation into a non-existent crime.

The *New York Times*, one of the biggest, most influential purveyors of false collusion stories, decided on a slightly different tack. In a meeting with *Times* staff, executive editor Dean Baquet made the surprising admission that the paper "built our newsroom" to cover a single story—the Russia collusion hoax. However, after Mueller's feeble testimony to Congress, "the story changed," said Baquet—in other words, the collusion narrative the *Times* had been pushing for nearly three years collapsed spectacularly. So what to do? Instead of calling for an internal investigation to see how the paper had botched the most intensely covered story in decades, Baquet advised it was time to "regroup, and shift resources and emphasis to take on a different story." That new story, any conservative could have guessed, would be Trump's racism.[45]

The media did immeasurable damage to the country through its false reports on Russian collusion. A YouGov poll showed that a majority of Democrats believed Russians tampered with their vote tallies to get Trump elected.[46] Mission accomplished! With the exception of the conservative press, the media pushed the false allegations with shocking uniformity. One notable dissenter was left-wing journalist Glenn Greenwald, who excoriated their reporting as "arrogant and willfully misleading."

Columnist Matthew Continetti observes that as the mainstream media's influence has declined, their efforts to control the narrative have intensified, and they have become more politicized and "less interested in the canons of professional journalism, such as presenting both sides of a story and refraining from baseless speculation." He chronicles the numerous times within a few short months in 2019 that the "liberal media matrix" advanced false headlines, including the slanders against the Covington Catholic high school students, the Jussie Smollett hoax, the Trump-Russia hoax in all its many plots and subplots, and the media's adoration of attorney Michael Avenatti, who represented Stormy Daniels until he didn't and was eventually indicted by a federal grand jury on thirty-six counts, including fraud.[47] No matter how many stories the media get wrong and how badly, they proceed undeterred—because their goal isn't news reporting; it's advancing the leftist agenda.

THE "TRUMP IS CRAZY" TROPE

Sometimes the left gets so carried away that it loses all sense of proportion, let alone respect for democratic norms. The *Washington Times* reported that a secret, five-person group was devising a plan to create a medical panel that would examine the health and fitness of presidential candidates, with the obvious intent of declaring Trump unfit for reelection. One member of the group is Dr. Bandy Lee, a Yale University psychiatrist and editor of *The Dangerous Case of Donald Trump*, a book of essays arguing that Trump is dangerous to the country due to his mental unfitness. "Based on the experience with the current president, we are calling for regular fitness for duty exams on presidential and vice-presidential candidates, preferably as a requirement sometime before they take on the job, and even preferably before they run," said Lee. Knowing that Congress would never go along, Lee's group suggested that candidates voluntarily agree to be examined.[48] With the left's habit of politicizing everything it touches, any Republican candidate *would be* insane to voluntarily submit to such an examination.

MSNBC's Lawrence O'Donnell, a notorious Trump hater, mused about Trump's mental state, even bringing on a psychiatrist to discuss several comments Trump had made. "The president struggled to pronounce a very simple word and he repeatedly could not do it. What does that mean?" asked O'Donnell. "We have grown accustomed to the vagaries and strangeness of Donald Trump's public behavior, but this was a day where the strangeness dominated, both the strangeness of the policy positions and the strangeness of the president's public behavior and public words.... Watching the president today, you had a right to wonder...whether there's something wrong with the working of the president's mind, especially if you watched him repeatedly struggle to say the word 'origin.'"[49]

Joe Scarborough made similar observations a few months before when he suggested that "if we had a cabinet that was filled with people with more character," or if "we had a House and a Senate that took their job seriously," they would have already taken action to remove Trump from office. "There would be people going up to the White House this morning saying, 'Mr. President, questions abound whether you were fit for this office. If this continues, we are going to ask your Cabinet to take a vote on whether you were fit for office and invoke the 25th Amendment.'. . . This is a man who obviously is not fit to hold the office, and we've known that for a very long time."[50]

Leftists freely politicize non-news shows as well. *Top Chef* host Padma Lakshmi slammed Trump over his immigration policies, mentioning his mental state. "And if you look at all the contributions immigrants have made, you're basically looking at what America is today, in whole, full stop—There's no crisis," said Lakshmi. "There's no crisis. The only crisis is that we have a lunatic with a lot of power. That is the only crisis."[51]

"MY DEEPEST WISH IS THAT YOUR BUSINESS FAILS"

The left's contempt for President Trump applies with equal fervor to his supporters. This was particularly apparent in the rush to judgment against the Covington Catholic High School students. Comedian Sarah Beattie, for example, tweeted, "I will bl*w whoever manages to punch that MAGA kid in the face." Reza Aslan tweeted, "Have you ever seen a more punchable face than this kid's?" And comedian Kathy Griffin called for the doxing of the Covington kids. "Name these kids," she demanded. "I want names. Shame them. If you think these [****ers] wouldn't dox you in a heartbeat, think again."[52] This is the same Kathy Griffin who falsely accused the Covington basketball players of displaying "the new Nazi sign"—which was the universally recognized "OK" hand gesture.[53]

Despite the constant media attacks on Trump supporters, *The Nation*'s Elie Mystal bemoaned the media's alleged sympathy for them. He clarified that he was talking about

> the poor, aggrieved white people who've allegedly been "left behind" by forces such as "globalization" and "Democrats." ... From the *New York Times* to CNN, we're being treated to deep dives on the white people who voted for Trump, found it hasn't paid off, and are now questioning their choices. I am here for none of it. If it took *missing a check* due to the government shutdown for you to realize that voting for a bigoted conman was unwise, I have no sympathy. If your business is being hurt by the tariffs ordered by the know-nothing "Tariff Man" you happily voted for, my deepest wish is that your business fails, thereby creating a market opportunity for a hardworking immigrant your president disparages.[54]

Translation: if you were stupid and self-interested enough to support the ogre Trump, you won't be forgiven.

"All of the 'economically aggrieved' Trump voters made the same immoral bargain," Mystal continued. "They calculated that allowing Trump to harass and terrorize 'other' people—nonwhites, women, gays, children, whatever—would result in more money in their pocket. Now they want me to be sad when the racist offset-check they were counting on doesn't clear? You must not know about me."

No, don't you dare sympathize with Trump voters because in Mystal's mind they are all evil, mercenary racists motivated solely to benefit themselves and gratify their own bigoted sentiments. Rather, Mystal instructs his readers to reserve their sympathy for those suffering people "who didn't vote for Trump.... Where are the stories about the innocent victims of Trump's policies, instead of stories about his enablers?"[55] Again, we see the same theme: leftist compassion is reserved exclusively for progressives. Even if a suffering person is part of any of the protected categories the left habitually exploits—minorities, women, gay, transgender—if the person is conservative, the left has no use for them. In the final chapter we'll look at the left's egregious hypocrisy and race-baiting on immigration.

CHAPTER SIXTEEN

Open Borders and Abolishing ICE: The Left's Immigration Agenda

Immigration is among the most controversial issues because progressives refuse to debate it in good faith and smear everyone who disagrees with them as racists. This tendency was noticed by columnist Damon Linker—no conservative—who observes that a surprisingly large number of liberals are "not claiming that cuts to legal immigration shouldn't be made, but that the very act of proposing and defending them in the first place is morally illegitimate. These liberals appear to believe that immigration restrictionists should be excluded on principle from participating in public debate and discussion about immigration policy in the United States."[1]

For example, liberals were outraged when *New York Times* columnist Ross Douthat argued they should negotiate immigration policy with White House policy adviser Stephen Miller.[2] *Salon* columnist Jeremy Binckes reminded Douthat that Miller is persona non grata. "President Donald Trump's immigration policy is, increasingly, in the hands of his policy adviser, Stephen Miller," he wrote. "To most, Miller's history and views should disqualify him from handling the sensitive topic."[3]

It's amusing that Binckes presumes to speak for "most"—most of whom? Trump campaigned as a border hawk, was elected on that platform, and then chose Miller to implement that policy. And in fact, Miller was a prominent public voice for Trump during the campaign. So it's clear Binckes does not mean "most" Americans object to Miller's views—Americans knew both his views and Trump's views when they elected Trump. No, it's clear that what Binckes means is that Miller is anathema to "most" people who live in the same ideological bubble as Binckes does. To *them*—liberal writers and reporters, left-wing activists, Democratic Party members and big-money donors, big-labor foot soldiers, Hollywood glitterati, the zealots of academia, and open-border Republican squishes—Miller is a non-person who can't be reasoned with or even talked to. Instead, he must be shunned and placed beyond the boundaries of respectable society because, as the left has made crystal clear, it believes the only moral position on immigration is open borders. As Linker further notes, "Increasingly, political argument is taking the same form, with liberals asserting that Trump Policy X is not just bad for reasons a, b, and c, but that it transgresses some unwritten standard of moral rightness that renders it prima facie unacceptable and illegitimate. Most often the rationale offered for this judgment amounts to the assertion that the policy, or the motive behind it, is racist (or nativist, xenophobic, or sexist, or homophobic, or transphobic)."[4]

We've seen that the left's moral certitude is a recurring theme that applies to numerous issues. They've unilaterally declared a consensus on climate change, casting all dissenters as abominable science deniers. To them, conservatives are cruel, greedy capitalists and religious hypocrites with no concern for the environment and no heart for the downtrodden or for suffering refugees.

In December 2018 Alexandria Ocasio-Cortez tweeted, "Joy to the World! Merry Christmas everyone—here's to a holiday filled with happiness, family, and love for all people. (Including refugee babies in mangers + their parents.)"[5] Putting aside her biblical illiteracy, AOC is implying conservatives are hypocritical Christians who fail to model Jesus's love.

Republicans are so heartless they would deny asylum to the persecuted and sadistically delight in separating children from their parents.

These are malicious lies. Republicans support granting asylum to people fleeing political persecution, which is what the laws are designed for, not for those escaping poverty. In supporting open borders, sanctuary cities, across-the-board amnesty, and a catch-and-release policy, Democrats are incentivizing border anarchy, human trafficking, and lawlessness. They are endangering American citizens and discriminating against immigrants who play by the rules. There is nothing compassionate about that.

THE NATIONAL CONSENSUS IS GONE

Throughout our history immigration has been legally controlled. We used to have a national consensus that immigration should be an orderly process, closely regulated to ensure that applicants demonstrate their genuine desire to become a part of America, embrace its ideals, and pledge their commitment to the Constitution. This is why the legal path to citizenship and its attendant naturalization process have involved training applicants in civics and inspiring patriotism for this nation. But this national consensus is gone. The Democratic Party now disclaims the nation's sovereign right to control its borders. It is astounding that any self-styled patriotic American could endorse an open-borders policy, which would inevitably disintegrate our national compact.

A nation cannot exist without borders and border enforcement. This is especially true of America because its uniqueness is in its founding ideas, which are enshrined in the Declaration of Independence and the Constitution. Our patriotic ancestors knew that our freedom tradition depends on adherence to the Constitution and on a citizenry dedicated to ordered liberty. They understood that freedom is meaningless unless undergirded by the rule of law, and they believed the government's first duty is to protect its citizens from domestic and foreign threats. They may have disagreed on whether and to what extent we should export our democratic principles, but never on whether we should preserve them for ourselves.

A nation cannot be sovereign without controlling its borders and preserving its culture and the cohesiveness of its national fabric. Indeed, national sovereignty is essential and perfectly biblical. "From one man (God) made all the nations, that they should inhabit the whole earth," declared the apostle Paul. "And he marked out their appointed times in history and the boundaries of their lands." But the left no longer embraces the American idea or America's right and duty to enforce its immigration laws, as well as the orderly, controlled system of immigration they establish. This partly stems from leftists' being more ashamed than proud of America's heritage.

Conservatives fervently believe in ethnic diversity. America is undeniably—and gloriously—an amalgam of countless ethnicities. But we also believe in the assimilation of all ethnicities into a common culture committed to the Constitution and rule of law—as opposed to a balkanized society of suspicious and competing groups.

Leftists don't particularly believe in American exceptionalism or the uniqueness of American culture except that it's uniquely exploitative and bigoted. They discourage assimilation because it works against their practice of identity politics. They conflate culture and race, believing that to celebrate a unique American culture is inherently racist.

Democrats must be pressed to explain how eviscerating our immigration laws would be in the best interest of America and its citizens, how flooding our borders with people we can't support or assimilate would help either those immigrants or current American citizens. If we care about preserving America as the freest and most prosperous and benevolent nation in the world, we cannot continue to ignore border security and thwart the rule of law. How compassionate would the world be without America?[6]

If leftists don't believe in a unique American culture or that America's ideas make it exceptional, then it follows that they wouldn't be as concerned with controlling the legal flow of immigration. If there is nothing special to preserve—if all cultures are equal and if our system of government isn't extraordinary—then what incentive exists to limit the number of people who enter the country? Additionally, the

Democratic Party realizes that the more people who enter the nation illegally, the greater their electoral prospects, especially if they can engineer an amnesty.

"CONTINUED DEMAGOGUERY IGNORES THE TRUE REALITY"

Congressman Dan Crenshaw asked Beto O'Rourke on Twitter, "If you could snap your fingers and make El Paso's border wall disappear, would you?" Crenshaw's question prompted MSNBC's Chris Hayes to ask O'Rourke the question. "Yes. Absolutely," replied O'Rourke. "I would take the wall down." He argued that the wall has not made Americans safer, has cost tens of billions of dollars to build and maintain, and has pushed migrants, asylum seekers, and refugees to the most inhospitable stretches of the border, "ensuring their suffering and death."[7] But Crenshaw noted that illegal crossings have dropped significantly since the wall was erected and that El Paso's mayor has attested that the fence works.

O'Rourke postures about harm to illegal immigrants but says nothing about the children that traffickers bring into the United States or about Amnesty International's estimates that 20,000 migrants are abducted each year in Mexico on their way to America's southern border.[8] He ignores the 15,482 heroin overdose deaths in this country in 2017 alone—some 288 deaths per week[9]—though 90 percent of U.S. heroin comes from Mexico, according to a Drug Enforcement Administration report.[10] He doesn't mention fentanyl, which was responsible for 29 percent of the 63,000 American overdose fatalities in the U.S. in 2016, though 80 percent of the drug's supply enters the country through Mexico. In February 2019, Border Patrol officials secured the largest-ever seizure of fentanyl at the border—more than 254 pounds, which is enough to kill 115 million people.[11]

Like many Democrats, O'Rourke thinks border walls are immoral. Congresswoman Vicky Hartzler offers this counterpoint: "This continued demagoguery ignores the true reality of the situation: illegal drugs are pouring over our border and fueling an opioid crisis that is killing thousands of Americans a year. The true immorality here is the reluctance to do anything about it."[12]

"I WAS GOING TO BE IN A BAD MOOD THE WHOLE DAY"

Fox News' Tucker Carlson offered a four-point summary of the political calculus underlying the Democrats' open-borders policy:

- ★ One: some studies, as noted, show there are 22 million illegal immigrants living in the nation.
- ★ Two: Democrats favor granting citizenship to all of them.
- ★ Three: Studies show the overwhelming majority of first-time immigrant voters vote Democrat.
- ★ Four: The biggest landslide in American presidential history involved a victory margin of only 17 million votes.[13]

Some reporters suggest both sides want to limit illegal immigration, so there is no reason the parties can't come together and reach a compromise solution. But that is pitiably naïve. Democrats support open borders and mass immigration. They have no interest in compromising, as evidenced by their continual shifting of the goalposts and refusal to agree to any Republican offers.

Democrats are steadfast opponents of the rule of law, encouraging illegal immigration through their support for amnesty across the board, their support for sanctuary cities, their callous disregard for criminal elements illegally crossing our borders, their demonization of ICE, their judges lawlessly thwarting President Trump's efforts to enforce federal immigration laws, their consistent obstruction of border enforcement, their endless game-playing over a wall, their denial that a border crisis exists, their downplaying the crimes—including vehicular homicides—committed by illegal aliens, and their lack of concern over illegal narcotics shipped into this country by illegal aliens and drug cartels. They further promote immigration anarchy by opposing measures such as Kate's Law, voter ID laws, adding a citizenship question on the census, deporting MS-13 gang members and other violent criminals, and closing loopholes for asylum that flood the legal system with meritless claims.

Having strenuously alleged that Trump was manufacturing a fake crisis on the border,[14] Democrats were caught flat-footed when their second favorite newspaper, the *Washington Post*, reported right before Trump's border address in January 2019 that there was indeed a border crisis.[15] *Post* reporter Nick Miroff said the numbers are "bonkers." At the rates occurring early in 2019, apprehensions could reach 765,000 by the end of the year, compared with 521,090 in 2018.[16] A CNN/SSRS poll showed that across party lines, Americans increasingly believe we have a border crisis, including 82 percent of Republicans, 70 percent of Democrats, 72 percent of independents, and 74 percent of all Americans.[17]

How could any reasonable person deny there's a crisis? Eighty-seven percent of illegal immigrant families who crossed the border during several months in early 2019 failed to show up for their deportation hearings, according to ICE acting chief, Nathalie R. Asher.[18] Likewise, Acting Homeland Security Secretary Kevin McAleenan testified to the Senate Judiciary Committee that 90 percent of asylum-seekers under a new program skipped their hearings.[19] NBC News reported that in February 2019 apprehensions of "undocumented" immigrants crossing the border were at their highest levels in twelve years.[20]

Eventually, the massive scale of the problem became impossible to ignore. President Obama's Department of Homeland Security secretary, Jeh Johnson, was one of the first Democrats to acknowledge the crisis when he stated on MSNBC's *Morning Joe*,

> When I was in office in Kirstjen Nielsen's job at her desk, I'd get to work around 6:30 in the morning and there'd be my intelligence book sitting on my desk, the PDB, and also the apprehension numbers from the day before. And I'd look at them every…morning, it would be the first thing I'd look at, and I probably got too close to the problem. [M]y staff will tell you if it was under 1,000 apprehensions the day before, that was a relatively good number. And if it was above 1,000, it was a relatively bad number, and I was going to be in a bad mood the whole day. On Tuesday, there were 4,000 apprehensions. I know that a thousand overwhelms the system. I cannot begin to imagine what 4,000 a day looks like. So, we are truly in a crisis.[21]

At the time, the *Washington Examiner*'s Byron York commented, "That is something Democrats in Congress will not admit. Perhaps they believe doing so would give a victory to Trump, which they cannot abide."[22]

After the DHS announced there were 100,000 apprehensions at the southern border in March 2019 and 76,000 in February, Brandon Judd, president of National Border Patrol Council, said the current influx of migrants flooding the southern border represented the "worst crisis" that U.S. Customs and Border Patrol agents have encountered since the agency was established in 1924. "This is the worst it's ever been and if we don't do something it's going to get worse," said Judd.[23] In April, the number of migrants apprehended increased to 109,144—the highest monthly total since 2007.[24]

York puts these numbers in perspective. While in the early- and mid-2000s the number of apprehensions on the southern border was around one million per year, it gradually decreased due to more aggressive border security policies and a major economic downturn. In 2011 they hit a low point of 327,577, but started to creep back up to 479,371 in 2014. Probably because of Trump's election and his tough immigration stance, the numbers dropped again to 303,916 in 2017. But once it became clear that the Democrats and the courts would obstruct Trump's efforts, the numbers rose again to levels approaching those of the early- and mid-2000s.

There is a major difference, however, between the situation then and now. Before, those apprehended were mostly single, adult men trying to avoid detection who were soon returned across the border. So one million apprehensions did not mean anywhere near that number remained in the United States. Today, those caught are far more likely to be families and unaccompanied children who are not trying to sneak in but want to turn themselves over to the Border Patrol, understanding that U.S. law prevents them from being returned or held more than a few days. "In short order," writes York, "they are released into the United States."[25]

Border patrol agents apprehended more than 100,000 people trying to enter the nation illegally in October and November 2018 alone. For the entire year of 2018, more than half a million people tried to enter the country illegally, which is a substantial increase from 2017. These are conservative numbers that exclude people who eluded border patrol and successfully crossed into America.

There are already between 12 million and 22 million illegals in the country today.[26] The United States stands nearly alone in tolerating these staggering numbers. ProCon.org found that in 2010 some 4 percent of the U.S. population consisted of illegals, while the average for thirteen other countries it analyzed was 1.3 percent.[27] *Investor's Business Daily* notes that past presidents—even Clinton and Obama—all acknowledged illegal immigration as a significant problem. "We simply cannot allow people to pour into the United States undetected, undocumented, unchecked, and circumventing the line of people who are waiting patiently, diligently, and lawfully to become immigrants into this country," said Obama.[28] He acknowledged the crisis again in 2014, though he obstructed all reasonable proposals to address it. In 2006, Senator Chuck Schumer and numerous other top Democrats voted for the Secure Fence Act, which provided for a physical barrier along more than 700 miles of the southern border that had no fencing.[29] But now, the only crisis the Democrats acknowledge is any attempt to solve the problem. Their dramatic shift from supporting to opposing border security is one of the most stunning examples of the party's pandering to its extremist base and serving their own interests instead of the nation's.[30]

THE WELFARE BENEFITS CRISIS

Speaking of an immigration-related crisis, some 63 percent of "noncitizens," including green card holders, receive welfare benefits that were designed to assist poor and sick Americans, according to the Census Bureau. Some 70 percent of those who have been here ten years or more receive benefits. To address this problem, President Trump proposed new "public charge" rules that would make it harder for immigrants to qualify for green cards if they use or would likely use welfare programs.

In the data, "noncitizens" include illegal immigrants, long-term temporary visitors such as guest workers, and permanent residents who have not been naturalized. These groups receive welfare, sometimes on behalf of U.S.-born children, despite barriers to keep them from doing so. This is because most legal immigrants have been in the country long enough to qualify for benefits, and the restrictions don't apply to all programs and especially not to noncitizen children. Further, some states provide welfare to new immigrants, and noncitizens, including even illegal immigrants, can receive benefits on behalf of their U.S.-born children who are granted U.S. citizenship and full welfare eligibility at birth.[31]

Leftists often tout the virtues of illegal immigrants compared to American citizens—absurdly, AOC asserts that illegals "are acting more American than any person who seeks to keep them out ever will be."[32] In fact, illegal immigration sucks enormous resources away from needy American citizens. A whopping 4.7 million noncitizen households received welfare according to the 2014 report. Noncitizen households are almost twice as likely to receive welfare (63 percent) as native-headed households (35 percent). Some 45 percent of noncitizen households use food assistance programs compared to 21 percent of citizens' households, and 50 percent of them receive Medicaid compared to 23 percent of citizens. Thirty-one percent of noncitizen-headed households receive cash welfare compared to 19 percent of citizen households.[33] If you think these statistics bother Democrats, you are mistaken. At a Democratic presidential debate, when candidates were asked whether their healthcare proposals would cover illegal immigrants, every one of them raised their hand.[34]

As noted, Democrats adamantly oppose a census citizenship question, arguing that illegal immigrants could be targeted by law enforcement if they admit their status. But that's a smokescreen because Trump's proposal wouldn't require them to specify whether they have legal status, only whether they are citizens. In fact, the Democrats didn't object to such a question as recently as 2010. The real reason they oppose it is that a higher noncitizen response rate leads to increased political power for Democrats because the census determines the apportionment of U.S. House seats, presidential electors, and intrastate seats, not to mention the allocation of hundreds of billions of dollars of federal funds.

"Disproportionate numbers of noncitizens, who tend to reside in heavily blue areas," writes Ben Weingarten, "mean disproportionate political representation and largesse for those blue areas." The Constitution doesn't necessarily mandate this result, but it is the current practice. The cases concerning whether "persons" in the appropriate constitutional provisions includes noncitizens haven't been conclusively determined. Congressman Warren Davidson has proposed a constitutional amendment, the Fair Representation Amendment, to clarify the issue, providing that representatives shall be apportioned solely "by counting the number of persons in each State who are citizens of the United States." Davidson correctly notes that the practice of counting noncitizens dilutes the influence of citizens, especially in states with lower noncitizen populations.[35]

BORDER WALLS WORK—SO DEMOCRATS OPPOSE THEM

Truth be told, the Democrats are no more serious about border security today than they were in 1986, when they falsely promised President Reagan that they'd secure the border in exchange for amnesty for some three million illegal immigrants. Democrats are experts at seducing Republicans into abandoning their principled commitments. Over and over again, in contentious political skirmishes, Republicans immediately act to honor their side of the bargain and accept the Democrats' promise of future action. But that future never comes. During the 2018–2019 government shutdown battle, Democrats wouldn't even agree to offer Trump as much as yesteryear's Democrats offered Reagan and Bush 41. They accused Trump of intransigence, despite his multiple compromise overtures and despite their refusal to make any concessions beyond the anemic $1.3 billion they had already committed for the wall. They simply demanded that Trump unilaterally abandon his signature campaign promise for their disingenuous assurance to contemplate certain half measures on border enforcement at an unspecified future time.

Among their arguments against the border wall, Democrats said it would be an inefficient use of federal funds—as if fiscal responsibility were part of their vocabulary. They also maintained that focusing on border enforcement was imprudent because most illegal immigration occurs from people overstaying their visas. Even if that's true, it's ridiculous to oppose border enforcement just because some illegals enter by other means.

Though Democrats claim the wall won't work, they really oppose it precisely because it *would* work, as experience has shown. One illuminating example is San Diego. Before construction of forty-six miles of reinforced fencing along the border there in 1986, there were 629,656 arrests.

In 2016, by contrast, there were just 31,891 arrests.[36] San Diego's illegal crossings decreased by 95 percent after it built the wall and instituted personnel and technological measures.[37] Likewise, after a physical barrier was constructed at Yuma, crossings there dropped by 90 percent.[38]

Through its vast experience Israel has learned about the effectiveness of border walls. David Rubin, originally from New York, lived in Israel for almost three decades and was mayor of the city of Shiloh. The author of *Trump and the Jews*, he is a supporter of Trump's border wall based on his knowledge and experience with the wall between Israel and Egypt, which successfully reduced illegal crossings. He attributes the Democrats' opposition to Trump's wall to their disdain for Trump and dismisses Schumer's and Pelosi's contention that a physical wall is pointless. "I don't think you can stop illegal immigration with just scanners and patrols," said Rubin. ". . . Empirically it doesn't work. We've seen that what works is a physical border with high-tech measures. That, along with patrols and enhanced tech, are the elements that you need to have if you truly want to put a stop to illegal immigration. If somebody is opposed to having those three elements, then I don't think they really want to stop it."[39]

The effectiveness of Israel's border walls is irrefutable. The country's walls and other security policies nearly eliminated illegal border crossings.[40] "Israel...had a real problem with illegal immigrants coming in from the southern border, about 16,000 in one year," explained Senator Ron Johnson. "In two years, they constructed a 143-mile fence, about $2.9 million per mile, and it cut that illegal immigration rate from about 16,000 to I think 18. Cut it by 99 percent."

Lauding the success of border walls, President Trump tweeted, "There are now 77 major or significant walls built around the world, with 45 countries planning or building walls. Over 800 miles of walls have been built in Europe since only 2015. They have all been recognized as close to 100% successful."[41] While the *New York Times* lamely attempted to debunk some of Trump's claims in a so-called "fact check," their rebuttals were mostly quibbles over semantics. They also cited "experts" to provide brilliant observations such as, "People will find ways to cross walls."[42]

"Trump's numbers ring true," writes the *Daily Caller*'s Evie Fordham. "There are 77 major walls or fences around the world, and many of them were built after the 9/11 terrorist attacks, according to a tally by University of Quebec geography professor Elisabeth Vallet cited by the *Washington Post*. Roughly 50 of the structures were constructed after World War II.... *USA Today* also reported: 'Since the start of Europe's migrant crisis in 2015, at least 800 miles of fences have been erected by Austria, Bulgaria, Greece, Hungary, Macedonia, Slovenia and others—a swift and concrete reaction as more than 1.8 million people descended on Europe from war zones from Afghanistan to Syria.'"[43]

Other countries besides Israel understand that walls work. India built a series of walls that successfully blocked Pakistani terrorists from entering, and many believe the barriers have prevented war between the two nuclear powers. The United Nations erected a highly effective wall dividing Cyprus to separate Turkish and Greek fighters. Morocco built a 1,700-mile system of border barriers to prevent the Algerian funded terrorist group Polisario Front from infiltrating, and its effectiveness helped to end the Western Sahara War after sixteen years. The Brits built walls in Northern Ireland to separate and pacify Protestant and Catholic neighborhoods. After ISIS subsumed northern Iraq, the Saudis built an effective 600-mile border fence and ditch system stretching from Jordan to Kuwait. Kenya was successful in reducing invasions of Somali terrorists with their 440-mile border fencing.[44] Other nations built walls specifically to prevent illegal immigration, such as India on its border with Bangladesh, Spain to keep out African migrants, and Greece, Turkey, and Hungary.[45]

Walls help reduce not only the entry of illegals but also the flow of drugs. Having substantial barriers instead of open frontier allows enforcement agents to place their resources at points of entry to interdict illegal narcotics. With open frontiers, agents are spread thin trying to stop bogus asylum seekers from entering between points of entry, explains *Conservative Review*'s Daniel Horowitz. While most drug seizures occur at points of entry, that doesn't mean that more drugs don't enter between points of entry without being detected, he argues. Horowitz concedes that interior enforcement against illegal immigration is also important to stopping the drug flow but notes that, sadly, Democrats vehemently oppose those measures as well.[46]

"THE ENTHUSIASM OF THE DEMOCRATIC PARTY IS FOR PROTECTING IMMIGRANTS [NOT BORDERS]"

It's crystal clear that Democrats don't really want to stop illegal immigration, as exemplified by their lawless establishment of sanctuary cities. The left always seems to have limitless compassion for lawbreakers and little concern for the law-abiding. Examples abound, such as the case of Gustavo Garcia, an illegal immigrant whose lengthy criminal record began in 2002. Garcia was detained in a Tulare County, California, jail for ten hours for being under the influence of a controlled substance. Before he was released, ICE officials notified deputies that he was a violent criminal who'd been deported twice, but California's sanctuary laws prevented the sheriff's office from detaining him for ICE. Two days later he shot and killed a man, wounded two others, and critically injured a motorist, then died in a high-speed pursuit following a shoot-out with police.[47]

As reported by the *Daily Caller*, Tulare County sheriff Mike Boudreaux commented, "'We have one man that essentially [has] been on a personal reign of terror.'... The sheriff expressed deep 'frustration' about being hamstrung by the state's sanctuary laws. 'The Tulare County Sheriff's Office is equally as frustrated with this situation,' Boudreaux said, citing ICE's lament about the needless suffering caused by releasing Garcia. 'Because of California law, detainers can no longer be recognized by local law enforcement.'" Never held accountable for their heinous enabling of such tragedies, leftists continue to masquerade as compassionate altruists.

Axios CEO Jim VandeHei unwittingly summed up the liberal position during an appearance on MSNBC. "I think the [Democrat] party's changed on immigration. I think the feeling that they have to appear to be really strong by supporting a lot more border security, that that has waned, and that the enthusiasm of the Democratic [P]arty is for protecting immigrants."[48] What he means is protecting *illegal* immigrants—and this is difficult to refute when you consider such head-scratchers as New York Democrats passing legislation to fund college for illegal immigrants. At an estimated cost of $27 million, the Dream Act would make thousands of "Dreamers" eligible for financial aid to attend public colleges in New York. The bill is "a slap in the face for all the hard-working taxpayers who play [by] the rules and struggle for the costs of a college education," said Republican state senator Daphne Jordan. Other Republican legislators agreed the bill would transfer money to illegals from legal residents who often have difficulty paying their own or their children's tuition. In addition, New York Democrats say they will consider permitting illegal immigrants to acquire driver's licenses and giving them improved housing. Governor Cuomo said he might favor compelling insurers to provide free contraceptive care for illegals.[49]

In New York City, Mayor Bill de Blasio announced that the city will spend up to $100 million per year to provide healthcare for people without health insurance, including illegal immigrants, at city-owned facilities. Republican state assemblywoman Nicole Malliotakis raised the obvious objection: "Our citizens have a hard enough time covering their own healthcare costs and now Mayor de Blasio also wants them to pay for the healthcare of 300,000 citizens of other countries. The mayor must stop abusing the middle class and treating us like his personal ATM."[50]

In California, Democratic State Assembly member Dr. Joaquin Arambula intends to reintroduce a bill to provide Medicaid coverage to illegal immigrants over the age of nineteen. If he prevails, the full benefits of the California Medical Assistance Program (Medi-Cal)—hospitalization, prescription drugs, oral care, and vision care—would be available for all low-income earners, including illegals. The state projected that 1.2 million illegals would qualify for the program, costing $3 billion a year. California governor Gavin Newsom supports the measure.[51]

On the federal level, congressional Democrats showed their aversion to border security by demanding, as a condition to reopening the government during the shutdown, a 17 percent reduction in ICE detention beds sought by the administration, an action which Republicans argued would result in more criminals on the streets.[52] "This is a poison pill that no administration, not this one, not the previous one, should ever accept," said Senate majority leader Mitch McConnell. "Imagine the absurdity of this: House Democrats want to set a limit on how many criminal aliens our government can detain."[53] Dozens of U.S. sheriffs came to Capitol Hill to protest the ICE bed cap. "We are at wits end on this," said Bristol County, Massachusetts, sheriff Thomas M. Hodgson. "This really is a catastrophe."

Two national sheriff's groups, the National Sheriffs' Association and the Major County Sheriffs of America, maintained that some 8,300 criminal aliens would have to be immediately released if the cap went into effect. They said 90 percent of illegal immigrants in ICE's custody in the nation's interior (as opposed to at its border facilities) had criminal records.[54] This is the type of result that occurs when Republicans are forced to compromise with Democrats, which illustrates the fallacy in the conventional wisdom that compromise is inherently virtuous. Here, it would lead to criminals being released on American streets. But Republicans signed on to the deal despite this provision, as Democrats were intransigent and it was the only way they could secure $1.3 billion in funding for border security—which wasn't nearly enough.

"THE AMERICA LAST PARTY"

Everything about the moralizing Democrats' immigration policy smacks of open borders—the *New York Times* made their stance explicit with a column titled, "There's Nothing Wrong with Open Borders."[55] The left often frames this argument in moral terms, such as Nancy Pelosi proclaiming, "A wall is an immorality between countries." But why is it immoral for a sovereign nation to protect its border and its citizens? Why is a wall immoral when other forms of border enforcement are not, such as a so-called "technological" border that Pelosi claims to support?[56] Was it immoral when she and virtually all other Democratic Party leaders gave impassioned speeches in recent years stressing the imperative of border security and preventing illegal immigration? Isn't one of the central duties of government to protect its own citizens and ensure their rights? How twisted must one's moral compass be to believe that protecting noncitizens is more important than protecting citizens? It is not immoral to enforce our borders; it is immoral *not to*.

Similarly, how is it fair—or moral—for Democrats to favor blanket amnesty for illegals when so many other immigrants play by the rules and abide by the rule of law? In early June 2019, House Democrats voted for the American Dream and Promise Act, which would grant full citizenship to almost three million illegals—most brought here illegally by their parents but also incorporating some adults who entered illegally, including criminals with violent records. Congressman Steve Scalise said the bill is "only a dream for criminals" because it blocks access to state and federal gang databases, prevents felons and gang members from being referred to ICE for deportation, grants amnesty to violent criminals, and provides no funds for border security. "It's simple: Republicans want safety from crime, and Democrats want sanctuary for criminals," tweeted Scalise.[57] The night before a Democratic presidential debate in June, Elizabeth Warren called for total decriminalization of border violations, understanding that if the violations are only civil there will be no detentions, so anyone who wants to come to the United States would likely be able to do so with virtual impunity.[58]

Pelosi's insistence that a border wall is immoral makes a mockery of our legal immigration system. Mollie Hemingway aptly quoted Bill Clinton on this point: "We are a nation of immigrants, but we're also a nation of laws. It is wrong and ultimately self-defeating for a nation of immigrants to permit the kind of abuse of our immigration laws we have seen in recent years and we must do more to stop it."[59] The logical extension of Pelosi's argument is that it's immoral for a sovereign nation to exist—because if it's immoral to prevent entry of foreigners, then it's immoral at any level, meaning there can be no morally justifiable exclusion. Since the media agree with her, they did not press Pelosi on the outrageousness, incoherence, and moral bankruptcy of her claim. Congressman Dan Crenshaw highlighted the folly of the Democrats' stance. "The extreme rhetoric surrounding the border security debate has turned radical ideas into aggressive action," he tweeted. "Vandalizing buildings & targeting our border agents is a fast way to discredit your argument. Incredible that enforcing our laws is somehow seen as morally corrupt."[60] Democrats have lurched so far left—so far from the rule of law—that they brazenly support lawbreaking and lawbreakers.

With the media's support, however, Democrats continue to trespass on the moral high ground on immigration and demonize Republicans, despite the indefensibility of their position. In a fiery exchange between Congressman Matt Gaetz and CNN host Chris Cuomo, Cuomo suggested it's convenient for Republicans that illegal aliens kill Americans because it advances the Republican argument against illegal immigration. Gaetz responded, "You think it's convenient for us that people are dead at the hands of illegal aliens?" Cuomo replied, "Yes.... You put a premium on certain lives and not others."[61]

Columnist George Neumayr exposes the immorality of the moralizing leftists' open-borders advocacy:

> They assert out of thin air the inalienable right of foreigners to claim citizenship, as if governments exist not to serve the good of the people who form them but the abstract rights of those outside of that government. If the Republicans are the America First party, the Democrats increasingly resemble the America Last party, fighting not to preserve a stable, secure, and orderly government for Americans but to sustain a fantasy against common sense that prioritizes the demands of foreigners. Where is the morality in that? It is simply injustice to one's own citizens dressed up as "humanitarianism"—a policy as unjust as parents who, in determining the security of their home, give greater consideration to strangers than their own children.[62]

Neumayr notes that leftists abandon their zealotry for these principles when applied to them personally, which is why all the well-fed politicians have walls, fences, and gates around their own homes. This is a microcosm of leftist advocacy across the board—they are, as we've shown, more generous than anyone else with other people's money but statistically less generous than conservatives in private charitable contributions.

Another glaring example of leftists' hypocrisy is their meltdown when President Trump announced his plan to send illegal immigrants to sanctuary cities. Some 170 cities and counties have sanctuary laws that prohibit law enforcement officials from assisting federal immigration authorities, and some cities actually impede enforcement. Trump would obviously prefer not to release illegal immigrants anywhere in the United States, but ICE lacks detention facilities and there is a shortage of judges to adjudicate asylum and deportation cases. So why not release them into cities that claim they want them?[63] Cher, the great conscience of the left, was having none of it. "I Understand Helping struggling Immigrants," she tweeted, "but MY CITY (Los Angeles) ISN'T TAKING CARE OF ITS OWN. WHAT ABOUT THE 50,000+Citizens WHO LIVE ON THE STREETS. PPL WHO LIVE BELOW POVERTY LINE, & HUNGRY? If my State Can't Take Care of Its Own How Can it Take Care of More."[64] Sounds like a pretty good argument against the leftists who run Los Angeles and liberalism in general, but that would be completely lost on Cher.

"WHY HASN'T THIS MADE HEADLINES?"

While Democrats shamelessly downplay criminality among illegal aliens, reportedly one in five U.S. prison inmates is a "criminal alien."[65] Data from the Administrative Office of the U.S. Courts indicate that of the nation's ninety-four federal districts, the top five for the highest number of defendants convicted and sentenced to prison in fiscal year 2018 were those along the U.S.-Mexico border. These districts cover the southern border from the Pacific to the Gulf of Mexico. The lesson, writes columnist Terence Jeffrey, is that "[t]he political leaders of this nation have known for years that the sort of criminal activity that is prosecuted in federal courts—as demonstrated by the government's own data on federal court convictions—is disproportionately focused along the nation's southern border. And they have not fixed it."[66]

A recent report from the Government Accountability Office suggests 91 percent of U.S. criminal aliens from 2011 to 2016 were from Mexico, Guatemala, Honduras, and El Salvador. Among them, there were 4.9 million arrests for 7.5 million offenses. The arrests include some one million drug crimes, a half million assaults, 133,800 sex offenses, 24,200 kidnappings, 33,000 homicide-related offenses, and 1,500 terrorism-related crimes. U.S. taxpayers spent more than $15 billion to imprison these criminals in federal, state, and local facilities. Investigative reporter Sharyl Attkisson asks, "Why hasn't this made headlines?"[67]

Why, indeed? In 2017 and 2018, ICE officers made 266,000 arrests of aliens with criminal records, including those charged or convicted of 100,000 assaults, 30,000 sex crimes, and 4,000 violent killings.[68]

According to John Jones, chief of the Intelligence Counterterrorism Division with the Texas Department of Public Safety, in the last seven years in Texas alone, more than 4,000 illegal aliens have been jailed for sexual assault and 62 percent of these involved assaults against children.[69] How would AOC and other proponents of eliminating ICE propose we deal with all these people, if at all? Then again, why would AOC and other Democrats worry about the ridiculousness of their position when they've managed to convince all but 37 percent of Americans that a border wall is wrong?

This shows the power of media and Democratic propaganda—as recently as 2013, an ABC News/*Washington Post* survey found that 65 percent of Americans supported building a 700-mile fence along the border with Mexico and adding 20,000 border patrol agents. Fifty-two percent even supported the wall if it would cost $46 billion, which is much higher than President Trump's request. Earlier polls showed similar results. In 2006, a *Time*/SRBI poll found that 52 percent of *Democrats* favored "building a security fence along the 2000-mile US-Mexican border."[70]

Democrats have done a masterful but disgraceful job portraying those who support border enforcement as racists. They oppose almost anything Trump supports, even if they recently favored it. They won't even agree to compromise if Trump makes major concessions, because they won't allow him any political victory on immigration. In fact, it's clear they don't want to solve the problem, preferring to keep it as a roiling issue that's useful for demonizing Republicans. It is stunning that Democrats now uniformly oppose the national sovereignty of the United States. Former Georgia gubernatorial candidate Stacey Adams has even said she is open to noncitizens and minors voting in municipal elections.[71] It's easy to predict that this position will quickly become much more popular within her party.

"BLACK AMERICANS ARE DISPROPORTIONATELY IMPACTED BY ILLEGAL IMMIGRATION"

If alien criminality doesn't bother the left, how about the effects of illegal immigration on jobs and wages? U.S. Civil Rights commissioner Peter Kirsanow observes that black Americans are disproportionately impacted by illegal immigration, with black males being more likely to face competition from illegals. "What happens is you eliminate the rungs on the ladder because a sizable number of black men don't have access to entry-level jobs," said Kirsanow. "It is not just the competition and the unemployment of blacks. It also depresses the wage levels." Kirsanow's comments are consistent with a Civil Rights Commission study in 2010 showing illegal immigration has depressed both wages and employment rates for low-skilled Americans, including a disproportionate number of black men.[72]

While Democrats portray all illegal immigrants as helpless victims, they can't explain the mobs who stormed the border in San Diego at the beginning of 2019. Some 150 people tried to climb over and under the border fence, and some became hostile and violent, throwing rocks at border agents. When the Border Patrol fired tear gas, smoke, and pepper spray at the rock throwers—who were part of a caravan from Central America—leftists condemned the officials, not the rioters. Homeland Security spokeswoman Katie Waldman reported that none of the attackers were injured and that they appeared to be staging a photo-op in front of "conveniently invited media."

A similar incident occurred in November 2018, when congressional Democrats and their media enablers also decried the use of tear gas as cruel.[73] While depicting all members of these caravans as victims of America, Democrats didn't disclose that nearly one-third of women in such groups report they were sexually abused during their journey to the border. Sixty-eight percent of the migrant and refugee populations entering Mexico report being victims of violence during their transit, often at the hands of gangs, other criminal organizations, and Mexican security forces assigned to protect them—all according to a 2017 report from Doctors Without Borders.[74]

The left constantly prioritizes illegals over the safety and interests of American citizens. Oakland mayor Libby Schaaf, after receiving a courtesy call from ICE informing her of an upcoming raid on illegal aliens in her city, warned the illegals in advance. The raid predictably failed to locate large numbers of criminal illegals in the area.[75] "What she did is no better than a gang lookout yelling, 'Police!' when a police cruiser comes in the neighborhood, except she did it to a whole community," said then-acting ICE director Thomas Homan. "There's over 800 significant public safety threat criminals...that we are unable to locate because of that warning, so that community's a lot less safe than it would have been." A year later Mayor Schaaf defended her actions and called for ICE to be abolished.[76]

Such calls for dismantling ICE are spreading fast through the Democratic Party. AOC put the onus on President Trump to explain why ICE *shouldn't* be abolished. "No one should feel unsafe in the United States of America. And that includes our amazing and beautiful and productive immigrant community and moreover, the one thing the president has not talked about is the fact he has systematically engaged in the violation of international human rights borders—human rights on our border.... The president should be really defending why we are funding such an agency at all because right now what we are seeing is death."[77] The demonization of ICE agents as murderers is a natural outgrowth of these demands. Democratic congresswoman Mary Gay Scanlon explicitly made this claim during a House Judiciary Committee meeting on border security, when she compared U.S. border officials to Nazis "back in Germany" who were "just following orders."[78]

AOC engaged in further demagoguery in June 2019 with an Instagram Live video. "The U.S. is running concentration camps on our southern border and that is exactly what they are," she declared. ". . . If that doesn't bother you...I want to talk to the people that are concerned enough with humanity to say that 'never again' means something."[79] AOC, of course, knows Democratic administrations used these same detention facilities—but unsurprisingly, they avoided historically illiterate comparisons to the Holocaust, in which six million Jews were killed through gassing, starvation, and death squads. By comparison, in border detention facilities, authorities provide detained illegal immigrants with meals, healthcare, clothing, and shelter, and eventually release them.[80]

Unfortunately, there is no prospect for compromise on the horizon on immigration. Democrats will continue to demonize Trump and his "deplorable" supporters as heartless Nazis because they defend America's sovereignty, rule of law, and what is left of its uniqueness and exceptionalism. They will remain intransigent because the issue is a major weapon to cast Republicans as racist and is a ticket for millions of new Democratic voters.

Conclusion

As I was contemplating a fitting close for this book, I looked back at my conclusion for the first of my two books on the Obama presidency, *Crimes Against Liberty*, and was struck by its opening paragraph, which I had forgotten. I referenced a distressing post on a conservative forum by an everyday patriot grieving for the loss of our nation as we know it. The author wrote,

> In the 55 years of my life as a proud citizen of the United States of America, this is the first time I've felt that a president of our country holds his fellow Americans and the United States in contempt. I don't think I've ever felt such an overwhelming feeling of rejection as I do with this administration. It's as though everything that I was raised so proudly to hold dear and true has been denigrated. Every single day we hear something else that is a slap in the face of every patriot. I pray

> that we will see relief in November because I know that I'm not the only American who feels the frustration. It is unimaginable to me what might happen if we cannot find some relief in November.

Obama is a leftist who attained the highest office in our land and was committed to fundamentally transforming America away from its founding principles. Regrettably, he made great strides toward his goal. He popularized leftism and emboldened Democrats to brazenly advocate their extremist policies. Through Obama's presidency the nation shifted leftward at warp speed, especially on cultural issues, and we are seeing the fruits of that seismic shift today, from abortion to transgenderism.

We have also witnessed a regressive cultural shift on race relations. One would have thought that with the election of an African-American president the nation would recognize it had made abundant progress in race relations, but Obama could not appreciate or acknowledge this evolution. Instead of using his position to bring racially diverse Americans closer together, he used race as a political cudgel to demonize conservatives and advance his own agenda. Following his lead, the left and most of the Democratic Party exploited race in every conceivable context for political gain. The divisive issue of race—along with gender—is now everywhere, and the left is bludgeoning conservatives every day with accusations of racism on multiple fronts—from academia, to Hollywood, to corporate ad campaigns. It would seem that a charge so cheaply and frequently made would lose its effectiveness, but if that's the case the left and its media echo chamber haven't received the message. If anything, they are ratcheting up the attacks.

In addition, Obama accelerated America's slow march to socialism to a rapid gallop, enabling the previously unthinkable and inspiring his fellow leftists to emerge from the shadows and unabashedly promote this utterly discredited ideology. Wide swaths of the Democratic Party are openly advocating socialism and the rest of the party essentially supports it in principle.

Now please return to the quote above and focus on these words: "I don't think I've ever felt such an overwhelming feeling of rejection as I do with this administration. It's as though everything that I was raised so proudly to hold dear and true has been denigrated. Every single day we hear something else that is a slap in the face of every patriot.... I know that I'm not the only American who feels the frustration."

Fast-forwarding to today, let's apply these words to the left's fevered war against everything we hold dear. They have taken the baton from Obama and are sprinting to the finish line. With startling zeal, leftists denounce this country and every American who is trying to preserve what has made it glorious. As we've seen, the left ferociously demonizes people simply for wearing caps evincing support for President Trump, who is fighting for them and the America they love.

It's sobering that this book contains hundreds of examples of the left's reckless extremism yet barely scratches the surface. No one can reasonably deny that extremism is a feature, not a bug, infecting the Democratic Party. We can safely assume that once the Democratic primary process is complete their candidate will be far less candid about his or her leftism, but we must not fall for such deception or allow our fellow voters to do so.

If Trump's policy successes were sure to be the determining factor, we would have nothing to fear in 2020, but the left will distract voters from the objective evidence and terrify them with false projections of race- and gender-infused totalitarianism under a second Trump term. The left will distort his record and deny that his policies are benefiting all groups, especially minorities. Additionally, beware of those who might grudgingly concede Trump's triumphs but argue that America's prosperity is not worth the polarization he has allegedly caused. Just remember that on that score Trump and conservatives did not draw first blood. The left is relentlessly assaulting our constitutional system and traditional values and viciously attacking those who resist. We are not the ones causing the division, and we mustn't be chased from the political battlefield by false, malicious charges of racism and sexism or because we value phony harmony over America's freedom tradition. You can be sure the left will never quit for a moment and that a Democratic victory in 2020 would usher in far more divisiveness and radicalism than we see today.

The 2020 election will be a referendum on capitalism versus socialism, on life versus infanticide, on gender sanity versus insanity, on equal opportunity versus forced equal outcomes, on color blindness versus race-baiting, on free speech versus censorship, on freedom of thought versus political correctness, on American sovereignty versus open borders and globalism, and on liberty versus authoritarianism.

Many even on the right downplayed the danger Obama represented to the Republic, and this blind complacency arguably led to the Tea Party and eventually to the rise of President Trump. Those who continue to dismiss or underestimate the designs and determination of the left do so at their own peril and ours.

We must remain vigilant and rise up and fight the left with greater force and perseverance than they are exerting, and that is no small order. Be encouraged that we are fighting for what is right and for the unique American idea, which has produced the freest, most prosperous and benevolent nation in history, and let us fortify one another with our mutual resolve.

God bless President Trump and all patriots who cherish this nation as a shining city on a hill and who have dedicated themselves to the cause of its continued greatness.

Acknowledgments

This is my tenth book—every one of them with Regnery Publishing, with which I've had a wonderful and gratifying relationship. I sincerely appreciate Marji Ross for her loyalty, support, and flexibility. She is a consummate professional at the top of her game and Regnery's continued success bears witness to it. My friend Harry Crocker has been with me from the beginning, and there is no one better in this industry. I can always rely on him to answer any questions or handle any issues at all stages of the process. Thanks again to Tom Spence in contracts and to Alyssa Cordova and her excellent team of publicists. Special thanks, also, to the art department for their amazing cover art.

Profuse thanks to my friend, Jack Langer, for editing this book, which makes this the seventh book we've worked on together. Jack has been a joy to work with and has made every one of my books read more clearly and smoothly. I marvel at his uncanny ability to strip unnecessary words from the manuscript, even when I think I've already purged them all through many rounds of self-editing. Jack is simply gifted—a brutal hunter of superfluous words—and I am blessed that he uses his gift to enhance all my books, and I pray he remains my editor for as long as I'm privileged to write books. Jack also challenges me to elaborate when a passage needs further explanation and to substantiate points when necessary. The result is a much cleaner and more cogent text. Jack's work ethic is extraordinary, and he is invariably responsive to any questions or concerns I have. It's been a joy to work with him and I can't thank him enough for making these books immeasurably better.

Thanks, as always, to my wife, and life partner, Lisa, for always being supportive, patient, and understanding in this demanding process.

My longtime friend Sean Hannity has always been supportive of all my books and other professional endeavors. As I've said many times, Sean remains a humble, kind, and generous man despite his celebrity and phenomenal success. I am proud to call him my very close friend and eternally appreciative of his encouragement. I couldn't have a more loyal ally.

I greatly appreciate the strong friendship and steadfast support of Mark Levin, upon whom I can always depend. I am extremely grateful for his support of this project—as always.

I must emphasize that my brother Rush is always at the top of my list. Rush is, above all, a loving brother—the best brother one could have. Again, sincere thanks to him for inspiring me, for opening up doors for me directly and indirectly, and for doing wonderful work for this nation we both love from the bottom of our hearts. He has always supported me and my career pursuits, unfailingly encouraging and cheering me on. I am blessed and grateful to have such a generous, caring, and thoughtful brother, who makes a difference every day in working to keep this nation true to its founding principles. He doesn't get nearly the credit he deserves and takes way more heat than anyone should have to endure. From the beginning of his national radio show, Rush has been the tip of the spear for the modern conservative movement and remains so today, persevering through it all and always at the top of his field.

Thanks, also, to my lifelong friend, Peter Kinder, for thoughtfully sending me relevant articles in the final few weeks of the process to make sure I didn't miss the latest examples of leftist insanity.

Most of all, I am grateful to God—the Father, the Son, and the Holy Spirit—for His countless blessings.

Notes

INTRODUCTION

1. Niv Elis, "Ocasio-Cortez: $10 Trillion Needed for Effective Climate Plan," *The Hill*, June 5, 2019; Douglas Holtz-Eakin, Dan Bosch, Ben Gitis, Dan Goldback, and Philip Rossetti, "The Green New Deal: Scope, Scale, and Implications," American Action Forum, February 25, 2019, https://www.americanactionforum.org/research/the-green-new-deal-scope-scale-and-implications/.
2. Joshua Caplan, "PHOTOS: Democrats Stuck on Bus after Donald Trump Cancels Foreign Trip," *Breitbart*, January 17, 2019, https://www.breitbart.com/politics/2019/01/17/photos-democrats-stuck-bus-donald-trump-cancels-foreign-trip/.
3. President Donald J. Trump, "President Donald J. Trump's State of the Union Address," The White House, February 5, 2019, https://www.whitehouse.gov/briefings-statements/president-donald-j-trumps-state-union-address-2/.
4. Leah Barkoukis, "Here's What Dems Refused to Stand for during SOTU Address," *Townhall*, February 6, 2019, https://townhall.com/tipsheet/leahbarkoukis/2019/02/06/heres-what-dems-refused-to-stand-for-during-sotu-n2540831.

CHAPTER ONE

1. William Cummings, "Alexandria Ocasio-Cortez, Ilhan Omar and Rashida Tlaib Fire Back at Nancy Pelosi's 'Twitter World' Quip," *USA Today*, July 8, 2019.
2. Rod Thomson, "What That Gallup Poll Actually Found: Democrats Don't Like America," The Revolutionary Act, July 3, 2019, https://therevolutionaryact.com/about-that-gallup-poll-on-low-american-pride-headlines-were-wrong/.
3. Adam Shaw, "Top 2020 Democrats Under Fire for 'Collective Bashing of America' After Cuomo Gaffe," Fox News, August 18, 2018, https://www.foxnews.com/politics/top-2020-democrats-under-fire-for-collective-bashing-of-america-after-cuomo-gaffe.
4. Stephen Schlesinger, "Obama: Every Country Is Exceptional," *Huffington Post*, November 23, 2013.

5. Robin Abcarian, "Michelle Obama Criticized for Remarks," *Los Angeles Times*, February 20, 2008.
6. Shaw, "Top 2020 Democrats Under Fire."
7. Ian Schwartz, "Eric Holder to Trump: 'Exactly When Did You Think America Was Great?'" RealClearPolitics, March 27, 2019, https://www.realclearpolitics.com/video/2019/03/27/eric_holder_to_trump_exactly_when_did_you_think_america_was_great.html.
8. Ryan Saavedra, "Ocasio-Cortez: State of America Is 'Garbage,' Reagan Pitted Whites Against Minorities," *Daily Wire*, March 9, 2019, https://www.dailywire.com/news/44467/ocasio-cortez-state-america-garbage-reagan-pitted-ryan-saavedra.
9. 347 U.S. 483 (1954).
10. Richard Vedder, "Racial Segregation on American Campuses: A Widespread Phenomenon," *Forbes*, November 15, 2018.
11. 410 U.S. 113, 93 S. Ct. 705, 35 L. Ed. 2d. 147 (1973).
12. 317 U.S. 111, 63 S. Ct. 82, 87 L. Ed. 122 (1942).
13. Breck Dumas, "ABC, CBS, and NBC Announce They Will Snub President Trump's 'Salute to America' Celebration," The Blaze, July 3, 2019, https://www.theblaze.com/news/networks-will-snub-trump-salute-to-america.
14. Andrew O'Reilly, "Flag burned in front of White House as tensions mount ahead of Trump's 'Salute to America'," Fox News, July 4, 2019, https://www.foxnews.com/politics/flag-burned-in-front-of-wh-as-tensions-mount-ahead-of-trumps-salute-to-america; Quin Hilyer, "Don't Let Unpatriotic Ingrates Mar Your Fourth of July," *Washington Examiner*, July 3, 2019.
15. Michael Medved, "Reject the Lie of White 'Genocide' Against Native Americans," *Townhall*, September 19, 2007.
16. Thomas Sowell, "Twisted History," *Townhall*, December 17, 2003.
17. Terry LaBan, "Did America Steal Its Land from the Native Americans?" *Quora*, April 3, 2018.
18. Allen C. Guelzo, "The Constitution Was Never Pro-Slavery," *National Review*, April 18, 2019.
19. Guelzo, "The Constitution Was Never Pro-Slavery."
20. Ibid.
21. Mark J. Perry, "Thomas Sowell on Slavery and This Fact – There are More Slaves Today than Were Seized from Africa in Four Centuries," *Carpe Diem* (blog), AEI, October 18, 2017.
22. Perry, "Thomas Sowell on Slavery and This."
23. Ibid.
24. Michael Barone, "Will Black Voters Keep Democrats from Going Too Far to the Left?" *Townhall*, April 5, 2019.
25. Stephanie Akin, "Black Voters Propelled Blue Wave, Study Finds," *Roll Call*, November 19, 2018.

26. Jake Tapper, "A Biden Problem: Foot in Mouth," ABC News, January 7, 2007, https://abcnews.go.com/Politics/story?id=2838420&page=1&page=1.
27. Joe Weisenthal, "Racist Comments from Harry Reid Mean, Yep, Another Democratic Loss in the Senate," *Business Insider*, January 10, 2010.
28. Shelby Steele, "Why the Left Is Consumed with Hate?" *Wall Street Journal*, September 23, 2018.
29. James Piereson, "A Not-So-Great Society," *Weekly Standard*, September 30, 2016.
30. Ronald Pestritto, "Woodrow Wilson: Godfather of Liberalism," The Heritage Foundation, July 31, 2012, https://www.heritage.org/political-process/report/woodrow-wilson-godfather-liberalism.
31. Robert Higgs, "How FDR Made the Depression Worse," *The Free Market 13, no. 2*, Mises Institute, February 1, 1995; Thomas Sowell, "FDR's Policies Prolonged Great Depression," *Rapid City Journal*, November 3, 2010; Harold L. Cole and Lee E. Ohanian, "How Government Prolonged the Depression," *Wall Street Journal*, February 2, 2009.
32. James Piereson, "A Not-So-Great Society," *Weekly Standard*, September 30, 2016.
33. Francis Whitney, *An Outline of American History*, United States Information Agency.
34. Piereson, "A Not-So-Great Society."
35. Bradford Richardson, "Race Relations Reach All-time Low Under Obama: Poll," *Washington Times*, July 19, 2016.
36. John Nolte, "Nolte: Academic Study Shows Donald Trump Has Made America Less Racist," *Breitbart*, May 20, 2019.
37. Ben White, "Trump Inherits Obama Boom," *Politico*, July 8, 2019.
38. Nigel Barber, "Why Liberal Hearts Bleed and Conservatives Don't," *Psychology Today*, October 8, 2012.
39. Barber, "Why Liberal Hearts Bleed and Conservatives Don't."
40. Matt Grossman, "U.S. Policy Has Gone Liberals' Way for 70 Years," *Washington Post*, April 8, 2014.
41. Grossman, "U.S. Policy Has Gone Liberals' Way for 70 Years."
42. Ibid.
43. Ibid.
44. Carlos Garcia, "Nike Cancels Fourth of July Shoe, Because Colin Kaepernick Said It Was Offensive," The Blaze, July 1, 2019, https://www.theblaze.com/news/kaepernick-nixes-patriotic-nike-shoe.
45. "Colorado targets Christian baker again despite Supreme Court's cake ruling," *Daily Signal*, August 15, 2018, https://www.dailysignal.com/2018/08/15/colorado-targets-christian-baker-again-despite-supreme-courts-cake-ruling/.
46. "Oberlin helped students defame a bakery, a jury says. The punishment: $33 million," *New York Times*, June 19, 2019.

47. Ronald Reagan, "A Time for Choosing," speech presented during the 1964 U.S. presidential election campaign on behalf of Republican candidate Barry Goldwater, October 27, 1964.
48. Niall Ferguson, "The Democrats Will Commit Political Suicide by Embracing Socialism," *Globe and Mail*, February 11, 2019.
49. Robert B. Charles, "Progressive Democrats are Lost – More Each Day," Association of Mature American Citizens, May 21, 2019, https://amac.us/progressive-democrats-are-lost-more-each-day/.
50. Lukas Mikelionis, "Dozens of Dems Vote 95 Percent of Time with AOC Despite Pelosi's Claim that Bloc is 'Like Five People,'" Fox News, April 16, 2019, https://www.foxnews.com/politics/dems-vote-ocasio-cortez-pelosi.

CHAPTER TWO

1. Christa J. Porter, Candace E. Maddox, "Using Critical Race Theory and Intersectionality to Explore a Black Lesbian's Life in College: An Analysis of Skye's Narrative," *The National Association of Student Affairs Professionals Journal* 15(2), Spring 2014, 25–40.
2. Christine Emba, "Intersectionality," *Washington Post*, September 21, 2015.
3. David Gillborn, "Intersectionality, Critical Race Theory, and the Primacy of Racism: Race, Class, Gender, and Disability in Education," *Sage Journals*, 21(3), February 25, 2010, 277-287.
4. Jennifer Kim, "Intersectionality 101: Why 'We're Focusing on Women' Doesn't Work for Diversity & Inclusion," Medium, April 10, 2018, https://medium.com/awaken-blog/intersectionality-101-why-were-focusing-on-women-doesn-t-work-for-diversity-inclusion-8f591d196789.
5. Mary Romero, *Introducing Intersectionality* (Cambridge, UK: Polity Press, 2018), iv.
6. Romero, *Introducing Intersectionality*, iv.
7. Jennifer Kim, "Mistakes to Avoid While Celebrating Women's History Month or Discussing 'Women's Issues,'" Medium, March 20, 2018, https://medium.com/awaken-blog/mistakes-to-avoid-while-celebrating-womens-history-month-or-discussing-women-s-issues-655c27e24122.
8. Ange-Marie Hancock, *Intersectionality, An Intellectual History* (New York: Oxford University Press, 2016), 4–5.
9. Andrea Grimes, "Patricia Arquette's Spectacular Intersectionality Fail," Rewire.News, February 23, 2015, https://rewire.news/article/2015/02/23/patricia-arquettes-spectacular-intersectionality-fail/.
10. Christine Emba, "Intersectionality," *Washington Post*, September 21, 2015.
11. Marissa Papanek, Nazy Javid, "UPDATE: Eureka Women's March Organizers Stand by Decision," KRCR News, December 28, 2018, https://

krcrtv.com/north-coast-news/eureka-local-news/organizers-cancel-womens-march-jan-19-due-to-overwhelmingly-white-participants.

12. Brodigan, "Amputee Actress Criticizes the Rock for Playing an Amputee," *Louder with Crowder*, July 17, 2018.
13. Papanek and Javid, "UPDATE: Eureka Women's March Organizers Stand by Decision."
14. Emma Green, "Are Jews White?" *The Atlantic,* December 5, 2016.
15. Georgi Boorman, "Women's March Cofounder's Refusal to Condemn Racism Implicates Intersectionalism," *The Federalist*, January 16, 2019, https://thefederalist.com/2019/01/16/womens-march-founder-tamika-mallory-wont-condemn-anti-semitism/.
16. Boorman, "Women's March Cofounder's Refusal to Condemn Racism."
17. Hank Berrien, "Intersectionality Fight: Founder of Women's March Calls for Sarsour and Mallory to Step Down," *Daily Wire*, November 19, 2018, https://www.dailywire.com/news/38522/intersectionality-fight-founder-womens-march-calls-hank-berrien.
18. Caitlin Flanagan, "Kirsten Gillibrand's Invocation of 'Intersectionality' Backfires," *The Atlantic*, December 21, 2018.
19. Flanagan, "Kirsten Gillibrand's Invocation of 'Intersectionality' Backfires."
20. Joseph Wulfsohn, "CNN Commentator to Republican Guest: 'White Men Who Think Like You' Are the 'Greatest Terrorist Threat' in US," Fox News, August 20, 2019, https://www.foxnews.com/media/cnn-angela-rye-white-men-greatest-terrorist-threat.
21. Jessica Bennett, "Don Lemon & April Ryan Have Tense Debate Over Sen. Kamala Harris," *Ebony*, February 12, 2019.
22. Renee Graham, "Yes, Kamala Harris is 'Black Enough,'" *Boston Globe*, February 19, 2019.
23. Morgan Jenkins, "I Want to Be Excited About Kamala Harris. The Reality Is a Little More Complicated," Yahoo Lifestyle, January 24, 2019, https://www.yahoo.com/lifestyle/want-excited-kamala-harris-reality-201005826.html.
24. Jeff Yang, "Tulsi Gabbard's Attack Raises Existential Question for Kamala Harris' Campaign," CNN, August 3, 2019, https://www.cnn.com/2019/08/02/opinions/tulsi-gabbard-kamala-harris-attack-democratic-debates-yang/index.html.
25. Jonathan Martin, Alan Blinder, and Campbell Robertson, "Justin Fairfax Puts Virginia Democrats in Bind on Impeachment," *New York Times*, February 9, 2019.
26. John Eligon, "'You're Not Supposed to Betray Your Race': The Challenge Faced by Black Women Accusing Black Men," *New York Times*, March 22, 2019.
27. Daniella Greenbaum David, "Rep. Ilhan Omar Whines That Criticizing Her Anti-Semitism Is – Wait for It – Racist," *The Federalist*, February 12, 2019.

28. Greenbaum David, "Rep. Ilhan Omar Whines."
29. Sister Toldjah, "Rep. Tlaib: My Anti-Semitic Views Are Being 'Shushed' Because I'm a Woman of Color," *RedState*, February 12, 2019, https://www.redstate.com/sister-toldjah/2019/02/12/rep.-tlaib-my-anti-semitic-views-shushed-woc.
30. "Persecution at a Glance," Open Doors USA, undated, https://www.opendoorsusa.org/christian-persecution/.
31. Ian Haworth, "Intersectionality Discriminates Discrimination," *Daily Wire*, December 23, 2018, https://www.dailywire.com/news/39625/haworth-intersectionality-discriminates-ian-haworth.
32. Marina Medvin, "Library Journal Laments "Proliferate Whiteness" of Authors with Books 'Physically Taking Up Space in Our Libraries,'" *Townhall*, April 18, 2019, https://townhall.com/columnists/marinamedvin/2019/04/18/library-journal-laments-proliferate-whiteness-of-authors-with-books-physically-taking-up-space-in-our-libraries-n2545012.
33. Cydney Henderson, "Rosanna Arquette Slammed for Saying She 'Feels So Much Shame' over Being White, Privileged," *USA Today*, August 8, 2019.
34. Brent Bozell and Tim Graham, "The Dictionary Adds 'White Fragility,'" *Townhall*, April 12, 2019, https://townhall.com/columnists/brentbozellandtimgraham/2019/04/12/the-dictionary-adds-white-fragility-n2544673.
35. Alex Parker, "The Plain! The Plain! Peter Dinklage Deemed Too White to Play Tattoo, As SJW's Make Further Imbeciles Of Themselves," *RedState*, August 31, 2018, https://www.redstate.com/alexparker/2018/08/31/peter-dinklage-herve-villechaize-yellowface/.
36. Kelly Wynne, "Fox News Streaming Service Allows Viewers to Watch 'Racists" on Their Computer, Chelsea Handler Says As She Attacks Hannity, Ingraham," *Newsweek*, October 18, 2018.
37. Alex Parker, "Non-Racist, Non-Sexist Left Shames White Women for the Scourge of a Crushed Blue Wave," *RedState*, November 8, 2018, https://www.redstate.com/alexparker/2018/11/08/white-women-midterm-elections/.
38. Gideon Resnick, "Bernie Sanders on Andrew Gillum and Stacey Abrams: Many Whites Made 'Uncomfortable' Voting for Black Candidates," *Daily Beast*, November 8, 2018, https://www.thedailybeast.com/bernie-sanders-on-andrew-gillium-and-stacey-abrams-many-whites-uncomfortable-voting-for-black-candidates.
39. Benny Johnson, "Protesters Chase Graham To His Car Saying They Will Remove Him From Office – Lindsey Responds," *Daily Caller*, October 5, 2018, https://dailycaller.com/2018/10/05/graham-car-protesters-response/.

40. Kathleen Joyce, "Forever 21 Apologizes for Using White Man to Model 'Black Panther'-Inspired Sweater," Fox News, December 19, 2018, https://www.foxnews.com/lifestyle/forever-21-apologizes-after-store-was-criticized-for-using-white-man-to-model-black-panther-inspired-sweater.
41. Amanda Prestigiacomo, "Watch: Columbia Student 'Under Investigation' For Praising White People Responds to Backlash," *Daily Wire*, December 13, 2018, https://www.dailywire.com/news/39324/watch-columbia-student-under-investigation-amanda-prestigiacomo.
42. Prestigiacomo, "Watch: Columbia Student 'Under Investigation.'"
43. Ben Shapiro, "Stacey Abrams Wants a Divided America," *Newsweek*, February 7, 2019.
44. Peggy McIntosh "White Privilege: Unpacking the Invisible Backpack," National Interpreter Education Center, 1989, http://www.interpretereducation.org/wp-content/uploads/2016/03/white-privilege-by-Peggy-McIntosh.compressed.pdf.
45. McIntosh, "White Privilege: Unpacking the Invisible Backpack."
46. Ibid.
47. Boorman, "Women's March Refusal to Condemn Racism."
48. Michael O'Fallon, "Jordan B. Peterson: Identity Politics & The Marxist Lie of White Privilege," Sovereign Nations, January 30, 2018, https://sovereignnations.com/2018/01/30/jordan-peterson-marxist-lie-white-privilege/.
49. Georgi Boorman, "How the Theory of White Privilege Leads to Socialism," *The Federalist*, June 26, 2018, https://thefederalist.com/2018/06/26/theory-white-privilege-leads-socialism/.
50. Jason Barker, "Happy Birthday, Karl Marx. You Were Right!" *New York Times*, April 30, 2018.
51. Edna Bonacich, "Racism in Advanced Capitalist Society: Comments on William J. Wilson's The Truly Disadvantaged," *The Journal of Sociology & Social Welfare*, December 1989; Boorman, "How the Theory of White Privilege Leads to Socialism."
52. Bonacich, "Racism in Advanced Capitalist Society," 44.
53. Dr. Dean Chavers, "5 Fake Indians: Checking a Box Doesn't Make You Native," Indian Country Today, October 15, 2014, https://newsmaven.io/indiancountrytoday/archive/5-fake-indians-checking-a-box-doesn-t-make-you-native-Z9mn2ErpHEWl5BDNU9LJRw/.
54. Victor Davis Hanson, "The White-Privilege Tedium," *National Review*, October 23, 2019.
55. Bonacich, "Racism in Advanced Capitalist Society."
56. Jayne Metzgar, "Hate Hoaxes Are What Happen When Your Religion Is Identity Politics," *The Federalist*, February 20, 2019, https://thefederalist.com/2019/02/20/hate-hoaxes-happen-religion-identity-politics/.

CHAPTER THREE

1. Michael Barone, "Will Black Voters Keep Democrats from Going Too Far to the Left?" Rasmussen Reports, April 5, 2019, http://www.rasmussenreports.com/public_content/political_commentary/commentary_by_michael_barone/will_black_voters_keep_democrats_from_going_too_far_to_the_left.
2. Emily Birnbaum, "Candace Owens Blasts Hearing on White Nationalism in House Testimony," *The Hill*, April 9, 2019.
3. Tommy Curry, "Critical Race Theory," *Encyclopedia Britannica*, June 9, 2016.
4. "Critical Race Theory," The Bridge, https://cyber.harvard.edu/bridge/CriticalTheory/critical4.htm.
5. "What is Critical Race Theory?" UCLA School of Public Affairs/Critical Race Studies, June 2009.
6. David Gillborn, "Intersectionality, Critical Race Theory, and the Primacy of Racism: Race, Class, Gender, and Disability in Education," *Sage Journals*, 21(3), February 25, 2010, 277–87.
7. Tommy Curry, "Critical Race Theory," *Encyclopedia Britannica*, June 9, 2016.
8. Christa J. Porter, Candace E. Maddox, "Using Critical Race Theory and Intersectionality to Explore a Black Lesbian's Life in College: An Analysis of Skye's Narrative," Michigan State University, Spring 2014.
9. William Voegeli, "Racism, Revised," *Claremont Review of Books*, November 6, 2018.
10. Ashley Feinberg, "The New York Times Unites vs. Twitter," *Slate*, August 15, 2019, https://slate.com/news-and-politics/2019/08/new-york-times-meeting-transcript.html.
11. Mara Gay (@MaraGay), "In the days and weeks to come, we will publish essays demonstrating that nearly everything that has made America exceptional grew out of slavery," Twitter, August 13, 2019, 3:19 p.m., https://twitter.com/maragay/status/1161401966167298054.
12. David Marcus, "Ocasio-Cortez Joins De Blasio in Call To Punish Asian Students," *The Federalist*, March 20, 2019, https://thefederalist.com/2019/03/20/ocasio-cortez-joins-de-blasio-call-punish-asian-students/.
13. Victor Davis Hanson, "The Game of Pseudo-Authenticity," *American Greatness*, January 13, 2019, https://www.amgreatness.com/2019/01/13/the-game-of-pseudo-authenticity/.
14. Davis Hanson, "The Game of Pseudo-Authenticity."
15. Zack Beauchamp, "Trump's 2019 State of the Union Was an Ode to an Imaginary America," Vox, February 5, 2019, https://www.vox.com/policy-and-politics/2019/2/5/18213123/trumps-2019-state-of-the-union-populism.

16. Beauchamp, "Trump's 2019 State of the Union Was an Ode."
17. Howard Dean (@GovHowardDean), "#CovingtonCatholic High School seems like a hate factory to me. Why not just close it? Check out this thread," Twitter, January 19, 2019, 10:15 p.m., https://twitter.com/GovHowardDean/status/1086869687609290752.
18. Robby Soave, "The Media Wildly Mischaracterized That Video of Covington Catholic Students Confronting a Native American Veteran," *Reason*, January 20, 2019.
19. Curtis Houck, "Weekend CNN, MSNBC Spend Over 53 Minutes Trying to Smear Covington Students," NewsBusters, January 21, 2019, https://www.newsbusters.org/blogs/nb/curtis-houck/2019/01/21/weekend-cnn-msnbc-spend-over-53-minutes-trying-smear-covington.
20. Kyle Drennen, "UPDATED: Good, Bad & Ugly: How the Media Covered False Smear of Covington Kids," NewsBusters, January 22, 2019, https://www.newsbusters.org/blogs/nb/kyle-drennen/2019/01/22/good-bad-ugly-how-media-covered-false-smear-covington-kids.
21. Clay Waters, "NYT Hot Take: 'Racist' MAGA Teens 'Mocked a Native American Veteran,'" NewsBusters, January 21, 2019, https://www.newsbusters.org/blogs/nb/clay-waters/2019/01/21/nyt-hot-take-racist-maga-teens-surrounded-and-mocked-native-american.
22. Houck, "Weekend CNN, MSNBC Spend Over 53 Minutes."
23. Hank Berrien, "Covington Student's Attorney: Bill Maher Could Be Next One We Sue," *Daily Wire*, February 26, 2019, https://www.dailywire.com/news/43961/covington-students-attorney-bill-maher-could-be-hank-berrien.
24. PopZette Staff, "These Celebrities Continue to Criticize the Covington High School Students," LifeZette, January 22, 2019, https://www.lifezette.com/2019/01/these-celebrities-continue-to-criticize-the-covington-high-school-students/.
25. Amber Athey, "CNN Silent on Contributor Fantasizing About Punching Covington Boy," *Daily Caller*, January 22, 2019, https://dailycaller.com/2019/01/22/cnn-bakari-sellers-punching-covington-nicholas-sandmann/.
26. Cheryl Magness, "All the Adults Involved Failed the Covington Catholic School Boys, and Should Be Ashamed," *The Federalist*, January 21, 2019, https://thefederalist.com/2019/01/21/adults-involved-failed-covington-catholic-school-boys-ashamed/.
27. WCPO Staff, "Bishop: Diocese of Covington felt 'Bullied and Pressured,' Into Condemning Students Too Quickly," WCPO Cincinnati, January 25, 2019, https://www.wcpo.com/news/local-news/bishop-foys-speaks-to-covington-catholic-students-offers-support-i-am-on-your-side.
28. Kathleen Parker, "The Covington Controversy Shows a Picture Isn't Always Worth a Thousand Words," *Washington Post*, January 22, 2019, https://www.washingtonpost.com/opinions/

the-covington-controversy-shows-a-picture-isnt-always-worth-a-thousand-words/2019/01/22/851faeb6-1e9c-11e9-8b59-0a28f2191131_story.html?noredirect=on.

29. Kyle Smith, "Nathan Phillips Lied. The Media Bought It," *National Review*, January 20, 2019.
30. Katrina Trinko, "The Smearing of Teens in MAGA Hats Shows Identity Politics' Danger," *Daily Signal*, January 21, 2019, https://www.dailysignal.com/2019/01/21/the-smearing-of-teens-in-maga-hats-shows-identity-politics-danger/.
31. Chauncey Devega, "White Victimology, White Privilege and the Covington Catholic Rules of Race," *Salon*, January 25, 2019, https://www.salon.com/2019/01/25/white-victimology-white-privilege-and-the-covington-catholic-rules-of-race/.
32. Devega, "White Victimology, White Privilege and the Covington Catholic Rules of Race."
33. A judge dismissed Sandmann's suit against the *Washington Post*, though an appeal is likely. Carrie Sheffield, "Covington High School Student Sues WaPo for Defamation," Accuracy in Media, February 21, 2019, https://www.aim.org/aim-column/covington-high-school-student-sues-wapo-for-defamation/; Max Londberg, "Libel suit filed against Kathy Griffin, Elizabeth Warren and others who tweeted about Covington Catholic incident," *Cincinnati Enquirer*, August 2, 2019.
34. Mark Lilla, "How the Modern Addiction to Identity Politics Have Fractured the Left," *New Statesman America*, September 18, 2017.
35. Lilla, "How the Modern Addiction to Identity Politics Have Fractured the Left."
36. Ibid.
37. Ibid.
38. Ibid.
39. Roger Kimball, "The National Gallery of Identity Politics," *Wall Street Journal*, December 18, 2018.
40. B.S., "The Rise of Universities' Diversity Bureaucrats," *The Economist*, May 8, 2018.
41. B.S., "The Rise of Universities' Diversity Bureaucrats."
42. Ibid.
43. Scott Bledsoe, "Democrats Seek to Make Companies Hire People Based on Sex and Race," *The Federalist*, January 14, 2019, https://thefederalist.com/2019/01/14/democrats-seek-make-companies-hire-people-based-sex-race/.
44. George Leef, "What Do College 'Chief Diversity Officers' Accomplish?" The James G. Martin Center for Academic Renewal, October 26, 2018, https://www.jamesgmartin.center/2018/10/what-do-college-chief-diversity-officers-accomplish/.
45. Leef, "What Do College 'Chief Diversity Officers' Accomplish?"

46. Bledsoe, "Democrats Seek to Make Companies Hire People Based on Sex and Race."
47. Ibid.
48. Ibid.
49. Timothy Isaiah Cho (@tisaiahcho), "If the references in your pastor's sermons, the books used in small groups, the resources passed between the laity, the music sung in worship, & even the reflection quotes in your worship bulletins are predominantly by White men, your church is promoting a truncated Christianity," Twitter, January 31, 2019, 2:57 p.m., https://twitter.com/tisaiahcho/status/1091108240660656129?lang=en.
50. Peter Heck, "The Church of Social Justice Embarrasses Itself with Statements Like This," The Resurgent, February 5, 2019, https://theresurgent.com/2019/02/05/the-church-of-social-justice-embarrasses-itself-with-statements-like-this/.
51. Rob Bluey, "Alveda King on Her Uncle MLK's Forgotten Legacy," *Daily Signal*, January 21, 2019, https://www.dailysignal.com/2019/01/21/alveda-king-on-her-uncle-mlks-forgotten-legacy-everything-we-did-was-founded-on-the-bible/.
52. Tali Arbel, "Researchers Say Amazon Face-Detection Technology Shows Bias," AP News, January 25, 2019, https://www.apnews.com/74fc5742 49894bf5add36c6e9f22a4fe; Jazz Shaw, "Amazon's Facial Recognition Software Found To Be Racist,, Sexist," *Hot Air*, January 27, 2019, https://hotair.com/archives/jazz-shaw/2019/01/27/amazons-facial-recognition-software-found-racist-sexist/.
53. Caroline Klein and David Allan, "Robot racism? Yes, says a study showing humans' biases extend to robots," CNN, August 1, 2019, https://www.cnn.com/2019/08/01/tech/robot-racism-scn-trnd/index.html.
54. Maxim Staff, "Bella Hadid Kissed a Female Robot in a Calvin Klein Ad and the Internet Lost Its Mind," *Maxim*, May 19, 2019.

CHAPTER FOUR

1. Hugh T. Ferguson, "Biden: Kavanaugh accuser 'should not have to go through what Anita Hill went through,'" *Politico*, September 21, 2018.
2. Associated Press, "Joe Biden criticizes 'white man's culture' and his own role in Anita Hill's hearing," *Los Angeles Times*, March 27, 2019; Jessica Kwong, "Joe Biden faces fresh backlash on Twitter after addressing his role in Anita Hill Hearing," *Newsweek*, March 27, 2019.
3. Bob Kinzel & VPR News, "He's in for 2020: Bernie Sanders Is Running for President Again," Vermont Public Radio, February 19, 2019, https://www.vpr.org/post/hes-2020-bernie-sanders-running-president-again.
4. Neera Tanden (@neeratanden), "At a time where folks feel under attack because of who they are, saying race or gender or sexual orientation or identity doesn't matter is not off, it's simply wrong,"

Twitter, February 19, 2019, 4:30 a.m., https://twitter.com/neeratanden/status/1097835900468424704?lang=en.

5. Liam Quinn, "Stephen Colbert Mocks 'Old White Guy' Bernie Sanders After 2020 Announcement," Fox News, February 20, 2019, https://www.foxnews.com/entertainment/stephen-colbert-mocks-old-white-guy-bernie-sanders-after-2020-announcement.
6. "cultural appropriation," Lexico, https://www.lexico.com/en/definition/cultural_appropriation.
7. "What is Cultural Appropriation and Why Is It Offensive?" *The Week UK*, January 30, 2019.
8. Ugo Giguere, "White Comedian Rejected for Show in Montreal After Dreadlocks Deemed 'Cultural Appropriation,'" *National Post*, January 16, 2019.
9. Presse Canadienne, "UQAM Co-Op Excludes White Comedian from Shows Because of His Dreadlocks," *Montreal Gazette*, January 15, 2019.
10. Rheana Murray, "Teen Who Wore Traditional Chinese Dress to Prom Sparks Fury on Social Media," *Today*, May 4, 2018, https://www.today.com/style/teen-who-wore-traditional-chinese-dress-prom-faces-backlash-t128426.
11. Reuters, "Nancy Pelosi Says Trump Wants to 'Make America White Again,'" *The Guardian*, July 9, 2019, https://www.theguardian.com/global/video/2019/jul/09/nancy-pelosi-says-trump-wants-to-make-america-white-again-video.
12. Hansi Lo Wang, "See 200 Years of Twists and Turns of Census Citizenship Questions," NPR, April 23, 2019, https://www.npr.org/2019/04/23/630562915/see-200-years-of-twists-and-turns-of-census-citizenship-questions.
13. Frank Camp, "LeBron James Claims 'Old White' NFL Team Owners have 'Slave Mentality,'" *Daily Wire*, December 31, 2018, https://www.dailywire.com/news/39636/lebron-james-says-old-white-nfl-team-owners-have-frank-camp.
14. FNR Tigg, "NBA Teams Reportedly Looking to Get Rid of the Term 'Owner'," *Complex*, June 3, 2019, https://www.complex.com/sports/2019/06/nba-teams-looking-to-get-rid-of-term-owner.
15. "CBP Southwest Border Total Apprehensions/Inadmissibles," U.S. Customs and Border Protection, May 8, 2019.
16. Hank Berrien, "Dem Senator Implies Trump's a Racist for Not Building a Wall on Canadian Border," *Daily Wire*, December 21, 2018, https://www.dailywire.com/news/39594/dem-senator-implies-trumps-racist-not-building-hank-berrien.
17. Matt Vespa, "Dem Congresswoman: Actually, Trump's Border Wall Is about Getting Rid of People of Color, Or Something," Townhall, January 14, 2019, https://townhall.com/tipsheet/mattvespa

/2019/01/14/dem-congresswoman-actually-trumps-border-wall-is-about-getting-rid-of-people-o-n2538989.

18. Hannity Staff, “Omar Erupts Again: Ilhan Omar Blames Border Crisis on ‘White Nationalism,’” seanhannity.com, March 29, 2019, https://hannity.com/media-room/omar-erupts-again-ilhan-omar-blames-border-crisis-on-white-nationalism/.
19. Eddie Scarry, “Democrats Can’t Back Down on the Wall because We Called It Racist, Freshman Dem Admits,” *Washington Examiner*, January 15, 2019.
20. Kyle Moss, “Meghan McCain Accuses ‘View’ Co-Hosts of Attempting To ‘Broad-Stroke’ Republicans as Racist,” *Yahoo Finance*, January 15, 2019, https://finance.yahoo.com/news/meghan-mccain-accuses-view-co-hosts-attempting-broad-stroke-republicans-racist-223915104.html.
21. Brandon Morse, “MSNBC Host Nicolle Wallace Claims ‘There Isn’t a Strain of Racism on the Left,’ So Perhaps She Can Explain the Following Examples,” *RedState*, January 16, 2019, https://www.redstate.com/brandon_morse/2019/01/16/msnbc-host-nicolle-wallace-claims-isnt-strain-racism-left-perhaps-explain-following-examples/.
22. John Fritze, “Bernie Sanders Likens West Baltimore to ‘Third World’ Country,” *Baltimore Sun*, December 8, 2015.
23. Baltimore Sun Editorial Board, “Baltimore’s Perpetual Trash Problem,” *Baltimore Sun*, April 11, 2019.
24. Sam Dorman, “Resurfaced video shows Elijah Cummings calling Baltimore ‘drug infested,’ likening residents to ‘zombies,’” Fox News, July 31, 2019, https://www.foxnews.com/media/resurfaced-video-shows-elijah-cummings-calling-baltimore-drug-infested-likening-residents-to-zombies.
25. Cydney H. Dupree, “White Liberals Present Themselves as Less Competent in Interactions with African-Americans,” *Yale Insights*, November 15, 2018.
26. Walter Williams, “Insulting Blacks,” Creators Syndicate, September 11, 2007, https://www.creators.com/read/walter-williams/09/07/insulting-blacks.
27. Corinne Bendersky, “Making U.S. Fire Departments More Diverse and Inclusive,” *Harvard Business Review*, December 7, 2018.
28. Hank Berrien, “UCLA Professor: Too Many White Male Firefighters Out There,” *Daily Wire*, December 19, 2018, https://www.dailywire.com/news/39520/ucla-professor-too-many-white-male-firefighters-hank-berrien.
29. Nell Greenfieldboyce “Academic Science Rethinks All-Too-White ‘Dude Walls’ of Honor,” NPR, August 25, 2019, https://www.npr.org/sections/health-shots/2019/08/25/749886989/academic-science-rethinks-all-too-white-dude-walls-of-honor.

30. William Voegeli, "Racism, Revised," *Claremont Review of Books*, November 6, 2018.
31. Walter Williams, "Acceptable Racism," *Jewish World Review*, December 12, 2018.
32. Colby Hall, "CNN's Harry Enten Ranks Dem 2020 Hopefuls: 'Not Sure it's the Time to Nominate a White Male,'" Mediaite, December 13, 2018, https://www.mediaite.com/tv/cnns-harry-enten-ranks-democratic-presidential-hopefuls-not-sure-its-the-time-to-nominate-a-white-male/.
33. Stephanie Taylor, "Linden Family Mourns 9-Year-Old Who Took Her Own Life," *Tuscaloosa News*, December 8, 2018.
34. Steven Johnson, "Silent Sam Protesters at Chapel Hill Embrace a New Tactic: a 'Grade Strike,'" *Chronicle of Higher Education*, December 7, 2018.
35. Fiona Moriarty-McLaughlin, "U Oregon Students Demand Removal of Pioneer Statue," *Campus Reform*, June 20, 2019, https://www.campusreform.org/?ID=13357.
36. Ethan Berman, "Public University Removes White Instructor for Telling Students to 'Be Respectful in Class,'" *College Fix*, December 6, 2018, https://www.thecollegefix.com/public-university-removes-white-instructor-for-telling-students-to-be-respectful-in-class/.
37. "President Eighmy Announces the Outcome of the Investigations into Classroom Incident," UTSA Today, November 14, 2018, https://www.utsa.edu/today/2018/11/story/EighmyUpdate3.html.
38. Clara Chin, "Office Hours Harm Minorities," *The Dartmouth*, April 14, 2017.
39. Douglas Ernst, "ESPN Host Implies Trump Is Racist for Serving Black, White Clemson Players Fast Food," *Washington Times*, January 16, 2019.
40. Anemona Hartocollis, "Asian-Americans Suing Harvard Say Admissions Files Show Discrimination," *New York Times*, January 16, 2019.
41. Brett Molina, "CNN Analyst Areva Martin Accused Radio Host David Webb of 'White Privilege.' Webb is Black," *USA Today*, January 16, 2019.
42. Douglas Ernst, "BuzzFeed's '37 Things White People Need To Stop Ruining In 2018' Article Blasted As Racist," *Washington Times*, December 28, 2017.
43. Ekow N. Yankah, "Can My Children Be Friends with White People," *New York Times*, November 11, 2017.
44. Brian Niemietz, "Bernie Sanders Calls President Trump a Racist on Martin Luther King Day," *Daily News*, January 21, 2019.
45. Pat Buchanan, "Democrats' America: The Heart of Darkness," *Townhall*, January 25, 2019, https://townhall.com/columnists/patbuchanan/2019/01/25/democrats-america-the-heart-of-darkness-n2540211.

46. Issac Bailey, "Why Trump's MAGA Hats Have Become a Potent Symbol of Racism," CNN, March 12, 2019, https://www.cnn.com/2019/01/21/opinions/maga-hat-has-become-a-potent-racist-symbol-bailey/index.html.
47. Sumantra Maitra, "No, A Catholic Kid Wearing a MAGA Hat Isn't a Ku Klux Klansman," *The Federalist*, January 22, 2019, https://thefederalist.com/2019/01/22/no-catholic-kid-wearing-maga-hat-isnt-like-kkk/.
48. Adam Serwer, "How Creed Forever Changed the Rocky Series," *The Atlantic*, November 28, 2018.
49. Molly Prince, "Democrats Highlight Kamal Harris's Race as Her Removal from the Senate Judiciary Committee Appears Likely," *Daily Caller*, November 26, 2018, https://dailycaller.com/2018/11/26/kamala-harriss-race-judiciary-committee/.
50. Gideon Resnick, "Kamala Harris Will Remain on Judiciary Committee Despite Democratic Senate Losses," *Daily Beast*, December 11, 2018, https://www.thedailybeast.com/kamala-harris-will-remain-on-judiciary-committee-despite-democratic-senate-losses.
51. Leda Fisher, "Should White Boys Still Be Allowed to Talk?" *The Dickinsonian*, February 7, 2019.
52. Jennifer Kabbany, "University Hosts No-Whites-Allowed Faculty and Staff Listening Sessions—to Promote Inclusivity," *College Fix*, April 24, 2019, https://www.thecollegefix.com/university-hosts-no-whites-allowed-faculty-and-staff-listening-sessions-to-promote-inclusivity/.
53. Paul Bois, "Jennifer Lopez Responds to Backlash after Motown Tribute Deemed Not Woke Enough," *Daily Wire*, February 11, 2019, https://www.dailywire.com/news/43316/jennifer-lopez-responds-backlash-after-motown-paul-bois.
54. Isis Davis-Marks, "Evil is Banal," *Yale Daily News*, February 7, 2019.
55. Ian Schwartz, "Don Lemon to Howard Schultz: It Is Not Okay To Say 'I Don't See Color' In 2019," RealClearPolitics, February 13, 2019, https://www.realclearpolitics.com/video/2019/02/13/don_lemon_to_howard_schultz_it_is_not_okay_to_say_i_dont_see_color_in_2019.html.
56. Diana Soriano, "White Privilege Lecture Tells Students White People 'Dangerous' If They See Race," *College Fix*, March 6, 2019, https://www.thecollegefix.com/white-privilege-lecture-tells-students-white-people-dangerous-if-they-dont-see-race/.
57. Aaron Colen, "Warren, Harris Publicly Support Reparations for Blacks Impacted by Slavery and Discrimination," The Blaze, February 21, 2019, https://www.theblaze.com/harris-warren-publicly-support-reparations-for-blacks-impacted-by-slavery-and-discrimination.
58. Jim Geraghty, "Kamala Harris Says America Hasn't Yet Had an Honest Conversation about Race," *National Review*, March 11, 2019.

59. John McWhorter, "Victimhood Chic: What the Jussie Smollett Story Reveals," *The Atlantic*, February 20, 2019.

CHAPTER FIVE

1. Dale O'Leary and Peter Sprigg, "Understanding and Responding to the Transgender Movement," Family Research Council, June 2015, https://www.frc.org/transgender.
2. O'Leary and Sprigg, "Understanding and Responding to the Transgender Movement."
3. Ibid.
4. Jeff Johnston, "What is 'Gender Identity'?" *Daily Citizen* (blog), Focus on the Family, 2016, https://dailycitizen.focusonthefamily.com/what-is-gender-identity/.
5. Dorothy Cummings McLean, "Jordan Peterson: Gender Ideology is 'Completely Insane,'" LifeSite News, March 23, 2018, https://www.lifesitenews.com/news/jordan-peterson-gender-theory-has-become-unquestionable-doctrine-thats-comp.
6. Selwyn Duke, "Feminists Screaming about 'Transgenderism,' Their Own Demon Child," The American Thinker, February 22, 2019, https://qoshe.com/american-thinker/selwyn-duke/feminists-screaming-about-transgenderism-their-own-demon-child/28469783.
7. Sam Killermann, *A Guide to Gender; The Social Justice Advocate's Handbook, 2nd Edition* (Austin, TX: Impetus Books, 2017), Kindle Edition, location 2651 of 4188.
8. RadFemFatale, "Feminism is Not About Gender Equality," Medium, October 12, 2017, https://medium.com/@radfemfatale/feminism-is-not-about-gender-equality-efc2ccb1e46b.
9. RadFemFatale, "Feminism is Not About Gender Equality."
10. Ibid.
11. Jennifer Weiner, "The Torture of Dressing for Your Office Holiday Party," *New York Times*, December 8, 2018.
12. Jane Pilcher & Imelda Whelehan, *Key Concepts in Gender Studies, 2nd Edition* (Thousand Oaks, California: Sage Publications Ltd. 2017), 99.
13. Charlotte Higgins, "The Age of Patriarchy: How an Unfashionable Idea Became a Rallying Cry for Feminism Today," *The Guardian*, June 22, 2018.
14. Higgins, "The Age of Patriarchy."
15. Dorothy Cummings McLean, "Take Your Kids Out of Class: Tucker Carlson and Jordan Peterson Discuss the Decline of Masculinity," LifeSite News, March 8, 2018, https://www.lifesitenews.com/news/take-your-kids-out-of-class-tucker-carlson-and-jordan-peterson-discuss-the.

16. Liberty Banner, "Jordan Peterson vs Crazy Cathy Areu on Toxic Masculinity," YouTube, July 12, 2018, https://www.youtube.com/watch?v=hTwnC2xSNt0.
17. James Barrett, "Watch: Jordan Peterson Takes On Feminist's 'Patriarchy' Arguments," *Daily Wire*, December 24, 2018, https://www.dailywire.com/news/39649/watch-jordan-peterson-takes-feminists-patriarchy-james-barrett.
18. Barrett, "Watch: Jordan Peterson Takes On Feminist's 'Patriarchy' Arguments."
19. Maya Salam, "What is Toxic Masculinity?" *New York Times*, January 22, 2019.
20. Salam, "What is Toxic Masculinity?"
21. F. Diane Barth, "Toxic Masculinity Is Terrible Shorthand for a Real Problem Plaguing Men," NBC News, January 14, 2019, https://www.nbcnews.com/think/opinion/toxic-masculinity-terrible-shorthand-real-problem-plaguing-men-ncna957941.
22. Lewis Howes, *The Mask of Masculinity: How Men Can Embrace Vulnerability, Create Strong Relationships, and Live Their Fullest Lives* (Emmaus, PA: Rodale Books, 2017).
23. Colleen Clemens, "What We Mean When We Say, 'Toxic Masculinity,'" *Teaching Tolerance*, December 11, 2017.
24. Liberty Banner, "Jordan Peterson vs Crazy Cathy Areu on Toxic Masculinity."
25. Ibid.
26. Stephanie Pappas, "APA Issues First-Even Guidelines for Practice With Men and Boys," *American Psychological Association* 50 (1), 2019, 34.
27. Rod Dreher, "Manhood as Mental Disorder," *The American Conservative*, January 8, 2019.
28. David French, "Grown Men Are the Solution, Not the Problem," *National Review*, January 7, 2019.
29. Michael Gurian, "Blaming Masculinity Will Only Make the Male Crisis Worse," *The Federalist*, January 14, 2019, https://thefederalist.com/2019/01/14/blaming-masculinity-will-make-male-crisis-worse/.
30. Gurian, "Blaming Masculinity Will Only Make the Male Crisis Worse."
31. Hans Fiene, "Gillette's Toxic Masculinity Ad Accidentally Makes a Case for Patriarchy," *The Federalist*, January 17, 2019, https://thefederalist.com/2019/01/17/gillettes-toxic-masculinity-ad-accidentally-makes-case-patriarchy/.
32. D.C. McAllister, "We Don't Need Less Traditional Masculinity, We Need More," *The Federalist*, January 15, 2019, https://thefederalist.com/2019/01/15/dont-need-less-traditional-masculinity-need/.

33. Melissa Langsam Braunstein, "How Our Anti-Boy Culture Affects Mothers Like Me," *The Federalist*, January 16, 2019, https://thefederalist.com/2019/01/16/anti-boy-culture-affects-mothers-like/.
34. Damian Reilly, "Masculinity Isn't Toxic – Corporate Moralizing Is," *The Spectator USA*, January 17, 2019.
35. Reilly, "Masculinity Isn't Toxic – Corporate Moralizing Is."
36. Jessica Chasmar, "Proctor and Gamble CEO: 'There is an Issue with Toxic Masculinity,'" *Washington Times*, January 25, 2019.
37. Jeff Johnston, "What is 'Gender Identity'?" Focus on the Family, 2016.
38. Johnston, "What is 'Gender Identity'?"
39. Norman L. Geisler, in Baker Encyclopedia of Christian Apologetics (Grand Rapids, MI: Baker Books, 1999), 147.
40. 1 Corinthians 6:19–20.
41. Rhys Mahurin, "Dr. Money and the History of Separating Sex and Gender," Timber Times, April 27, 2018.
42. Lee Airton, *Gender: Your Guide* (New York, New York: Adams Media, 2016), Kindle Edition, location 331 of 3976.
43. Mahurin, "Dr. Money and the History of Separating Sex and Gender."
44. Ibid.
45. Bill Muehlenberg, "Gender Insanity vs. Gender Reality," Culture Watch, January 12, 2018, https://billmuehlenberg.com/2018/01/12/gender-insanity-vs-gender-reality/.
46. Muehlenberg, "Gender Insanity vs. Gender Reality."
47. Bill de Blasio and Carmelyn P. Malalis, Gender Identity Expression Factsheet, NYC Commission on Human Rights, May 2016.
48. Miranda Katz, "No, NYC Did Not Just Introduce a $250,000 Fine for Any Incorrect Use of Gender Pronouns," Gothamist, May 19, 2016, https://gothamist.com/2016/05/19/gender_pronouns_false_fine.php.
49. Casey Parks, "Gresham-Barlow School District Agrees to Pay Transgender Teacher, Add Gender-Neutral Bathrooms After Complaint," The Oregonian, May 20, 2016.
50. Graham Moomaw, "Virginia High School Teacher Fired for Refusing to Use Transgender Student's New Pronouns," *Richmond Times-Dispatch*, December 6, 2018.
51. Will Oremus, "Facebook No Longer Limits Your Gender to 'Male' or 'Female,'" *Future Tense*, (blog), *Slate*, February 13, 2014, http://www.slate.com/blogs/future_tense/2014/02/13/facebook_gender_options_male_female_and_custom_plus_preferred_pronouns.html.
52. Rhiannon Williams, "Facebook's 71 Gender Options Come to UK Users," *Telegraph UK*, June 27, 2014.
53. Daniel Avery, "Joe Biden Says 'There Are at Least Three' Genders in Iowa Campaign Stop," *Newsweek*, August 11, 2019.

54. Tyson Langhofer, "Psychological Research Explains Why Increasing Gender Choices Increases Our Misery," *The Federalist*, February 7, 2019, https://thefederalist.com/2019/02/07/psychological-research-explains-increasing-gender-choices-increases-misery/.
55. Walt Heyer, "Fifty-Six Shades of Gender Insanity," *The Federalist*, March 10, 2015, https://thefederalist.com/2015/03/10/fifty-six-shades-of-gender-insanity/.
56. "cisgender," *Merriam-Webster Dictionary*, 2019.
57. "dysphoria," *Oxford English Dictionary*, 2019.
58. Heyer, "Fifty-Six Shades of Gender Insanity."
59. Ibid.
60. Walt Heyer, "Kids Aren't Born Trans," CNS News, April 5, 2019, https://www.cnsnews.com/commentary/walt-heyer/kids-arent-born-trans.
61. Walt Heyer, "Kids Aren't Born Transgender, So Don't Let Advocates Bamboozle You," *Daily Signal*, March 29, 2019, https://www.dailysignal.com/2019/03/29/kids-arent-born-transgender-so-dont-let-advocates-bamboozle-you/.
62. Heyer, "Kids Aren't Born Transgender, So Don't Let Advocates Bamboozle You."
63. Sam Dorman, "Paglia: 'Transgender Mania' is a Symptom of West's Cultural Collapse," CNS News, November 3, 2015, https://www.cnsnews.com/news/article/sam-dorman/camille-paglia-transgender-mania-symptom-cultural-collapse.
64. Gravitahn, "Lesson from History: Transgender Mania is Sign of Cultural Collapse – Camille Paglia," YouTube, December 14, 2016, https://www.youtube.com/watch?v=I8BRdwgPChQ.
65. Matt Barber, "The Entire 'LGBT' Narrative Just Crumbled," The Stream, August 29, 2016, https://stream.org/entire-lgbt-narrative-just-crumbled/.
66. Jack Turban, "Hannah Is a Girl. Doctors Finally Treat Her Like One," *New York Times*, April 8, 2017.
67. Ben Shapiro, "The Insanity of the Left's Child Gender-Confusion Agenda," *Townhall*, April 12, 2017, https://townhall.com/columnists/benshapiro/2017/04/12/the-insanity-of-the-lefts-child-genderconfusion-agenda-n2312030.
68. Shapiro, "The Insanity of the Left's Child Gender-Confusion Agenda."
69. Jane Robbins, "Doctors Speak Out Against Medical Profession's Utter Lack of Caution for Trans Kids," *The Federalist*, January 31, 2019, https://thefederalist.com/2019/01/31/pediatricians-speak-medical-professions-utter-lack-caution-trans-kids/.
70. Charlene Aaron, "'Drag Queen Story Hours' Expose Pre-Schoolers to What Some Parents Call 'Gender Insanity'," CBN News, August 14, 2018, https://www1.cbn.com/cbnnews/us/2018/august/

drag-queen-story-hours-expose-pre-schoolers-to-what-some-parents-call-gender-insanity.

71. Chris Enloe, "Library Apologizes for Allowing Child Sex Offender to Entertain Children at 'Drag Queen Storytime,'" The Blaze, March 17, 2019, https://www.theblaze.com/news/houston-library-apologizes-drag-queen-storytime.
72. Charlene Aaron, "'Drag Queen Story Hours' Expose Pre-Schoolers to What Some Parents Call 'Gender Insanity'," CBN News, August 14, 2018, https://www1.cbn.com/cbnnews/us/2018/august/drag-queen-story-hours-expose-pre-schoolers-to-what-some-parents-call-gender-insanity.
73. Delaina Dixon, "This Mother and Son Are Becoming Father and Daughter, Both Will Transition," Bravo TV, March 16, 2017, https://www.bravotv.com/blogs/this-mother-and-son-are-becoming-father-and-daughter.
74. Asian J. Androl, "Mother and Daughter Became Father and Son: A Case Report," *Asian Journal of Andrology* 17(5), Sept-Oct. 2015, 855–56.
75. Kwame Anthony Appiah, "Should I Go to a Gender-Reveal Party?" *New York Times Magazine*, September 25, 2018.
76. Albert Mohler, "The Audacity of Gender-Reveal Parties: Another Step Towards Cultural Insanity," *AlbertMohler.com*, October 15, 2018, https://albertmohler.com/2018/10/15/audacity-gender-reveal-parties-another-step-towards-cultural-insanity/.
77. Mohler, "The Audacity of Gender-Reveal Parties: Another Step Towards Cultural Insanity."
78. Cummings McLean, "Jordan Peterson: Gender Ideology is 'Completely Insane.'"
79. Jordan B. Peterson, 12 Rules for Life (Toronto, Canada: Random House Canada, 2018), 293.
80. Johnston, "What is 'Gender Identity'?"
81. Jeff Johnston, "Male and Female: Biology Matters," Focus on the Family, 2016.
82. "Drugs Can Affect Men and Women Differently," CBS News, February 7, 2014, http://www.cbsnews.com/news/drugs-can-affect-men-and-women-differently/.
83. Larry Cahill, "Equal ≠ The Same: Sex Differences in the Human Brain," *Cerebrum*, March–April 2014.
84. Alice Eagly et al., "Feminism and Psychology: Analysis of a Half-Century of Research on Women and Gender," *American Psychologist* 67 (3), 2012, 211–230.
85. John Stossel, "War on Women," *Townhall*, March 12, 2014, https://townhall.com/columnists/johnstossel/2014/03/12/war-on-women-n1807016.

86. "Boys & Girls Are Different: Men, Women & the Sex Difference," ABC News Special Episode Guide, https://www.tvguide.com/tvshows/abc-news-special/episode-855020/298075/; stosselftw, "John Stossel – Men and Women," YouTube, September 7, 2007, https://www.youtube.com/watch?v=T20R_bf-B4s.
87. Cahill, "Equal ≠ The Same: Sex Differences in the Human Brain."
88. Ibid.
89. Ibid.
90. Carol Ann Rinzler, *Why Eve Doesn't Have an Adam's Apple: A Dictionary of Sex Differences* (New York: Facts on File, 1996), 4; Cahill, "Equal ≠ The Same: Sex Differences in the Human Brain"; Johnston, "Male and Female: Biology Matters."
91. Alexandra Wilts, "Trump's 'Dangerous" Tax Reforms Could Kill 10,000 People A Year, Says Former Treasury Secretary Larry Summers," *Independent UK*, December 4, 2017.
92. Mary Dooe, "Larry Summers 'May Have Done a Service to Women,' with His Sexist Remarks," PRI, January 31, 2015, https://www.pri.org/stories/2015-01-31/larry-summers-may-have-done-service-women-his-sexist-remarks; Stuart Taylor, Jr., "Why Feminist Careerists Neutered Larry Summers," *The Atlantic*, February 2005.
93. Michael Barone, "Ruth Marcus: Larry Summers Was Right About Men and Women in Math and Science," *US News & World Report*, December 4, 2008.
94. Ruth Marcus, "Was Larry Summers Right?" RealClearPolitics, December 3, 2008, https://www.realclearpolitics.com/articles/2008/12/was_larry_summers_right.html.
95. Kara Swisher, "Google Has Fired the Employee Who Penned a Controversial Memo on Women and Tech," *Recode* (blog), Vox, August 7, 2017, https://www.vox.com/2017/8/7/16110696/firing-google-ceo-employee-penned-controversial-memo-on-women-has-violated-its-code-of-conduct.

CHAPTER SIX

1. Brian Stelter (@brianstelter), "She's got a target on her back because she ticks every box that makes conservatie mven uncomfortable—@LEBassett talking about @AOC," Twitter, January 27, 2019, 3:01 p.m., https://twitter.com/brianstelter/status/1089659775254618113?lang=en.
2. Peter Beinart, "There's a Reason Many Voters Have Negative Views of Warren—But the Press Won't Tell You Why," *The Atlantic*, January 2, 2019.
3. A. B. Stoddard, "No, Democrats, the Likability Question Isn't Sexist," RealClearPolitics, January 14, 2019, https://www.realclearpolitics.com/articles/2019/01/14/no_democrats_the_likability_question_isnt_sexist_139164.html.

4. "2020 Democratic Presidential Nomination," RealClearPolitics, August 9, 2019.
5. Pat Buchanan, "2020: Socialist America or Trump's America?" *Townhall*, April 5, 2019, https://townhall.com/columnists/patbuchanan/2019/04/05/2020-socialist-america-or-trumps-america-n2544301.
6. Naomi Rao, "Shades of Gray," *Yale Herald*, October 14, 1994.
7. Sumantra Maitra, "Nominee for Kavanaugh's Old Seat Tarred for Eschewing Identity Politics," *The Federalist*, January 22, 2019, https://thefederalist.com/2019/01/22/trumps-nominee-kavanaughs-old-seat-tarred-eschewing-identity-politics/.
8. Marcela Howell, Sung Yeon Choimorrow, and Jessica Gonzalez-Rojas, "Neomi Rao Will Not Protect Rights of Women of Color," *The Hill*, February 24, 2019.
9. Mary Margaret Olohan, "ACLU Told CA Teachers to Help Students Obtain Abortions Without Parental Notification, Video Reveals," *Daily Caller*, July 7, 2019, https://dailycaller.com/2019/07/07/sex-education-aclu-video/.
10. Ashe Schow, "Elton John: It's 'Bulls***' To Criticize A Heterosexual Man for Playing a Homosexual Man in a Film," *Daily Wire*, May 18, 2019, https://www.dailywire.com/news/47390/elton-john-its-bulls-criticize-heterosexual-man-ashe-schow.
11. Hannah Yasharoff, "Scarlett Johansson Defends Casting: 'I Should Be allowed to Play Any Person, Tree or Animal,'" *USA Today*, July 14, 2019.
12. William Shatner (@WilliamShatner), "I would think that censorship of classics because certain 'types' need to judge things through their own 2018 myopic glasses and demand they be stricken from history is important. Or is this 1984 only 34 years too late?" Twitter, December 11, 2018, 8:19 a.m., https://twitter.com/williamshatner/status/1072526404359737345?lang=en.
13. Paul Bois, "SJWs Roast William Shatner for Defending 'Baby, It's Cold Outside,'" *Daily Wire*, December 12, 2018, https://www.dailywire.com/news/39290/sjws-roast-william-shatner-defending-baby-its-cold-paul-bois
14. Laura Bassett, "Conservative Men Are Obsessed with Alexandria Ocasio-Cortez. Science Tells Us Why," *HuffPost*, January 14, 2019 https://www.huffpost.com/entry/conservatives-afraid-alexandria-ocasio-cortez_n_5c38cb74e4b05cb31c421cc3.
15. Joseph A. Wulfsohn, "CNN Host Joan Walsh Says Trump is 'Sexist' for Suggesting Melania Could Make Salads," Fox News, January 15, 2019, https://www.foxnews.com/entertainment/cnn-host-joan-walsh-says-trump-is-sexist-for-suggesting-melania-could-make-salads.

16. Jeremy W. Peters, Jo Becker, and Julie Hirschfeld Davis, "Trump Rescinds Rules on Bathrooms for Transgender Students," *New York Times*, February 22, 2017.
17. Colleen Jenkins and Daniel Trotta, "Seeking End to Boycott, North Carolina Rescinds Transgender Bathroom Law," Reuters, March 30, 2017, https://www.reuters.com/article/us-north-carolina-lgbt/seeking-end-to-boycott-north-carolina-rescinds-transgender-bathroom-law-idUSKBN1711V4.
18. Jonathan Drew, "North Carolina's Transgender Rights Battle Isn't Over," *USA Today*, June 25, 2018.
19. Emanuella Grinberg and Dani Stewart, "3 Myths That Shape the Transgender Bathroom Debate," CNN, March 7, 2017, https://www.cnn.com/2017/03/07/health/transgender-bathroom-law-facts-myths/index.html.
20. Jamie Shupe, "Criminal Records Show Women Are Prudent to Not Want Men in Their Bathrooms," *The Federalist*, December 19, 2018, https://thefederalist.com/2018/12/19/criminal-records-show-women-prudent-not-want-men-bathrooms/.
21. Jonathon Van Maren, "Female Students Rebel against Transgender Bathrooms, Refuse to Use Same Facilities as Boys," LifeSite News, February 27, 2019, https://www.lifesitenews.com/blogs/female-students-rebel-against-transgender-bathrooms-refuse-to-use-same-facilities-as-boys.
22. "Man Dressed as Woman Arrested for Spying into Mall Bathroom Stall, Police Say," NBC 4 Washington, November 17, 2015, https://www.nbcwashington.com/news/local/Man-Dressed-as-Woman-Arrested-for-Spying-Into-Mall-Bathroom-Stall-Police-Say-351232041.html.
23. John Cadiz Klemack and Jonathan Lloyd, "Man Disguised as Woman Recorded 'Hours' of Mall Restroom Video: Investigators," NBC 4 Los Angeles, May 15, 2013, https://www.nbclosangeles.com/news/local/Secret-Recording-Store-Mall-Antelope-Valley-Palmdale-Restroom-207541101.html.
24. Ben Johnson, "'Transgender' Man May Continue Using Girls' Locker Room, Says College," LifeSite News, November 10, 2012, https://www.lifesitenews.com/news/transgender-man-may-continue-using-locker-room-with-six-year-old-girls.
25. Caleb Stephen, "CNN's Cuomo: 12-year-old Girl Doesn't Want to See Penis in Girls' Room Because of 'Intolerant' Dad," LifeSite News, February 27, 2017, https://www.lifesitenews.com/opinion/cnns-cuomo-on-trans-bathrooms-this-isnt-about-a-scared-girl.-it-is-about-an.
26. Fred Lucas, "Supreme Court Upholds Trump Transgender Military Policy—For Now," *Daily Signal*, January 22, 2019, https://www.

dailysignal.com/2019/01/22/supreme-court-upholds-trump-transgender-military-policy-for-now/.

27. "Obama Judge Rules Medicaid Must Pay for Transgender Sex Reassignment Surgery," Judicial Watch, August 22, 2019, https://www.judicialwatch.org/corruption-chronicles/obama-judge-rules-medicaid-must-pay-for-transgender-sex-reassignment-surgery/.
28. Doug Mainwaring, "11-Year-Old 'Drag Kid' Dances in Popular NYC Gay Club as Patrons Toss Money at Him," LifeSite News, December 17, 2018, https://www.lifesitenews.com/news/11-year-old-drag-kid-dances-in-popular-nyc-gay-club-as-patrons-toss-money-a.
29. Matt Walsh (@MattWalshBlog), "The Left is applauding the sexual abuse of this child. This is why decent and rational people want nothing at all to do with Leftism. It openly promotes, advocates, and celebrates child sexual abuse," Twitter, December 17, 2018, 9:58 a.m., https://twitter.com/MattWalshBlog/status/1074725642497941504.
30. Doug Mainwaring, "10-year-old Girl Suspended for Asking to be Exempted from LGBT School Lesson," LifeSite News, July 1, 2019, https://www.lifesitenews.com/news/10-year-old-girl-suspended-for-asking-to-be-exempted-from-lgbt-school-lesson.
31. "9-year-old Austin Drag Queen Spreading Message of Love," ABC13, June 21, 2019, https://abc13.com/society/9-year-old-austin-drag-queen-spreading-message-of-love/5356269/.
32. Emily Zanotti, "Activists Suggest the Next James Bond Should Be Transgender," *Daily Wire*, December 23, 2018, https://www.dailywire.com/news/39637/activists-suggest-next-james-bond-should-be-emily-zanotti.
33. Steph Harmon, "Bond's number is up: black female actor 'is the new 007,'" *The Guardian*, July 15, 2019.
34. Paul Bois, "University of Oklahoma Introduces a Feminist James Bond Course," *Daily Wire*, December 27, 2018, https://www.dailywire.com/news/39729/university-oklahoma-introduces-feminist-james-bond-paul-bois.
35. Jessica Schladebeck, "Tom Ford on Why All Men Should Be Penetrated Once: 'I Think It Would Help Them Understand Women," *Daily News*, December 7, 2016.
36. Alex Parker, "Federal Judge Orders Male Inmate Transferred to Women's Prison Because He Identifies as Female," *RedState*, December 29, 2018, https://www.redstate.com/alexparker/2018/12/29/deon-strawberry-hampton-transgender-transferred-prison/.
37. Jillian Jorgensen, "City Orders Jails To House Transgender Inmates in Lockups Consistent with Their Gender Identity," *Daily News*, April 16, 2018.
38. Jenny Singer, "Dear Men: Dating You Is Hell," *The Forward*, December 30, 2018.

39. "Frequently Asked Questions: Stephens College Admissions and Enrollment Policy," 2019, http://komu.s3.amazonaws.com/files/faq_admissions_policy__(1).pdf.
40. Amanda Prestigiacomo, "He Played Handball for Australia's Men's Team. Now Transgender, He's Dominating Women's Handball," *Daily Wire*, December 7, 2018, https://www.dailywire.com/news/39158/transgender-player-dominating-womens-handball-amanda-prestigiacomo.
41. Carlos Gracia, "Marathon Champion Says Women's Sports Should Be Protected from Transgender Athletes—Activists Go on the Attack," The Blaze, March 29, 2019, https://www.theblaze.com/news/paula-radcliffe-transgender.
42. Libby Emmons, "Tennis Legend Martina Navratilova Attacked for Saying Only Women Should Compete in Women's Sports," *The Federalist*, February 22, 2019, https://thefederalist.com/2019/02/22/tennis-legend-martina-navratilova-fire-saying-women-compete-womens-sports/.
43. Piers Morgan, "It's Grotesquely Unfair for Transgender Women to Compete in Women's Sports, and Outrageous for Trans People to Bully and Vilify LGBT Heroine Martina Navratilova for Stating the Obvious," *Daily Mail*, March 4, 2019.
44. Sister Toldjah, "Martina Learns That Nothing Short of Total Surrender Will Appease Transgender Activists (UPDATE: Martina Responds)," *RedState*, March 4, 2019, https://www.redstate.com/sister-toldjah/2019/03/04/martina-learns-nothing-short-total-surrender-will-appease-transgender-activists/.
45. Kelsey Bolar, "8th Place: A High School Girl's Life after Transgender Students Join Her Sport," *Daily Signal*, May 6, 2019, https://www.dailysignal.com/2019/05/06/8th-place-high-school-girls-speak-out-on-getting-beat-by-biological-boys/.
46. Amanda Prestigiacomo, "Transgender Woman Wins Discrimination Suit, $20,000 for Being Cut from Women's Football Team," *Daily Wire*, December 31, 2018, https://www.dailywire.com/news/39735/transgender-woman-wins-discrimination-suit-after-amanda-prestigiacomo.
47. Associated Press, "Bill Targeting Transgender Athlete Policy Fails in South Dakota," NBC News, February 26, 2019, https://www.nbcnews.com/feature/nbc-out/bill-targeting-transgender-athlete-policy-fails-south-dakota-n976116.
48. Associated Press, "Bill Targeting Transgender Athlete Policy Fails in South Dakota."
49. Margot Cleveland, "LGBT Activists Teaching Judges To Yank Kids From Parents Who Won't Transgender Them," *The Federalist*, February

12, 2019, https://thefederalist.com/2019/02/12/lgbt-activists-teaching-judges-yank-kids-parents-wont-transgender/.

50. Amanda Prestigiacomo, "Actress Debra Messing Posts Empowering 'Vagina' Cupcakes, Gets Trashed as Transphobic and Issues Apology," *Daily Wire*, March 11, 2019, https://www.dailywire.com/news/44518/actress-debra-messing-posts-empowering-vagina-amanda-prestigiacomo.
51. Hadley Heath Manning, "How the Left Pretends To Champion Women While Actually Erasing Them," *The Federalist*, January 17, 2019, https://thefederalist.com/2019/01/17/left-pretends-champion-women-actually-erasing/.
52. Charles L. Greene II, "Logo Proposal Community Response," Mount Holyoke, December 2018, https://www.mtholyoke.edu/communications/logo-proposal-community-response.
53. Stefanie Stiles, "Why Do Feminists Say Women Aren't a Success If They Focus on Family?" *The Federalist*, January 21, 2019, https://thefederalist.com/2019/01/31/feminists-insist-women-arent-success-focus-family/.
54. Elizabeth Bauer, "The Future of Feminism Is ... East Germany?" *The Federalist*, February 28, 2019, https://thefederalist.com/2019/02/28/we-have-seen-the-future-of-feminism-and-it-is-east-germany/.
55. Marissa Michaels, "PSRJ, PSGE Host Third Annual Menstruation Celebration to Destigmatize Periods," *Daily Princetonian*, December 2, 2018.
56. Frank Camp, "How the Deconstruction of Sex-Related Biology Could Tear Us Apart," *Daily Wire*, December 29, 2018, https://www.dailywire.com/news/39775/camp-how-deconstruction-sex-related-biology-could-frank-camp.
57. Andrew Nicoll, "Crumbs! Scottish Parliament Staff Banned from Saying Gingerbread 'Man' at Holyrood Coffee Shop because It's Not Gender Neutral – As They Rename Biscuits 'Gingerbread People,'" The Scottish Sun, December 14, 2018, https://www.thescottishsun.co.uk/news/scottish-news/3621770/gingerbread-man-biscuits-holyrood-scottish-parliament-cafe-gender-neutral/.
58. Martin Beckford, "Mother, 38, Is Arrested in Front of Her Children and Locked in a Cell for Seven Hours After Calling a Transgender Woman a Man on Twitter," *Daily Mail*, February 9, 2019.
59. Sophie Lewis, "Miss Spain Makes History as First Transgender Woman to Compete in Miss Universe Pageant," CBS News, December 18, 2019, https://www.cbsnews.com/news/miss-spain-makes-history-as-first-transgender-woman-to-compete-in-miss-universe-pageant/.
60. Matt Walsh, "A Male Miss Universe Contestant Is Being Applauded by the Same People Who Complain about Appropriation," *Daily Wire*,

December 17, 2018, https://www.dailywire.com/news/39413/walsh-miss-universe-matt-walsh.

61. Sarah Templeton, "New Auckland Santa Statue Takes 'Unintentional' Aim at Simon Bridges," Newshub, November 29, 2018, https://www.newshub.co.nz/home/lifestyle/2018/11/mary-poppins-inspired-auckland-santa-statue-takes-aim-at-simon-bridges.html.
62. Madeline Farber, "'Modern' Santa? Some Want Father Christmas to Be Gender-Neutral, Have Tattoos, Survey Finds," Fox News, December 21, 2018, https://www.foxnews.com/lifestyle/modern-santa-some-want-father-christmas-to-be-gender-neutral-have-tattoos-survey-finds.
63. Chad Felix Greene, "The Stigma of Being Conservative Is Worse Than That of Being Gay," *The Federalist*, December 11, 2018, https://thefederalist.com/2018/12/11/stigma-conservative-politics-worse-stigma-gay/.
64. Joy Pullmann, "Left Savages Gay Writer for Saying People Stigmatize His Conservatism," *The Federalist*, December 17, 2018, https://thefederalist.com/2018/12/17/left-savages-gay-writer-saying-people-stigmatize-conservatism-sexuality/.
65. Frank Camp, "Deadspin Sportswriter Tells Gay Conservatives To 'Shut The F*** Up,'" *Daily Wire*, December 13, 2018, https://www.dailywire.com/news/39350/deadspin-writer-tells-gay-conservatives-shut-f-frank-camp.
66. Walt Heyer, "Mom Dresses Six-Year-Old Son as Girl, Threatens Dad with Losing His Son for Disagreeing," *The Federalist*, November 26, 2018, https://thefederalist.com/2018/11/26/mom-dresses-six-year-old-son-girl-threatens-dad-losing-son-disagreeing/.
67. Emanuella Grinberg, "These Bills Could Make Life Harder for Transgender People, Civil Rights Groups Say," CNN, February 28, 2019, https://www.cnn.com/2019/02/27/us/transgender-bills-2019/index.html.
68. Emily Wilson, "San Francisco Creates World's First Ever Transgender Cultural District," *Daily Beast*, December 11, 2018, https://www.thedailybeast.com/san-francisco-creates-worlds-first-ever-transgender-cultural-district.
69. Dr. Susan Berry, "Vermont To Allow Taxpayer-Funded Transgender Sex Reassignment Surgeries for Children," *Breitbart*, June 13, 2019, https://www.breitbart.com/politics/2019/06/13/vermont-taxpayer-funded-transgender-sex-reassignment-surgeries-children/.
70. Leon Wolf, "Wisconsin Medicaid Will Begin Covering Gender Reassignment Surgery Today," The Blaze, January 1, 2019, https://www.theblaze.com/news/wisconsin-medicaid-will-begin-covering-gender-reassignment-surgery-today.

71. Jana J. Pruet, "Jury Awards Transgender Women $780K after Judge Rules Ban on Reassignment Surgery Is Discriminatory," The Blaze, October 12, 2018, https://www.theblaze.com/news/2018/10/12/jury-awards-transgender-women-780k-after-judge-rules-ban-on-reassignment-surgery-is-discriminatory.
72. Joan Biskupic, "Federal Judge Rules Male-Only Draft Is Unconstitutional," CNN, February 25, 2019, https://www.cnn.com/2019/02/25/politics/male-only-draft-unconstitutional/index.html.
73. Linda Harvey, "Top 10 Progressive Endorsements of Child Abuse in 2018," BarbWire, December 28, 2018.
74. video on Daily Motion, https://www.google.com/url?sa=t&rct=j&q=&esrc=s&source=web&cd=1&ved=2ahUKEwifkeSrmbzhAhXn24MKHaz2CSgQFjAAegQIBhAB&url=https%3A%2F%2Fwww.dailymotion.com%2Fvideo%2Fx5nlhzi&usg=AOvVaw1KsAp3aLro-V6toi2eMoz7.
75. Tyler O'Neil, "Transgender Writer Embraces Cannibalism: Wants to Drink 'Transphobe Bone Broth," PJ Media, February 25, 2019, https://pjmedia.com/trending/transgender-writer-embraces-cannibalism-wants-to-drink-transphobe-bone-broth/.
76. Colleen Kratofil, "'Januhairy Is the New Movement Empowering Women to Grow Out Their Body Hair," *People*, January 9, 2019.
77. Breck Dumas, "DC Restaurant Fined $7K for Questioning Transgender Activist Who Used Women's Restroom," The Blaze, January 18, 2019, https://www.theblaze.com/news/dc-restaurant-fined-for-questioning-gender.
78. Dave Urbanski, "'Transkids' Site Sells Fake Penises for Girls Who Identify As Boys – and They're Called 'Packers,'" The Blaze, January 4, 2019, https://www.theblaze.com/news/site-sells-fake-penises-for-girls-who-identify-as-boys.
79. Chris Enloe, "Gillette Is at It Again: This Time Featuring Samson, a Transgender Man Shaving for the First Time," The Blaze, May 26, 2019, https://www.theblaze.com/news/gillette-commercial-transgender.
80. Maressa Brown, "Dads Could Soon Nurse Babies with the Help of a 'Chestfeeding' Kit," *Parents*, October 25, 2018.
81. Francesca Specter, "New 'Chestfeeding Kit' Enables Fathers to Breastfeed Their Baby," Yahoo News, February 12, 2019, https://news.yahoo.com/woman-designs-first-chestfeeding-kit-enables-fathers-breastfeed-babies-115441439.html.
82. Lydia Wheeler, "Dem Lawmaker Wants Federal Laws Rewritten with Gender Neutral Terms," *The Hill*, January 3, 2019.
83. Mike Ciandella, "To Promote Gender Equality, California Governor's Wife Won't Go by 'First Lady,'" The Blaze, January 8, 2019, https://www.theblaze.com/news/california-governors-wife-will-not-go-by-first-lady.

84. Hasan Chowdhury, "Microsoft Word Will Change Your Words To Be 'Gender Inclusive,'" *The Telegraph*, May 7, 2019.
85. Alex Parker, "Lesbian Couple Identifying as Straight Couple Prepares To Transition 5-Yr-Old Son into a Daughter," *RedState*, January 16, 2019, https://www.redstate.com/alexparker/2019/01/16/greg-jody-rogers-transition-jayden/.
86. Paul Bois, "Ocasio-Cortez: I Acknowledge My Privilege Being Born 'Cisgendered,'" *Daily Wire*, February 1, 2019, https://www.dailywire.com/news/42944/ocasio-cortez-i-acknowledge-my-privilege-being-paul-bois.
87. Scott Whitlock, "WashPost Covers 'Menstrual Equity' But Ignores Major Pro-Life Rally," NewsBusters, February 4, 2019, https://www.newsbusters.org/blogs/nb/scott-whitlock/2019/02/04/washpost-covers-menstrual-equity-ignores-major-pro-life-rally.
88. Rachel Frazin, "Women Sue Yale To Gender-Integrate Fraternities," *The Hill*, February 12, 2019.
89. "The Equality Act," *Heritage Explains* (blog), The Heritage Foundation, 2019, https://www.heritage.org/gender/heritage-explains/the-equality-act.
90. Bolar, "8th Place: A High School Girl's Life after Transgender Students Join Her Sport."
91. Peter Heck, "Let the Games Begin: Transgenderism Poised to Ruin the Olympics," The Resurgent, March 6, 2019, https://theresurgent.com/2019/03/06/let-the-games-begin-transgenderism-poised-to-ruin-the-olympics/.
92. Rita Loffredo, "White Male Professors To Be Given Female Minority Scholar Mentors in Anti-Bias Effort," *College Fix*, August 16, 2018, https://www.thecollegefix.com/white-male-professors-to-be-given-female-minority-scholar-mentors-in-anti-bias-effort/.
93. Cherie Vandermillen, "CA Democrats Introduce LGBTQ Bill that Would Protect Pedophiules Who Rape Children," Pulpit and Pen, February 22, 2019, https://pulpitandpen.org/2019/02/22/ca-democrats-introduce-lgbtq-bill-that-would-protect-pedophiles-who-rape-children/.
94. Katy Grimes, "CA Democrats Author Bill To Protect Sex Offenders Who Lure Minors," California Globe, February 19, 2019, https://californiaglobe.com/legislature/ca-democrats-author-bill-to-protect-sex-offenders-who-lure-minors/.
95. Neil Munro, "Students Rebel Against Transgender Ideology in Iowa, Alaska," *Breitbart*, April 15, 2019, https://www.breitbart.com/politics/2019/04/15/students-rebel-against-transgender-ideology-in-nebraska-alaska/.
96. Tara Campbell, "Transgender Rights Clash Prompts Walkout at CB Abraham Lincoln High," WOWT News, April 11, 2019, https://www.

wowt.com/content/news/Transgender-rights-clash-prompts-walkout-at-CB-Abraham-Lincoln-High-508449271.html.

97. Heather Madden, "To the Left's Dismay, Women Aren't a Political Monolith," *Washington Examiner*, December 29, 2018.
98. "Candidate Gender Perceptions Survey," Independent Women's Voice, July 2018, http://pdf.iwvoice.org/IWV_Candidate_Gender_Perceptions_SurveySummary_July2018.pdf.

CHAPTER SEVEN

1. "Fox News Poll 2/13/19," Fox News, https://www.foxnews.com/politics/fox-news-poll-2-13-19.
2. Scott Rasmussen, "Is Socialism a Threat to America, to Democrats or Both?" *Townhall*, February 21, 2019, https://townhall.com/columnists/scottrasmussen/2019/02/21/is-socialism-a-threat-to-america-to-democrats-or-both-n2541951.
3. Thomas J. DiLorenzo, *The Problem with Socialism*, (Washington, D.C.: Regnery Publishing, 2016), 1.
4. Kathleen Elkins, "Most Young Americans Prefer Socialism to Capitalism, New Report Finds," CNBC, August 14, 2018, https://www.cnbc.com/2018/08/14/fewer-than-half-of-young-americans-are-positive-about-capitalism.html.
5. Felix Salmon, "Gen Z Prefers 'Socialism' to 'Capitalism,'" *Axios*, January 27, 2019, https://www.axios.com/socialism-capitalism-poll-generation-z-preference-1ffb8800-0ce5-4368-8a6f-de3b82662347.html.
6. Emily Ekins, "Millennials Don't Know What 'Socialism' Means," *Reason*, July 16, 2014.
7. Timothy Meads, "New Poll Shows Gen Z Is Pretty Confused about Socialism, Capitalism, and More," *Townhall*, August 19, 2019, https://townhall.com/tipsheet/timothymeads/2019/08/19/new-poll-shows-gen-z-is-pretty-confused-about-socialism-capitalism-and-more-n2551861.
8. Scott Rasmussen, "Is Socialism a Threat to America, to Democrats or Both?" *Townhall*, February 21, 2019, https://townhall.com/columnists/scottrasmussen/2019/02/21/is-socialism-a-threat-to-america-to-democrats-or-both-n2541951.
9. John Nichols, "Socialism Is More Popular Than You Think, Mr. President," *The Nation*, February 7, 2019.
10. Hank Berrien, "Why Leftists Want Free College: Poll Shows Americans Between 18-24 Favor Socialism Over Capitalism," *Daily Wire*, January 28, 2019, https://www.dailywire.com/news/42704/why-leftists-want-free-college-poll-shows-hank-berrien.
11. Mitchell Langbert, "Homogeneous: The Political Affiliations of Elite Liberal Arts College Faculty," National Association of Scholars, Summer

2018, https://www.nas.org/academic-questions/31/2/homogenous_the_political_affiliations_of_elite_liberal_arts_college_faculty.
12. Langbert, "Homogeneous: The Political Affiliations of Elite Liberal Arts College Faculty."
13. "Heterodox Academy," Heterodox Academy, https://heterodoxacademy.org.
14. Langbert, "Homogeneous: The Political Affiliations of Elite Liberal Arts College Faculty."
15. Ibid.
16. Burton Folsom, "Why Do Millenials Want Socialism?" *Townhall*, February 28, 2019, https://townhall.com/columnists/burtonfolsom/2019/02/28/why-do-millennials-want-socialism-n2542364.
17. George Novack, "Radical Intellectuals in the 1930s," *International Socialist Review* 29 (2), March–April 1968, 21–34, https://www.marxists.org/archive/novack/works/1967/sep/x01.htm.
18. Novack, "Radical Intellectuals in the 1930s."
19. Ibid.
20. Ronald Radosh, "Why Democratic Socialists Support Totalitarian Regimes," *Washington Free Beacon*, January 28, 2019, https://freebeacon.com/national-security/why-democratic-socialists-support-totalitarian-regimes/.
21. C. M. Lopez, "The Left's Love Affair with Tyrants, Murderers, and Terrible People," Association of Mature American Citizens, January 19, 2018, https://amac.us/lefts-love-affair-tyrants-murderers-terrible-people/.
22. Kristine Phillips, "Obama: History Will Judge Fidel Castro's 'Enormous Impact' on Cubans," *Washington Post*, November 26, 2016.
23. Brad Polumbo and Patrick Hauf, "Bernie Sanders' Support for Socialist Dictators is Disgraceful," *The Federalist*, March 4, 2019, https://thefederalist.com/2019/03/04/bernie-sanders-support-socialist-dictators-disgraceful-disqualifying/.
24. *Merriam-Webster*, s.v. "socialism (*n.*)," accessed March 4, 2019, https://www.merriam-webster.com/help/citing-the-dictionary.
25. Friedrich A. Hayek, *The Road to Serfdom: Text and Documents – The Definitive Edition* (*The Collected Works of F. A. Hayek, Volume 2*) (Chicago: University of Chicago Press, 1944, 2007), 54–56.
26. DiLorenzo, *The Problem with Socialism*, 5.
27. Kimberly Amadeo, "Auto Industry Bailout: Was the Big 3 Bailout Worth It?" The Balance, November 27, 2018, https://www.thebalance.com/auto-industry-bailout-gm-ford-chrysler-3305670.
28. U.S. Department of the Treasury, "Auto Industry," updated January 8, 2015, https://www.treasury.gov/initiatives/financial-stability/TARP-Programs/automotive-programs/pages/default.aspx.
29. Amadeo, "Auto Industry Bailout: Was the Big 3 Bailout Worth It?"

30. "GM Layoffs: A Tragedy Caused by Embracing Government Subsidies, Not Markets," *Investor's Business Daily*, November 29, 2018, https://www.investors.com/politics/editorials/venezuela-maduro-guaido-pence/.
31. Mary Barra, "General Motors CEO: We Call for Federal Electric and Zero-emission Vehicle Policies," *USA Today*, October 26, 2018.
32. "GM Layoffs: A Tragedy Caused by Embracing Government Subsidies, Not Markets."
33. Barra, "General Motors CEO: We Call for Federal Electric and Zero-emission Vehicle Policies."
34. "GM Surrenders to The Green Lobby – Calls on Feds to Mandate Electric Cars," *Investor's Business Daily*, October 26, 2018, https://www.investors.com/politics/editorials/gm-electric-cars-mandate/.
35. Milton Friedman and Rose Friedman, *Free to Choose: A Personal Statement*, (Orlando, FLA: Houghton Mifflin Harcourt, 1980), 285.
36. Friedman and Friedman, *Free to Choose: A Personal Statement*, 286.
37. Ibid., 311.
38. Ibid., 91.
39. Gerald F. Seib, "In Crisis, Opportunity for Obama," *Wall Street Journal*, November 21, 2008.
40. Friedman and Friedman, *Free to Choose: A Personal Statement*, 92.
41. Christopher Chantrill, "US Government Spending History from 1900," US Government Spending, accessed March 4, 2019, https://www.usgovernmentspending.com/past_spending.
42. Christopher Chantrill, "Debt and Deficit Facts," US Government Spending, accessed March 4, 2019, https://www.usgovernmentdebt.us/debt_deficit_history.
43. "United States Gross Federal Debt to GDP," Trading Economics, accessed March 4, 2019, https://tradingeconomics.com/united-states/government-debt-to-gdp.
44. Thomas Sowell, *Basic Economics: A Common Sense Guide to the Economy*, Fifth Edition (New York, New York: Basic Books, 2015), 440.
45. Irving Kristol, "Socialism: An Obituary for an Idea," *The Alternative: An American Spectator* 10 (1), October 1976.
46. Friedman and Friedman, *Free to Choose: A Personal Statement*, 283.
47. Kristian Neimietz, "You Can't Argue Against Socialism's 100 Percent Record of Failure," Foundation for Economic Education, April 16, 2018, https://fee.org/articles/you-cant-argue-against-socialisms-100-percent-record-of-failure/.
48. Angie Drobnic Holan, "Obama Statements on Single-Payer Have Changed a Bit," PolitiFact, July 16, 2009, https://www.politifact.com/truth-o-meter/statements/2009/jul/16/barack-obama/obama-statements-single-payer-have-changed-bit/.

49. Matthew Continetti, "What To Do about the Rebirth of Socialism, *Washington Free Beacon*, February 15, 2019, https://freebeacon.com/columns/what-to-do-about-the-rebirth-of-socialism/.
50. Kristol, "Socialism: An Obituary for an Idea."
51. Continetti, "What To Do About the Rebirth of Socialism."
52. Kristol, "Socialism: An Obituary for an Idea."
53. Ibid.
54. Rev. Peter A. Speckhard, "The Nature of Capitalism," January Letters 49, *First Things*, January 2003, 4.
55. Jack Kemp, "Jack Kemp in His Own Words," Jack Kemp Foundation, February 20, 2019, https://www.jackkempfoundation.org/gameplan/jack-kemp-in-his-own-words/.
56. Ludwig von Mises, *Socialism: An Economic and Sociological Analysis* (New Haven, CT: Yale University Press, 1951), 457.
57. von Mises, *Socialism: An Economic and Sociological Analysis*, 457.
58. Ibid.
59. Ibid.
60. Thomas Sowell, "The Job-Creation Snow Job," *National Review*, December 8, 2009.
61. Robert Higgs, "How FDR Made the Depression Worse," *The Free Market* 13 (2), February 1995; "Thomas Sowell: FDR's Policies Prolonged Great Depression," *Rapid City Journal*, November 3, 2010; Harold L. Cole and Lee E. Ohanian, "How Government Prolonged the Depression," *Wall Street Journal*, February 2, 2009.
62. Jay W. Richards, *Money, Greed, and God: Why Capitalism Is the Solution and Not the Problem* (New York, New York: Harper One, 2010), 7.
63. Richards, *Money, Greed, and God: Why Capitalism Is the Solution and Not the Problem*, 104.
64. Thomas Del Beccaro, "Trickle Down Economics Does Not Exist," *Forbes*, January 4, 2018.
65. David Weinberger, "Fact-Checking President Obama on 'Trickle-Down' Ecomomics," *Daily Signal*, December 12, 2011, https://www.dailysignal.com/2011/12/12/fact-checking-president-obama-on-trickle-down-economics/.
66. Daniel Mitchell, "The Historical Lessons of Lower Tax Rates," The Heritage Foundation, August 13, 2003, https://www.heritage.org/taxes/report/the-historical-lessons-lower-tax-rates.
67. William A. Niskanen and Stephen Moore, "Cato Institute Policy Analysis No. 261: Supply-Side Tax Cuts and the Truth about the Reagan Economic Record," Cato Institute, October 22, 1996, https://www.academia.edu/35446555/Cato_Institute_Policy_Analysis_No._261_Supply-Side_Tax_Cuts_and_the_Truth_about_the_Reagan_Economic_Record.

68. Steven Horwitz, "There is No Such Thing as Trickle-Down Economics," Foundation for Economic Education, September 24, 2016, https://fee.org/articles/there-is-no-such-thing-as-trickle-down-economics/.
69. David R. Henderson, "The Troubling Logic of 'You Didn't Build That,'" Foundation for Economic Education, November 12, 2018, https://fee.org/articles/the-troubling-logic-of-you-didnt-build-that/.
70. Kevin D. Williamson, *The Politically Incorrect Guide to Socialism* (Washington, D.C.: Regnery Publishing, 2011), 21–22.
71. Sowell, *Basic Economics: A Common Sense Guide to the Economy*, 111.
72. Patrick Tyrell, "The Empty Promises of Socialism," The Heritage Foundation, October 26, 2018, https://www.heritage.org/international-economies/commentary/the-empty-promises-socialism.
73. Sowell, *Basic Economics: A Common Sense Guide to the Economy*, 111.
74. John Grgurich, "Who's More Generous, Liberals or Conservatives?" The Fiscal Times, October 17, 2014, https://www.thefiscaltimes.com/2014/10/17/Who-s-More-Generous-Liberals-or-Conservatives.
75. Democratic Audit UK, "Republicans Give More to Charity – But Not Because They Oppose Income Distribution," Democratic Audit, November 17, 2017, http://www.democraticaudit.com/2017/11/17/republicans-give-more-to-charity-but-not-because-they-oppose-income-redistribution/.
76. Bradford Richardson, "Religious People More Likely to Give to Charity, Study Shows," *Washington Times*, October 30, 2017.
77. Jonathan Gruber and Daniel M. Hungerman, "Faith-Based Charity and Crowd Out During the Great Depression," (May 2005), *NBER Working Paper No. 211332*, https://ssrn.com/abstract=723301.
78. Andy Puzder, "Andy Puzder: If Socialists Really Wanted to Help People They'd Be Capitalists," Fox News, March 12, 2019, https://www.foxnews.com/opinion/andy-puzder-democratic-socialist-fantasies-are-just-that-fantasies-and-if-you-dont-believe-me-ask-venezuela.
79. Thomas Del Beccaro, "Trickle Down Economics Does Not Exist," *Forbes*, January 4, 2018.
80. Thomas Lifson, "Bernie Sanders Tells Fox News Town Hall That He Won't Pay His 'Fair Share' In Taxes Unless He is Forced To," American Thinker, April 16, 2019, https://www.americanthinker.com/blog/2019/04/bernie_sanders_tells_fox_news_town_hall_that_he_wont_pay_his_fair_share_in_taxes_unless_he_is_forced_to.html.
81. 2 Thess. 3:10. NIV.
82. 1 Thess. 4:11-12. NIV.
83. 1 Thess. 5:14. NIV.

84. Matt. 6:2, 3; Gal. 2:10; 1 Tim. 5:4; Heb. 13:16; James 2:15–16; 1 John 3:17. See John F. MacArthur, *The MacArthur New Testament Commentary.... Thessalonians* (Chicago: Moody Press, 2002), 307.
85. MacArthur, *The MacArthur New Testament Commentary* (Chicago: Moody Press, 2002), 307.

CHAPTER EIGHT

1. Milton Friedman and Rose Friedman, *Free To Choose: A Personal Statement* (Orlando, FLA: Houghton Mifflin Harcourt, 1980), 2–3.
2. Friedrich A. Hayek, *The Road to Serfdom* (Chicago: University of Chicago Press, 1944), 69.
3. "Venezuela Election: Maduro Wins Second Term Amid Claims of Vote Rigging," BBC News, May 21, 2018, https://www.bbc.com/news/world-latin-america-44187838; John Otis, "'Maduro Would Beat Jesus' Venezuelans Lament Rigged System as Election Looms," *The Guardian*, May 19, 2018.
4. Thomas Del Beccaro, "Dear Pope Francis, Catholicism Owes a Debt to Capitalism," *Forbes*, April 22, 2015.
5. Jay W. Richards, *Money, Greed, and God: Why Capitalism Is the Solution and Not the Problem* (New York, New York: Harper One, May 4, 2010), 121.
6. Ronald Reagan, "Remarks at the Annual Meeting of the Board of Governors of the International Monetary Fund and World Bank Group," *Public Papers of the Presidents of the United States: Ronald Reagan, 1987*, 1093.
7. Thomas J. DiLorenzo, *The Problem with Socialism* (Washington, D.C.: Regnery Publishing, 2016), 30.
8. Lauren Reiff, "The Curious Allegation of Capitalist Greed," Medium, September 29, 2018, https://medium.com/@laurennreiff/the-curious-allegation-of-capitalist-greed-87633bf6b0c0.
9. Walter E. Williams, "Socialism Is Evil," Free Republic, July 28, 2004, http://www.freerepublic.com/focus/f-news/1252930/posts.
10. George Bennett, "Democrat Pelosi in Boca: Tax bill is 'theft,' bonuses are 'crumbs,'" *Palm Beach Post*, January 25, 2018.
11. Mark J. Perry, "Why Socialism Always Fails," *Carpe Diem,* (blog), AEI, March 22, 2016, http://www.aei.org/publication/why-socialism-always-fails/.
12. Ronald Reagan, "Remarks at the Annual Meeting of the Board of Governors of the International Monetary Fund and World Bank Group," *Public Papers of the Presidents of the United States: Ronald Reagan, 1987*, 1093.
13. Thomas Sowell, *Basic Economics: A Common Sense Guide to the Economy*, Fifth Edition (New York, New York: Basic Books, 2015), 19.

14. Richards, *Money, Greed, and God: Why Capitalism Is the Solution and Not the Problem*, 21.
15. Michael S. Heiser, *Problems in Bible Interpretation: Difficult Passages* (Bellingham, WA: Lexham Press, 2017).
16. Bruce B. Barton and Grant R. Osborne, *Acts* (Wheaton, IL: Tyndale House, 1999), 69.
17. "Does the Bible Support Communism?" Got Questions Ministries, https://www.gotquestions.org/communism-Bible.html.
18. William H. Baker, in A. S. Moreau, H. Netland, and C. van. Engen, *Evangelical Dictionary of World Missions* (Grand Rapids, MI: Baker Books, 2000), 886.
19. Heiser, *Problems in Bible Interpretation: Difficult Passages* (Bellingham, WA: Lexham Press, 2016).
20. Norman L. Geisler & Thomas A. Howe, *When Critics Ask: A Popular Handbook on Bible Difficulties* (Wheaton, Ill.: Victor Books, 1992), 429–30.
21. Augustus Hopkins Strong, *Systematic Theology* (Philadelphia: American Baptist Publication Society: 1907), 894.
22. Mark L. Ward, *Biblical Worldview: Creation, Fall, Redemption* (M. L. Ward Jr. & D. Cone, eds.) (Greenville, SC: BJU Press, 2016), 262.
23. See: Lev. 25:35, Mark 10:21, Eph. 4:28, Phil. 2:4, 1 Tim. 6:18, 1 John 3:17.
24. Robert A. Morey, *A Christian Student's Survival Guide* (Millerstown, PA: Faith Defenders, 2010), 212.
25. William H. Baker, in A. S. Moreau, H. Netland, & C. van. Engen, *Evangelical Dictionary of World Missions*, 886.
26. Ron Nash, "Legalized Theft," *Tabletalk Magazine*, March 1998.
27. Fredrich A. Hayek, *The Road to Serfdom* (Chicago: University of Chicago Press, 1944), 38–39.
28. Hopkins Strong, *Systematic Theology*, 894.
29. *The Black Book of Communism* (Cambridge, MA: Harvard Univ. Press, 1999).
30. Walter E. Williams, "Capitalism vs. Socialism," Creators Syndicate, May 20, 2018, https://www.creators.com/read/walter-williams/05/18/capitalism-vs-socialism.
31. DiLorenzo, *The Problem with Socialism*, 16.
32. Mamta Badkar, "Ten Hyper-Inflation Stories of the 20th Century," *Business Insider*, March 19, 2011, http://businessinsider.com/10-hyperinflation-stories-of-the-20th-century-2011-3?op=1.
33. Thomas J. DiLorenzo, *The Problem with Socialism*, 7–8.
34. Maxim Lott, "How Socialist Turned Venezuela From the Wealthiest Country in South America into an Economic Basket Case," Fox News, January 26, 2019, https://www.foxnews.com/world/

how-socialism-turned-venezuela-from-the-wealthiest-country-in-south-america-into-an-economic-basket-case.

35. "Venezuela's Army Death Squads Kill Thousands – UN," AP, Reuters, April 7, 2019, https://www.dw.com/en/venezuelas-army-death-squads-kill-thousands-un/a-49477147.
36. Katy Watson, "Venezuela: The Country That Has Lost Three Million People," BBC News, December 30, 2018, https://www.bbc.com/news/world-latin-america-46524248.
37. Christopher Gage, "It'll Work This Time," American Greatness, February 8, 2019, https://amgreatness.com/2019/02/08/itll-work-this-time/; Jamie Nugent and Joshua Curzon, "Venezuela Campaign – 10 Fallacies About the Situation in Venezuela," Adam Smith Institute, February 3, 2019, https://www.adamsmith.org/blog/venezuela-campaign-10-fallacies-about-the-situation-in-venezuela.
38. Jamie Nugent, "Venezuela Campaign: A State of Ill-Health," Adam Smith Institute, September 9, 2018, https://www.adamsmith.org/blog/venezuela-campaign-a-state-of-ill-health.
39. Jim Wyss, "Once Hailed by the UN for Feeding the Poor, Venezuela Sees Hunger Rate Triple," *Miami Herald*, November 12, 2018.
40. Douglas French, "How Can Venezuela Be So Rich in Resources, but So Low in Supplies," *Christian Science Monitor*, April 24, 2012.
41. Nugent and Curzon, "Venezuela Campaign – 10 Fallacies About the Situation in Venezuela."
42. DiLorenzo, *The Problem with Socialism*, 77.
43. Stefan Karlsson, "The Sweden Myth," Mises Daily Articles, Mises Institute, August 7, 2006, https://mises.org/library/sweden-myth.
44. Johan Norberg, "Swedish Models," *National Interest*, January 6, 2006; Williamson, *The Politically Incorrect Guide to Socialism*, 106.
45. Karlsson, "The Sweden Myth."
46. Ryan Bourne, "Capitalism's Critics Need to Be Told About Its 200 Years of Success," *UK Telegraph*, June 11, 2018.
47. Thomas Del Beccaro, "Dear Pope Francis, Catholicism Owes A Debt to Capitalism," *Forbes*, April 22, 2015.
48. Will and Ariel DuRant, *The Lessons of History* (New York, New York: Simon & Schuster Paperbacks: 2010), Kindle location 633 of 1846.
49. Dierdre Nansen McCloskey, "The Industrial Revolution," Prudentia, 2008, http://www.deirdremccloskey.com/articles/revolution.php.
50. Ana Swanson, "Why the Industrial Revolution Didn't Happen in China," *Washington Post*, October 28, 2016.
51. Kelsey Piper, "Human History, In One Chart," Vox, November 8, 2018, https://www.vox.com/future-perfect/2018/11/8/18052076/human-history-in-one-chart-industrial-revolution.
52. Swanson, "Why the Industrial Revolution Didn't Happen in China."
53. Sowell, *Basic Economics: A Common Sense Guide to the Economy*, 4.

54. Jeff Charles, "Socialism: Equality of Outcome, Or Poverty and Tyranny," Liberty Nation, October 3, 2018, https://www.libertynation.com/socialism-equality-of-outcome-or-poverty-and-tyranny/.
55. Bill Schneider, "Is This Obama's 'Malaise' Moment?" Reuters, June 24, 2014, https://www.reuters.com/article/idIN226475345320140624; Aaron Blake, "The New American 'Malaise'," *Washington Post*, December 12, 2014; Rush Limbaugh, "The Obama Malaise," *The Rush Limbaugh Show*, December 12, 2014.
56. Richard M. Salsman, "President Obama's Hopeless 'Malaise' Moment," *Forbes*, November 20, 2011.
57. Adam Smith, *An Inquiry into the Nature and Causes of the Wealth of Nations* (M. J. Adler & P. W. Goetz, eds.) Second Edition, (Chicago; Auckland; Geneva; London; Madrid; Manila; Paris; Rome; Seoul; Sydney; Tokyo; Toronto: Robert P. Gwinn; Encyclopædia Britannica, Inc., 1952, 1990), Vol. 36, 217.
58. Friedman and Friedman, *Free To Choose: A Personal Statement*, 2.
59. Ibid., 24–25.
60. Sowell, *Basic Economics:A Common Sense Guide to the Economy*, 11.
61. Ibid., 13.
62. Sterling Terrell, "3 Reasons Why Socialism Is Bad," Thought Catalog, September 20, 2014, https://thoughtcatalog.com/sterling-terrell/2014/09/3-reasons-why-socialism-is-bad/.
63. Perry, "Why Socialism Always Fails."
64. Richards, *Money, Greed, and God: Why Capitalism Is the Solution and Not the Problem*, 76.
65. F. A. Hayek, *The Fatal Conceit: The Errors of Socialism* (Chicago, IL: The University of Chicago Press, 1988), 14.
66. Sowell, *Basic Economics: A Common Sense Guide to the Economy*,14.
67. Ibid., 89.
68. Ibid., 110–11.
69. Andy Puzder, "Andy Puzder: If Socialists Really Wanted to Help People They'd Be Capitalists," Fox News, March 12, 2019, https://www.foxnews.com/opinion/andy-puzder-democratic-socialist-fantasies-are-just-that-fantasies-and-if-you-dont-believe-me-ask-venezuela.
70. Hayek, *The Fatal Conceit, The Errors of Socialism*, 6.
71. Ibid., 7–8.
72. "Fox News Poll 2/13/19," Fox News, https://www.foxnews.com/politics/fox-news-poll-2-13-19.

CHAPTER NINE

1. Tim Hains, "Ocasio-Cortez: 'The World Is Going to End in 12 Years If We Don't Address Climate Change,'" video clip, RealClearPolitics, January 22, 2019, https://www.realclearpolitics.com/video/2019/01/22/ocasio-cortez_the_world_is_going_to_end_in_12_years_if_we_dont_address_climate_change.html.
2. David Montgomery, "AOC's Chief of Change," *Washington Post*, July 10, 2019.
3. Javier Blas, "The U.S. Just Became a Net Oil Exporter for the First Time in 75 Years," *Bloomberg*, December 6, 2018, https://www.bloomberg.com/news/articles/2018-12-06/u-s-becomes-a-net-oil-exporter-for-the-first-time-in-75-years; Hon. Kathleen Hartnett White, "OPINION: What's in the GND? A Lot of Spending – And Global Ambitions," *Daily Caller*, February 7, 2019, https://dailycaller.com/2019/02/07/hartnett-green-new-deal/.
4. James Conca, "Any Green New Deal Is Dead Without Nuclear Power," *Forbes*, May 21, 2019.
5. Green New Deal Information Sheet, https://assets.documentcloud.org/documents/5729035/Green-New-Deal-FAQ.pdf.
6. Rich Lowry, "Millennial Socialism 101," *Salem News*, January 13, 2019.
7. "Draft Text for Proposed Addendum to House Rules for 116th Congress of the United States," https://docs.google.com/document/d/1jxUzp9SZ6-VB-4wSm8sselVMsqWZrSrYpYC9slHKLzo/preview.
8. Eliza Relman, "Alexandria Ocasio-Cortez says her Green New Deal climate plan would cost at least $10 trillion," *Business Insider*, June 5, 2019, https://www.businessinsider.com/alexandria-ocasio-cortez-says-green-new-deal-cost-10-trillion-2019-6.
9. Marlo Lewis Jr., "How Much Will the Green New Deal Cost Your Family?" Competitive Enterprise Institute, February 22, 2019, https://cei.org/blog/how-much-will-green-new-deal-cost-your-family.
10. Clark Mindock, "Alexandria Ocasio-Cortez Claims Capitalism is 'Irredeemable,'" *Independent*, March 11, 2019, https://www.independent.co.uk/news/world/americas/us-politics/aoc-capitalism-irredeemable-alexandria-ocasio-cortez-south-southwest-sxsw-a8816956.html.
11. Nicolas Loris, "UN's Plan on Climate Change: End Capitalism," CNS News, October 22, 2018, https://www.cnsnews.com/commentary/nicolas-loris/uns-plan-climate-change-end-capitalism.
12. Timothy Cama, "Poll: Majorities of Both Parties Support GND," *The Hill*, December 17, 2018.
13. James Rainey, "More Americans Believe in Global Warming – But They Won't Pay Much to Fix It," NBC News, January 24, 2019, https://www.nbcnews.com/news/us-news/more-americans-believe-global-warming-they-won-t-pay-much-n962001.

14. "Is the Public Willing to Pay to Help Fix Climate Change?" The Associated Press-NORC Center for Public Affairs Research, http://www.apnorc.org/projects/Pages/Is-the-Public-Willing-to-Pay-to-Help-Fix-Climate-Change-.aspx.
15. Kevin Dayaratna, Nicolas Loris and David Kreutzer, "Consequences of Paris Protocol: Devastating Economic Costs, Essential Zero Environmental Benefits," The Heritage Foundation, April 13, 2016, https://www.heritage.org/environment/report/consequences-paris-protocol-devastating-economic-costs-essentially-zero.
16. Craig Richardson, "The 'GND' Is a Prescription for Poverty," *Washington Examiner*, January 28, 2019.
17. Richardson, "The 'GND' Is a Prescription for Poverty."
18. Philip Rosetti, "What it Costs to Go 100 Percent Renewable," American Action Forum, January 25, 2019, https://www.americanactionforum.org/research/what-it-costs-go-100-percent-renewable/.
19. Nick Loris, "Heritage Expert: The GND is a Raw Deal for the American People," The Heritage Foundation, February 7, 2019, https://www.heritage.org/press/heritage-expert-the-green-new-deal-raw-deal-the-american-people.
20. Veronique de Rugy, "Politicians Can't Get Enough Energy Cronyism," Mercatus Center, George Washington University, August 17, 2017, https://www.mercatus.org/%5Bnode%3A%5D/commentary/politicians-cant-get-enough-energy-cronyism.
21. David Shepardson and Bernie Woodall, "Electric Vehicle Sales Fall Far Short of Obama Goal," Reuters, January 20, 2016, https://www.reuters.com/article/us-autos-electric-obama-insight/electric-vehicle-sales-fall-far-short-of-obama-goal-idUSKCN0UY0F0.
22. Susan Ferrechio, "Will Ocasio-Cortez's 'Green New Deal' Even Get a Vote?" *Washington Examiner*, February 11, 2019.
23. Elias Hubbard, "Senate Democrats Dodge Vote on Green New Deal Resolution," Click Lancashire, March 26, 2019, http://clicklancashire.com/2019/03/27/senate-democrats-dodge-vote-on-green-new-deal-resolution.html.
24. Ben Walsh, "Stephanie Kelton Wants You to Rethink the Deficit," *Barron's*, September 13, 2018.
25. Bob Bryan, "A New Survey Shows that Zero Top US Economists Agreed with the Basic Principles of an Economic Theory Supported by Alexandria Ocasio-Cortez," *Business Insider*, March 13, 2019, https://www.businessinsider.sg/economist-survey-alexandria-ocasio-cortez-modern-monetary-theory-2019-3/.
26. Josh Mound, "AOC's 70-% Tax Plan Is Just the Beginning," *Jacobin*, January 28, 2019.
27. Matthew Sheffield, "Poll: A Majority of Americans Support Raising the Top Tax Rate to 70 Percent," *The Hill*, January 15, 2019.

28. Avie Schneider, "U.S. Unemployment Rate Drops To 3.7 Percent, Lowest in Nearly 50 Years," NPR, October 5, 2018, https://www.npr.org/2018/10/05/654417887/u-s-unemployment-rate-drops-to-3-7-percent-lowest-in-nearly-50-years.
29. Stephen Moore, "Why the Left Hates Prosperity," *Washington Times*, October 28, 2018.
30. Phillip W. Magness, "The Rich Never Actually Paid 70 Percent," American Institute for Economic Research, January 7, 2019, https://www.aier.org/article/rich-never-actually-paid-70-percent.
31. Magness, "The Rich Never Actually Paid 70 Percent."
32. Ibid.
33. Jim Powell, "Two of The All-Time Greatest Successes In Cutting Taxes and Spending," *Forbes*, August 10, 2011.
34. Adam Michel, "Alexandria Ocasio-Cortez Wants to Raise Taxes Drastically. Here's Why It Would Backfire," *Daily Signal*, January 8, 2019, https://www.dailysignal.com/2019/01/08/alexandria-ocasio-cortez-wants-to-raise-taxes-drastically-heres-why-it-would-backfire/.
35. Brian Riedl, "America Might Be Ready for Democratic Socialism. It's Not Ready for the Bill," Vox, August 7, 2018, https://www.vox.com/the-big-idea/2018/8/7/17658574/democratic-socialism-cost-medicare-college-sanders-deficits-taxes.
36. Riedl, "America Might Be Ready for Democratic Socialism. It's Not Ready for the Bill."
37. Brian Riedl, "Why 70 Percent Tax Rates Cannot Finance Socialism," *National Review*, January 8, 2019.
38. Paul Krugman, "The Economics of Soaking the Rich," *New York Times*, January 5, 2019.
39. William L. Anderson, "Paul Krugman's Conversion to a 70-Percent Income Tax," Mises Institute, January 15, 2019, https://mises.org/wire/paul-krugmans-conversion-70-percent-income-tax-0.
40. Daniel J. Mitchell, "The Historical Lessons of Lower Tax Rates," The Heritage Foundation, July 19, 1996, https://www.heritage.org/taxes/report/the-historical-lessons-lower-tax-rates-0.
41. Mitchell, "The Historical Lessons of Lower Tax Rates."
42. Adam Michel, "Alexandria Ocasio-Cortez Wants to Raise Taxes Drastically. Here's Why It Would Backfire," *Daily Signal*, January 8, 2019, https://www.dailysignal.com/2019/01/08/alexandria-ocasio-cortez-wants-to-raise-taxes-drastically-heres-why-it-would-backfire/.
43. Christine Goss, "The Job Guarantee Rests on the Lie That People Can Escape Insecurity," *The Federalist*, February 12, 2019, https://thefederalist.com/2019/02/12/green-new-deals-job-guarantee-rests-lie-people-can-escape-risk/.
44. Benjy Sarlin, "Elizabeth Warren's Plan to Tax the Super-Rich Has Been Tried Before. Here's What Happened," NBC News, January 29,

2019, https://www.nbcnews.com/politics/2020-election/elizabeth-warren-s-plan-tax-super-rich-has-been-tried-n963971.

45. Sarlin, "Elizabeth Warren's Plan to Tax the Super-Rich Has Been Tried Before."
46. Aparna Mathur, Abby McCloskey, "Universal Child Care Is the Wrong Approach," AEI, February 22, 2019, http://www.aei.org/publication/universal-child-care-is-the-wrong-approach/.
47. Jeff Stein, "Sen. Elizabeth Warren Proposes Universal Child Care, Paid for By Tax on Ultra-Millionaiers," *Washington Post*, February 19, 2019.
48. Andrew Wilford, "WILFORD: Sanders Just Dropped Another Confiscatory Tax Proposal," *Daily Caller*, February 2, 2019, https://dailycaller.com/2019/02/02/wilford-sanders-tax/.
49. Demian Brady, "Issue Brief: Death and a Thousand Paper Cuts: The Compliance Burden of the Estate Tax," National Taxpayers Union Foundation, October 26, 2017, https://www.ntu.org/foundation/detail/death-and-a-thousand-paper-cuts-the-compliance-burden-of-the-estate-tax.
50. Andrew O'Reilly, "Sanders Calls for Wiping Out $1.6 Trillion in Student Debt by Taxing Wall Street," Fox News, June 24, 2019, https://www.foxnews.com/politics/sanders-unveils-plan-to-eliminate-1-6-trillion-in-student-debt-by-taxing-wall-street-banks.
51. Tom Precious, "'Serious as a Heart Attack': Cuomo Warns of Falling State Revenue," *Buffalo News*, February 4, 2019.
52. Brad Slager, "Andrew Cuomo Announces Loss of Billions in Tax Revenue, Looks for Others To Blame," *RedState*, February 9, 2019, https://www.redstate.com/bradslager/2019/02/09/andrew-cuomo-announces-loss-of-billions-in-tax-revenue-looks-for-others-to-blame/.
53. Victor Davis Hanson, "California's Rendezvous with Reality," *Townhall*, February 28, 2019, https://townhall.com/columnists/victordavishanson/2019/02/28/californias-rendezvous-with-reality-n2542316.
54. "The Impact of A $15 Minimum Wage," Employment Policies Institute, January 2019.
55. Rachel Greszler, "Lawmakers Are Pushing a $15 Minimum Wage. Here Are 3 Disastrous Consequences That Would Result," *Daily Signal*, January 17, 2019.
56. James Sherk, "Raising Minimum Starting Wages to $15 per Hour Would Eliminate Seven Million Jobs," The Heritage Foundation, July 26, 2016.
57. "The Impact of A $15 Minimum Wage," Employment Policies Institute, January 2019, https://www.epionline.org/studies/the-impact-of-a-15-minimum-wage/.
58. Rachel Greszler, "Lawmakers Are Pushing a $15 Minimum Wage. Here Are 3 Disastrous Consequences That Would Result," *Daily Signal*, January 17, 2019, https://www.dailysignal.com/2019/01/17/

lawmakers-are-pushing-a-15-minimum-wage-here-are-3-disastrous-consequences-that-would-result/.

59. Greszler, “Lawmakers Are Pushing a $15 Minimum Wage.”
60. Ibid.
61. Ibid.
62. Betsy McCaughey, “Maxine Waters Means Nightmares for Wall Street, Suburbs,” *New York Post*, January 22, 2019.
63. Press Release, “Waters Statement at Historic Diversity and Inclusion Subcommittee Hearing,” U.S. House Committee on Financial Services, February 28, 2019.
64. Carlos Garcia, “WaPo Blames San Francisco’s Problems on Capitalism – And Gets Ridiculed Ruthlessly on Social Media,” The Blaze, May 22, 2019, https://www.theblaze.com/news/san-francisco-blames-capitalism.
65. Wesley J. Smith, “Medicare-for-All’s Bitter Pill,” *National Review*, March 11, 2019.
66. “Medicare for All Act of 2019,” 116th Congress, 1st Session, Jayapal.house.gov.
67. This analysis was of the earlier plan by Bernie Sanders, but the same would hold true of this current plan. Haeyoun Park and Margot Sanger-Katz, “How Medicare for All Would Affect You,” *New York Times*, September 14, 2017.
68. “Medicare for All Act of 2019,” 116th Congress, 1st Session, jayapal.house.gov.
69. Wesley J. Smith, “Medicare-for-All’s Bitter Pill,” *National Review*, March 11, 2019.
70. “Medicare for All Act of 2019,” 116th Congress, 1st Session, Jayapal.house.gov
71. The 2018 Annual Report of the Board of Trustees, “Federal Hospital Insurance and Federal Supplementary Medical Insurance Trust Funds,” June 5, 2018; Steven T. Mnuchin and other Trustees, “Status of the Social Security and Medicare Programs,” Social Security Administration, 2018.
72. Fred Lucas, “Trump’s 2020 Budget Seeks More Border Wall Funding, Work Requirements for Welfare,” *Daily Signal*, March 11, 2019, https://www.dailysignal.com/2019/03/11/trumps-2020-budget-seeks-more-border-wall-funding-work-requirements-for-welfare/.
73. Fred Lucas, “Bernie Sanders Says ‘Many Thousands’ Will Die as Budget Chief Predicts Stronger Medicare,” *Daily Signal*, March 13, 2019, https://www.dailysignal.com/2019/03/13/bernie-sanders-says-many-thousands-will-die-as-budget-chief-predicts-stronger-medicare/.
74. Lucas, “Bernie Sanders Says ‘Many Thousands’ Will Die.”
75. Steven T. Mnuchin and other Trustees, “Status of the Social Security and Medicare Programs,” Social Security Administration, 2018.
76. Berkeley Lovelace Jr., “Trump Presidency Smacks Down the “New Normal” of 2% Growth, Top House Tax Writer Brady Says,” CNBC,

January 31, 2018, https://www.cnbc.com/2018/01/31/trump-smacks-down-new-normal-of-2-percent-growth-says-rep-kevin-brady.html.

77. George F. Will, "Is Anemic Growth the New Normal?" *Washington Post*, July 8, 2016.
78. Kevin Hoffman, "Roskam Says Obama Admin the First to Never Top 3% In Annual GDP Growth," Politifact, March 16, 2017, https://www.politifact.com/illinois/statements/2017/mar/16/peter-roskam/rep-roskam-gdp-growth-obama/.
79. Frank Hill, "Hill: 2% Real GDP Growth Is Not 'the New Normal,'" *North State Journal*, August 1, 2018; Genevieve Wood, "State of the Union 2019: The Trump Economy is a Success Story Not Even His Harshest Critics Can Deny," Fox News, January 29, 2019, https://www.foxnews.com/opinion/state-of-the-union-2019-the-trump-economy-is-a-success-story-not-even-his-harshest-critics-can-deny.
80. Louis Woodhill, "Barack Obama's Sad Record on Economic Growth," RealClearMarkets, February 1, 2016, https://www.realclearmarkets.com/articles/2016/02/01/barack_obamas_sad_record_on_economic_growth_101987.html.
81. S. Noble, "Obama's Legacy: US Will Never Again See .3% Growth," Independent Sentinel, April 18, 2016, https://www.independentsentinel.com/obamas-legacy-us-will-never-again-see-3-growth/.
82. Michael Hiltzik, "If Trump Thinks He Can Get More Than 3% Economic Growth, He's Dreaming," *Los Angeles Times*, May 19, 2017.
83. Hiltzik, "If Trump Thinks He Can Get More Than 3% Economic Growth, He's Dreaming."
84. Anthony B. Kim, "Under Trump, US Economic Freedom Rises Significantly," *Daily Signal*, January 25, 2019, https://www.dailysignal.com/2019/01/25/under-trump-us-economic-freedom-has-risen-significantly/.
85. "An Analysis of Trump's Policy Proposals in State of the Union Address," The Heritage Foundation, February 6, 2019, https://www.heritage.org/immigration/commentary/analysis-trumps-policy-proposals-state-the-union-address.
86. David Urban, "David Urban: Trump Has Kept His Promise to Revive Manufacturing," TribLive, August 17, 2019, https://triblive.com/opinion/david-urban-trump-has-kept-his-promise-to-revive-manufacturing/.
87. "2019 Index of Economic Freedom," The Heritage Foundation, 2019, https://www.heritage.org/index/about.
88. "An Analysis of Trump's Policy Proposals in State of the Union Address," The Heritage Foundation, February 6, 2019.
89. Ibid.
90. "United States Labor Force Participation Rate," Trading Economics, January 2019, https://tradingeconomics.com/united-states/labor-force-participation-rate; Andy Puzder, "Labor Market Is Thriving Far Better Under Trump Than Under Obama," *The Hill*, October 9, 2017.

91. Cockburn, "Jeremy Corbyn's Strange Flirtations with the American Left," *Spectator USA*, February 4, 2019.
92. Dominic Green, "Meet Alexandria Ocasio-Corbyn," *Spectator USA*, February 4, 2019.
93. Green, "Meet Alexandria Ocasio-Corbyn."
94. Cockburn, "Jeremy Corbyn's Strange Flirtations with the American Left."
95. David Weigel, "Britain's Jeremy Corbyn: I Got My Ideas from Bernie Sanders," *Washington Post*, July 13, 2017.
96. Green, "Meet Alexandria Ocasio-Corbyn."
97. Georgi Boorman, "Women's March Refusal to Condemn Racism Eviscerates Intersectionalism," *The Federalist*, January 16, 2019, https://thefederalist.com/2019/01/16/womens-march-founder-tamika-mallory-wont-condemn-anti-semitism/.
98. Ryan Saavedra, "Linda Sarsour Calls for People to Stop 'Humanizing' Jews," *Daily Wire*, September 8, 2018, https://www.dailywire.com/news/35631/linda-sarsour-calls-dehumanization-jews-report-ryan-saavedra.
99. Hank Berrien, "Report: First Time Women's March Leaders Met, Two Leaders Asserted Anti-Semitic Conspiracy Theories," *Daily Wire*, December 10, 2018, https://www.dailywire.com/news/39245/report-first-time-womens-march-leaders-met-two-hank-berrien.
100. Berrien, "Report: First Time Women's March Leaders Met, Two Leaders Asserted Anti-Semitic Conspiracy Theories."
101. Matt Vespa, "She Said What? Ilhan Omar Has Anti-Semitism Trouble Again," *Townhall*, March 4, 2019, https://townhall.com/tipsheet/mattvespa/2019/03/04/ilhan-omar-has-antisemitism-trouble-again-n2542514.
102. Tom Elliott, "Rep. Ilan Omar Uses Holocaust Remembrance Day to Downplay Holocaust," Grabien News, January 27, 2019, https://news.grabien.com/story-rep-ilan-omar-uses-holocaust-remembrance-day-downplay-holoca.
103. Farley Weiss, "Reps. Ilhan Omar and Rashida Tlaib Should've Been Punished for Their Anti-Semitism," *USA Today*, March 13, 2019.
104. Tom Elliot, "Rep. Ilhan Omar Goes on Anti-Semitic Twitter Rampage; Advocacy Group Demands Apology," Grabien News, February 10, 2019, https://news.grabien.com/story-rep-ilhan-omar-goes-anti-semitic-twitter-rampage.
105. Elliot, "Rep. Ilhan Omar Goes on Anti-Semitic Twitter Rampage."
106. David Harsanyi, "The Democrats' Anti-Semitism Problem Isn't Going Away," *The Federalist*, February 12, 2019, https://thefederalist.com/2019/02/11/democrats-anti-semitism-problem-isnt-going-away/.
107. Harsanyi, "The Democrats' Anti-Semitism Problem Isn't Going Away."

108. Weiss, "Reps. Ilhan Omar and Rashida Tlaib Should've Been Punished for Their Anti-Semitism."
109. "Trump: Congresswoman Omar's Apology for Israel Remark 'Lame,'" *Philadelphia Tribune,* February 13, 2019.
110. Mike Brest, "Mike Pence Condemns Rep. Omar for pushing 'Anti-Semitic Tropes,'" *Daily Caller*, February 12, 2019, https://dailycaller.com/2019/02/12/pence-omar-anti-semitism/.
111. Khorri Atkinson, "Ilhan Omar Reignites Anti-Semitism Controversy in Exchange with Top House Dem," *Axios*, March 3, 2019, https://www.axios.com/ilhan-omar-anti-semitism-nita-lowey-6ff9eb97-b3e4-4274-b472-b5bd5c455167.html.
112. Vespa, "She Said What!? Ilhan Omar Has Anti-Semitism Trouble Again."
113. Courtney O'Brien, "Resolution Against Anti-Semitism Delayed Because Dems Want it Expanded to Include This," *Townhall*, March 5, 2019, https://townhall.com/tipsheet/cortneyobrien/2019/03/05/resolution-against-antisemitism-delayed-because-n2542652.
114. Matt Vespa, "Fireworks: House Dems Have 'Full-Scale Brawl' Over Resolution That Indirectly Rebukes Ilhan Omar's Reported Anti-Semitism," *Townhall*, March 6, 2019, https://townhall.com/tipsheet/mattvespa/2019/03/06/fireworks-house-dems-blow-up-over-resolution-that-indirectly-rebukes-ilhan-omar-n2542701.
115. William Cummings and Christal Hayes, "House Overwhelmingly Passes Resolution Condemning Hate After Rep. Ilhan Omar's Comments," *USA Today*, March 7, 2019.
116. Steve Postal, "Omar, Tlaib, and Anti-Semitism," American Thinker, March 6, 2019, https://www.americanthinker.com/articles/2019/03/omar_tlaib_and_antisemitism.html.
117. Thomas Lifson, "House Dems Just Can't Bring Themselves to Condemn AntiSemitism," American Thinker, March 6, 2019, https://www.americanthinker.com/blog/2019/03/house_dems_just_cant_bring_themselves_to_condemn_antisemitism.html.
118. William Cummings and Christal Hayes, "House Overwhelmingly Passes Resolution Condemning Hate After Rep. Ilhan Omar's Comments," *USA Today*, March 7, 2019.
119. Matt Vespa, "He Went There: Top Democrat Downplays Holocaust Survivors to Defend Ilhan Omar's Anti-Semitic Antics," *Townhall*, March 7, 2019, https://townhall.com/tipsheet/mattvespa/2019/03/07/top-dem-defends-omars-anti-semitic-antics-her-experience-is-more-personal-than-n2542755.
120. Michael Goodwin, "Dems Have Only Themselves to Blame for Ilhan Omar's Anti-Semitic Comments," *New York Post*, March 6, 2019.
121. Alex Shepherd, "Trump's Attack on Socialism Is a Colossal Blunder," *New Republic*, February 19, 2019.

CHAPTER TEN

1. Rodney Hawkins, "Biden Tells African-American Audience GOP Ticket Would Put Them 'Back in Chains,'" CBS News, August 14, 2012, https://www.cbsnews.com/news/biden-tells-african-american-audience-gop-ticket-would-put-them-back-in-chains/.
2. David Catron, "Mississippi Rejects Democrat Race-Baiting," *The American Spectator*, November 28, 2018, https://spectator.org/mississippi-rejects-democrat-race-baiting/.
3. Salena Zito, "America Needs A Good Laugh," *Washington Examiner*, December 16, 2018.
4. Domenico Montanaro, "Warning to Democrats: Most Americans against U.S. Getting More Politically Correct," NPR, December 19, 2018, https://www.npr.org/2018/12/19/677346260/warning-to-democrats-most-americans-against-u-s-getting-more-politically-correct.
5. Virginia Kruta, "Booker Campaign Calls for Cancellation of Trump Rally—'A Breeding Ground for Racism,'" *Daily Caller*, August 6, 2019, https://dailycaller.com/2019/08/06/booker-campaign-call-end-trump-rallies/.
6. CBS Austin Staff, "Austin Boy Called 'Little Hitler' after Selling Hot Cocoa to Raise Money for Border Wall," KATU 2, February 18, 2019, https://katu.com/news/nation-world/austin-boy-called-little-hitler-after-selling-hot-cocoa-to-raise-money-for-border-wall.
7. Jenna Amatulli, "Jane Curtin: 'My New Year's Resolution Is to Make Sure the Republican Party Dies,'" *HuffPost*, January 1, 2019, https://www.huffpost.com/entry/jane-curtin-new-years-resolution-republican-party_n_5c2b9348e4b05c88b70366cc.
8. Nick Givas, "Washington Post Columnist Warns of Need to 'Burn Down the Republican Party' to Wipe Out Trump Supporters," Fox News, August 26,2016, https://www.foxnews.com/media/trump-republican-party-2020-burn-down.
9. Todd Starnes, "UC Davis Students Protest Photo of Slain Police Officer Holding Blue Lives Matter Flag," Fox News, January 13, 2019, https://www.foxnews.com/opinion/todd-starnes-uc-davis-students-protest-photo-of-slain-police-officer-holding-blue-lives-matter-flag.
10. Hank Berrien, "CNN Bashes Troops Who Support Trump. Sarah Sanders Fires Back," *Daily Wire*, December 27, 2018, https://www.dailywire.com/news/39727/cnn-bashes-troops-who-support-trump-sarah-sanders-hank-berrien.
11. Souad Mekhennet and Greg Miller, "Jamal Khashoggi's Final Months in Exile in the Long Shadow of Saudi Arabia," *Washington Post*, December 22, 2018.
12. David Rutz, "Brzezinski Blasts Pompeo over Response to Khashoggi Murder: He's Like a 'Wannabe Dictator's Buttboy,'" *Washington Free*

Beacon, December 12, 2018, https://freebeacon.com/politics/brzezinski-blasts-pompeo-over-response-to-khashoggi-murder-hes-acting-like-a-dictators-buttboy/.

13. Michelangelo Signorile, "Homophobia Isn't Funny, So Why Do Liberal Comics Keep Using It?" *HuffPost*, August 14, 2018, https://www.huffpost.com/entry/opinion-casual-homophobia-comedy-trump-jokes_n_5b698a50e4b0de86f4a5143d.
14. Mark Bauerlein, "A Long History of Violence among U.S. Liberals," *Philadelphia Inquirer*, July 25, 2017.
15. Jamie Ehrlich, "Maxine Waters Encourages Supporters to Harass Trump Administration Officials," CNN, June 25, 2018, https://www.cnn.com/2018/06/25/politics/maxine-waters-trump-officials/index.html.
16. Ehrlich, "Maxine Waters Encourages Supporters to Harass Trump Administration Officials."
17. Erin Jensen, "White House Correspondents' Dinner: Michelle Wolf Obliterates Sarah Huckabee Sanders," *USA Today*, April 29, 2018.
18. Aris Folley, "California Restaurant Owner Won't Serve Customers Wearing MAGA Hats," *The Hill*, January 31, 2019.
19. Nicholas Fondacaro, "Cuomo Argues in Favor of Allowing the Banning of MAGA Hat Wearers from Businesses," NewsBusters, February 1, 2019, https://www.newsbusters.org/blogs/nb/nicholas-fondacaro/2019/02/01/cuomo-argues-favor-allowing-banning-maga-hat-wearers.
20. Sarah Taylor, "Woman Assaults Young Man Wearing MAGA Hat at Mexican Eatery, Says She's Actually the Victim," The Blaze, February 24, 2019, https://www.theblaze.com/news/woman-assaults-man-maga-hat.
21. Joseph Curl, "GOP Senator Reveals Vulgar, Threatening Messages She Received Before Kavanaugh Confirmation Vote," *Daily Wire*, December 19, 2018, https://www.dailywire.com/news/39513/gop-senator-reveals-vulgar-threatening-messages-joseph-curl.
22. Kyle Perisic, "The Person Doxxing ICE Employees Is a Professor at NYU," *Daily Caller*, June 20, 2018, https://dailycaller.com/2018/06/20/antifa-doxxing-professor-nyu-ice/.
23. Kyle Perisic, "NYU Remains Silent on Professor Who Doxxed ICE Employees," *Daily Caller*, July 10, 2018, https://dailycaller.com/2018/07/10/nyu-professor-doxx-ice/.
24. Kyle Perisic, "Twitter Suspends Reporters Who Doxxed Stephen Miller, But Not the Prof Who Doxxed Ice Employees," *Daily Caller*, June 21, 2018, https://dailycaller.com/2018/06/21/twitter-reporters-doxxed-stephen-miller-ice-employees/.
25. Lucia I. Suarez Sang, "Portland Antifa Protesters Caught on Video Bullying Elderly Motorist, Woman in Wheelchair," Fox News, October 10, 2018.

26. Ashe Schow, "'I Could Have Died That Day': Marines Testify about Brutal Attack by Antifa," *Daily Wire*, December 17, 2018, https://www.dailywire.com/news/39428/i-could-have-died-day-marines-testify-about-brutal-ashe-schow.
27. Christopher Cadelago, "White House Reports Peter Fonda Tweet on Barron Trump to Secret Service," *Politico*, June 20, 2018.
28. Jim Geraghty, "Tom Perez: The Leftist Radical Who Could Be Hillary's Running Mate," *National Review*, June 2, 2016.
29. Alex Parker, "Racist University of Georgia Teaching Assistant: Whites 'May Have to Die' for Black Freedom," *RedState*, January 21, 2019, https://www.redstate.com/alexparker/2019/01/21/university-of-georgia-irami-osei-frimpong-white-people-die/.
30. Virginia Kruta, "Ocasio-Cortez Says 'Where We Are' as Americans Is 'Garbage,'" *Daily Caller*, March 10, 2019, https://dailycaller.com/2019/03/10/ocasio-cortez-where-we-are-america-garbage/.
31. Aaron Gleason, "Mob Gets Actor to Apologize for Suggesting Lefties Read Ben Shapiro," *The Federalist*, December 26, 2018, https://thefederalist.com/2018/07/20/mob-gets-filmmaker-delete-tweet-suggesting-lefties-read-ben-shapiro/.
32. Jodi Smith, "Mark Duplass Tweets Misguided and Ill-Informed Support of Ben Shapiro and James Gunn Is There," *Pajiba* (blog), July 18, 2018, https://www.pajiba.com/web_culture/mark-duplass-tweets-misguided-and-illinformed-support-of-ben-shapiro.php.
33. Caitlin Yilek, "Joe Biden Takes Heat for Calling Mike Pence a 'Decent Guy,'" *Washington Examiner*, February 28, 2019.
34. Jennifer Konerman, "The Late-Night Host, Back from Paternity Leave, Also Responds to the Media Calling Him a 'Hollywood Elitist' for Discussing Health Care," *Hollywood Reporter*, May 8, 2017.
35. John Hawkins, "The Liberal Lie So Big It May One Day Split the Country," *Townhall*, May 13, 2017, https://townhall.com/columnists/johnhawkins/2017/05/13/the-liberal-lie-so-big-it-may-one-day-split-the-country-n2326353.
36. Saagar Enjeti (@esaagar), Twitter, April 9, 2019.
37. Editorial, "Media Bias: Pretty Much All of Journalism Now Leans Left, Study Shows," *Investor's Business Daily*, November 16, 2018.
38. Editorial, "Media Bias: Pretty Much All of Journalism Now Leans Left, Study Shows."
39. Steve Warren, "NYC Boycott Bombs as Chick-fil-A Booms Despite the Protest of Its Christian, Family Values," CBN News, April 4, 2018, https://www1.cbn.com/cbnnews/finance/2018/april/chick-fil-as-formula-for-success-grows-despite-the-protest-of-some-to-its-christian-family-values.
40. Brooke Phillips, "San Antonio Bans Chick-fil-A from Airport," News 4 San Antonio, March 21, 2019, https://news4sanantonio.com/news/

local/city-councilman-motions-to-ban-chick-fil-a-from-san-antonio-international-airport.

41. Dan Gainor, "Chick-fil-A, One Year Later," *Focus on the Family*, June/July 2013.
42. Elizabeth Bauer, "Activists Demand Companies Advertise LGBT Behaviors or Lose Ranking," *The Federalist*, February 5, 2019, https://thefederalist.com/2019/02/05/activists-demand-companies-advertise-lgbt-behaviors-lose-ranking/.
43. Rick Nathanson, "Ruling Hark Back to 2006 Albuquerque Case," *Albuquerque Journal*, June 5, 2018.
44. Karla Dial, "Elane Photography: 'Paying the Price' For Religious Freedom," *Focus on the Family*, 2013.
45. "Washington Floral Artist to Ask US Supreme Court to Protect Her Freedom," Alliance Defending Freedom news release, February 16, 2017, https://www.adflegal.org/detailspages/press-release-details/washington-floral-artist-to-ask-us-supreme-court-to-protect-her-freedom.
46. Adam Liptak, "In Narrow Decision, Supreme Court Sides with Baker Who Turned Away Gay Couple," *New York Times*, June 4, 2018.
47. Jack Crowe, "Masterpiece Cakeshop Owner Sued Again after Refusing to Bake 'Gender Transition' Cake," *National Review*, June 11, 2019.
48. Dial, "Elane Photography: 'Paying the Price' For Religious Freedom."
49. David Crary, Rachel Zoll, and Michael Liedtke, "Mozilla CEO Resignation Raises Free-Speech Issue," *USA Today*, April 4, 2014.
50. Ian McCullough, "Did Mozilla CEO Brendan Eich Deserve to Be Removed From His Position?" *Forbes*, April 11, 2014.
51. Michael Brown, "Vimeo Allows Jihadists and Porn but Not the Christian Testimony of Former Gays," Christian Today, March 28, 2017.
52. Brown, "Vimeo Allows Jihadists and Porn but Not the Christian Testimony of Former Gays."
53. Jeff Johnston, "Silencing Discussion About Male-Female Differences," *Focus on the Family*, 2017.
54. Scott Morefield, "Tom Brokaw Argues That Hispanics Should 'Work Harder at Assimilation,' Pays A Heavy Price on Twitter," *Daily Caller*, January 27, 2019, https://dailycaller.com/2019/01/27/tom-brokaw-hispanics-assimilation-twitter/.
55. Rob McLean and Brian Stelter, "NBC Calls Tom Brokaw's Assimilation Comments 'Inaccurate and Inappropriate,'" CNN, January 28, 2019, https://www.cnn.com/2019/01/27/media/tom-brokaw-nbc-meet-the-press/index.html.
56. Brandi Miller, "If Kevin Hart Were Really Sorry, He'd Prove It," *HuffPost*, December 8, 2018, https://www.huffpost.com/entry/opinion-kevin-hart-apologies_n_5c0bfe47e4b0ab8cf693dc63.
57. Rich Kiamco, "Like Kevin Hart, I also Made a Bad Joke on State. Unlike Hart, I Learned from the Experience," *USA Today*, December 14, 2018.

58. Emma Dumain, "Racist? Immoral? The Shutdown Fight Becomes a Rhetorical War," McClatchy DC Bureau, January 7, 2019, https://www.mcclatchydc.com/latest-news/article224032920.html.
59. Kim Hart, "Exclusive Poll: Most Democrats See Republicans as Racist, Sexist," *Axios*, November 12, 2018, https://www.axios.com/poll-democrats-and-republicans-hate-each-other-racist-ignorant-evil-99ae7afc-5a51-42be-8ee2-3959e43ce320.html.
60. Betsy McCaughey, "Dems Are at It Again – This Time, Smearing Wall Supporters as 'Deplorables," *New York Post*, December 25, 2018.
61. Dumain, "Racist? Immoral? The Shutdown Fight Becomes a Rhetorical War."
62. Dartunorro Clark, "Kamala Harris Thinks Trump Is a Racist. GOP Chairwoman Calls Her 'Desperate,'" NBC News, February 26, 2019, https://www.nbcnews.com/politics/2020-election/kamala-harris-thinks-trump-racist-gop-chairwoman-calls-her-desperate-n976271.
63. Tim Haines, "Sen. Sharrod Brown: Republicans Following 'Racist' Trump 'Like Lemmings Off A Cliff'," RealClearPolitics, March 10, 2019, https://www.realclearpolitics.com/video/2019/03/10/sen_sherrod_brown_republicans_following_racist_trump_like_lemmings_off_a_cliff.html.
64. Matt Wilstein, "'The View' Goes Off the Rails on 'Racist' Republicans: 'I'm John McCain's Daughter!'" *Daily Beast*, January 15, 2019, https://www.thedailybeast.com/the-view-goes-off-the-rails-on-racist-republicans-im-john-mccains-daughter.
65. "An Open Letter to America's CEOs," Restore Public Trust, April 6, 2019, https://restorepublictrust.org/wp-content/uploads/2019/04/20190406-RPT-OpenLetterCorporateAmerica-FINAL-1.pdf.
66. James Barrett, "Watch: Students Want 'Clarence Thomas' Building Renamed. Then They're Asked to Explain Why," *Daily Wire*, January 1, 2019, https://www.dailywire.com/news/39215/watch-students-oppose-clarence-thomas-building-james-barrett.
67. Noella Chye & Rosie Bradbury, "Cambridge Rescinds Offer of Visiting Fellowship to Controversial Professor Jordan Peterson," *Varsity*, March 20, 2019.
68. Toby Young, "Cambridge's Shameful Decision to Rescind Jordan Peterson's Visiting Fellowship," *Spectator USA*, March 21, 2019.
69. Charlotte Townsend, "If You're A Conservative Woman on My Campus, Get Used to Bullying," *The Federalist*, March 21, 2019, https://thefederalist.com/2019/03/21/youre-conservative-woman-campus-get-used-bullying/.
70. Bradford Betz, "Yale Law School Policy May Discriminate Against Christian Groups, Sen. Ted Cruz Says," Fox News, April 8, 2019, https://www.foxnews.com/politics/sen-ted-cruz-opens-investigation-into-yale-law-school-over-supposed-blacklisting-of-christian-organizations; Gregg Re, "Hawley Suggests Trump Admin Strip Yale

of Federal Funding If 'Targeting' of Religious Students Continues," Fox News, April 9, 2019, https://www.foxnews.com/politics/hawley-suggests-trump-admin-strip-yale-of-federal-funding-if-targeting-of-religious-students-continues.

71. Re, "Hawley Suggests Trump Admin Strip Yale of Federal Funding If 'Targeting' of Religious Students Continues."
72. Hank Berrien, "Famed Atheist Deletes Patreon Account Over Banning of Anti-Leftists," *Daily Wire*, December 17, 2018, https://www.dailywire.com/news/39400/famed-atheist-deletes-patreon-account-over-banning-hank-berrien.
73. C. Edward Kelso, "Jordan Peterson and Dave Rubin Leaving Patreon in Protest Against Censorship, CoinSpice, January 1, 2019, https://coinspice.io/news/jordan-peterson-and-dave-rubin-leaving-patreon-in-protest-against-censorship/.
74. Dave Rubin, "Why I Left the Left," PragerU, February 6, 2017, https://www.prageru.com/video/why-i-left-the-left/.

CHAPTER ELEVEN

1. Brian Joondeph, "Coffee Will Kill You, Until it Won't, and Other Fake Health News," American Thinker, June 18, 2019, https://www.americanthinker.com/articles/2019/06/coffee_will_kill_you_until_it_wont_and_other_fake_health_news.html.
2. Matt Stiles, "Rise in Homeless Numbers Prompts Outrage and Alarm across L.A. County," *Los Angeles Times*, June 5, 2019; Megan Cerullo, "Homelessness on the Rise in Some U.S. Cities," CBS News, December 11, 2018, https://www.cbsnews.com/news/homelessness-on-the-rise-in-some-u-s-cities/.
3. Robert E. Moffit, "House Democrats Unveil Plan to Bring Total Government Control over American Health Care," The Heritage Foundation, February 28, 2019, https://www.heritage.org/medicare/commentary/house-democrats-unveil-plan-bring-total-government-control-over-american-health.
4. Jennie Taer, "'Meatless Mondays'...NYC Mayor Takes a Page from Kim Jong-UN's Menu," *SaraCarter* (blog), March 16, 2019, https://saraacarter.com/meatless-mondays-ny-mayor-takes-a-page-from-kim-jong-uns-menu/.
5. Michael M. Grynbaum, "New York's Ban on Big Sodas Is Rejected by Final Court," *New York Times*, June 26, 2014.
6. Whitney Filloon, "California Bans Restaurants from Automatically Giving Out Plastic Straws," Eater, September 21, 2018, https://www.eater.com/2018/9/21/17886256/california-straw-ban-plastic.
7. Post Editorial Board, "Banning Plastic Straws is More Scam then Science," *New York Post*, July 2, 2018.

8. Joel B. Pollack, "House Democrats Want 'Oversight' over Fox News' Editorial Decisions," *Breitbart*, April 2, 2019, https://www.breitbart.com/the-media/2019/04/02/house-democrats-want-oversight-over-fox-news-editorial-decisions/.
9. William Turton, "How Our Administrative State Undermines the Constitution," *The Federalist*, February 8, 2019, https://thefederalist.com/2019/02/08/administrative-state-undermines-constitution/.
10. Turton, "How Our Administrative State Undermines the Constitution."
11. Ibid.
12. Enrico Cantoni and Vincent Pons, "Strict ID Laws Don't Stop Voters: Evidence from a U.S. Nationwide Panel, 2008–2016," The National Bureau of Economic Research, February 2019, https://www.nber.org/papers/w25522.
13. Kevin Mooney, "Noncitizen Voting Called 'Next Battle Space' in Fight for Election Integrity," *Daily Signal*, March 4, 2019, https://www.dailysignal.com/2019/03/04/noncitizen-voting-called-next-battle-space-in-fight-for-election-integrity/.
14. Margot Cleveland, "Nearly 58,000 Noncitizens Illegally Voted in Texas. More Nationwide?" *The Federalist*, January 28, 2019, https://thefederalist.com/2019/01/28/nearly-58000-noncitizens-illegally-voted-texas-many-nationwide/.
15. Ryan Saavedra, "Breaking: Democrats Introduce Bill to Eliminate Electoral College," *Daily Wire*, January 3, 2019, https://www.dailywire.com/news/39931/breaking-democrats-introduce-bill-eliminate-ryan-saavedra.
16. David Harsanyi, "Why Democrats Fear the Electoral College," *Townhall*, March 22, 2019, https://townhall.com/columnists/davidharsanyi/2019/03/22/why-democrats-fear-the-electoral-college-n2543492.
17. Allen Guelzo, "In Defense of the Electoral College," *National Affairs*, Winter 2018.
18. John Bowden, "Pelosi Says She Backs Lowering Voting Age to 16," *The Hill*, March 14, 2019.
19. "The Facts About H.R. 1 – the For the People Act of 2019," The Heritage Foundation, February 1, 2019, https://www.heritage.org/election-integrity/report/the-facts-about-hr-1-the-the-people-act-2019.
20. Peter Hasson, "Majority of House Democrats Vote to Let 16-Year-Olds Vote for President," *Daily Signal*, March 8, 2019, https://www.dailysignal.com/2019/03/08/majority-of-house-democrats-vote-to-let-16-year-olds-vote-for-president/.
21. Courtney O'Brien, "CNN Anchors Say Dems Wanting Prisoners to Vote Are 'Way Out There,'" *Townhall*, April 24, 2019, https://townhall.com/tipsheet/cortneyobrien/2019/04/24/cnn-anchors-say-dems-wanting-prisoners-to-vote-are-way-out-there-n2545283.

22. "The Facts About H.R. 1 – the For the People Act of 2019," The Heritage Foundation.
23. "Stop Democrats from Using Your Tax Dollars to Elect Their Candidates," American Commitment, https://action.americancommitment.org/ctas/5c7d681cc64b6-urge-congress-action.
24. Jarrett Stepman, "The Left Wants to Transform Our Election System. It's a Recipe for 1-Party Rule," *Daily Signal*, February 18, 2019, https://www.dailysignal.com/2019/02/18/the-left-wants-to-transform-our-election-system-its-a-recipe-for-1-party-rule/.
25. Stephen Dinan, "ACLU Blasts Democrats' Election Bill as Unconstitutional," *Washington Times*, March 4, 2019.
26. Zachary B. Wolf, "Government Overhaul: Democrats Eye Packing Supreme Court, Changing Voting System," CNN, March 21, 2019, https://www.cnn.com/2019/03/21/politics/change-us-government-system-democrats-2020/index.html.
27. Rich Logos, "The Democrats' 2020 Census Goal: Turn Purple States Irreversibly Blue," The American Thinker, February 25, 2019, https://www.americanthinker.com/articles/2019/02/the_democrats_2020_census_goal_turn_purple_states_irreversibly_blue.html.
28. Liam Quinn, "Trump Rips 'Radical' Democrats, Says Census 'Meaningless' without Citizenship Question," Fox News, April 1, 2019, https://www.foxnews.com/politics/president-trump-attacks-radical-democrats-says-census-meaningless-without-citizenship-question.
29. Eric W. Orts, "The Path to Give California 12 Senators, and Vermont Just One," *The Atlantic*, January 2, 2019.
30. Madeline Osburn, "How A 1946 Law Is Still Dissolving Legislative Power Today," *The Federalist*, February 21, 2019, https://thefederalist.com/2019/02/21/1946-law-still-dissolving-legislative-power-today/.
31. Ema O'Connor, "A Pennsylvania Court Blocked Trump's Birth Control Rules Across the US – Again," *BuzzFeed*, January 14, 2019.
32. Ben Weingarten, "Stop Activists from Controlling the Country with Universal Injunctions," *The Federalist*, February 15, 2019, https://thefederalist.com/2019/02/15/president-trump-needs-stop-activists-controlling-country-universal-injunctions/.
33. 5 U.S. 137 (1803).
34. Hans A. von Spakovsky, "The Liberal Mythology of the 'Activist' Supreme Court," The Heritage Foundation, June 16, 2010, https://www.heritage.org/commentary/the-liberal-mythology-the-activist-supreme-court.
35. Jeffrey Cimmino, "Kirsten Gillibrand Compares Pro-Life Beliefs to Racism, 'Not Acceptable,'" Fox News, June 11, 2019, https://www.foxnews.com/politics/kirsten-gillibrand-compares-pro-life-beliefs-to-racism-not-acceptable.

36. Andrew Kugle, "Gillibrand: Pro-Life People Are Ineligible to Be Judges," *Washington Free Beacon*, June 14, 2019, https://freebeacon.com/politics/gillibrand-pro-life-people-are-ineligible-to-be-judges/.
37. Amanda Prestigiacomo, "NJ Dems Propose Legislation to Potentially Remove Trump's Name From 2020 Ballot," *Daily Wire*, February 4, 2019, https://www.dailywire.com/news/43027/nj-proposing-measure-would-potentially-remove-amanda-prestigiacomo.
38. The Editorial Board, "California Bans Trump," *Wall Street Journal*, July 31, 2019.
39. Victor Davis Hanson, "Left's Proposed Voting Changes Are about Power, Not Principles," *Daily Signal*, March 28, 2019, https://www.dailysignal.com/2019/03/28/lefts-proposed-voting-changes-are-about-power-not-principles/.
40. Joe Simonson, "Beto O'Rourke Wonders If the Constitution Still Works," *Daily Caller*, January 15, 2019, https://dailycaller.com/2019/01/15/beto-orourke-constitution-outdated/.

CHAPTER TWELVE

1. Ryan Saavedra, "Watch: Democrat Ted Lieu Admits He Wants to Censor Speech, Laments He Can't," *Daily Wire*, December 13, 2018, https://www.dailywire.com/news/39312/watch-democrat-ted-lieu-admits-he-wants-censor-ryan-saavedra.
2. Streiff, "Democrat Congressman Calls for Banning MAGA Hats after March for Life Confrontation," *RedState*, January 20, 2019, https://www.redstate.com/streiff/2019/01/20/democrat-congressman-calls-banning-maga-hats-march-live-confrontation/.
3. Editors, "A Lesson in Free Speech," *Washington Times*, April 15, 2019.
4. Alana Goodman, "Wounded SEAL Dan Crenshaw Mocked by Left as 'Captain Shithead,' Nazi, 'Eyeless F—k'," *Washington Examiner*, April 13, 2019.
5. Charlotte Henry, "Tim Cook Says 'No Home' for Hate on Apple's Platforms," The Mac Observer, December 4, 2019, https://www.macobserver.com/news/cook-adl-award/.
6. Andrew Klavan, "Mac-Fascism," *Daily Wire*, December 7, 2018, https://www.dailywire.com/news/39151/klavan-mac-fascism-andrew-klavan.
7. Kevin Mooney, "Geologist Accuses Apple of Political Bias in Removing App Countering Climate Alarmism," *Daily Signal*, March 11, 2019, https://www.dailysignal.com/2019/03/11/inconvenient/.
8. Madeline Osburn, "Twitter Is Now Banning Conservatives for Investigative Journalism about Big Tech's Abortion Activism," *The Federalist*, June 13, 2019, https://thefederalist.com/2019/06/13/twitter-now-banning-conservatives-investigative-journalism-big-techs-abortion-activism/.

9. Hank Berrien, "Report: YouTube Search Results For 'Abortion' Change After Leftist Writer Complains They're Too Pro-Life," *Daily Wire*, December 24, 2018, https://www.dailywire.com/news/39650/report-search-results-abortion-change-youtube-hank-berrien.
10. Allum Bokhari, "'The Smoking Gun': Google Manipulated YouTube Search Results for Abortion, Maxine Waters, David Hogg," *Breitbart*, January 16, 2019, https://www.breitbart.com/tech/2019/01/16/google-youtube-search-blacklist-smoking-gun/.
11. Bokhari, "'The Smoking Gun': Google Manipulated YouTube Search Results for Abortion, Maxine Waters, David Hogg."
12. Brandon Morse, "YouTube Looking to Remove the Dislike Button after Social Justice Ads Get Disliked into Oblivion," *RedState*, February 4, 2019, https://www.redstate.com/brandon_morse/2019/02/04/youtube-looking-remove-dislike-button-social-justice-ads-get-disliked-oblivion/.
13. Peter Hasson, "'Disrespectful': Google Employees Melt Down over the Word 'Family,'" *Daily Caller*, January 16, 2019, https://dailycaller.com/2019/01/16/google-family-triggered-meltdown/.
14. Matthew Boyle, "'Silent Donation': Corporate Emails Reveal Google Executives' Efforts to Turn Out Latino Voters Who They Thought Would Vote for Clinton," *Breitbart*, September 10, 2018, https://www.breitbart.com/politics/2018/09/10/silent-donation-corporate-emails-reveal-google-executives-efforts-to-swing-election-to-hillary-clinton-with-latino-outreach-campaign/.
15. Allum Bokhari, "The Google Tape: Google Global Affairs VP Kent Walker – 'History Is on Our Side'," *Breitbart*, September 12, 2018, https://www.breitbart.com/tech/2018/09/12/the-google-tape-google-global-affairs-vp-kent-walker-history-is-on-our-side/; Allum Bokhari, "Leaked Video: Google Leadership's Dismayed Reaction to Trump Election," *Breitbart*, September 12, 2018, https://www.breitbart.com/tech/2018/09/12/leaked-video-google-leaderships-dismayed-reaction-to-trump-election/.
16. Peter Hasson, "Exclusive: Google Employees Debated Burying Conservative Media in Search," *Daily Caller*, November 29, 2018, https://dailycaller.com/2018/11/29/google-censorship-conservative-media/.
17. Stephanie Haney and George Martin, "Google's Left-Wing Agenda Revealed: Undercover Video Shows Top Exec Pledging Company Would 'Stop the Next Trump Situation' and Exposes Search Giant's Secret Plan for Radical Social Engineering," *Daily Mail*, July 6, 2019.
18. Beth Baumann, "WATCH: Cruz Loses His Patience with Google Exec During Hearing on Big Tech," *Townhall*, June 25, 2019, https://townhall.com/tipsheet/bethbaumann/2019/06/25/watch-cruzs-snarky-response-to-google-execs-take-on-big-tech-censorship-n2548975.

19. Paul Mirengoff, "Psychologist: Google Generated At Least 2.6 Million Votes for Hillary," *Power Line* (blog), August 9, 2019, https://www.powerlineblog.com/archives/2019/08/psychologist-google-generated-at-least-2-6-million-votes-for-hillary.php.
20. Alex Thompson, "Twitter Appears to Have Fixed "Shadow Ban" of Prominent Republicans Like the RNC Chair and Trump Jr.'s Spokesman," Vice News, July 25, 2018.
21. Jack Shafer, "The Conservative Revolt against Twitter," *Politico*, November 26, 2018.
22. Shafer, "The Conservative Revolt against Twitter."
23. Amanda Prestigiacomo, "James Woods Is in 'Twitter Jail.' Here's the Tweet That Got Him Suspended," *Daily Wire*, April 30, 2019, https://www.dailywire.com/news/46558/james-woods-twitter-jail-heres-tweet-got-him-amanda-prestigiacomo.
24. Richard Hanania, "It Isn't Your Imagination: Twitter Treats Conservatives More Harshly Than Liberals," Quillette, February 12, 2019, https://quillette.com/2019/02/12/it-isnt-your-imagination-twitter-treats-conservatives-more-harshly-than-liberals/.
25. Jessica Guynn, "Ted Cruz threatens To Regulate Facebook, Google and Twitter over Charges of Anti-Conservative Bias," *USA Today*, April 10, 2019.
26. Charles Fain Lehman, "DOJ Initiates Antitrust Investigation of Big Tech," *Washington Free Beacon*, July 24, 2019, https://freebeacon.com/issues/doj-initiates-antitrust-investigation-of-big-tech/.
27. Emily Zanotti, "Monterey Bay Aquarium Forced to Apologize after a Joke Tweet about a Fat Otter," *Daily Wire*, December 20, 2018, https://www.dailywire.com/news/39567/monterey-bay-aquarium-forced-apologize-after-joke-emily-zanotti.
28. ABC News, "Jameela Jamil Shuts Down Body Shaming Avon Ad, Gets Company to Take it Down," WTOP, January 21, 2019, https://wtop.com/celebrities/2019/01/actress-jameela-jamil-criticizes-body-shaming-avon-ad-gets-apology/.
29. Jenna Amatulli, "Jameela Jamil Announces Company Launch to Change How People Talk about Bodie," *HuffPost*, January 3, 2019, https://www.huffpost.com/entry/jameela-jamil-company-launch-body-positivity_n_5c2d31b3e4b0407e9087cde0.
30. Ben Shapiro, "Harvard Rescinds Admission to Conservative Kyle Kashuv over Private Racist Remarks He Wrote At 16, Despite Apology and Evidence of Growth. This is Disgusting," *Daily Wire*, June 17, 2019, https://www.dailywire.com/news/47971/hold-harvard-rescinds-admission-conservative-kyle-ben-shapiro.
31. Ilana Kaplan, "Millennials Watching 'Friends' on Netflix Shocked by Storylines," *Independent*, January 11, 2018.

32. Angelica Florio, "These 13 Jokes From 'Seinfeld' Are Super Offensive Now – Yes, That Includes the 'Soup Nazi,'" *Bustle*, December 31, 2018, https://www.bustle.com/p/these-13-jokes-from-seinfeld-are-super-offensive-now-yes-that-includes-the-soup-nazi-10191949.
33. Jack Shepherd, "Dwayne 'The Rock' Johnson Hits Out at 'Snowflakes' for 'Looking for a Reason to Be Offended,'" *Independent*, January 11, 2019.
34. Dana Rose Falcone, "Jerry Seinfeld: College Students Don't Know What the Hell They're Talking About," *Entertainment Weekly*, June 8, 2015.
35. Scott Jaschik, "Professors and Politics: What the Research Says," Inside Higher Ed, February 27, 2017, https://www.insidehighered.com/news/2017/02/27/research-confirms-professors-lean-left-questions-assumptions-about-what-means; Howard Kurtz, "College Faculties a Most Liberal Lot, Study Finds," *Washington Post*, March 29, 2005.
36. Karin Agness, "The Five Strategies the Left Uses to Silence Conservative Women on Campus," *Campus Reform*, March 25, 2015, https://www.campusreform.org/?ID=6390.
37. Dr. Nina M. Lozano (@DrNinaMReich), "Ben Shapiro espouses hate speech, and is linked to numerous hate groups. As a LMU Professor, I will be organizing protests, and alerting the media of LMU's decision to support hate speech—which is completely antithetical to our University Mission," Twitter, January 29, 2019, 10:37 p.m., https://twitter.com/drninamreich/status/1090499121926950912?lang=en.
38. Ian Miles Cheong, "Milo Yiannopoulos Undeterred by UC Berkeley Cancellation of 'Free Speech Week,'" *Daily Caller*, September 23, 2017, https://dailycaller.com/2017/09/23/milo-yiannopoulos-undeterred-by-uc-berkeley-cancellation-of-free-speech-week/.
39. David L. Hudson, "Free Speech on Public College Campuses Overview," Freedom Forum Institute, March 2018, https://www.freedomforuminstitute.org/first-amendment-center/topics/freedom-of-speech-2/free-speech-on-public-college-campuses-overview/.
40. Stuart Smith, "CSU Students Question ASCSU Senate about Use of Student Fees to Bring Dennis Prager to Campus," *Rocky Mountain Collegian*, October 4, 2018.
41. Betsy McCaughey, "Trump Takes on Campus Speech Police," *Townhall*, March 6, 2019, https://townhall.com/columnists/betsymccaughey/2019/03/06/trump-takes-on-campus-speech-police-n2542655.
42. Brett Samuels, "Trump Signs Executive Order on Campus Free Speech," *The Hill*, March 31, 2019.
43. Connor Friedersdorf, "The New Intolerance of Student Activism," *The Atlantic*, November 9, 2015.

44. Foundation for Individual Rights in Education, "Yale University Students Protest Halloween Costume Email (VIDEO 3)," YouTube, November 6, 2015, https://youtu.be/9IEFD_JVYd0.
45. Friedersdorf, "The New Intolerance of Student Activism."
46. Robby Soave, "Harvard Caves to Student Mob, First Ronald Sullivan for Being Harvey Weinstein's Lawyer," *Reason*, May 12, 2019.
47. Michelle Malkin, "Malkin: Harvard's Insatiable Identity-Politics Cannibals," *Daily Wire*, May 18, 2019, https://www.dailywire.com/news/47385/malkin-harvards-insatiable-identity-politics-michelle-malkin.
48. Kenny Xu, "If Princeton Students Are Scared to Hear Conservatives, They Aren't Elite," *The Federalist*, January 16, 2019, https://thefederalist.com/2019/01/16/princeton-students-scared-hear-conservative-arent-elite/.
49. Smagar, "Tucson Festival of Books: Trump-Friendly Voices Not Wanted?" *RedState*, February 23, 2019, https://www.redstate.com/diary/smagar/2019/02/23/tucson-festival-books-trump-friendly-voices-not-wanted/.
50. Mark Hemingway, "How to Succeed in Advertising Boycotts without Really Trying," RealClearPolitics, February 21, 2019, https://www.realclearpolitics.com/articles/2019/02/21/how_to_succeed_in_advertising_boycotts_without_really_trying.html.
51. Maeve McDermott, "Bill Maher Mocks Rashida Tlaib's 'Boycott': 'Some People Have One Move Only,'" *USA Today*, August 22, 2019.
52. Sarah Whitten, "Starbucks to Close All Company-Owned Stores on the Afternoon of May 29 for Racial-Bias Education Day," CNBC, April 17, 2018, https://www.cnbc.com/2018/04/17/starbucks-to-close-all-stores-on-may-29-for-racial-bias-education-day.html.
53. Brian K. Miller, "If This Man's Speech Isn't Protected, No One's Is," RealClearPolitics, January 3, 2019, https://www.realclearpolitics.com/articles/2019/01/03/if_this_mans_speech_isnt_protected_no_ones_is_139070.html.
54. Peter Hasson, "Democratic Operatives Used Misleading Facebook Pages to Suppress GOP Turnout in Midterms," *Daily Caller*, January 8, 2019, https://dailycaller.com/2019/01/08/democrat-facebook-campaign-supress/.
55. Tim Haines, "James O'Keefe: Clinton Campaign, DNC Coordinated with Organizations to Incite Violence at Trump Events," RealClearPolitics, October 17, 2016, https://www.realclearpolitics.com/video/2016/10/17/new_okeefe_video_clinton_campaign_dnc_coordinated_with_organizations_to_beat_up_trump_supporters.html.
56. Kim Strassel, "Russia, the NRA, and Fake News," *Wall Street Journal*, March 22, 2018.

57. Margot Cleveland, "Bruce Ohr Revealed Political Operatives Got FBI to Investigate the NRA," *The Federalist*, March 14, 2019, https://thefederalist.com/2019/03/14/bruce-ohr-testimony-revealed-political-operatives-got-fbi-investigate-nra/.
58. Chuck Ross, "FEC Chief Supported Russia-NRA Campaign Finance Probe Based Solely on 'Vague' News Article," *Daily Caller*, August 17, 2019, https://dailycaller.com/2019/08/17/fec-democratic-chair-nra-russia-vague-story/.
59. Cleveland, "Bruce Ohr Revealed Political Operatives Got FBI to Investigate the NRA."

CHAPTER THIRTEEN

1. David Sivak, "Fact Check: Have There Been 60 Million Abortions Since Roe v. Wade?" Check Your Fact, July 3, 2018, https://checkyourfact.com/2018/07/03/fact-check-60-million-abortions/.
2. Wm. Robert Johnston, "Reasons Given for Having Abortions in the United States," Johnston Archive, January 18, 2016, http://www.johnstonsarchive.net/policy/abortion/abreasons.html.
3. Georgi Boorman, "Video: Just Eight Weeks after Conception, Tiny Baby Kicks Arms and Legs," *The Federalist*, January 17, 2019, https://thefederalist.com/2019/01/17/video-just-eight-weeks-conception-tiny-baby-kicks-arms-legs/.
4. Boorman, "Video: Just Eight Weeks after Conception, Tiny Baby Kicks Arms and Legs."
5. "Expert Tells Congress Unborn Babies Can Feel Pain Starting at 8 Weeks," One of Us, May 24, 2013, https://oneofus.eu/2013/05/expert-tells-congress-unborn-babies-can-feel-pain-starting-at-8-weeks/.
6. Boorman, "Video: Just Eight Weeks after Conception, Tiny Baby Kicks Arms and Legs."
7. Dr. Julie-Clare Becher, "Insights into Early Fetal Development," *Pregnancy Archive*, May–August 2018.
8. Lydia Saad, "Trimesters Still Key to U.S. Abortion Views," Gallup, June 13, 2018, https://news.gallup.com/poll/235469/trimesters-key-abortion-views.aspx.
9. Boorman, "Video: Just Eight Weeks after Conception, Tiny Baby Kicks Arms and Legs."
10. Caleb Parke, "Liberal Student Arrested for Punching Pro-Lifer on UNC Campus, Triggered by Images of Aborted Children," Fox News, May 9, 2019, https://www.foxnews.com/us/liberal-student-arrested-punching-pro-lifer.
11. Micaiah Bilger, "Woman Writes: 'I Had an Abortion Last Week Just Because I Wanted To," Life News, February 1, 2017, https://www.lifenews.com/2017/02/01/woman-writes-i-had-an-abortion-last-week-just-because-i-wanted-to/.

12. Sarah Terzo, "Some Pro-Choice Activists Admit Abortion Kills Life: 'I Knew It Was a Baby,'" Live Action, January 31, 2013, https://www.nationalrighttolifenews.org/2013/01/some-pro-choice-activists-admit-abortion-kills-life-i-knew-it-was-a-baby/.
13. Terzo, "Some Pro-Choice Activists Admit Abortion Kills Life: 'I Knew It Was a Baby."
14. Paul Bois, "WATCH: Planned Parenthood Admits Unborn Children Are Babies in Sex-Ed Video," *Daily Wire*, December 14, 2018, https://www.dailywire.com/news/39379/watch-planned-parenthood-admits-unborn-children-paul-bois.
15. Bois, "WATCH: Planned Parenthood Admits Unborn Children Are Babies in Sex-Ed Video."
16. Planned Parenthood, "In-Clinic Abortion Planned Parenthood Video," YouTube, March 8, 2017, https://www.youtube.com/watch?time_continue=20&v=L0OEDPtn-QM.
17. Sarah Terzo, "'I Know It's Murder': Shocking Quotes from Abortionists Openly Admitting They're Killing Babies," Life Site News, March 25, 2013, https://www.lifesitenews.com/opinion/abortionists-agree-abortion-is-killing.
18. Paul Bois, "WATCH: Mom Sings Creepy Lullaby Her Baby 'Gave' Before She Aborted It," *Daily Wire*, December 12, 2018, https://www.dailywire.com/news/39300/watch-mom-sings-creepy-lullaby-her-baby-gave-she-paul-bois.
19. Grace Carr, "Physician Says There Isn't Single Scenario Where Late-Term Abortion Protects Mother's Health," *Daily Signal*, February 12, 2019, https://www.dailysignal.com/2019/02/12/physician-says-there-isnt-single-scenario-where-late-term-abortion-protects-mothers-health/.
20. Matt Walsh, "WALSH: NPR Gave 'Guidance' on What Words to Use When Discussing Abortion. I've Got Better Suggestions," *Daily Wire*, May 23, 2019, https://www.dailywire.com/news/47588/walsh-npr-gave-guidance-what-words-use-when-matt-walsh.
21. Victoria Marshall, "Nikki Haley Responds after Whoopi Goldberg Calls Her Pro-Life Stance 'Anti-Human,'" *Townhall*, June 7, 2019, https://townhall.com/tipsheet/victoriamarshall/2019/06/07/whoopi-goldberg-calls-haleys-prolife-position-antihuman-haley-responds-n2547715.
22. Charles C. Camosy, "The War of Words on Abortion," *New York Times*, January 9, 2019.
23. Dr. Albert Mohler, "After Trying to Reinvent Itself, Planned Parenthood Doubles Down on Their 'Core Mission' as an Abortion Provider," AlbertMohler.com, January 10, 2019, https://albertmohler.com/2019/01/10/briefing-1-10-19/.
24. Amanda Prestigiacomo, "WATCH: Feminist Promotes, Brags about Abortion to CHILDREN in Shocking Video," *Daily Wire*, December 31, 2018, https://www.dailywire.com/news/39796/watch-feminist-promotes-brags-about-abortion-amanda-prestigiacomo.

25. Prestigiacomo, "WATCH: Feminist Promotes, Brags about Abortion to CHILDREN in Shocking Video."
26. Rich Smith, "Shout Your Abortion Is Launching Their Book Tonight at the Neptune," The Stranger, December 5, 2018, https://www.thestranger.com/slog/2018/12/05/36760177/shout-your-abortion-is-launching-their-book-tonight-at-the-neptune.
27. Liz Wolfe, "The 'Shout Your Abortion' Coffee Table Book Fights Off the Real Abortion Conversation," *The Federalist*, December 18, 2018, https://thefederalist.com/2018/12/18/the-shout-your-abortion-coffee-table-book-hides-the-real-abortion-conversation/.
28. Becky Yeh, "New Video Debunks Planned Parenthood's 3 Percent Abortion Myth," Live Action, September 14, 2016, https://www.liveaction.org/news/new-video-debunks-planned-parenthoods-3-percent-abortion-myth/.
29. "Planned Parenthood Ousts President, Seeking a More Political Approach," *New York Times*, July 16, 2019.
30. Mohler, "After Trying to Reinvent Itself, Planned Parenthood Doubles Down on Their 'Core Mission' as an Abortion Provider."
31. Emily Jashinsky, "In Abortion Debate on House Floor, Democrat Dismisses Republicans as 'Sex-Starved Males,'" *The Federalist*, June 12, 2019, https://thefederalist.com/2019/06/12/abortion-debate-house-floor-democrat-dismisses-republicans-sex-starved-males/.
32. Ben Kew, "Gloria Steinem Compares Pro-Life Movement to Nazism: Hitler 'Campaigned Against Abortion,'" *Breitbart*, February 27, 2019, https://www.breitbart.com/entertainment/2019/02/27/gloria-steinem-compares-pro-life-movement-to-nazism-hitler-campaigned-against-abortion/.
33. Brianna Heldt, "Emory University Hosts Lecture Touting Abortion as a 'Moral Good,'" *Townhall*, March 1, 2019, https://townhall.com/tipsheet/briannaheldt/2019/03/01/emory-university-hosts-lecture-touting-abortion-as-a-moral-good-n2542451.
34. Rebecca Todd Peters, "In My Words: Trusting Women to Make Abortion Decisions Is a Christian Norm," Elon University, July 31, 2018, https://www.elon.edu/E-Net/Article/164677.
35. Todd Peters, "In My Words: Trusting Women to Make Abortion Decisions Is a Christian Norm."
36. Micaiah Bilger, "Girl Scouts Gives Its Highest Award to Teen Who Organized Campaign Promoting Abortion," Life News, March 5, 2019, https://www.lifenews.com/2019/03/05/girl-scouts-gives-its-highest-award-to-teen-who-organized-campaign-promoting-abortion/.
37. "Quality, Respectful Abortion Care," Planned Parenthood of New York City, https://www.plannedparenthood.org/planned-parenthood-new-york-city/campaigns/care-no-matter-what.

38. "My Abortion Saved," My Abortion. My Life., https://www.myabortionmylife.org/billboards.
39. Natalie Kitroeff and Jessica Silver-Greenberg, "Planned Parenthood Is Accused of Mistreating Pregnant Employees," *New York Times*, December 20, 2018.
40. Kitroeff and Silver-Greenberg, "Planned Parenthood Is Accused of Mistreating Pregnant Employees."
41. Jacob Airey, "Knowles" Why Is the Media Surprised Planned Parenthood Mistreats Pregnant Employees?" *Daily Wire*, December 23, 2018, https://www.dailywire.com/news/39623/knowles-why-media-surprised-planned-parenthood-jacob-airey.
42. Lauretta Brown, "Senate Democrats Halt Bill That Would Have Permanently Banned Taxpayer Funding of Abortion," *Townhall*, January 18, 2019, https://townhall.com/tipsheet/laurettabrown/2019/01/18/senate-democrats-halt-bill-that-would-have-permanently-banned-taxpayer-funding-of-abortion-n2539235.
43. Rebecca Downs, "Democratic Candidates Showcase Their Abortion Extremism on Debate Stage," *Townhall*, June 28, 2019, https://townhall.com/columnists/rebeccadowns/2019/06/28/democratic-candidates-showcase-their-abortion-extremism-on-debate-stage-n2549165.
44. Lauretta Brown, "New Poll: Three Quarters of Americans Support Restrictions on Abortion," *Townhall*, January 15, 2019, https://townhall.com/tipsheet/laurettabrown/2019/01/15/new-poll-three-quarters-of-american-support-restrictions-on-abortion-n2539062.
45. "Bernie Sanders: 'Yes' on Aborting Babies until Birth," Grabien, April 15, 2019, https://grabien.com/story.php?id=231361.
46. Brown, "New Poll: Three Quarters of Americans Support Restrictions on Abortion."
47. Alexandra Desanctis, "New York State Senate Passes Expansive Abortion Bill," *National Review*, January 22, 2019.
48. Newsroom, "Governor of New York Nixes Nearly All Protections for Preborn Babies," Live Action, January 22, 2019, https://www.liveaction.org/news/new-york-nixes-protections-preborn/.
49. Hank Berrien, "NY Governor Cuomo Celebrates Allowing Abortion up until Birth, Orders World Trade Center Lit Pink," *Daily Wire*, January 23, 2019, https://www.dailywire.com/news/42529/ny-governor-cuomo-celebrates-allowing-abortion-hank-berrien.
50. Dr. Susan Berry, "Actress Ilana Glazer Says NY Abortion Law 'Making the World a Better Place,'" *Breitbart*, March 12, 2019, https://www.breitbart.com/entertainment/2019/03/12/actress-ilana-glazer-says-ny-abortion-law-making-the-world-a-better-place/.

51. Brianna Heldt, "Illinois Follows New York in Considering Extreme Late-Term Abortion Bill," *Townhall*, February 27, 2019, https://townhall.com/tipsheet/briannaheldt/2019/02/27/illinois-follows-new-york-in-considering-extreme-lateterm-abortion-bill-n2542337.
52. John Klar, "Vermont's Terrifying Abortion Law Removes Protections for Pregnant Victims," *The Federalist*, March 20, 2019, https://thefederalist.com/2019/03/20/vermonts-terrifying-abortion-law-removes-protections-pregnant-victims/.
53. Madeline Osburn, "Virginia Democrats Propose Bill Allowing Abortions until Birth," *The Federalist*, January 30, 2019, https://thefederalist.com/2019/01/30/virginia-democrats-propose-bill-allowing-abortions-birth/.
54. Alexandra DeSanctis, "Virginia Government Defends Letting Infants Die," *National Review*, January 30, 2019.
55. DeSanctis, "Virginia Government Defends Letting Infants Die."
56. David French, "Yes, the Virginia Abortion Bill Is Just as Barbaric as You've Heard," *National Review*, January 30, 2019; Osburn, "Virginia Democrats Propose Bill Allowing Abortions Until Birth."
57. P. R. Lockhart, "'Abortion as Black Genocide': Inside the Black Anti-Abortion Movement," Vox, January 19, 2019, https://www.vox.com/identities/2018/1/19/16906928/black-anti-abortion-movement-yoruba-richen-medical-racism.
58. Amanda Prestigiacomo, "Anne Hathaway Scolds Pro-Life 'White Women' over Abortion Laws," *Daily Wire*, May 23, 2019, https://www.dailywire.com/news/47592/anne-hathaway-scolds-pro-life-white-women-over-amanda-prestigiacomo.
59. Jonathon Van Maren, "The Abortion Industry Is Having One of Its Worst Years Eve.... Thanks to Pro-Life Efforts," LifeSite, April 1, 2019, https://www.lifesitenews.com/blogs/the-abortion-industry-is-having-one-of-its-worst-years-everthanks-to-pro-life-efforts.
60. Jacob Airey, "'Unplanned' Actress Fires Back at Alyssa Milano's Attack on Georgia's Pro-Life Bill," *Daily Wire*, March 29, 2019, https://www.dailywire.com/news/45284/unplanned-actress-fires-back-alyssa-milanos-attack-jacob-airey.
61. Aaron Colen, "TV Networks Are Refusing to Sell Ads fort Pro-Life Movie 'Unplanned,'" The Blaze, March 29, 2019, https://www.theblaze.com/news/tv-networks-are-refusing-to-sell-ads-for-pro-life-movie-unplanned.
62. Brian Stelter and Shannon Liao, "Disney, Netflix and WarnerMedia Say New Abortion Law May Push Their Movies Out of Georgia," CNN Business, May 30, 2019, https://www.cnn.com/2019/05/30/business/disney-bob-iger-abortion-georgia/index.html.
63. Kimberly Leonard, "Democrats Block Senate Bill Requiring Medical Care for Babies That Survive Abortion," *Washington Examiner*, February 4, 2019.

64. Leonard, "Democrats Block Senate Bill Requiring Medical Care for Babies that Survive Abortion."
65. Lindsay Elizabeth, "Surprising Number of Babies Surviving Botched Abortions Underscores Need for 'Born Alive' Laws," CBN News, August 24, 2019, https://www1.cbn.com/cbnnews/us/2019/august/surprising-number-of-babies-surviving-botched-abortions-underscores-need-for-born-alive-laws.
66. Katie Yoder, "20 Celebs Join Planned Parenthood to Bash Trump's Title X," *Townhall*, March 15, 2019, https://townhall.com/columnists/katieyoder/2019/03/15/20-celebs-join-planned-parenthood-to-bash-trumps-title-x-n2543177.
67. Seth Newkirk, "Supreme Court May Allow Mothers to Kill Babies for Being Disabled or a Girl," *The Federalist*, January 9, 2019, https://thefederalist.com/2019/01/09/supreme-court-allows-mothers-kill-babies-disabled-girl/.
68. Kristen Waggoner, "Cory Booker: Neomi Rao Is Unfit for Office If She Supports Natural Marriage," *The Federalist*, February 8, 2019, https://thefederalist.com/2019/02/08/cory-booker-neomi-rao-unfit-office-supports-natural-marriage/.
69. Alexandra Desanctis, "Feinstein: 'I Have Never and Will Never Apply a Religious Litmus Test to Nominees,'" *National Review*, September 12, 2017.
70. John H. Garvey and Amy Coney Barrett, "Catholic Judges in Capital Cases," *Marquette Law Review*, 81, (2005): 303–350.
71. Dawn Ennis, "Christian Soccer Player Who Refused to Wear Pride Jersey Not on U.S. World Cup Roster," Outsports, May 3, 2019, https://www.outsports.com/2019/5/3/18527844/uswnt-jaelene-hinkle-women-soccer-world-cup-homophobia-roster-pride-jersey-christian-religion.
72. Jocelyn Davis, "Why It's Not Discrimination for Christian Agencies to Only Recruit Christian Foster and Adoptive Parents," *The Federalist*, December 19, 2018, https://thefederalist.com/2018/12/19/not-discrimination-christian-agencies-recruit-christian-foster-adoptive-parents/.
73. Ashe Schow, "New York State Issues Ultimatum to Faith-Based Adoption Agency," *Daily Wire*, December 13, 2018, https://www.dailywire.com/news/39338/new-york-state-issues-ultimatum-faith-based-ashe-schow.
74. Bre Payton, "Catholic Senior Living Center Bans Residents from Saying 'Merry Christmas,'" *The Federalist*, December 20, 2018, https://thefederalist.com/2018/12/20/catholic-senior-living-center-bans-residents-saying-merry-christmas/.
75. Alexander Pease, "Keynote Speaker at Harvard Diversity Conference Says Christians Should be 'Locked Up,'" *College Fix*, April 26, 2019,

https://www.thecollegefix.com/keynote-speaker-at-harvard-diversity-conference-says-christians-should-be-locked-up/.

76. Doug Mainwaring, "In Calling Pope Francis a 'Homophobe,' Late Night Comic Condemns All Faithful Catholics," LifeSite, December 12, 2018, https://www.lifesitenews.com/blogs/in-calling-pope-francis-a-homophobe-late-night-comic-condemns-all-faithful.
77. Nicole Darrah, "Nebraska Principal Reportedly Bans Candy Canes, Says 'J Shape' Stands for Jesus," Fox News, December 6, 2018, https://www.foxnews.com/us/nebraska-principal-reportedly-bans-candy-canes-says-j-shape-stands-for-jesus.
78. Cydney Henderson, "Lady Gaga Slams Mike Pence as the 'Worst Representation of What it Means to Be a Christian,'" *USA Today*, January 22, 2019.
79. Cortney O'Brien, "John Kings Shocks Panelists by Questioning Karen Pence's Secret Service Protection," *Townhall*, January 18, 2019, https://townhall.com/tipsheet/cortneyobrien/2019/01/18/john-king-take-away-karen-pences-secret-service-protection-n2539291.
80. Rachel del Guidice, "Liberals Bash Karen Pence for Teaching at Christian School," *Daily Signal*, January 16, 2019, https://www.dailysignal.com/2019/01/16/liberals-bash-karen-pence-for-teaching-at-christian-school/.
81. Albert Mohler, "Growing Secular Antipathy to Christianity on Display as New York Times Reporter Looks to 'Expose' Christian Schools," AlbertMohler.com, January 30, 2019, https://albertmohler.com/2019/01/30/briefing-1-30-19/; Dr. Susan Berry, "New York Times Wants to 'Expose Christian Schools,'" *Breitbart*, January 25, 2019, https://www.breitbart.com/politics/2019/01/25/new-york-times-wants-to-expose-christian-schools/.
82. Joy Pullman, "Progressive Va. School Refuses to Play Sports with Icky Christian Kids," *The Federalist*, January 30, 2019, https://thefederalist.com/2019/01/30/progressive-va-school-refuses-to-play-sports-with-icky-christian-kids/.
83. Brent Bozell and Tim Graham, "The Media Was Still Unglued in 2018," *Townhall*, December 26, 2019, https://townhall.com/columnists/brentbozellandtimgraham/2018/12/26/the-media-was-still-unglued-in-2018-n2538027.
84. Veronica Neffinger, "Kevin Sorbo Banned from Comicon Due to Conservative Political Leanings," Christian Headlines, January 15, 2018, https://930amtheanswer.com/articles/blogs/religion-today-blog/kevin-sorbo-banned-from-comicon-due-to-conservative-political-leanings.
85. Jack Crowe, "Judge Blocks Rule Change that Would Allow More Employers to Refuse Contraception Coverage," *National Review*, January 14, 2019.

86. James Wesolek, "Texas Democrats Seek to Ban Christianity Using So-Called Anti-Discrimination Laws," *The Federalist*, January 28, 2019, https://thefederalist.com/2019/01/28/texas-democrats-seek-ban-christianity-using-called-anti-discrimination-laws/.
87. Alex Pappas, "Dems Won't Strike 'So Help You God' from House Committee Oath after Outcry," Fox News, January 30, 2019, https://www.foxnews.com/politics/dems-wont-strike-so-help-you-god-from-house-committee-oath-after-outcry.
88. Susan Jones, "Judiciary Chairman Jerrold Nadler Omits 'So Help Me God' From Oath as He Swears in Witnesses," CNS News, February 6, 2019, https://www.cnsnews.com/news/article/susan-jones/republican-chides-democrat-judiciary-chairman-you-omitted-so-help-me-god.
89. William Newton, "Big Exhibition of J.R.R. Tolkien's Artwork Leaves Out His Christianity," *The Federalist*, February 6, 2019, https://thefederalist.com/2019/02/06/big-new-york-exhibition-j-r-r-tolkiens-artwork-leaves-christianity/.
90. Nicole Russell, "Federal Court: U-Iowa Discriminated Against Christian Student Groups," *The Federalist*, February 11, 2019, https://thefederalist.com/2019/02/11/federal-court-university-iowa-illegally-discriminated-christian-student-groups/.
91. Joy Pullman, "Left to State Supreme Court Candidate: You Can't Be a Good Judge because You're a Christian," *The Federalist*, February 18, 2019, https://thefederalist.com/2019/02/18/leftists-wi-supreme-court-candidate-cant-good-judge-youre-christian/.
92. *Christian Legal Soc. Chapter of Univ. of Cal., Hastings College of Law v. Martinez*, 561 U.S. 661 (2010).
93. "Are U.S. Colleges Hostile to Christian Students?" Belief Net, https://www.beliefnet.com/news/home-page-news-and-views/are-us-colleges-hostile-to-christian-students.aspx?.
94. Michael Gryboski, "NJ Teacher Suspended for Giving Student a Bible, Sharing a Verse," Christian Post, January 16, 2013, https://www.christianpost.com/news/nj-teacher-suspended-for-giving-student-a-bible-sharing-verse-88401/.
95. Jason Hanna and Steve Almasy, "Washington High School Coach Placed on Leave for Praying on Field," CNN, October 30, 2015, https://www.cnn.com/2015/10/29/us/washington-football-coach-joe-kennedy-prays/index.html.
96. Todd Starnes, "Atlanta Fire Chief: I Was Fired because of My Christian Faith," Fox News, January 7, 2015, https://www.foxnews.com/opinion/atlanta-fire-chief-i-was-fired-because-of-my-christian-faith.
97. Mary Eberstadt, "Regular Christians Are No Longer Welcome in American Culture," *Time*, June 29, 2016.

98. Rob Cooper, "Forcing a Religion on Your Children Is as Bad as Child Abuse, Claims Atheist Professor Richard Dawkins," *Daily Mail*, April 22, 2013.
99. Brianna Heldt, "Students Faces Suspension for Posting Bible Verses in Her School," *Townhall*, March 14, 2019, https://townhall.com/tipsheet/briannaheldt/2019/03/14/student-faces-suspension-for-posting-bible-verses-in-her-high-school-n2543138.
100. Josh Hammer, "Students at a Small Christian School Are Apparently 'Shaking' after Mike Pence Was Invited as Commencement Speaker," *Daily Wire*, April 15, 2019, https://www.dailywire.com/news/46003/students-small-christian-school-are-apparently-josh-hammer.

CHAPTER FOURTEEN

1. Ralph Benko, "The Left's War with Trump: Is America an Insane Monster or Is America the Beautiful?" *Forbes*, October 1, 2017.
2. Frank Bruni, "Donald Trump's Phony America," *New York Times*, March 4, 2019.
3. Thomas Jipping, "Are Senate Democrats in the Grip of TDS?" RealClearPolitics, February 23, 2019, https://www.realclearpolitics.com/articles/2019/02/23/are_senate_democrats_in_the_grip_of_tds_139554.html.
4. Paul Bedard, "Liberal Media Scream: Bill Maher Cheers Economic Collapse If It Dooms Trump," *Washington Examiner*, August 5, 2019.
5. "Pelosi: 'I Want Women to See That You Do Not Get Pushed Around," CNN, https://www.cnn.com/videos/politics/2018/11/09/badass-women-of-washington-nancy-pelosi-dana-bash-orig.cnn.
6. Sophie Weiner, "Nancy Pelosi and Her Supporters Are Going All Out to Save Her Job," Splinter, November 13, 2018, https://splinternews.com/nancy-pelosi-and-her-supporters-are-going-all-out-to-sa-1830400181.
7. Kyle Olson, "Maxine Meltdown! Waters Begs Americans to 'Turn the Television Off' During Trump SOTU," The American Mirror, February 5, 2019, http://www.theamericanmirror.com/maxine-sotu-meltdown-trump-not-worthy-of-being-listened-to-i-hope-people-turn-the-television-off/.
8. Liam Quinn, "Rep. Maxine Waters Attacks Trump as 'Unworthy,' Slams Summit With 'Terrorist and Killer" Kim Jong Un," Fox News, March 5, 2019, https://www.foxnews.com/politics/rep-maxine-waters-attacks-president-trump-as-unworthy-slams-summit-with-terrorist-and-killer-kim-jong-un.
9. Henry Rodgers, "Kamala Harris Says the Country Needs a President Who Can Prosecute Trump," *Daily Caller*, February 24, 2019, https://dailycaller.com/2019/02/24/kamala-harris-trump-prosecution/.
10. Aaron Colen, "Obama is Human, President Trump is 'Really Not,' Says Rep. Ilhan Omar," The Blaze, March 11, 2019, https://www.

theblaze.com/news/obama-is-human-president-trump-is-really-not-says-rep-ilhan-omar.

11. Paul Crookston, "Sen. Doug Jones (D) Was Lawyer for Dem Who Said Trump Jr. Should've Been Aborted," *Washington Free Beacon*, May 3, 2019, https://freebeacon.com/politics/sen-doug-jones-d-was-lawyer-for-dem-who-said-trump-jr-shouldve-been-aborted/.
12. Joseph Curl, "Actor Fires Back at People Hoping Dorian Will Destroy Trump's Florida Resort," *Daily Wire*, August 30, 2019, https://www.dailywire.com/news/51224/actor-fires-back-people-hoping-dorian-will-destroy-joseph-curl.
13. Melanie Arter, "DHS Secretary to Gutierrez: 'Calling Me a Liar Are Fighting Words," CNS News, December 20, 2018, https://www.cnsnews.com/news/article/melanie-arter/dhs-secretary-dem-congressman-calling-me-liar-are-fighting-words.
14. Bethany Blankley, "Yet Another Politician Gets It Wrong About Baby Jesus…Again…," Patheos, December 21, 2018, https://www.patheos.com/blogs/hedgerow/2018/12/yet-another-politician-gets-it-wrong-about-baby-jesus-again/.
15. Blankley, "Yet Another Politician Gets It Wrong About Baby Jesus…Again…"
16. Paul Crookston, "John Kerry Tells Davos Crowd Trump Should Resign," *Washington Free Beacon*, January 22, 2019, https://freebeacon.com/politics/john-kerry-tells-davos-crowd-trump-should-resign/.
17. Christopher Bedford, "Van Jones: John Lewis, Sheila Jackson Lee Opposed Criminal Justice Reform Because 'They Just Didn't Want Trump to Have A Victory,'" *Daily Caller*, January 27, 2019, https://dailycaller.com/2019/01/27/van-jones-john-lewis-sheila-jackson-lee-criminal-justice-reform-trump/.
18. Ken Meyer, "Harry Reid Says Trump is 'Amoral', Compares Him to Mobsters Who Shoot People 'In the Head,'" Mediaite, January 2, 2019, https://www.mediaite.com/online/harry-reid-says-trump-is-amoral-compares-him-to-mobsters-who-shoot-people-in-the-head/.
19. Chris Cillizza, "Harry Reid Lied About Mitt Romney's Taxes. He's Still Not Sorry," *Washington Post*, September 15, 2016.
20. Robert Reich, "State of Disunion: Democrats Must Not Give in to Trump's Hateful Speech," *The Guardian*, February 4, 2019.
21. Steve Cortes, "Trump Didn't Call Neo-Nazis 'Fine People' in Charlottesville. Here's Proof," RealClearPolitics, March 21,2019, https://www.realclearpolitics.com/articles/2019/03/21/trump_didnt_call_neo-nazis_fine_people_heres_proof_139815.html.
22. Alexandria Ocasio-Cortex (@AOC), "The President defended Neo-Nazis who murdered a woman in Charlottesville. The Dept of Justice sued him for not renting to Black tenants. He launched his campaign by called Mexicans 'rapists.' He banned Muslims. The President is racist. And that should make

you uncomfortable," Twitter, January 8, 2019, 2:05 p.m., https://twitter.com/AOC/status/1082760135359905793?ref_src=twsrc%5Etfw%7Ctwcamp%5Etweetembed%7Ctwterm%5E1082760135359905793&ref_url=https%3A%2F%2Fthehill.com%2Fhomenews%2Fhouse%2F424435-ocasio-cortez-trump-is-racist-and-that-should-make-you-uncomfortable.

23. Tim Hains, "Carl Bernstein: Border Wall Is a Symbol That Says 'Brown People, We Don't Want You,'" RealClearPolitics, January 8, 2019, https://www.realclearpolitics.com/video/2019/01/08/carl_bernstein_border_wall_is_a_symbol_that_says_brown_people_we_dont_want_you.html.
24. Ryan Foley, "MSNBC's Hayes: Trump's Base Wants 'an Ethnically Pure America,'" NewsBusters, Janurary 12, 2019, https://www.newsbusters.org/blogs/nb/ryan-foley/2019/01/12/msnbcs-hayes-trumps-base-wants-ethnically-pure-america.
25. David Marcus, "Does AOC Have Any Basis for Smearing Trump as an Anti-Semite?" *The Federalist*, January 21, 2019, https://thefederalist.com/2019/01/21/does-aoc-have-any-basis-for-smearing-trump-as-an-anti-semite/.
26. Chris Enloe, "House Democrat Admits 'Sole Focus' Is Unseating President Trump, Not Legislative Accomplishments," The Blaze, April 28, 2019, https://www.theblaze.com/news/house-democrat-sole-focus-unseat-trump.
27. Mark Hensch, "Comey Farewell: 'A President Can Fire an FBI Director for Any Reason,'" *The Hill*, May 10, 2017.
28. Byron York, "What, Precisely, Do Democrats Want to Impeach Trump For?" *Washington Examiner*, January 6, 2019.
29. Tim Hains, "Rep. Al Green: 'I'm Concerned If We Don't Impeach This President, He Will Get Re-Elected," RealClearPolitics, May 6, 2019, https://www.realclearpolitics.com/video/2019/05/06/al_green_im_concerned_if_we_dont_impeach_this_president_he_will_get_re-elected.html.
30. Ryan Bort, "Rep. Rashida Tlaib Calls Trump a 'Motherf-cker' White Promising Impeachment," *Rolling Stone*, January 4, 2019.
31. Joe Concha, "Joy Behar Defends Freshman Dem's Impeachment Remarks: 'I Identify with Her," *The Hill*, January 4, 2019.
32. Concha, "Joy Behar Defends Freshman Dem's Impeachment Remarks: 'I Identify with Her.'"
33. Brian Flood, "Joy Behar: Media Jumped Gun on Covington Video Because 'We're Desperate to Get Trump Out of Office," Fox News, January 23, 2019, https://www.foxnews.com/entertainment/joy-behar-media-jumped-gun-on-covington-video-because-were-desperate-to-get-trump-out-of-office.
34. Brian Flood, "Joy Behar's Joyless 2018: 'The View' Star's Most over-the-Top-Anti-Trumpiness of the Year," Fox News, December 19, 2018,

https://www.foxnews.com/entertainment/the-view-star-joy-behars-anti-trump-statements-of-2018.

35. Brian Flood, "Melania Trump Rep Slams 'The View' for 'Shameful' Body Double Segment," Fox News, March 12, 2019, https://www.foxnews.com/entertainment/melania-trump-rep-slams-the-view-for-shameful-body-double-segment.
36. "I'd Like to Punch Him in the Face," *Washington Post*, October 25, 2016.
37. Alicia Melville-Smith, "Robert De Niro Calls Trump an 'Idiot' and a 'National Disaster," *Buzzfeed*, October 8, 2016, https://www.buzzfeednews.com/article/aliciamelvillesmith/robert-de-niro-calls-trump-a-pig-a-bozo-and-a-bullshit-artis.
38. Rebecca Rubin, "Robert De Niro Says 'F—- Trump' at Tony Awards, Gets Standing Ovation," *Variety*, June 10, 2018.
39. Damian Jones, "Robert De Niro Hits Out at Donald Trump Again," NME, April 5, 2018, https://www.nme.com/news/film/robert-de-niro-hits-out-at-donald-trump-again-2283192.
40. Kelsey Harkness, "Art Exhibit Invites People to Throw Trash at Ivanka Trump Lookalike," *The Federalist*, February 4, 2019, https://thefederalist.com/2019/02/04/art-exhibit-invites-people-throw-trash-vacuuming-ivanka-trump-lookalike/.
41. Julio Rosas, "More Patriots Players Say They Won't Visit the White House If Invited: 'I Highly Doubt it,'" Mediaite, February 5, 2019, https://www.mediaite.com/online/more-patriots-players-say-they-wont-visit-the-white-house-if-invited-i-highly-doubt-it/.
42. Emily Zanotti, "SAD: Harry Potter Actor Won't Root for Tom Brady in the Super Bowl over Trump Hat," *Daily Wire*, January 27, 2019, https://www.dailywire.com/news/42697/sad-harry-potter-actor-wont-root-tom-brady-super-emily-zanotti.
43. Andrew Mark Miller, "Girl Who Bragged about Berating Man with MAGA Hat Doesn't Understand Why People Are Upset with Her," Diamond and Silk, April 30, 2019, https://www.diamondandsilk.com/blog/2019/04/30/girl-who-bragged-about-berating-man-with-maga-hat-doesnt-understand-why-people-are-upset-with-her-4/.
44. "Alabama Abortion Law: Jim Carrey Paints Portrait of Alabama Gov. Kay Ivey Being Aborted," AL.com, May 20, 2019, https://www.al.com/news/2019/05/alabama-abortion-law-jim-carrey-paints-controversial-portrait-of-alabama-gov-kay-ivey.html.
45. James Barrett, "Jim Carrey Targets Trump Admin Women in More Bizarre & Bitter Posts," *Daily Wire*, December 28, 2018, https://www.dailywire.com/news/39745/jim-carrey-targets-trump-admin-women-more-bizarre-james-barrett.
46. Lee Moran, "Jim Carrey Shares Cartoon Theory of Devolution about Donald Trump's Supporters," *HuffPost*, January 5, 2019, https://

www.huffpost.com/entry/jim-carrey-donald-trump-supporters_n_5c30571ee4b0bcb4c25bdcb4.

47. John Bowden, "Mark Hamill Says Darth Vader Better Than Trump: 'He Saw the Error of His Ways'," *The Hill*, December 27, 2018.
48. Zachary Leeman, "Chelsea Handler Says Trump Supporters Don't Care That He Is a 'Criminal'," LifeZette, March 5, 2019, https://www.lifezette.com/2019/03/chelsea-handler-says-trump-supporters-dont-care-that-he-is-a-criminal/.
49. Jessica Chasmar, "Chelsea Handler Says Trump Election Drove Her to Therapy: 'I Had a Midlife Identity Crisis," *Washington Times*, April 8, 2019.
50. Hillary Lewis, "Meryl Streep on Why People 'Should Be Afraid' of Trump," *Hollywood Reporter*, December 9, 2018.
51. "Maher: 'Trump Is Holding This Country Hostage, You Don't Deal with Terrorists,'" CNS News, January 20, 2019, https://www.cnsnews.com/video/maher-trump-holding-country-hostage-you-dont-deal-terrorists.
52. Alex Rogers, "Democratic Leaders Dig in on Wall Fight: 'Trump Must Stop Holding the American People Hostage,'" CNN Politics, January 9, 2019, https://www.cnn.com/2019/01/08/politics/democratic-response-trump-speech-pelosi-schumer/index.html.
53. Scott Whitlock, "MSNBC Dismisses Trump's 'Immigrant Crime Stuff' 'Scam' Speech," NewsBusters, January 8, 2019, https://www.newsbusters.org/blogs/nb/scott-whitlock/2019/01/08/msnbc-dismisses-trumps-immigrant-crime-stuff-scam-speech.
54. "Menendez: Trump 'Lies' and Plays 'Fast' with 'Half-Truths' About the Border," Grabien, January 8, 2019, https://grabien.com/story.php?id=216149.
55. Josh Feldman, "Chuck Todd Previews Trump Address: POTUS 'Manufactured One Heck of a Political Crisis for Himself,'" Mediaite, January 8, 2019, https://www.mediaite.com/tv/chuck-todd-previews-trump-address-potus-manufactured-one-heck-of-a-political-crisis-for-himself/.
56. "Rep. Clarke on the Shutdown: Trump 'Has Fashioned Himself After a Banana Republic Dictator, a Con Man,'" Grabien, January 8, 2019, https://grabien.com/story.php?id=216153.
57. Greg Price, "Peter Strzok Was Asked 'What Does Trump Support Smell Like?' and If They're 'Hillbillies' During Wild House Hearing," *Newsweek*, July 12, 2018.
58. Kristine Phillips, "Politico Reporter Apologizes for Calling CNN Haters at Trump Rally 'Garbage People' with Bad Teeth," *Washington Post*, August 2, 2018.
59. Hank Berrien, "WATCH: Kimmel Mocks Donors to GoFundMe Page for Border Wall: 'Dopey People… These People Are Dipping into Their Meth Money for This,'" *Daily Wire*, December 21, 2018, https://www.

dailywire.com/news/39610/watch-kimmel-mocks-donors-gofundme-page-border-hank-berrien.

60. Kevin Williamson, "Why Outrage Over Sean Spicer's Casting on Dancing with the Stars Is a Double Standard," *New York Post*, August 24, 2019.
61. Jennifer Epstein, "Immigration Groups Ask Fortune 500 CEOs to Blacklist Trump Aides," Bloomberg, April 5, 2019, https://www.bloomberg.com/news/articles/2019-04-05/immigration-groups-ask-fortune-500-ceos-to-blacklist-trump-aides.
62. Alex Parker, "'Hail Satan': Satanists Fight Trump, & Satanic Temple Founder Says He's Comin' For All You Theocrats," *RedState*, March 9, 2019, https://www.redstate.com/alexparker/2019/03/09/lucien-greaves-penny-lane-indiewire-hail-satan-interview-donald-trump-theocracy-theocratic-right/.

CHAPTER FIFTEEN

1. Rich Noyes, "Networks Trashed Trump with 90% Negative Spin in 2018, But Did It Matter?" NewsBusters, January 15, 2019, https://www.newsbusters.org/blogs/nb/rich-noyes/2019/01/15/networks-trashed-trump-90-negative-spin-2018-did-it-matter.
2. Bill D'Agostino, "Networks: 2,201 Minutes on Russia Scandal, Zero for No Collusion Report," NewsBusters, February 14, 2019, https://www.newsbusters.org/blogs/nb/bill-dagostino/2019/02/14/networks-2202-minutes-russia-scandal-zero-no-collusion-report.
3. Kristine Marsh, "CNN's Navarro Tells Fed Workers: Rack Up Bills at Trump Hotels, Refuse to Pay," NewsBusters, January 25, 2019, https://www.newsbusters.org/blogs/nb/kristine-marsh/2019/01/25/cnns-navarro-tells-fed-workers-rack-bills-trump-hotels-and-refuse.
4. John Cage, "Boston Globe Writer Urgers Waiters to 'Tamper' with Food of Republicans," *Washington Examiner*, April 12, 2019.
5. Victor Morton, "Donald Trump Jr. Condemns Jemele Hill over 'Getcho Hand out My Pocket' State of the Union Tweet," *Washington Times*, February 6, 2019.
6. Brent Bozell and Tim Graham, "These Boots Are Made for Double Standards," *Townhall*, December 28, 2018, https://townhall.com/columnists/brentbozellandtimgraham/2018/12/28/these-boots-are-made-for-double-standards-n2538154.
7. Devan Cole, "Michelle Obama on 2017 Inauguration: 'Bye, Felicia,'" CNN Politics, December 20, 2018, https://www.cnn.com/2018/12/19/politics/michelle-obama-jimmy-fallon-inauguration/index.html.
8. Bridget Read, "Melania Trump Unveils the 2018 White House Christmas Decorations, and They're Straight Out of Gilead," *Vogue*, November 26, 2018.

9. "What's Up with This Year's Surreal White House Christmas Portrait?" *Vogue*, December 18, 2018.
10. Dan, "Video: Kimmel Cracks Another Joke about Ivanka Trump and It Backfired Horribly," Daily Headlines, December 14, 2018, http://dailyheadlines.com/video-kimmel-cracks-another-joke-about-ivanka-trump-and-it-backfired-horribly/.
11. Quin Hillyer, "CNN Opinions Dressed as Facts Really are 'Fake News,'" *Washington Examiner*, January 8, 2019.
12. Beth Baumann, "'We Know Their Narrative': Laura Logan Trashes Mainstream Media during 'Hannity' Interview," *Townhall*, May 4, 2019, https://townhall.com/tipsheet/bethbaumann/2019/02/20/we-know-their-narrative-lara-logan-trashes-mainstream-media-during-hannity-i-n2541977.
13. Mollie Hemingway, "Media's Angry Response to President Trump's Oval Office Speech Comes Up Short," *The Federalist*, January 9, 2019, https://thefederalist.com/2019/01/09/medias-angry-response-to-president-trumps-oval-office-speech-comes-up-short/.
14. Amber Athey, "KUSI Accuses CNN of Declining an Interview After Finding Out Reporter Was Pro-Wall," *Daily Caller*, January 11, 2019, https://dailycaller.com/2019/01/11/kusi-cnn-interview-border-wall/.
15. Mike Brest, "Border Security Experts Explain Why Only One Cable Network Wants to Talk to Them," *Daily Caller*, January 14, 2019, https://dailycaller.com/2019/01/14/judd-homan-border-wall-cnn-msnbc/.
16. Adam Michel, "Don't Believe the Fake News. Tax Cuts for Everyday Americans Are Real," *Daily Signa*l, February 13, 2019, https://www.dailysignal.com/2019/02/13/dont-believe-the-fake-news-tax-cuts-for-everyday-americans-are-real/.
17. Ryan Saavedra, "WATCH: ABC News Mocks Trump as They Fantasize about His Death," *Daily Wire*, December 6, 2018, https://www.dailywire.com/news/39124/watch-abc-news-mocks-trump-they-fantasize-about-ryan-saavedra.
18. Jacob Airey, "Klavan: Media Uses Bush Funeral to Attack Trump," *Daily Wire*, December 7, 2018, https://www.dailywire.com/news/39139/klavan-media-uses-bush-funeral-attack-trump-jacob-airey.
19. Emily Zanotti, "Daily Beast Writer Smears Patriots as 'The Preferred Team of White Nationalists," *Daily Wire*, February 3, 2019, https://www.dailywire.com/news/42994/daily-beast-writer-smears-patriots-preferred-team-emily-zanotti.
20. Lloyd Marcus, "It Is Outrageous that Supporting Trump Is Dangerous," American Thinker, April 3, 2019, https://tmp.americanthinker.com/articles/2019/04/it_is_outrageous_that_supporting_trump_is_dangerous.html.
21. Ethel C. Fenig, "Chicago's Mayor Blames Trump for Jussie Smollett Hoax," American Thinker, March 30, 2019, https://www.

americanthinker.com/blog/2019/03/chicagos_mayor_blames_trump_for_jussie_smollett_hoax.html.

22. Mike Brest, "The Atlantic Writer Suggests Trump Is to Blame for College Bribery Scandal," *Daily Caller*, March 14, 2019, https://dailycaller.com/2019/03/14/atlantic-trump-bribery-scandal-college/.
23. Joseph A. Wulfsohn, "NBC News Panel Blames Trump for Gov. Ralph Northam's Blackface Scandal," Fox News, February 5, 2019, https://www.foxnews.com/entertainment/nbc-news-panel-blames-trump-for-gov-ralph-northams-blackface-scandal.
24. Mike Lillis, "Citing Virginia Race Scandals, Dem Vows Vote to Impeach Trump," *The Hill*, February 8, 2019.
25. John Nolte, "Nolte: Nine Reasons to Be Skeptical of BuzzFeed's Cohen Report," *Breitbart*, January 18, 2019, https://www.breitbart.com/the-media/2019/01/18/nolte-nine-reasons-to-be-skeptical-of-buzzfeeds-cohen-report/.
26. Nolte, "Nolte: Lying Media Shell-Shocked by Robert Mueller's Fact Check," *Breitbart*, January 19, 2019, https://www.realclearpolitics.com/2019/01/21/lying_media_shell-shocked_by_mueller039s_fact_check_463911.html
27. Devlin Barrett, Matt Zapotosky, and Karoun Demirjian, "In a Rare Move, Mueller's Office Denies BuzzFeed Report That Trump Told Cohen to Lie About Moscow Project," *Washington Post*, January 18, 2019.
28. Michael Barone, "Does the Media Deserve to Be Respected and Believed?" *Townhall*, January 25, 2019, https://townhall.com/columnists/michaelbarone/2019/01/25/does-the-media-deserve-to-be-respected-and-believed-n2540213.
29. "Trump Denies Calling Meghan 'Nasty' Despite Audio Recording," BBC, June 2, 2019, https://www.bbc.com/news/world-us-canada-48491602.
30. William Saletan, "The Least Pro-Life President Ever," *Slate*, February 8, 2019, https://slate.com/news-and-politics/2019/02/trump-is-not-pro-life.html.
31. Brent Bozell and Tim Graham, "The Media Was Still Unglued in 2018," *Townhall*, December 26, 2019, https://townhall.com/columnists/brentbozellandtimgraham/2018/12/26/the-media-was-still-unglued-in-2018-n2538027.
32. Matt Vespa, "Where Was the Media Outrage When 18 Migrants Died in Custody under the Obama Administration?" *Townhall*, December 27, 2018, https://townhall.com/tipsheet/mattvespa/2018/12/27/where-was-the-media-outrage-when-18-migrants-died-in-custody-under-the-obama-administration-n2538105.
33. Hank Berrien, "WATCH: CBS Anchor to DHS Official: How Could You Let Sick Immigrant Child Out of Hospital? Official: Uh, Have You Heard of Doctors?" *Daily Wire*, December 26, 2018, https://

www.dailywire.com/news/39699/watch-cbs-anchor-dhs-official-how-could-you-let-hank-berrien.

34. Vespa, "Where Was the Media Outrage When 18 Migrants Died in Custody under the Obama Administration?"
35. Brad Wilmouth, "On MSNBC, Radio Host Mark Thompson Claims Baby Jesus Might Have Died Under Trump," NewsBusters, January 3, 2019, https://www.newsbusters.org/blogs/nb/brad-wilmouth/2019/01/03/msnbc-thompson-claims-baby-jesus-might-have-died-under-trump.
36. Brad Wilmouth, "MSNBC Blames Trump for 'Forcing' Illegals to Cross Desert," NewsBusters, January 2, 2019, https://www.newsbusters.org/blogs/nb/brad-wilmouth/2018/12/30/msnbc-blames-trump-forcing-illegals-cross-desert.
37. Daniel Horowitz, "The Media Never Cares When Americans Are Killed by Illegal Immigrants," *Conservative Review*, December 31, 2018, https://www.conservativereview.com/news/the-media-never-cares-when-americans-are-killed-by-illegal-immigrants/.
38. Cortney O'Brien, "Huh: Don Lemon Suggests There Be an On Air 'Delay' During Trump's Speech," *Townhall*, January 8, 2019, https://townhall.com/tipsheet/cortneyobrien/2019/01/08/don-lemon-suggests-there-be-an-on-air-delay-during-trumps-speech-n2538666.
39. Joseph Curl, "SHOCKER: Former Top Editor of New York Times Admits Newspaper Is Anti-Trump," *Daily Wire*, January 2, 2019, https://www.dailywire.com/news/39857/shocker-former-editor-new-york-times-admits-joseph-curl.
40. Jim Clayton, "MSNBC Witches Fantasize About Ivanka Being Arrested," Conservative Daily News, December 18, 2018, https://www.conservativedailynews.com/2018/12/msnbc-witches-fantasize-about-ivanka-being-arrested/.
41. Ken Meyer, "CNN Security Analyst: Mueller Report Will Disclose How Trump and Family Are Compromised by Russians," Mediaite, January 14, 2019, https://www.mediaite.com/tv/cnn-security-analyst-mueller-report-will-disclose-how-trump-and-family-are-compromised-by-russians/.
42. Daniel Chaitin, "Carl Bernstein: Draft of Mueller's Final Report Says Trump Helped Putin 'Destablize' the US," *Washington Examiner*, January 13, 2019.
43. Josh Feldman, "Jon Meacham on Stunning NYT Trump Report: 'This is What the Founders Were Worried About,'" Mediaite, January 12, 2019, https://www.mediaite.com/tv/jon-meacham-on-stunning-nyt-trump-report-this-is-what-the-founders-were-worried-about/.
44. David Harsayni, "The Media Have Done Irreparable Damage to the Country," *The Federalist*, March 25, 2019, https://thefederalist.com/2019/03/25/media-irreparable-damage-to-the-country/.

45. Ashley Feinberg, "The New York Times Unites vs. Twitter," *Slate*, August 15, 2019, https://slate.com/news-and-politics/2019/08/new-york-times-meeting-transcript.html.
46. Tom Rogan, "Whoever Convinced Most Democrats That Putin Hacked the Election Tallies Is Doing Putin's Bidding," *Washington Examiner*, November 19, 2019.
47. Matthew Continetti, "The Liberal Media 'Matrix,'" *Washington Free Beacon*, April 12, 2019, https://freebeacon.com/columns/the-liberal-media-matrix/.
48. Kimberly Leonard, "Secret Group Wants Psychiatric Panel to Judge the Mental Health of Trump," *Washington Examiner*, February 8, 2019.
49. Josh Feldman, "Lawrence O'Donnell: Right to Wonder Today If There's 'Something Wrong' with 'The President's Mind,'" Mediaite, April 2, 2019, https://www.mediaite.com/tv/lawrence-odonnell-you-had-the-right-to-wonder-today-if-theres-something-wrong-with-the-presidents-mind/.
50. Ken Meyer, "Scarborough Calls for 25th Amendment: Trump's Presser Shows He's 'Obviously' Not Fit for Office," Mediaite, January 3, 2019, https://www.mediaite.com/tv/scarborough-calls-for-25th-amendment-trumps-presser-shows-hes-obviously-not-fit-for-office/.
51. "Top Chef Host: The Only Crisis in America Is We Have a Lunatic with a Lot of Power," Grabien, https://grabien.com/story.php?id=226221.
52. Matthew Vadum, "The Left's Smirking MAGA Kid Hoax," Canada Free Press, January 22, 2019, https://canadafreepress.com/article/the-lefts-smirking-maga-kid-hoax.
53. Alex Griswold, "Kathy Griffin Falsely Accuses Covington Catholic Basketball Players of Throwing Up 'Nazi Sign,'" *Washington Free Beacon*, January 22, 2019, https://freebeacon.com/politics/kathy-griffin-falsely-accuses-covington-catholic-basketball-players-nazi-sign/.
54. Elie Mystal, "Dear Media, Please Cut the Sob Stories about Trump Voters Hurt by Trump Policies," The Nation, January 8, 2019.
55. Mystal, "Dear Media, Please Cut the Sob Stories about Trump Voters Hurt by Trump Policies."

CHAPTER SIXTEEN

1. Damon Linker, "Liberals Have Lost Their Minds over Immigration," *The Week*, January 30, 2018.
2. Amber Athey, "Liberals Livid with New York Times For Pro-Stephen Miller Opinion Piece," *Daily Caller*, January 29, 2018, https://dailycaller.com/2018/01/29/liberals-livid-with-new-york-times-for-pro-stephen-miller-opinion-piece/.
3. Jeremy Binckes, "To Ross Douthat, White Immigration Is the Only Good Immigration," *Salon*, January 29, 2018, https://www.salon.

com/2018/01/29/to-ross-douthat-white-immigration-is-the-only-good-immigration/.

4. Damon Linker, "Liberals Have Lost Their Minds over Immigration."
5. Niv Elis, "Ocasio-Cortez Sends Christmas Greeting to 'Refugee Babies in Mangers,'" *The Hill*, December 25, 2018.
6. Part of this paragraph was borrowed from an earlier column I wrote: David Limbaugh, "How Compassionate Is the Democrats' Open-Borders Policy?" Creators Syndicate, December 28, 2018, https://www.creators.com/read/david-limbaugh/12/18/how-compassionate-is-the-democrats-open-borders-policy.
7. Madeline Osburn, "O'Rourke: I'd Destroy the Entire Border Wall If I Could," *The Federalist*, February 15, 2019, https://thefederalist.com/2019/02/15/orourke-id-destroy-entire-border-wall/.
8. Chip Roy, "Lawless Borders Are a Humanitarian Crisis," *The Federalist*, January 9, 2019, https://thefederalist.com/2019/01/09/lawless-borders-humanitarian-crisis-past-time-finally-solve/.
9. "Heroin Overdose Data," Centers for Disease Control and Prevention, December 19, 2018, https://www.cdc.gov/drugoverdose/data/heroin.html.
10. "2018 National Drug Threat Assessment," U.S. Department of Justice Drug Enforcement Administration, October 2018, https://www.dea.gov/sites/default/files/2018-11/DIR-032-18%202018%20NDTA%20%5Bfinal%5D%20low%20resolution11-20.pdf.
11. Beth Bailey, "By Weaponing Border Policy, Democrats Play Games with Lives," *The Federalist*, February 15, 2019, https://thefederalist.com/2019/02/15/weaponizing-border-policy-democrats-play-political-games-peoples-lives/.
12. Congresswoman Vicki Hartzler, "Why We Need to Take Action on Border Security," *Townhall*, February 21, 2019, https://townhall.com/capitol-voices/congresswomanvickyhartzler/2019/02/21/why-i-stand-by-president-trumps-emergency-declaration-to-build-a-border-wall-n2542026.
13. Walter E. Williams, "History Lesson Explains Shifting Political Stances on Illegal Immigration," *Daily Signal*, January 16, 2019, https://www.dailysignal.com/2019/01/16/a-history-lesson-on-the-shifting-political-stances-on-illegal-immigration/.
14. Charles Hurt, "Pelosi, Schumer Have a Border-Security Problem with the American People," *Washington Times*, January 8, 2019.
15. Brandon Morse, "Wow! The Washington Post Just Gave Trump a Huge Helping Hand on the Border Crisis in Time for His Address," *RedState*, January 8, 2019, https://www.redstate.com/brandon_morse/2019/01/08/wow-washington-post-just-gave-trump-huge-helping-hand-border-crisis-time-address/.
16. Matt Vespa, "No Border Crisis? Even This WaPo Reporter Said February's Illegal Alien Apprehension Numbers Were 'Bonkers,'"

Townhall, March 6, 2019, https://townhall.com/tipsheet/mattvespa/2019/03/06/no-border-crisis-even-this-wapo-reporter-said-februarys-illegal-alien-apprehension-numbers-were-bonkers-n2542667.

17. Jennifer Agiesta, "CNN Poll: Three-Quarters of Americans Say There's a Crisis at the Border," CNN, July 2, 2019, https://www.cnn.com/2019/07/02/politics/cnn-poll-immigration-border-crisis/index.html.
18. Stephen Dinan, "87% of Illegal Immigrant Families Are No-Shows for Deportation: ICE," *Washington Times*, May 9, 2019.
19. Jack Crowe, "DHS Secretary: 90 Percent of Recent Asylum-Seekers Skipped Their Hearings," *National Review*, June 11, 2019.
20. Julia Ainsley, "February Had Highest Total of Undocumented Immigrants Crossing U.S. Border in 12 Years," NBC News, March 5, 2019, https://www.nbcnews.com/politics/immigration/highest-february-total-undocumented-immigrants-crossing-u-s-border-12-n979546.
21. Thomas Lifson, "Watch the Long Faces as Jeh Johnson, Obama's DHS Secretary, Tells MSNBC That the Border is 'Truly in Crisis,'" American Thinker, March 30, 2019, https://www.americanthinker.com/blog/2019/03/watch_the_long_faces_as_jeh_johnson_obamas_dhs_secretary_tells_msnbc_that_the_border_truly_in_a_crisis.html.
22. Byron York, "How Bad Does Border Have to Be for Democrats to Admit It's an Emergency?" *Townhall*, April 2, 2019, https://townhall.com/columnists/byronyork/2019/04/02/how-bad-does-border-have-to-be-for-democrats-to-admit-its-an-emergency-n2544171.
23. Jack Crowe, "Border Patrol Union President: 'This Is the Worst Crisis' in Agency's History," *National Review*, April 2, 2019.
24. "Southwest Border Migration FY 2019," U.S. Customs and Border Protection, May 8, 2019, https://www.cbp.gov/newsroom/stats/sw-border-migration.
25. York, "How Bad Does Border Have to Be for Democrats to Admit It's an Emergency?"
26. Editorial, "Yes, There Is a Crisis at the Border – The Numbers Show It," *Investor's Business Daily*, January 10, 2019.
27. "Illegal Immigration Around the World: 13 Countries Compared to the United States," ProCon.org, March 12, 2013, https://immigration.procon.org/view.resource.php?resourceID=005235.
28. John Wagner, "Trump Touted Obama's 2005 Remarks on Immigration. Here's What Obama Actually Said," *Washington Post*, October 24, 2018; Editorial, "Yes, There Is a Crisis at the Border – The Numbers Show It."
29. Jarrett Stepman, "Fact-Checking 5 of Trump's Claims in Border Speech," *Daily Signal*, January 9, 2019, https://www.dailysignal.com/2019/01/09/fact-checking-5-of-trumps-claims-in-border-speech/.
30. Sumantra Maitra, "Don't Let Ocasio-Cortez Dance around the Facts of Immigration," *The Federalist*, January 9, 2019, https://thefederalist.

com/2019/01/09/dont-let-ocasio-cortez-party-dance-around-facts-immigration/.

31. Paul Bedard, "Census Confirms: 63 Percent of 'Non-Citizens' on Welfare, 4.6 Million Households," *Washington Examiner*, December 3, 2018.
32. Ian Schwartz, "Alexandria Ocasio-Cortez: Illegal Immigrants Act More American Than Citizens Trying to Keep Them Out," RealClearPolitics, January 8, 2019, https://www.realclearpolitics.com/video/2019/01/08/alexandria_ocasio-cortez_illegal_immigrants_act_more_american_than_citizens_trying_to_keep_them_out.html.
33. Bedard, "Census Confirms: 63 Percent of 'Non-Citizens' on Welfare, 4.6 Million Households."
34. Doug P., "This Will Be in a Trump Ad: Guess How Many Dems Raised Their Hands after Being Asked If Illegals Would Be Covered Under Their Health Plans," Twitchy, June 27, 2019, https://twitchy.com/dougp-3137/2019/06/27/this-will-be-in-a-trump-ad-guess-how-many-dems-raised-their-hands-after-being-asked-if-illegals-would-be-covered-under-their-health-plans/.
35. Ben Weingarten, "Why Don't Democrats Want Noncitizens Recorded on the Census?" *The Federalist*, February 21, 2019, https://thefederalist.com/2019/02/21/dont-democrats-want-census-find-many-noncitizens-live-united-states/.
36. Roy, "Lawless Borders Are A Humanitarian Crisis."
37. Adam Isacson and Maureen Meyer, "WOLA Report: Lessons from San Diego's Border Wall," WOLA, December 14, 2017, https://www.wola.org/analysis/wola-report-lessons-san-diegos-border-wall/.
38. Matt Gaetz, "Rep. Gaetz: Border Walls Work, and Democrats Know It," *USA Today*, February 4, 2019.
39. Frank Camp, "The Daily Wire Speaks with Author and Former Israeli Mayor David Rubin about the Effectiveness of Border Walls," *Daily Wire*, December 21, 2018, https://www.dailywire.com/news/39603/daily-wire-speaks-author-and-former-israeli-mayor-frank-camp.
40. Miriam Valverde, "Border Fence in Israel Cut Illegal Immigration by 99 Percent, GOP Senator Says," PolitiFact, February 13, 2017, https://www.politifact.com/truth-o-meter/statements/2017/feb/13/ron-johnson/border-fence-israel-cut-illegal-immigration-99-per/.
41. President Donald J. Trump (@realDonaldTrump), "There are now 77 major or significant walls built around the world, with 45 countries planning or building walls. Over 800 miles of walls have been built in Europe since only 2015. They have all been recognized as close to 100% successful. Stop the crime at our Southern Border!" Twitter, January 16, 2019, 4:33 a.m., https://twitter.com/realdonaldtrump/status/1085515276228153345?lang=en.

42. Palko Karasz, "Fact Check: Trump's Tweet on Border Walls in Europe," *New York Times*, January 17, 2019.
43. Evie Fordham, "Trump Touts Other Border Walls around the Globe as 'Close to 100 Percent Successful,'" *Daily Caller*, January 16, 2019, https://dailycaller.com/2019/01/16/trump-border-wall-world/.
44. Michael Rubin, "Trump's Border Wall Is Standard Practice in Other Parts of the World," *Washington Examiner*, January 23, 2018.
45. Rubin, "Trump's Border Wall Is Standard Practice in Other Parts of the World."
46. Daniel Horowitz, "3 Reasons Why the Media's 'Walls Won't Work to Stop Drugs' Argument Is Wrong," *Conservative Review*, January 14, 2019, https://www.conservativereview.com/news/3-reasons-why-the-medias-walls-wont-work-to-stop-drugs-argument-is-wrong/.
47. James Barrett, "WATCH: Body Cam Footage of Cops' Shootout with Illegal Alien Protected from ICE by CA's Sanctuary Laws Just Two Days Earlier," *Daily Wire*, December 21, 2018, https://www.dailywire.com/news/39584/watch-body-cam-footage-cops-shootout-illegal-alien-james-barrett.
48. Mark Finkelstein, "Jim VandeHei on MSNBC: Dem 'Enthusiasm' to Protect Illegals, Not Borders," NewsBusters, January 2, 2019, https://www.newsbusters.org/blogs/nb/mark-finkelstein/2019/01/02/axios-vandehei-dem-enthusiasm%E2%80%94protect-illegal-immigrants-not.
49. Jason Hopkins, "New York Democrats Pass Bill to Fund College for Illegal Immigrants," *Daily Signal*, January 28, 2019, https://www.dailysignal.com/2019/01/28/new-york-democrats-pass-bill-to-fund-college-for-illegal-immigrants/.
50. Karen Matthews, "Mayor Says NYC Will Expand Health Coverage to 600,000 People," AP News, January 8, 2019, https://www.apnews.com/f7217b88cb5f415788ea45b591ee1ee6
51. Kimberly Leonard, "California Democrats Plan to Extend Medicaid to Illegal Immigrants," *Washington Examiner*, December 3, 2018.
52. Henry Rodgers, "Democrats and Republicans Reach 'Agreement in Principle' on Border Security," *Daily Caller*, February 11, 2019, https://dailycaller.com/2019/02/11/democrats-republicans-agreement-border-wall/.
53. Henry Rodgers, "Democrats Remain Defiant, Double Down on Ice Bed Cap as Border Negotiations Close," *Daily Caller*, February 12, 2019, https://dailycaller.com/2019/02/12/dems-ice-bed-cap-border-deal/.
54. Paul Bedard, "Sheriffs Storm Capitol Hill to Demand Border Wall, ICE Funding," *Washington Examiner*, February 11, 2019.
55. Farhad Manjoo, "There's Nothing Wrong with Open Borders," *New York Times*, January 16, 2019.
56. Frank Camp, "CAMP: How Is the Democratic Border Security Solution Morally Different from Trump's Wall?" *Daily Wire*,

December 21, 2018, https://www.dailywire.com/news/39607/camp-how-democratic-border-security-solution-frank-camp.

57. Katie Pavlich, "Democrats (Again) Side with Criminal Illegal Aliens in Amnesty Bill," *Townhall*, June 5, 2019, https://townhall.com/tipsheet/katiepavlich/2019/06/05/the-democrats-daca-bill-is-full-of-loopholes-for-criminals-n2547479.
58. Thomas Lifson, "One Eve of Tonight's Dem Debate, Elizabeth Warren Calls for Decriminalizing Border Violations," American Thinker, June 26, 2019, https://www.americanthinker.com/blog/2019/06/on_eve_of_tonights_dem_debate_elizabeth_warren_calls_for_decriminalizing_border_violations.html.
59. Mollie Hemingway (@MZHemingway), Twitter, February 21, 2019.
60. Dan Crenshaw (@DanCrenshawTX), "The extreme rhetoric surrounding the border security debate has turned radical ideas into aggressive actions. Vandalizing buildings & targeting our border agents is a fast way to discredit your argument. Incredible that enforcing our laws is somehow see as morally corrupt," Twitter, February 20, 2019 9:46 a.m., https://twitter.com/dancrenshawtx/status/1098277792347799554?lang=en.
61. Kristine Marsh, "Outrageous! Chris Cuomo: Republicans Want Illegals to Kill Americans Because It's 'Convenient'," NewsBusters, February 8, 2019, https://www.newsbusters.org/blogs/nb/kristine-marsh/2019/02/08/outrageous-chris-cuomo-republicans-want-illegals-kill-americans.
62. George Neumayr, "The Immorality of the Open Borders Party," *American Spectator*, January 18, 2019.
63. Fred Lucas, "Answers to 4 Big Questions About Sending Immigrants to Sanctuary Cities," *Daily Signal*, April 16, 2019, https://www.dailysignal.com/2019/04/16/answers-to-4-big-questions-about-trumps-interest-in-sending-illegal-immigrants-to-sanctuary-cities/.
64. Julio Rosas, "Cher Asks How Can Los Angeles Take More Immigrants: 'MY CITY… ISNT TAKING CARE OF ITS OWN,'" Mediaite, April 15, 2019, https://www.mediaite.com/online/cher-asks-how-can-los-angeles-take-more-immigrants-my-city-isnt-taking-care-of-its-own/.
65. Sharyl Attkisson, "One in Five US Prison Inmates Is a 'Criminal Alien,'" *The Hill*, September 19, 2018.
66. Terence P. Jeffrey, "5 Federal Courts on Mexican Border Lead Nation in Criminal Convictions," CNS News, April 3, 2019, https://www.cnsnews.com/commentary/terence-p-jeffrey/5-federal-courts-mexican-border-lead-nation-criminal-convictions.
67. Attkisson, "One in Five US Prison Inmates Is a 'Criminal Alien.'"
68. "Fiscal Year 2018 ICE Enforcement and Removal Operations Report," U.S. Immigration and Customs Enforcement, 2018, https://www.ice.gov/doclib/about/offices/ero/pdf/eroFY2018Report.pdf.
69. Daniel Greenfield, "Democrats Fighting to Protect 2,500 Illegal Aliens Locked Up For Molesting Kids In Texas," Sons of Liberty Media,

January 13, 2019, https://sonsoflibertymedia.com/democrats-fighting-to-protect-2500-illegal-aliens-locked-up-for-molesting-kids-in-texas/.

70. Emily Ekins, "Americans Used to Support a Border Wall. What Changed Their Minds?" *The Federalist*, January 14, 2019, https://thefederalist.com/2019/01/14/americans-used-support-border-wall-changed-minds/.
71. Paul Crookston, "Stacey Abrams 'Wouldn't Oppose' Non-Citizens, Minors Voting in Local Elections," *Washington Free Beacon*, January 11, 2019, https://freebeacon.com/politics/stacey-abrams-wouldnt-oppose-non-citizens-minors-voting-in-local-elections/.
72. Fred Lucas, "How Illegal Immigration Harms Black Americans, According to Civil Rights Commissioner," *Daily Signal*, February 19, 2017, https://www.dailysignal.com/2017/02/19/how-illegal-immigration-harms-black-americans-according-to-civil-rights-commissioner/.
73. Stephen Dinan, "'Violent Mob' Repelled in Attempt to Storm U.S. Border in San Diego," *Washington Times*, January 1, 2019.
74. "Report: Forced to Flee Central America's Northern Triangle," Doctors Without Borders, May 11, 2017, https://www.doctorswithoutborders.org/what-we-do/news-stories/research/report-forced-flee-central-americas-northern-triangle.
75. Jazz Shaw, "Oakland Mayor Has 'No Regrets' over Tipping Off Illegal Aliens," Hot Air, December 29, 2018, https://hotair.com/archives/jazz-shaw/2018/12/29/oakland-mayor-no-regrets-tipping-off-illegal-aliens/.
76. Dan Cancian, "'I Did the Right Thing': Oakland Mayor Libby Schaaf Defends Tipping Off Immigrants Ahead of Ice Raid," *Newsweek*, December 28, 2018.
77. Mike Brest, "Ocasio-Cortez: Trump Needs to Explain Why ICE Should Still Be Funded," *Daily Caller*, January 9, 2019, https://dailycaller.com/2019/01/09/ocasio-cortez-trump-needs-to-explain-why-ice-should-still-be-funded/.
78. John Daniel Davidson, "Democratic Congresswoman Compares U.S. Border Officials to Nazis," *The Federalist*, February 26, 2019, https://thefederalist.com/2019/02/26/democratic-congresswoman-compares-u-s-border-officials-nazis/.
79. Ken Meyer, "Alexandria Ocasio-Cortez: 'The U.S. is Running Concentration on Our Southern Border,'" Mediaite, June 18, 2019, https://www.mediaite.com/tv/alexandria-ocasio-cortez-the-u-s-is-running-concentration-camps-on-our-southern-border/.
80. Timothy Meads, "AOC Makes Moronic Claim That the USA Has Concentration Camps on Southern Border," *Townhall*, June 18, 2019, https://townhall.com/tipsheet/timothymeads/2019/06/18/aoc-says-united-states-is-running-concentration-camps-on-southern-border-n2548442.

Index

A

B

C

F

G

H

I

L

M

N

O

P

S

T

U

Y

Z